Philosophy in the Modern World

A NEW HISTORY OF WESTERN PHILOSOPHY

VOLUME IV

Philosophy in the Modern World

ANTHONY KENNY

CLARENDON PRESS · OXFORD

OXFORD
UNIVERSITY PRESS

Great Clarendon Street, Oxford ox2 6DP

Oxford University Press is a department of the University of Oxford.
It furthers the University's objective of excellence in research, scholarship,
and education by publishing worldwide in

Oxford New York

Auckland Cape Town Dar es Salaam Hong Kong Karachi
Kuala Lumpur Madrid Melbourne Mexico City Nairobi
New Delhi Shanghai Taipei Toronto

With offices in

Argentina Austria Brazil Chile Czech Republic France Greece
Guatemala Hungary Italy Japan Poland Portugal Singapore
South Korea Switzerland Thailand Turkey Ukraine Vietnam

Oxford is a registered trade mark of Oxford University Press
in the UK and in certain other countries

Published in the United States
by Oxford University Press Inc., New York

© Sir Anthony Kenny 2007

The moral rights of the author have been asserted
Database right Oxford University Press (maker)

First published 2007

British Library Cataloguing in Publication Data

Data available

Library of Congress Cataloging in Publication Data

Data available

Typeset by SPI Publisher Services, Pondicherry, India
Printed in Great Britain
on acid-free paper by
Clays Ltd, St Ives plc

ISBN 978–0–19–875279–0

1

To the memory of Georg Henrik von Wright

SUMMARY OF CONTENTS

CONTENTS

CONTENTS

CONTENTS

INTRODUCTION

This is the final volume of a four-volume history of Western philosophy from its beginnings to its most recent past. The first volume, published in 2004, told the story of ancient philosophy, and the second volume, published in 2005, covered medieval philosophy from the time of St Augustine to the Renaissance. The third volume, *The Rise of Modern Philosophy*, treated of the major philosophers of the sixteenth, seventeenth, and eighteenth centuries, ending with the death of Hegel early in the nineteenth. This present volume continues the narrative up to the final years of the twentieth century.

There are two different kinds of reason for reading a history of philosophy. Some readers do so because they are seeking help and illumination from older thinkers on topics of current philosophical interest. Others are more interested in the people and societies of the distant or recent past, and wish to learn about their intellectual climate. I have structured this and previous volumes in a way that will meet the needs of both classes of reader. The book begins with three summary chapters, each of which follows a chronological sequence; it then contains nine chapters, each of which deals with a particular area of philosophy, from logic to natural theology. Those whose primary interest is historical may focus on the chronological surveys, referring if they wish to the thematic sections for amplification. Those whose primary interest is philosophical will concentrate rather on the later chapters, referring back to the chronological chapters to place particular issues in context.

Certain themes have occupied chapters in each of the four volumes of this series: epistemology, metaphysics, philosophy of mind, ethics, and philosophy of religion. Other topics have varied in importance over the centuries, and the pattern of thematic chapters has varied accordingly. The first two volumes began the thematic section with a chapter on logic and language, but there was no such chapter in volume III because logic went into hibernation at the Renaissance. In the period covered by the present volume formal logic and the philosophy of language occupied such a central position that each topic deserves a chapter to itself. In the earlier volumes, there was a chapter devoted to physics, considered as a branch of what used to be called 'natural philosophy'; however, since Newton physics has been a fully mature science independent of philosophical underpinning, and so there is no chapter on physics in the present volume. Volume III was the first to contain a chapter on political philosophy, since before the time of More and Machiavelli the political institutions of Europe were too different from those under which we live for the insights of political philosophers to be relevant to current discussions. This volume is the first and only one to contain a chapter on aesthetics: this involves a slight overlap with the previous volume, since it was in the eighteenth century that the subject began to emerge as a separate discipline.

The introductory chapters in this volume, unlike those in previous ones, do not follow a single chronological sequence. The first chapter indeed does trace a single line from Bentham to Nietzsche, but because of the chasm that separated English-speaking philosophy from Continental philosophy in the twentieth century the narrative diverges in the second and third chapter. The second chapter begins with Peirce, the doyen of American philosophers, and with Frege, who is commonly regarded as the founder of the analytic tradition in philosophy. The third chapter treats of a series of influential Continental thinkers, commencing with a man who would have hated to be regarded as philosopher, Sigmund Freud.

I have not found it easy to decide where and how to end my history. Many of those who have philosophized in the second half of the twentieth century are people I have known personally, and several of them have been close colleagues and friends. This makes it difficult to make an objective judgement on their importance in comparison with the thinkers who have occupied the earlier volumes and the earlier pages of this one. No doubt my choice of who should be included and who should be omitted will seem arbitrary to others no less qualified than myself to make a judgement.

In 1998 I published *A Brief History of Western Philosophy*. I decided at that time not to include in the book any person still living. That, conveniently, meant that I could finish the story with Wittgenstein, whom I considered, and consider, to be the most significant philosopher of the twentieth century. But since 1998, sadly, a number of philosophers have died whom anyone would expect to find a place in a history of modern philosophy—Quine, for instance, Anscombe, Davidson, Strawson, Rawls, and others. So I had to choose another way of drawing a *terminus ante quem*. As

I approached my seventy-fifth birthday the thought occurred to me of excluding all writers who were younger than myself. But this appeared a rather egocentric cut-off point. So finally I opted for a thirty-year rule, and have excluded works written after 1975.

I must ask the reader to bear in mind that this is the final volume of a history of philosophy that began with Thales. It is accordingly structured in rather a different way from a self-standing history of contemporary philosophy. I have, for instance, said nothing about twentieth-century neo-scholastics or neo-Kantians, and have said very little about several generations of neo-Hegelians. To leave these out of a book devoted to the philosophy of the last two centuries would be to leave a significant gap in the history. But the importance of these schools was to remind the modern era of the importance of the great thinkers of the past. A history that has already devoted many pages to Aquinas, Kant, and Hegel does not need to repeat such reminders.

As in writing previous volumes, I have had in mind an audience at the level of second- or third-year undergraduate study. Since many undergraduates interested in the history of philosophy are not themselves philosophy students, I have tried not to assume any familiarity with philosophical techniques or terminology. Similarly, I have not included in the Bibliography works in languages other than English, except for the original texts of writers in other languages. Since many people read philosophy not for curricular purposes, but for their own enlightenment and entertainment, I have tried to avoid jargon and to place no difficulties in the way of the reader other than those presented by the subject matter itself. But, however hard one tries, it is impossible to make the reading of philosophy an undemanding task. As has often been said, philosophy has no shallow end.

I am indebted to Peter Momtchiloff and his colleagues at Oxford University Press, and to two anonymous readers for the Press who removed many blemishes from the book. I am also particularly grateful to Patricia Williams and Dagfinn Føllesdal for assisting me in the treatment of twentieth-century Continental philosophers.

1

Bentham to Nietzsche

Bentham's Utilitarianism

Britain escaped the violent constitutional upheavals that affected most of Europe during the last years of the eighteenth, and the early years of the nineteenth, century. But in 1789, the year of the French Revolution, a book was published in England that was to have a revolutionary effect on moral and political thinking long after the death of Napoleon. This was Jeremy Bentham's *An Introduction to the Principles of Morals and Legislation*, which became the founding charter of the school of thought known as utilitarianism.

Bentham was born in 1748, the son of a prosperous London attorney. A tiny, bookish, and precocious child, he was sent to Westminster School at the age of 7 and graduated from The Queen's College, Oxford, at the age of 15. He was destined for a legal career, and was called to the Bar when 21, but he found contemporary legal practice distasteful. He had already been repelled by current legal theory when, at Oxford, he had listened to the lectures of the famous jurist William Blackstone. The English legal system, he believed, was cumbrous, artificial, and incoherent: it should be reconstructed from the ground up in the light of sound principles of jurisprudence.

The fundamental such principle, on his own account, he owed to Hume. When he read the *Treatise of Human Nature*, he tells us, scales fell from his eyes and he came to believe that utility was the test and measure of all virtue and the sole origin of justice. On the basis of an essay by the dissenting chemist Joseph Priestley, Bentham interpreted the principle of utility as meaning that the happiness of the majority of the citizens was the criterion by which the affairs of a state should be judged. More generally, the real standard of morality and the true goal of legislation was the greatest happiness of the greatest number.

During the 1770s Bentham worked on a critique of Blackstone's *Commentaries on the Laws of England*. A portion of this was published in 1776 as *A Fragment on Government*, which contained an attack on the notion of a social contract. At the same time he wrote a dissertation on punishment, drawing on the ideas of the Italian penologist Cesare Beccaria (1738–94). An analysis of the purposes and limits of punishment, along with the exposition of the principle of utility, formed the substance of the *Introduction to the Principles of Morals and Legislation*, which was completed in 1780, nine years before its eventual publication.

The *Fragment on Government* was the first public statement by Bentham of the principle that 'it is the greatest happiness of the greatest number that is the measure of right and wrong'. The book was published anonymously, but it had some influential readers, including the Earl of Shelburne, a leading Whig who was later briefly Prime Minister. When Shelburne discovered that Bentham was author of the work, he took him under his patronage, and introduced him to political circles in England and France. Most significant among Bentham's new English friends was Caroline Fox, a niece of Charles James Fox, to whom, after a long but spasmodic courtship, he made an unsuccessful proposal of marriage in 1805. Most important of the French acquaintances was Étienne Dumont, tutor to Shelburne's son, who was later to publish a number of his works in translation. For a time Bentham's reputation was greater in France than in Britain.

Bentham spent the years 1785–7 abroad, travelling across Europe and staying with his brother Samuel, who was managing estates of Prince Potemkin at Krichev in White Russia. While there he conceived the idea of a novel kind of prison, the Panopticon, a circular building with a central observation point from which the jailer could keep a permanent eye on the inmates. He returned from Russia full of enthusiasm for prison reform, and tried to persuade both the British and French governments to erect a model prison. William Pitt's government passed an Act of Parliament authorizing the scheme, but it was defeated by ducal landowners who did not want a prison near their estates, and by the personal intervention (so Bentham liked to believe) of King George III. The French National Assembly did not take up his offer to supervise the establishment of a Panopticon, but did confer on him an honorary citizenship of the Republic.

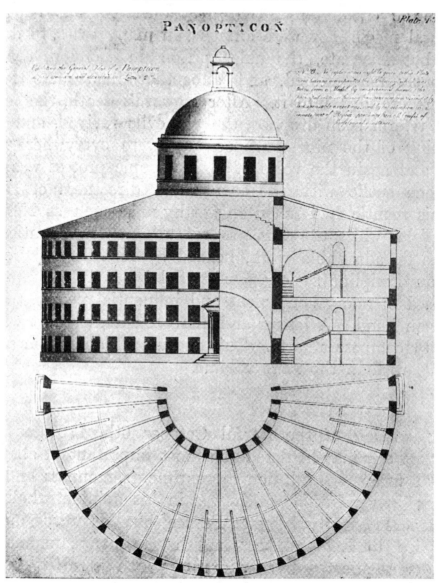

Bentham's plan for a perfect prison, the Panopticon.

Bentham's interest in legal theory and practice extended far beyond its original focus on criminal law. Exasperated by the confused state of civil law he wrote a long treatise *Of Laws in General*, which, like so many of his works, remained unpublished until long after his death. Reflecting on the Poor Laws he proposed that a network of Panopticons should be set up to serve as workhouses for the 'burdensome poor', managed by a national joint stock company, which would take a dividend once the inmates' labour had provided for their sustenance. No Panopticon, whether penal or commercial, was ever constructed. In 1813, however, Parliament voted Bentham the giant sum of £23,000 in compensation for his work on the scheme.

In 1808 Bentham became friends with a Scottish philosopher, James Mill, who was just starting to write a monumental *History of India*. Mill had a remarkable two-year-old son, John Stuart, and Bentham assisted in that prodigy's education. Partly because of Mill's influence Bentham, who had been working for some years on the rationale of evidence in the courts, now began to focus on political and constitutional reform rather than on criticisms of legal procedure and practice. He wrote a *Catechism of Parliamentary Reform*, which was completed in 1809, though it was not published until 1817, when it was followed up, a year or two later, with the draft of a radical reform bill. He spent years on the drafting of a constitutional code, which was unfinished when he died. By the end of his life, he had become convinced that the existing British constitution was a screen hiding a conspiracy of the rich against the poor. He therefore advocated the abolition of the monarchy and the House of Lords, the introduction of annual parliaments elected by universal suffrage, and the disestablishment of the Church of England.

Bentham's constitutional and liberal proposals extended well beyond the affairs of Britain. In 1811 he proposed to James Madison that he should draw up a constitutional code for the United States. He was active on the London Greek Committee, which sponsored the expedition on which Lord Byron met his death at Missolonghi in 1823. For a time he had hopes that his constitutional code would be implemented in Latin America by Simón Bolívar, the President of Colombia.

The group of 'philosophical radicals' who accepted the ideals of Bentham in 1823 founded the *Westminster Review* in order to promote utilitarian causes. They were enthusiasts for educational reform. Bentham devised a curriculum for secondary education which emphasized science and technology rather than Greek and Latin. He and his colleagues were active in the establishment of University College London, which opened its doors in 1828. This was the first university-level institution in Britain to admit students without religious tests. There, in accordance with his will, Bentham's remains were placed after his death in 1832, and there, clothed and topped with a wax head, they survive to this day—his 'auto-icon' as he termed it. A more appropriate memorial to his endeavours was the Great Reform Bill, widely extending the parliamentary franchise, which passed into law a few weeks before he died.

Among those who knew him well, even his greatest admirers agreed that he was a very one-sided person, powerful in intellect but deficient in feeling. John Stuart Mill described him as precise and coherent in thought, but lacking in sympathy for the most natural and strongest feelings of human beings. Karl Marx said that he took the English shopkeeper as the paradigm of a human being. 'In no time and in no country', Marx said, 'has homespun commonplace ever strutted about in so self-satisfied a way' (C 488). Bentham's knowledge of human nature was indeed very limited. 'It is wholly empirical,' Mill said, 'and the empiricism of one who has had little experience.' He never, in Mill's view, reached maturity. 'He was a boy to the last' (U 78).

The Development of John Stuart Mill

Mill himself was never allowed to be a boy. He did not go to school or mingle with other children, but was educated at home by his demanding father. He began to learn Greek at the age of three and by the age of twelve had read much of Plato in the original. At that age he began studying logic from the text of Aristotle, while helping to proofread his father's *History of India*. In the following year he was taken through a course in political economy. He was never allowed a holiday 'lest the habit of work should be broken, and a taste for idleness acquired'. But when he was fourteen he spent a year in France at the house of Bentham's brother Samuel, which gave him an opportunity to attend science lectures at Montpellier. Apart from that, he had no university education, but by the age of sixteen he was already far more well-read than most Masters of Arts.

5

What Mill, looking back, most valued in his extraordinary education was the degree to which his father left him to think for himself. 'Anything which could be found out by thinking I never was told, until I had exhausted my efforts to find it out for myself' (*A* 20). He reckoned that he started adult life with an advantage of a quarter of a century over his contemporaries who had been to public school and university. But his education turned him, in his own words, into 'a mere reasoning machine'. After several years spent campaigning for liberal causes alongside colleagues on the *Westminster Review*, while holding a day job as a clerk with the East India Company, Mill suffered a mental breakdown and fell victim to a deep depression in which even the most effective work for reform seemed quite pointless.

He was rescued from his crisis, on his own account, by the reading of Wordsworth in the autumn of 1828. The poems made him aware not only of natural beauty, but of aspects of human life that had found no place in Bentham's system.

They seemed to be the very culture of the feelings, which I was in quest of. In them I seemed to draw from a source of inward joy, of sympathetic and imaginative pleasure, which could be shared in by all human beings; which had no connexion with struggle or imperfection, but would be made richer by every improvement in the physical or social condition of mankind. From them I seemed to learn what would be the perennial sources of happiness, when all the greater evils of life shall have been removed. And I felt myself at once better and happier as I came under their influence. (*A* 89)

After his crisis and recovery, Mill did not cease to venerate Bentham and to regard his work as having superseded that of all previous moralists; but he became convinced that his system needed modification and supplementation in both its personal and its social aspects.

On the personal side, Mill's thought developed under the influence of English poets, of whom Coleridge soon overtook Wordsworth as the dominant presence in his mind. In mature life he was willing to pair Coleridge and Bentham as 'the two great seminal minds of England in their age'. On the social side, the new influences on Mill were French in origin—the nascent socialism of the Comte de Saint-Simon (1760–1825) and the embryonic positivism of Auguste Comte (1798–1857).

While the British utilitarians had been content to take private ownership and hereditary property as something given and indefeasible, the

Saint-Simonians argued that the capital and labour of a society should be managed as a whole for the general good of the community, with each of the citizens being obliged to contribute according to their ability, and entitled to be rewarded in proportion to their contribution. Mill was unconvinced by the socialist programme, but it made him aware of the need of a justification for the institutions of private property and the free market. He admired the Saint-Simonians' idealism, and was inspired by a number of their principles—in particular their insistence on the perfect equality of men and women.

Comte had begun his philosophical career as a Saint-Simonian, but went on to develop a system of his own to which he gave the name of 'positive philosophy'. The feature of this system that made a lasting impression on Mill was the theory that human knowledge and human societies passed through three historical stages: theological, metaphysical, and positive. These stages were, in the Saint-Simonian term, 'organic', or self-contained. In the first stage, societies gave supernatural explanations of phenomena and endeavoured to bring about effects in the world by magical or religious practices. This phase, according to Comte, lasted through the feudal system up to the Reformation. In the metaphysical phase, phenomena were explained by essences and forces, which turned out to be no less occult than the supernatural factors held to operate in the theological stage. It was the French Revolution that had brought this stage to conclusion, and the world was now about to enter upon the positive, or truly scientific, stage of science and society.

What Mill took from Comte and the Saint-Simonians was the idea of Progress. Between each organic period and the next there was, so Mill understood, a critical and disruptive period, and he believed that he was living in such a period. He now began to look forward

to a future which shall unite the best qualities of the critical with the best qualities of the organic periods; unchecked liberty of thought, unbounded freedom of individual action in all modes not hurtful to others; but also, convictions as to what is right and wrong, useful and pernicious, deeply engraven on the feelings by early education and general unanimity of sentiment. (A 100)

Once that state was achieved, further progress would be unnecessary: moral convictions would be so firmly grounded in reason and necessity that they would not, like all past and present creeds, need to be periodically thrown off.

Though a prolific journalist from an early age, Mill did not publish any books until his late thirties. But his first published book, in 1843, was a work of substance which achieved immediate and lasting fame. This was *A System of Logic* in six books, on which he had been working for several years, and which went through eight editions in his lifetime.

The book covers a wide variety of topics, unified by Mill's desire to present a nineteenth-century update of the British empiricist tradition. He presented a secular version of Berkeley's theological phenomenalism: matter is no more than a permanent possibility of sensation, and the external world is 'the world of possible sensations succeeding one another according to laws'. He agreed with Hume that we have no conception of mind itself, as distinguished from its conscious manifestations in ourselves, and he regarded it as a particularly difficult problem for a philosopher to establish the existence of minds other than his own. But unlike previous empiricists, Mill had a serious interest in formal logic and the methodology of the sciences.

The *System of Logic* begins with an analysis of language, and an account of different types of name (including proper names, pronouns, descriptions, general terms, and abstract expressions). All names, according to Mill, denote things: proper names denote the things they are names of, and general terms denote the things they are true of. But besides denotation, there is connotation: that is to say, a word like 'man' will denote Socrates (among others) but will also connote attributes such as rationality and animality.

Mill gave a detailed theory of inferences, which he divided into real and verbal. Syllogistic inference is verbal rather than real, because a syllogism gives us no new knowledge. Real inference is not deductive, but inductive, as when we reason 'Peter is mortal, James is mortal, John is mortal, therefore all men are mortal'. Such induction does not, as some logicians had thought, lead us from particular cases to a general law. The general laws are merely formulae for making inferences from known particulars to unknown particulars. Mill sets out five rules, or canons, of experiment to guide inductive scientific research. The use of such canons, Mill maintains, enables empirical inquiry to proceed without any appeal to a priori truths.[1]

---

[1] Mill's logic is discussed in detail in Ch. 4.

The *System of Logic* ranges far beyond the discussion of language and inference. Its sixth book, for instance, is entitled 'On the Logic of the Moral Sciences'. The principal such sciences are psychology, sociology, and what Mill called 'ethology', or the study of the formation of character. Social science includes the science of politics and the study of economics; but Mill's fullest treatment of these topics appeared in a different book, *Principles of Political Economy* of 1848.

In presenting his modernized empiricism Mill took one unprecedented, and important, step. The truths of mathematics have always presented a difficulty for thoroughgoing empiricists, since they seem to be among the most certain objects of our knowledge, and yet they seem to precede rather than result from experience. Mill maintained that arithmetic and geometry, no less than physics, consist of empirical hypotheses—hypotheses that have been very handsomely confirmed in experience, but hypotheses that are none the less corrigible in the light of later experience.

This thesis—implausible as it has appeared to most subsequent philosophers—was essential to Mill's overriding aim in *A System of Logic*, which was to refute a notion that he regarded as 'the great intellectual support of false doctrines and bad institutions', namely the notion that truths external to the mind may be known by intuition independent of experience. Mill indeed saw this issue as the most important in all philosophy. 'The difference between these two schools of philosophy, that of Intuition, and that of Experience and Association, is not a mere matter of abstract speculation; it is full of practical consequences, and lies at the foundation of all the greatest differences of practical opinion in an age of progress' (*A* 162).

The most aggressive campaign waged by Mill in this intellectual battle was carried out in one of his last works, *An Examination of Sir William Hamilton's Philosophy* (1865). Sir William Hamilton was a Scottish philosopher and reformer who was Professor of Logic and Metaphysics in Edinburgh from 1838 to 1856. In his lectures he attempted to present a new and improved version of the common-sense philosophy of Reid, just as Mill had tried to bring out a new and improved version of the empiricism of Hume. Mill saw in these lectures, when they were published, an ideal target at which to fire his explosive criticisms of all forms of intuitionism.

Mill's *Examination* achieved more fame than the text it was examining; but nowadays it too is not often studied. The works of Mill that have retained a large readership were, on his own account, not entirely his own

9

work. In 1851 he married Harriet, the widow of a London merchant, John Taylor, a bluestocking with whom he had enjoyed an intimate but chaste friendship for some twenty years. The marriage lasted only seven years before Harriet died at Avignon. According to Mill she should be counted as co-author of his pamphlets *On Liberty* (published in 1859) and *The Subjection of Women* (written in 1861 and published in 1869).

Harriet Taylor, inspirer, collaborator, and eventually wife of J.S. Mill

On Liberty seeks to draw limits to government interference with individual freedom. Its key principle is set out thus:

The sole end for which mankind are warranted, individually or collectively, in interfering with the liberty of action of any of their number, is self-protection. The only purposes for which power can be rightfully exercised over any member of a civilised community, against his will, is to prevent harm to others. His own good, either physical or moral, is not a sufficient warrant.

Over himself, Mill says, over his own body and mind, the individual is sovereign. The essay applies this principle in various areas, most conspicuously in support of freedom of opinion and freedom of expression.

The publication of *The Subjection of Women* was the culmination of a long campaign by Mill to secure female rights and improve women's lot. When James Mill, in his *Essay on Government*, had affirmed that women did not need a vote, because their interests coincided with that of their menfolk, young John Stuart, supported by Bentham, had dissented. In his *Thoughts on Parliamentary Reform* of 1859 he proposed that every educated householder, male or female, should be entitled to vote 'for why should the vote-collector make a distinction where the tax-gatherer makes none?' (*CW* xix. 328). In 1866 he presented a petition for female suffrage, and during the debates on the Second Reform Bill proposed an amendment—which attracted seventy-three votes—to strike out the words that restricted the franchise to males. But *The Subjection of Women* addressed issues much wider than that of the suffrage, and attacked the whole institution of marriage as interpreted by Victorian law and morality. So structured, he maintained, wedlock was simply a form of domestic servitude.

From 1865 to 1868 Mill was Member of Parliament for Westminster. In addition to feminist issues, he interested himself in Irish affairs and in electoral reform. He was critical of the British government's policy of coercion in Ireland, and published a pamphlet advocating a radical reform of the landholding system. He advocated proportional representation in parliamentary elections, as a safeguard against the exercise of tyranny by a majority against a minority. His thoughts on such matters had appeared in print in 1861 in *Considerations on Representative Government*.

During the last years of his life Mill dwelt at Avignon with his stepdaughter Helen Taylor. He died there in 1873 and was buried beside his wife. His

Autobiography and *Three Essays on Religion* were published posthumously by his stepdaughter.

Though Mill's liberalism never ceased to have admirers, his reputation as a systematic philosopher faded rapidly after his death. His logical work was looked on with disfavour by the founders of modern symbolic logic. His empiricism was swamped by the wave of idealism that engulfed Britain in the last decades of the nineteenth century. It was only when empiricism returned to favour in the 1930s that his writings began once more to be widely read. But the utilitarian tradition was kept alive without interruption by Henry Sidgwick (1838–1900), who published his principal work, *Methods of Ethics*, in the year after Mill's death.

Sidgwick was a Fellow of Trinity College, Cambridge, who in 1869 resigned his fellowship on conscientious grounds. He became Professor of Philosophy in the university in 1883. He was at first an uncritical admirer of Mill and welcomed his system as giving him relief from the arbitrary moral rules of his upbringing. But he came to hold that there was an inconsistency between two great principles of Mill's system: psychological hedonism (everyone seeks their own happiness) and ethical hedonism (everyone should seek the general happiness). One of the main tasks he set himself in *Methods of Ethics* was to resolve this problem, which he called 'the dualism of practical reason'.

In the course of his thinking Sidgwick abandoned the principle of psychological hedonism and replaced it with an ethical principle of rational egoism, that each person has an obligation to seek his own good. This principle, he believed, was intuitively obvious. Ethical hedonism, too, he decided, could only be based on fundamental moral intuitions. Thus, his system combined utilitarianism with intuitionism, which he regarded as the common-sense approach to morality. However, the typical intuitions of common sense were, he believed, too narrow and specific; the ones that were the foundation of utilitarian morality were more abstract. One such was that future good is as important as present good, and another is that from the point of view of the universe any single person's good is of no more importance than any other person's.

The remaining difficulty is to reconcile the intuitions of utilitarianism with those of rational egoism. Sidgwick came to the conclusion that no complete solution of the conflict between my happiness and the general happiness was possible on the basis of mundane experience (*ME*, p. xix). For most people, he accepted, the connection between the individual's interest and his duty is made through belief in God and personal immortality. As he himself was unwilling to invoke God in this context, he concluded sadly that 'the prolonged effort of the human intellect to frame a perfect ideal of rational conduct is seen to have been foredoomed to inevitable failure' (*ME*, end). He consoled himself by seeking, through the work of the Society for Psychical Research, founded in 1882, empirical evidence for the survival of the individual after death.

Schopenhauer's Philosophy of the Will

In setting out his principle of utility, Bentham had contrasted it with the principle of asceticism, which approves of actions in so far as they tend to diminish happiness. Bentham's target was Christian morality, but no Christian ever held the principle of asceticism in all its fullness. Of all philosophers the one who came closest to professing such a principle was the atheist Arthur Schopenhauer, who was just one year old when Bentham published his *Introduction*.

Schopenhauer was the son of a Danzig merchant, and was brought up to follow a business career until his father's death in 1803. He then resumed a life of study, beginning in 1810 a course of philosophy at the University of Göttingen, after a false start as a medical student. His favourite philosophers were Plato and Kant, but he did not admire Kant's disciple Fichte, whose lectures he heard at Berlin in 1811. In particular he was disgusted by Fichte's nationalism, and rather than join the Prussian struggle against Napoleon he withdrew to write a work *On the Fourfold Root of the Principle of Sufficient Reason*, which he presented as a doctoral dissertation to the University of Jena in 1813.

During the years 1814–18 he wrote his major work, *The World as Will and Idea*. The work is divided into four books, the first and third devoted to the world as Idea, and the second and fourth to the world as Will. By 'idea' (*Vorstellung*, sometimes translated 'representation') Schopenhauer does not mean a concept, but a concrete experience—the kind of thing that Locke and Berkeley called by the name 'idea'. According to Schopenhauer, the world exists only as idea, only in relation to consciousness: 'The world is my idea.' For each of us our own body is the starting point of our perception of the world, and other objects are known through their effects on each other.

Schopenhauer's account of the world as idea is not very different from the system of Kant. But the second book, in which the world is presented as will, is highly original. Science, Schopenhauer says, explains the motion of bodies in terms of laws such as inertia and gravitation. But science offers no explanation of the inner nature of these forces. Indeed no such explanation could ever be offered if a human being was no more than a knowing subject. However, I am myself rooted in the world, and my body is not just one object among others, but has an active power of which I am conscious. This, and this alone, allows us to penetrate the nature of things. 'The answer to the riddle is given to the subject of knowledge, who appears as an individual, and the answer is *will*. This and this alone gives him the key to his own existence, reveals to him the significance, shows him the inner mechanism of his being, of his action, of his movements' (*WWI* 100). Each of us knows himself both as an object and as a will, and this throws light on every phenomenon in nature. The inner nature of all objects must be the same as that which in ourselves we call will. But there are many different grades of will, reaching down to gravitation and magnetism, and only the higher grades are accompanied by knowledge and self-determination. Nonetheless, the will is the real thing-in-itself for which Kant sought in vain.

Since he agrees that inanimate objects do not act on reasons or act for motives, why does Schopenhauer call their natural tendencies 'will' rather than 'appetite' like Aristotle, or 'force' like Newton? If we explain force in terms of will, Schopenhauer replies, we explain the less known by the better known. The only immediate knowledge we have of the world's inner nature is given us by our consciousness of our own will.

But what is the nature of will itself? All willing, Schopenhauer tells us, arises from want, and so from deficiency, and therefore from suffering. If a wish is granted, it is only succeeded by another; we always have many more desires than we can satisfy. If our consciousness is filled by our will, we can never have happiness or peace; our best hope is that pain and boredom will alternate with each other.

In the third and fourth book of his masterpiece Schopenhauer offers two different ways of liberation from the slavery to the will. The first way of escape is through art, through the pure, disinterested contemplation of beauty. The second way of escape is through renunciation. Only by renouncing the will to live can we be totally freed from the tyranny of the will. The will to live is to be renounced not by suicide, but by asceticism. To make real moral progress we must leave behind not just wickedness (delighting in the suffering of others) and badness (using others as means to our ends) but also mere justice (treating others on equal terms with ourselves) and even goodness (willingness to sacrifice oneself for others). We must go beyond virtue to asceticism. I must come to have such a horror of this miserable world that I will no longer think it enough to love others as myself or to give up my own pleasures when they stand in the way of others' good. To reach the ideal I must adopt chastity, poverty, and abstinence, and welcome death when it comes as a deliverance from evil.

As models of self-abnegation, Schopenhauer held out Christian, Hindu, and Buddhist saints. However, his case for asceticism did not rest on any religious premises, and he accepted that the life of most saints was full of superstition. Religious beliefs, he thought, were mythical clothings of truths unattainable by the uneducated. But his system was expressly influenced by the Maya doctrine of Indian philosophy, the doctrine that individual subjects and objects are all mere appearance, the veil of Maya.

The World as Will and Idea had little immediate influence. In 1820 Schopenhauer went to Berlin, where the dominant philosopher in the university was Hegel, for whom he had little respect, sneering at 'the narcotic effect of long-spun periods without a single idea in them'. He deliberately advertised his lectures at the same time as Hegel's, but he was unable to woo the students away. The boycott of his lectures added fuel to his dislike of the Hegelian system, which he regarded as mostly nonsense, or, as he put it, 'atrocious and extremely wearisome humbug' (*WWI* 26).

Schopenhauer did not win any public recognition of his genius until 1839, when he won a Norwegian prize for an essay *On the Freedom of the Will*. This he published in 1841, along with another essay on the foundation of ethics, under the title *The Two Fundamental Problems of Ethics*. In 1844 he published an expanded edition of *The World as Will and Idea* and in 1851 a collection of essays entitled *Parerga and Paralipomena*. These enabled a wide public to appreciate the wit and clarity of his literary style, as well as to savour, with pleasure or distaste, his irreverent and politically incorrect opinions.

15

The unsuccessful Continental revolutions of 1848 took place just after Schopenhauer's sixtieth birthday. In his sixties he became popular with members of a generation that had become disillusioned with political attempts to make the world a better place. He was courted by the German academic establishment that he had flagellated in his writings. He was able to enjoy the comforts of the world that he had denounced as a degrading illusion. If people complained that his own life was very different from the ascetic ideal that he proclaimed, he would reply, 'it is a strange demand upon a moralist that he should teach no other virtue than that which he himself possesses'. He died in 1860.

Ethics and Religion in Kierkegaard

While Schopenhauer, in Frankfurt, was expanding *The World as Will and Idea*, a Danish philosopher in Copenhagen was bringing out a series of treatises that presented a similar call to asceticism on a quite different metaphysical basis. This was Søren Aabye Kierkegaard, born in 1813 into a tragic family. His mother and five of his six siblings died before he reached adulthood, and his father believed himself cursed for a blasphemy uttered long ago while a shepherd boy. Sent to Copenhagen University in 1830 to study theology, Kierkegaard acquired, like Schopenhauer, a familiarity with, and a hatred for, the philosophy of Hegel. He disliked theology, but in 1838 he underwent a religious conversion, accompanied by a mystical experience 'of indescribable joy'. In 1840 he became engaged to Regine Olsen, but he broke off the engagement a year later, deciding that his own and his family's history rendered him unsuitable for marriage. Henceforth he saw himself as a man with a vocation as a philosopher.

In 1841, after completing a dissertation on Socratic irony, Kierkegaard went to Berlin and attended the lectures of Schelling. His distaste for German idealism increased; but unlike Schopenhauer, he thought that its mistake was to undervalue the concrete individual. Like Schopenhauer, though, he sketched out for his readers a spiritual career that ends with renunciation. In his version, however, each upward phase in the career, far from being a diminution of individuality, is a stage in the affirmation of one's own unique personality.

Kierkegaard's system was expounded, between 1843 and 1846, in a series of works published under different pseudonyms. *Either/Or*, of 1843, presents two different life-views, one aesthetic and one ethical. From a starting point in which the individual is an unquestioning member of a crowd, the aesthetic life is the first stage towards self-realization. The aesthetic person pursues pleasure, but does so with taste and elegance. The essential feature of his character is that he avoids taking on any commitment, whether personal, social, or official, that would limit his options for seizing whatever is immediately attractive. As time goes on, such a person may realize that his demand for instant freedom is actually a limitation on his powers. If so, he moves on to the ethical stage, in which he takes his place within social institutions and accepts the obligations that flow from them. But however hard he tries to fulfil the moral law, he finds that his powers are unequal to it. Before God he is always in the wrong.

Both aesthetic and ethical ways of life have to be transcended in an ascent to the religious sphere. This message is conveyed in different ways in further pseudonymous works: *Fear and Trembling* in 1843, *The Concept of Anxiety* in 1844, and *Stages on Life's Way* in 1845. The series reached its climax with the publication of the lengthy *Concluding Scientific Postscript* in 1846, whose message is that faith is not the outcome of any objective reasoning as the Hegelians had claimed.

The transition from the ethical to the religious sphere is vividly portrayed in *Fear and Trembling*, which takes as its text the biblical story of God's command to Abraham to kill his son Isaac in sacrifice. An ethical hero, such as Socrates, lays down his life for the sake of a universal moral law; but Abraham breaks a moral law in obedience to an individual command of God. This is what Kierkegaard calls 'the teleological suspension of the ethical'—Abraham's act transgresses the ethical order to pursue a higher end (*telos*) outside it. But if an individual feels a call to violate the moral law, no one can tell him whether this is a mere temptation or a genuine command of God. He cannot even know or prove it to himself: he has to make a decision in blind faith.

After a second mystical experience in 1848 Kierkegaard adopted a more transparent method of writing, and published, under his own name, a number of Christian discourses and works such as *Purity of Heart is to Will One Thing* (1847) and *Works of Love* (1847). But he reverted to a pseudonym for *Sickness unto Death*, which presents faith as being the only alternative to despair, and as the necessary condition for a full realization of one's authentic existence or selfhood.

Much of the latter part of Kierkegaard's life was taken up in conflict with the established Danish Church, which he regarded as Christian only in name. He was highly critical of the Primate, Bishop J. P. Mynster, and after his death in 1854 published a bitter attack on him. He founded and funded an anticlerical broadsheet, *The Moment*, which ran for nine issues, after which he collapsed in the street and died, after a few weeks' illness, in November 1855. Against his wishes, and against the protests of his nephew, he was given a church funeral.

Dialectical Materialism

Schopenhauer and Kierkegaard both derived their philosophical impetus from a reaction against the system of Hegel. But the most violent and most influential rejection of Hegelianism was that of Karl Marx, who described his own philosophical mission as 'turning Hegel upside down'. The dialectical idealism of Hegel was in his vision to be replaced by a dialectical materialism.

Marx's father was a liberal Jew who had turned Protestant shortly before his son's birth in 1816. The young Karl went to school in Trier and attended Bonn University for one year, studying law and living riotously. He then went to Berlin University for five years, where he sobered up, took to writing poetry, and switched from law to philosophy. When Marx arrived in Berlin, Hegel was already dead, but he studied Hegelian philosophy with a left-wing group known as the Young Hegelians, which included Ludwig Feuerbach and was led by Bruno Bauer. From Hegel and Bauer, Marx learnt to view history as a dialectical process. Each stage of history was determined by its predecessor according to fundamental logical or metaphysical principles in a process that had a rigour similar to that of a geometrical proof.

The Young Hegelians attached great importance to Hegel's concept of alienation, that is to say, the state in which people view as exterior to themselves something that is truly an intrinsic element of their own being. The form of alienation Hegel himself emphasized was that in which individuals, all of whom were manifestations of a single Spirit, saw each

A posthumous drawing
of Kierkegaard, by
Vilhelm Marstrand

other as hostile rivals rather than elements of an underlying unity. Bauer,
and still more Feuerbach, regarded religion as the supreme form of
alienation, in which humans, who were the highest form of beings,
projected their own life and consciousness into an unreal heaven. 'Religion
is the separation of man from himself,' Feuerbach wrote; 'he sets God over
against himself as an opposed being' (*W* vi. 41).

For both Hegel and Feuerbach religion was a form of false consciousness. For Hegel this was to be remedied by the translation of religious myths into idealist metaphysics. For Feuerbach, however, Hegelianism was itself a form of alienation. Religion should be eliminated, not translated, and replaced by a naturalistic, and positive, understanding of the everyday life of human beings in society. Marx agreed that religion was a form of false consciousness, but he thought that both Hegel and Feuerbach had provided only inadequate remedies for alienation. Hegel's metaphysics represented man as a mere spectator of a process that he should in fact control. Feuerbach, on the other hand, had not realized that God was not the only alien essence men worshipped. Much more important was money, which represented the alienation of men's labour. In so far as private property was the basis of the State, Marx wrote in a critique of Hegel's political philosophy, the State too was an alienation of man's true nature. Alienation was not to be removed by philosophical reflection: what was needed was nothing less than social upheaval. 'The philosophers have only interpreted the world in various ways; the point is to change it' (*TF* 11).

Having obtained a doctorate from Jena University for a thesis on Democritus and Epicurus, in 1842 Marx broke with the Young Hegelians, went to live in Cologne, and began a career as a political journalist. He edited a radical newspaper, the *Rheinische Zeitung*. In 1843 he married a woman he had known since childhood, Jenny von Westphalen, the daughter of a baron in the service of the Prussian government. Though irritable and dictatorial, Marx—unusually among great philosophers—enjoyed, until Jenny's death in 1881, a happy married life. Shortly after the wedding, the *Rheinische Zeitung* was closed down by the Prussian government, under pressure from the Tsar of Russia.

The Marxes moved to Paris, where Karl found further work as a journalist, read his way through the English classics of political economy, and made a number of radical friends. The most important of these was Friedrich Engels, who had just returned from working for his father's cotton-spinning business in Manchester, where he had written a study of the English working classes. Marx and Engels, after a meeting at the Café de Régence in Paris, began to work out together the theory of 'communism', that is to say, the abolition of private property in favour of communal ownership. The major work on which the two men collaborated was *The*

German Ideology, which was completed in Brussels, whither Marx had migrated after being expelled from Paris for subversive journalism.

In this book Marx and Engels presented the materialist conception of history. Life determines consciousness, not consciousness life. The basic reality of history is the process of economic production, and to understand it one must understand the material conditions of this production. The varying modes of production give rise to the formation of social classes, to warfare between them, and eventually to the forms of political life, law, and ethics. The hand-mill, for instance, gives you a society presided over by a feudal lord, the steam mill produces a society dominated by the industrial capitalist. A dialectical process is leading the world through these various stages towards a proletarian revolution and the arrival of communism.

The German Ideology was not published until long after Marx's death, but its ideas were summarized in *The Poverty of Philosophy* of 1847 (a response to a work of P. J. Proudhon entitled *The Philosophy of Poverty*). A better-known presentation of the materialist conception of history was *The Communist Manifesto*, which Marx produced in February 1848 on the basis of drafts by Engels. This was intended as an epitome of the principles and ideals of the newly founded Communist League. The message of the *Manifesto* was summed up thus by Engels in the foreword to one of its later editions:

The whole history of mankind (since the dissolution of primitive tribal society, holding land in common ownership) has been a history of class struggles, contests between exploiting and exploited, ruling and oppressed classes; the history of these class struggles forms a series of evolutions in which, nowadays, a stage has been reached where the exploited and oppressed class—the proletariat—cannot attain its emancipation from the sway of the exploiting and ruling class—the bourgeoisie—without at the same time, and once and for all, emancipating society at large from all exploitation, oppression, class distinctions and class struggles. (*CM* 48)

The most famous sentences of the *Manifesto* were its last: 'Let the ruling classes tremble at a communistic revolution. The proletarians have nothing to lose but their chains. They have a world to win. Working men of all countries, unite!'

In the year in which the *Manifesto* was published there were armed uprisings in many cities, notably Paris, Berlin, Milan, and Rome. Marx and Engels briefly returned to Germany, urging the revolutionaries to set up a system of free state education, to nationalize transport and banking, and to impose a progressive income tax. After the collapse of the revolution, Marx was twice tried in Cologne, once on a charge of insulting the public prosecutor and once on a charge of incitement to revolt. He was acquitted on both counts but was expelled from Prussian territories. He returned briefly to Paris but was once more expelled from there. For the rest of his life he lived in London, often in abject poverty, which caused three of his six children to die of starvation.

In London, Marx worked tirelessly at developing the theory of dialectical materialism, often spending ten hours a day researching in the library of the British Museum. During the winter of 1857–8 he wrote a series of notebooks in which he summed up his economic thought of the previous decade: these were not made available to the world in general until 1953, when they appeared under the German title *Grundrisse*. On these drafts he based the *Contribution to a Critique of Political Economy* of 1859. The preface of that work contains a succinct and authoritative statement of the materialist theory of history.

Throughout his life Marx endeavoured to combine communist theory with communist practice. In 1864 he helped to found the International Working Men's Association, better known as the First International. It held six congresses in nine years, but it suffered from internal dissension, led by the anarchist Mikhail Bakunin, and fell into external disrepute because of its support for the savage and futile insurrection in Paris in 1870. It was dissolved in 1876.

Marx's writing career culminated in the massive *Capital*, which sought to explain in detail how the course of history was dictated by the forces and relations of production. The first volume of this was published in Hamburg in 1867; the second and third volumes remained unpublished when Marx died in 1883 and were posthumously published by Engels. Marx was buried beside his wife in Highgate Cemetery.

The theme of Marx's great work is that the capitalist system is in a state of terminal crisis. Capitalism, of its very nature, involves the exploitation of the working class. For the true value of any product depends upon the amount of labour put into it. But the capitalist appropriates part of this value, paying the labourer less than the product's real worth. As technology develops, and with it the labourer's productivity, a greater and greater proportion of the wealth generated by labour finds its way into the pockets of the capitalist.[2] This exploitation is bound to reach a point at which the proletariat finds it intolerable, and rises in revolt. The capitalist system will be replaced by the dictatorship of the proletariat, which will abolish private property and introduce a socialist state in which the means of production are totally under central government control. But the socialist state, in its turn, will wither away to be replaced by a communist society in which the interests of the individual will coincide with those of the community.

Marx's predictions of proletarian revolution followed by universal socialism and communism have, mercifully, been falsified by the course of history since his death. But whatever he may himself have thought, his theories are essentially philosophical and political rather than scientific; and judged from that standpoint they can claim both successes and failures. Marx erred in claiming that events are determined totally by economic factors. Even in countries that underwent socialist revolutions of a Marxist type, the power wielded by individuals such as Lenin, Stalin, and Mao gave the lie to the theory that only impersonal forces give history its shape. But, on the other hand, no historian, not even a historian of philosophy, would nowadays dare to deny the influence of economic factors on politics and culture.

If we look back, a century and a half later, on the proposals of *The Communist Manifesto*, we find a mixture of rash draconian measures enforceable only by tyranny (e.g. abolition of inheritance and compulsory agricultural labour), institutions that advanced countries now take for granted (progressive taxation and universal education), and experiments that have been adopted with greater or less success in different times and places (nationalization of railways and banks). Considered as a prophet, Marx has been discredited; and so has his claim that ideology is merely the smokescreen of the status quo. But the most convincing refutation of the thesis that consciousness is impotent to determine life is provided by Marx's own philosophy. For the history of the world since his death has been enormously influenced, for good or ill, by his own system of ideas, considered not as a scientific theory, but as an inspiration to political activism and a guideline for political regimes.

---

[2] Marx's theory of surplus value will be considered in detail in Ch. 11.

Darwin and Natural Selection

Ten years before his death Marx sent a copy of the second edition of the first volume of *Capital* to Charles Darwin, whose *On the Origin of Species* had been published fourteen years earlier. He received a courteous acknowledgement of this gift of 'the great work', but Darwin, like many another reader, found it impossible to proceed beyond the volume's early pages. In giving Marx's funeral oration Engels described the materialist conception of history as a scientific breakthrough comparable with the discovery of evolution by natural selection. This was an exaggeration, but Marx and Darwin did turn out to be the two most influential thinkers of the nineteenth century—and the two most heavily criticized, then and now.

Charles Darwin was born in Shrewsbury in 1809 and boarded at Shrewsbury School from 1818 to 1825. He enrolled as a medical student at Edinburgh in 1825 but did not complete his studies; instead he went to Christ's College in Cambridge and took a pass BA in 1831. The Professor of Botany recommended him to Captain Fitzroy of HMS *Beagle*, who appointed him ship's naturalist. During a five-year cruise in the southern hemisphere Darwin collected a mass of geological, botanical, zoological, and anthropological material. Initially he was more interested in geology than in zoology, and made discoveries about the nature of volcanic islands and the formation of coral reefs. He published a popular account of his maritime researches in 1839 in a volume best known as *The Voyage of the Beagle*. In the same year he married Emma Wedgwood and was elected to the Royal Society.

During the 1840s and 1850s, studying the flora and fauna of his estate in Kent, he developed the theory of natural selection, producing in 1844 a sketch of his ideas for private circulation. He had in mind to present the theory in a vast volume, to be completed some time in the 1860s. However, when another zoologist, Alfred Russell Wallace, had a similar theory of the 'survival of the fittest' presented to a learned society in 1858, Darwin decided to establish the independence and priority of his own ideas, and thus rushed into print an 'abstract' of his ideas, which was *On the Origin of Species*. In 1860 at a meeting of the British Association for the Advancement of Science, Thomas Henry Huxley successfully defended Darwinism in a famous debate with Samuel Wilberforce, the Bishop of Oxford.

In later years Darwin published a number of supplementary treatises on fertilization and variations of structure and behaviour within and across species. The best known of his later books was published in 1871, *The Descent of Man and Selection in Relation to Sex*. In that book, besides developing the theory of sexual selection, which was an important supplement to the theory of natural selection, he defended the thesis that human beings shared a common ancestor with orang-utans, chimpanzees, and gorillas. He died in 1882 and was buried in Westminster Abbey.

Darwin was not the first person to propose a theory of evolution. In the ancient world, as Darwin himself acknowledged, the Sicilian philosopher Empedocles had 'shadowed forth the principle of natural selection'.[3] But Empedocles had been savaged by Aristotle, who believed that species had existed from eternity, and he was ignored by Christians, who believed that animal species had been created by God for Adam in the Garden of Eden. The great Swedish naturalist Linnaeus (1707–78), whose classification of plant and animal species was to provide the platform on which Darwin's theory was built, believed that each species had been separately created and that the resemblances and differences between them revealed the design of the creator.

Linnaeus and other taxonomists had divided the plant and animal kingdoms into genera and species, to which they gave Latin names. All lions, for instance are members of the same species, *felis leo*. The lion species is a member of the genus of cats (*felis*), which includes other species such as the tiger (*felis tigris*) and the leopard (*felis pardus*). Within a given species the characteristics of individuals may vary widely, but the defining mark of a species is that its members can breed with other members to produce offspring of the same species. Unions between members of different species, on the other hand, are commonly sterile.

Rather than appeal to the inscrutable purposes of a creator, a number of naturalists had suggested that the resemblances between different species within a genus might be explained by descent from a distant common ancestor. This was proposed by Darwin's grandfather Erasmus Darwin (1731–1802), and also by the French zoologist J. B. Lamarck, who in 1815 maintained that any generation of a species might acquire a beneficial characteristic which it would then pass on to its offspring. Giraffes, stretching to reach the topmost leaves, would lengthen their necks and beget longer-necked offspring.

[3] See vol. I, p. 21.

Darwin, by resurrecting the ancient idea of natural selection, was able to put forward a quite different explanation of the resemblances and differences between species. The fundamental bases of his theory were three. First, organisms vary greatly in the degree to which they are adapted to the environment in which they live. Second, all species are capable of reproducing at a rate that would increase their numbers from generation to generation: even a single couple of slow-breeding elephants, after a period of 500 years, could have 15 million descendants. Third, the reason that species do not increase and multiply at this rate is that in each generation only a few offspring survive to breed. All the members of each species have to fight for existence, against the climate and against competing individuals and competing species, to obtain food for themselves and to avoid becoming food for others. It is this third factor that operates the selection that is the mechanism of evolution.

Owing to this struggle for life, any variation, however slight, and from whatever cause proceeding, if it be in any degree profitable to an individual of any species in its infinitely complex relations to other organic beings and to external nature, will tend to the preservation of that individual and will generally be inherited by its offspring. The offspring, also, will thus have a better chance of surviving, for, of the many individuals of any species which are periodically born, but a small number can survive. (OS 52)

Darwin distinguished three different kinds of selection. Artificial selection had long been practised by human husbandmen who selected for breeding the specimens, whether of potatoes or racehorses, that were best adapted to their purposes. Natural selection, unlike artificial selection, was not purposive. Advantageous variations were preserved and extended simply by natural pressures on the survival and reproduction of the individuals of a species. Within natural selection Darwin made a further distinction: between natural selection in the narrow sense, which determined whether an individual survived long enough to breed, and sexual selection, which determined with whom such a surviving individual would mate. Unlike Lamarck, Darwin did not believe that the variations in adaptation were acquired by parents in their lifetime: the variations that they passed on were ones they had themselves inherited. Though it was possible to establish some laws of variability, the origin of a particular advantageous variation could well be a matter of chance.

Natural selection can easily be illustrated, and observed, in the case of characteristics within a single species. Suppose that there is a population of moths, some happening to be dark and others happening to be pale, who live on birch trees and are preyed upon by birds. While the trees retain their natural silver colour, the better-camouflaged pale moths will have a better chance of survival, and will therefore come to form the greater part of the population. If, however, the trees become blackened with soot, the odds of survival will tilt in favour of the dark moths. As they survive in more than average numbers, it will appear from the outside that the species is changing its colour, from being characteristically pale to being characteristically dark.

Darwin believed that over a long period of time natural selection could go further and create whole new species of plants and animals. This would, indeed, be a process so slow as to be in the normal sense unobservable; but recent discoveries in geology made plausible the idea that the earth had existed for a sufficient length of time for species to come into and go out of existence in this manner. Evolution could thus explain not only the likenesses and differences between existing species, but also the difference between the species now extant and defunct species from earlier ages that were being discovered in fossil form throughout the world. Even the most complex organs and instincts, Darwin claimed, could be explained by the accumulation of innumerable slight variations, each good for the individual.

To suppose that the eye, with all its inimitable contrivances for adjusting the focus to different distances, for admitting different amounts of light, and for the correction of spherical and chromatic aberration, could have been formed by natural selection, seems, I freely confess, absurd in the highest possible degree. Yet reason tells me, that if numerous gradations from a perfect and complex eye to one very imperfect and simple, each grade being useful to its possessor, can be shown to exist; if further, the eye does vary ever so slightly, and the variations be inherited, which is certainly the case; and if any variation of modification in the organ be ever useful to an animal under changing conditions of life, then the difficulty of believing that a perfect and complex eye could be formed by natural selection, though insuperable by our imagination, can hardly be considered real. (OS 152)

The case for Darwin's theory was greatly strengthened after his death, first when the laws of population genetics established by Gregor Mendel became generally known, and then when the identification of DNA enabled molecular geneticists to elucidate the mechanisms of heredity. The story of Darwinism belongs to the history of science, not the history of philosophy; but no history of philosophy can omit to mention Darwin, because of the implications of his biological work on philosophy of religion and on general metaphysics.[4]

John Henry Newman

Though Darwin's ideas met with opposition in some ecclesiastical circles, they were accepted with equanimity by the greatest religious writer of the Victorian age, John Henry Newman. Shortly after the appearance of *On the Origin of Species* Newman observed that if one were to believe in the separate creation of each species one would also have to believe in the creation of fossil-bearing rocks. 'There is as much want of simplicity in the creation of distinct species', he wrote, 'as in those of the creation of trees in full growth or of rocks with fossils in them. I mean that it is as strange that monkeys should be so like men, with no historical connexion between them, as that there should be...no history or course of facts by which fossil bones got into the rocks.'[5] He was quite prepared 'to go the whole hog with Darwin' and he took no part in any controversy between science and religion. His claim to a place in the history of philosophy lies elsewhere.

Newman was born in London in 1801, and was an undergraduate at Trinity College, Oxford, from 1817 to 1820, and a Fellow of Oriel between 1822 and 1845. In 1828 he became Vicar of St Mary's, the university church, and acquired a lasting fame as a preacher. After an evangelical upbringing he became convinced, over the years, of the truth of the Catholic interpretation of Christianity. He was one of the founders of the 'Oxford Movement', which sought to have this interpretation accepted as authoritative within the Church of England. In 1845, however, he converted to Roman Catholicism and resigned his Oriel fellowship.

As a Roman Catholic priest he founded an oratory, or community of parochial priests, in Birmingham, where he was based for most of the rest of his life. In 1850 he was appointed the first Rector of a new Catholic university in Dublin, a post which he held until 1858. The lectures and addresses which he gave in that capacity became *The Idea of a University*, which when published became a classic of the theory of education.

[4] These implications are discussed in Chs. 7 and 12.
[5] Quoted by David Brown, *Newman: A Man for our Time* (London: SPCK, 1990), 5.

Newman wrote numerous theological works both before and after his conversion, but his claim to be a great writer was established for the general public by his *Apologia pro Vita Sua*, an autobiography written in response to charges against his integrity brought by the novelist Charles Kingsley. In addition to historical and devotional works he wrote one philosophical classic, *An Essay in Aid of a Grammar of Assent* of 1870, which developed epistemological ideas he had first presented in his University Sermons in St Mary's. Newman did not share the enthusiasm of Cardinal Manning, head of the Catholic Church in England, for the Vatican Council's definition of Papal Infallibility in 1870. Nonetheless, he was in 1879 made a cardinal by Pope Leo XIII. He lived a retired life until his death in 1890. One of his best-known works today is *The Dream of Gerontius*, a poetical drama and meditation on death, which was set to music by Edward Elgar in 1900.

Newman's interest in philosophy derived from his desire to prove to the world that not just belief in God, but the acceptance of a specific religious creed, was a completely rational activity. He faced squarely the question: how can religious belief be justified, given that the evidence for its conclusions seems inadequate for the total commitment of faith? He did not, like Kierkegaard, demand the adoption of faith in the absence of reasons, a blind leap over a precipice. He sought to show that adhesion to a creed was itself reasonable, even if no proof could be offered of its articles. In the course of dealing with this question in *The Grammar of Assent*, Newman had much to say of general philosophical interest about the nature of belief, in secular as well as religious contexts.

The general philosophical question posed by Newman is this: is it always wrong to give assent to a proposition in the absence of adequate evidence or argument? Locke had asserted that no proposition should be entertained with greater assurance than justified by the proofs it was built on. In response, Newman pointed to the fact that many of our most solid beliefs go well beyond the flimsy evidence we could offer for them. We all believe that Great Britain is an island; but how many of us have circumnavigated it, or met people who have? If we refused ever to give assents going beyond the force of evidence, the world could not go on, and science itself could make no progress.

Religious belief, then, cannot be condemned as irrational simply on account of being based on grounds that are no more than conjectural. In fact, Newman maintained, strong evidence for the truth of the Christian religion is to be found in the history of Judaism. He agreed, however, that this evidence carried weight only for those who were already prepared to receive it, people who believed in the existence of God and the possibility of revelation. If it is asked why one should believe in God in the first place, Newman responds by appealing to the inward experience of divine power, which is to be found in the voice of conscience.

Few who were not already believers have found convincing either Newman's argument from conscience or his appeal to the testimony of history. But the general epistemological account within which he embeds his apologetics has been admired by philosophers who were far from sharing his religious faith. It is arguably the best treatment of the topics of belief and certainty between Hume and Wittgenstein.[6]

Nietzsche

Just at the time when Newman was presenting his justification of the rationality of religious belief, there was appointed to a professorship in Basel a young man who was to make the twentieth century echo to his proclamation of the death of God. Friedrich Nietzsche was born into a devout Lutheran family in Saxony in 1844. He studied at the universities of Bonn and Leipzig; his training was not in philosophy but in classical philology, in which he displayed such facility that he became a full professor at the age of twenty-four, before he had even completed his doctorate. He taught at Basel from 1869 to 1879, with a brief interval of service in the ambulance corps during the Franco-Prussian War of 1870.

Nietzsche was profoundly influenced by two events shortly before he took up his chair. One was reading of Schopenhauer's *The World as Will and Idea*; the other was meeting Richard Wagner, whose *Tristan und Isolde* had fascinated him since he had heard it at the age of sixteen. His first published work, *The Birth of Tragedy* of 1872, showed the influence of both men. In it he drew a contrast between two aspects of the Greek psyche: the wild irrational passions personified in Dionysus, which found expression in music and tragedy, and the disciplined and harmonious beauty represented by Apollo, which found expression in epic and the plastic arts. The

---

[6] See Ch. 6 below.

triumph of Greek culture was to achieve a synthesis between the two—a synthesis that was disrupted by the rationalistic incursion of Socrates. The decadence which then overtook Greece had infected contemporary Germany, which could achieve salvation only through following the lead of Wagner, to whom the book was dedicated.

Between 1873 and 1876 Nietzsche published four essays, *Untimely Meditations* (or, in another English version, *Songs out of Season*). Two were negative, one a criticism of David Strauss, author of a famous life of Jesus, the other an attack on the pretensions of scientific history. Two were positive: one in praise of Schopenhauer and the other in eulogy of Wagner. But by 1878 Nietzsche had broken with Wagner (he was disgusted with *Parsifal*) and had lost his enthusiasm for Schopenhauer (whose pessimism he now found stifling). In *Human, All too Human*, he showed himself uncharacteristically sympathetic to utilitarian morality and for once appeared to value science as superior to art. But his enduring underlying conviction that art was the supreme task of life displayed itself in the form of the work, which is poetic and aphoristic rather than argumentative or deductive.

In 1879, afflicted by psychosomatic illness, Nietzsche took early retirement from his chair at Basel and brought his academic career to an end. For the next ten years he dwelt in various places in Italy and Switzerland in pursuit of better health, spending many a summer in Sils Maria in the Engadine. He published a series of works in which he hoped to replace the pessimism of Schopenhauer with an optimistic affirmation of life. In works such as *Daybreak* in 1881 and *The Gay Science* (or *Joyful Wisdom*) in 1882 he denounced, as elements hostile to life, Christian self-denial, altruistic ethics, democratic politics, and scientific positivism. He saw it as his task 'to erect a new image and idea of the free spirit'.

As a practical expression of the freedom of his spirit, Nietzsche in 1882 joined the German materialist Paul Rée and the Russian feminist Louise von Salomé in a cohabiting 'trinity'. This love triangle, however, did not last long and from 1883 to 1885 Nietzsche devoted himself to the production of his most famous work, the oracular *Thus Spake Zarathustra*. The unhappy ending of his relationship with Lou may be part cause of the book's most famous aphorism, 'You are going among women? Do not forget the whip!' But the work contained three more important ideas that were going to be of significance in the final period of Nietzsche's life. One is the idea that men as they now are will be superseded by a race of supermen:

The trinity of Salomé, Rée, and Nietzsche, photographed in 1882

'higher ones, stronger ones, more triumphant ones, merrier ones, built squarely in body and soul'. The second is the idea of the transvaluation of values: a complete overturning of traditional and especially Christian moral priorities. The third is the idea of eternal recurrence: in infinite time there are periodic cycles in which all that has ever happened happens once again.

These ideas were given an exposition that was less prophetical and more discursive in the philosophically most important of Nietzsche's works, *Beyond Good and Evil* of 1886 and *The Genealogy of Morals* in 1887. These texts set out a contrast between an aristocratic master-morality which places a high value on nobility, bravery, and truthfulness, and a slave-morality or herd-morality which values submissive traits such as humility, sympathy, and benevolence. Nietzsche saw these works as prolegomena to a systematic exposition of his philosophy, on which he worked energetically but was never able to complete. Several versions extracted from his notes were posthumously published, but only the first part of the work appeared in his lifetime, under the title *The Antichrist* (published in 1895).

The year 1888 was one of feverish production. In addition to *The Antichrist* Nietzsche published a ferocious attack on Wagner (*The Case of Wagner*) and wrote *The Twilight of the Idols* (published in 1889). He also wrote a semi-autobiographical work, *Ecce Homo*, in which can be detected signs of the mental instability (probably of syphilitic origin) that led to him being institutionalized in Jena in 1889. He ended his days insane, being nursed first by his mother and later at Weimar by his sister Elizabeth, who built up an archive of his papers. Nietzsche died in 1900; his sister took control of his *Nachlass* and exercised a degree of protective control over its publication.

During the twentieth century Nietzsche had a great influence in continental Europe, especially upon Russian literature and German philosophy. His opposition to submissive morality and to democratic socialism made him popular among Nazis, who saw themselves as developing a race of superior humans. Partly for this reason, he was long neglected by English-speaking philosophers; but in the latter part of the century, ethicists in the analytic tradition came to realize that his onslaught on traditional morality needed to be answered rather than ignored.[7]

---

[7] Nietzsche's writings on morality are considered in detail in Ch. 9.

2

Peirce to Strawson

C. S. Peirce and Pragmatism

The thinkers whom we have considered so far in these volumes have all come from Europe, North Africa, or the Middle East. The American continent, nowadays home to many of the world's most influential philosophers, was almost barren of philosophy until the latter part of the nineteenth century. In the eighteenth century acute contributions to different areas of philosophy were made by the Calvinist theologian Jonathan Edwards (1703–58) and the Enlightenment polymath Benjamin Franklin (1706–90). Early in the nineteenth century the essayist Ralph Waldo Emerson (1803–82) presented a form of idealism, called 'transcendentalism', which was briefly fashionable in the United States. But it was with the work of Charles Sanders Peirce (1839–1914) that American philosophy really came of age.

Peirce was the son of a formidable professor of mathematics at Harvard, and he took a *summa cum laude* degree in chemistry there in 1863. For thirty years he served on the US coastal survey, and he also undertook research at Harvard Observatory. The only book he published, *Photometric Researches*, was a work of astronomy. Around 1872 he joined William James, Chauncey Wright, Oliver Wendell Holmes, and others in a discussion group known as the Metaphysical Club. He gave several lecture courses at Harvard on the history and logic of science, and from 1879 until 1884 he was a lecturer on logic at the new, research-oriented Johns Hopkins University in Baltimore. But he was a difficult colleague, impatient of academic conventions, and his marriage to Melusina Fay, a pioneering feminist, broke down in 1883. He failed to obtain tenure, and he never again held an academic post or a full-time job. During the latter part of his life he lived in poverty in Pennsylvania with his devoted second wife, Juliette.

Peirce was a highly original thinker. Like many another nineteenth-century philosopher, he took as his starting point the philosophy of Kant, whose *Critique of Pure Reason* he claimed to know almost by heart. But he regarded Kant's comprehension of formal logic as amateurish. When he set himself to repair this deficiency he found it necessary to recast substantial parts of the Kantian system, such as the theory of categories. Unusually among his contemporaries, he knew and admired the writings of the medieval scholastics, in particular the works of Duns Scotus. The feature he most praised in scholastic philosophers (as in Gothic architects) was the complete absence in their work of self-conceit. He himself had a high opinion of his own merits, regarding Aristotle and Leibniz as his only peers in logic. His work ranged widely, not only over logic in the narrow sense, but also encompassing theory of language, epistemology, and philosophy of mind. He was the originator of one of the most influential of American schools of philosophy, namely pragmatism.

During his lifetime, Peirce's philosophy was presented to the public only in a series of journal articles. In 1868 he published in the *Journal of Speculative Philosophy* two articles with the title 'Questions Concerning Certain Faculties Claimed for Man': these set out an early version of his epistemology. The results are mainly negative: we have no power of introspection, and we have no power of thinking without signs. Above all we have no power of intuition: every cognition is determined logically by some prior cognition.

More influential was a series of 'illustrations of the logic of science' which appeared in the *Popular Science Monthly* in 1877–8. In these he enunciated his principle of fallibilism, that anything that claims to be human knowledge may, in the end, turn out to be mistaken. This, he insisted, does not mean that there is no such thing as objective truth. Absolute truth is the goal of scientific inquiry, but the most we can achieve is ever-improving approximations to it. One of the 1878 articles contains the first formulation of what was later called 'the principle of pragmatism'. This was to the effect that in order to attain clearness in our thoughts of an object, we need only consider what conceivable effects of a practical kind the object may involve (*EWP* 300).

In 1884 Peirce edited a collection of *Johns Hopkins Studies in Logic*. He wrote an essay on the logic of relations, and his system of quantificational logic

C.S. Peirce with his second wife Juliette

was presented by one of his students. The system included a novel notation for representing the syntax of relations: e.g. the compound sign 'Lij' could represent that Isaac loves Jessica, and the sign 'Gijk' could represent that Isaac gave Jessica to Kore. It also contained two signs for quantifiers, 'Σ' corresponding to 'some', and 'Π' corresponding to 'all'. The syntax of Peirce's 'General Algebra of Logic', as he called it, was equivalent to that of the system of logic that Gottlob Frege, unknown to him, had developed in Germany a few years previously.

In *The Monist* in 1891–2, 'A Guess at the Riddle', Peirce presented his metaphysics and philosophy of mind against the background of an overall evolutionary cosmology. The definitive statement of his pragmatism (which he now preferred to call 'pragmaticism', since he wished to disown some of the theses of his pragmatist disciples) was issued in a course of lectures at Harvard in 1903 and a further series of papers in *The Monist* in 1905.

In the last years of his life Peirce worked hard to develop a general theory of signs—a 'semiotic' as he called it—as a framework for the philosophy of thought and language. Many of these ideas, which some regard as his most important contribution to philosophy, were worked out between 1903 and 1912 in correspondence with an Englishwoman, Victoria Welby.

Peirce never completed the full synthesis of philosophy on which he worked for many years, and at his death left a mass of unpublished drafts, many of which were posthumously published once interest in his work blossomed in the twentieth century. His influence on other philosophers has not been in proportion to his genius. Peirce's work in logic was never presented in a fully rigorous form, and it was Frege who, through Russell, gave to the world the logical system that the two of them had independently conceived. Peirce's subtle version of pragmatism never seized the imagination of the world in the same way as the more popular version of his admirer William James. It is to the work of Frege and James, therefore, that we now turn.

The Logicism of Frege

Gottlob Frege (1848–1925) was known to few people in his lifetime, but after his death came to occupy a unique position in the history of philosophy. He was the inventor of modern mathematical logic, and an outstanding philosopher of mathematics. He is revered by many as the founder of the school of philosophy which has long been the dominant one in Anglophone universities: analytic philosophy, which focuses its concern on the analysis of meaning in language. It was his influence—mediated in Britain by Bertrand Russell and on the European mainland by Edmund Husserl—that gave philosophy the linguistic turn that characterized the twentieth century.

Frege was born into a Lutheran family of schoolteachers who lived in Wismar, on the Baltic coast of Germany. His father died when he was in his teens, and he was supported through school and university by his mother, now headmistress of the girls' school that had been founded by her husband. He entered Jena University in 1869, but after four semesters he moved to Göttingen, where he took his Ph.D., with a geometrical dissertation, in 1873. He returned to Jena as a *privatdozent*, or unsalaried lecturer, in 1874, and taught there in the mathematics faculty for forty-four years, becoming a professor in 1879. Apart from his intellectual activity his life was uneventful and secluded. Few of his colleagues troubled to read his books and articles, and for his most important work he had difficulty in finding a publisher.

Frege's productive career began in 1879 with the publication of a pamphlet entitled *Begriffsschrift* ('Concept Script'). The concept script that gave the book its title was a new symbolism designed to bring out clearly logical relationships that ordinary language obscures. Frege used it to develop a new system that has a permanent place at the heart of modern logic: the propositional calculus. This is the branch of logic that deals with those inferences that depend on the force of negation, conjunction, disjunction, etc. when applied to sentences as wholes. Its fundamental principle is to treat the truth-value (i.e. the truth or falsehood as the case may be) of sentences containing connectives such as 'and', 'if', and 'or' as being determined solely by the truth-values of the component sentences linked by the connectives. Composite sentences such as 'Snow is white and grass is green' are treated as being, in the logicians' technical term, *truth-functions* of their constituent simple propositions such as 'Snow is white' and 'Grass is green'.

Propositional logic had been studied in the ancient world by the Stoics and in the Middle Ages by Ockham and others;[1] but it was Frege who gave it its first systematic formulation. *Begriffsschrift* presents the propo-

---

[1] See vol. I, p. 141; vol. II, pp. 148–50.

sitional calculus in an axiomatic manner in which all the laws of propositional logic are derived, by a specified method of inference, from a number of primitive propositions. The actual symbolism that Frege invented for this purpose is difficult to print, and has long been superseded in the presentation of the calculus; but the operations that it expressed continue to be fundamental in mathematical logic.

It was not, however, the propositional calculus, but the predicate calculus, that was Frege's greatest contribution to logic. This is the branch of logic that deals with the internal structure of propositions rather than with propositions considered as atomic units. Frege invented a novel notation for quantification, that is to say, a method of symbolizing and rigorously displaying those inferences that depend for their validity on expressions such as 'all' or 'some', 'no' or 'none'. With this notation he presented a predicate calculus that greatly improved upon the Aristotelian syllogistic that had hitherto been looked upon as the be-all and end-all of logic. Frege's calculus allowed formal logic, for the first time, to cope with sentences containing multiple quantification, such as 'Nobody knows everything' and 'Every boy loves some girl'.[2]

Though *Begriffsschrift* is a classical text in the history of logic, Frege's purpose in writing it was concerned more with mathematics than with logic. He wanted to put forward a formal system of arithmetic as well as a formal system of logic, and most importantly, he wanted to show that the two systems were intimately linked. All the truths of arithmetic, he claimed, could be shown to follow from truths of logic without the need of any extra support. How this thesis (which came to be known as 'logicism') was to be demonstrated was sketched in *Begriffsschrift*, and set out more fully in two later works, *Grundlagen der Arithmetik* ('Foundations of Arithmetic') of 1884 and *Die Grundgesetze der Arithmetik* ('The Fundamental Laws of Arithmetic') of 1893 and 1903.

The most important step in Frege's logicist programme was to define arithmetical notions, such as that of number, in terms of purely logical notions, such as that of class. Frege achieves this by treating the cardinal numbers as classes of equivalent classes, that is to say, of classes with the same number of members. Thus the number two is the class of pairs, and the number three the class of trios. Such a definition at first sight appears

---

[2] See Ch. 4 below.

circular, but in fact it is not since the notion of equivalence between classes can be defined without making use of the notion of number. Two classes are equivalent to each other if they can be mapped onto each other without residue. Thus, to take an example of Frege's, a waiter may know that there are as many knives as there are plates on a table without knowing how many of each there are. All he needs to do is to observe that there is a knife to the right of every plate and a plate to the left of every knife.

Thus, we could define four as the class of all classes equivalent to the class of gospel-makers. But such a definition would be useless for the logicist's purpose since the fact that there were four gospel-makers is no part of logic. Frege has to find, for each number, not only a class of the right size, but one whose size is guaranteed by logic. He does this by beginning with zero as the first of the number series. This can be defined in purely logical terms as the class of all classes equivalent to the class of objects that are not identical with themselves: a class that obviously has no members ('the null class'). We can then go on to define the number one as the class of all classes equivalent to the class whose only member is zero. In order to pass from these definitions to definitions of the other natural numbers Frege needs to define the notion of 'succeeding' in the sense in which three succeeds two, and four succeeds three, in the number series. He defines 'n immediately succeeds m' as 'There exists a concept F, and an object falling under it x, such that the number of Fs is n and the number of Fs not identical with x is m'. With the aid of this definition the other numbers can be defined without using any notions other than logical ones such as identity, class, and class-equivalence.

Begriffsschrift is a very austere and formal work. *The Foundations of Arithmetic* sets out the logicist programme much more fully, but also much more informally. Symbols appear rarely, and Frege takes great pains to relate his work to that of other philosophers. According to Kant, our knowledge of both arithmetic and geometry depended on intuition: in the *Critique of Pure Reason* he had maintained that mathematical truths were synthetic a priori, that is to say that while they were genuinely informative, they were known in advance of all experience.[3] John Stuart Mill, as we have seen, maintained that mathematical propositions were empirical generalizations, widely applicable and widely confirmed, but a posteriori nonetheless.

---

[3] See vol. III, p. 103.

Frege agreed with Kant against Mill that mathematics was known a priori, and like Kant he thought that geometry rested on intuition. But his thesis that arithmetic was a branch of logic meant that it was not synthetic, as Kant had claimed, but analytic. It was based, if Frege was right, solely upon general laws that were operative in every sphere of knowledge and needed no support from empirical facts. Arithmetic had no separate subject matter of its own any more than logic had.

In the *Foundations* there are two theses that Frege regarded as important. One is that each individual number is a self-subsistent object. The other is that the content of a statement assigning a number is an assertion about a concept. At first sight these propositions seem to conflict with each other; but once we understand what Frege means by 'concept' and 'object' we see that they do not.

In saying that a number is an object, Frege is not suggesting that it is something tangible like a bush or a box. Rather, he is denying two things. First, he is denying that a number is a property of anything: in three blind mice, threeness is not a property of any mouse in the way that blindness is. Second, he is denying that number is anything subjective, an image or idea or any property of any mental item.

Concepts, for Frege, are mind-independent, and so there is no contradiction between the claim that numbers are objective and the claim that number statements are statements about concepts. By this second claim, Frege means that a statement such as 'The earth has one moon' assigns the number one to the concept *moon of the earth*. Similarly, 'Venus has no moons' assigns the number zero to the concept *moon of Venus*. In this latter case, it is quite clear that there does not exist any moon to have a number as its property. But all statements of number are to be treated in the same way.

But if number statements of this kind are statements about concepts, what kind of object is a number itself? Frege's answer is that a number is the extension of a concept. The number that belongs to the concept F, he says, is the extension of the concept 'like numbered to the concept F'. This is tantamount to saying that it is the class of all classes that have the same number of members as the class of Fs, as was explained above. So Frege's theory that numbers are objects depends on the possibility of taking classes as objects.

In the years after the publication of *Foundations*, Frege published a number of seminal papers on the philosophy of language. Three appeared in 1891–2:

'Function and Concept', 'Sense and Reference', 'Concept and Object'. Each of these presented original philosophical ideas of great importance with astonishing brevity and clarity. They were seen, no doubt, by Frege himself as ancillary to his concerns with the nature of mathematics, but at the present time they are regarded as founding classics of modern semantic theory.[4]

Between 1884 and 1893 Frege worked on the treatise that should have been the climax of his intellectual career, the *Grundgesetze der Arithmetik*, which was to set out in a complete and formal manner the logicist construction of arithmetic from logic. The task was to enunciate a set of axioms that would be recognizably truths of logic, to propound a set of undoubtedly sound rules of inference, and then from those axioms by those rules to derive, one by one, the standard truths of arithmetic. The derivation was to occupy three volumes, of which only two were completed, the first dealing with the natural numbers, and the second with negative, fractional, irrational, and complex numbers.

Frege's ambitious project aborted before it was completed. Between the publication of the first volume in 1893 and the second in 1903 Frege received a letter from an English philosopher, Bertrand Russell, pointing out that the fifth of the initial set of axioms rendered the whole system inconsistent. This axiom stated, in effect, that if every F is a G, and every G is an F, then the class of Fs is identical with the class of Gs; and vice versa. It was the axiom which, in Frege's words, allowed the transition from a concept to its extension, the transition from concepts to classes that was essential if it was to be established that numbers were logical objects.

The problem, as Russell pointed out, was that the system, with this axiom, permits without restriction the formation of classes of classes, and classes of classes of classes, and so on. Classes must themselves be classifiable. Now can a class be a member of itself? Most classes are not (the class of men is not a man) but some apparently are (e.g. the class of classes is surely a class). It seems, therefore, that we have two kinds of classes: those that are members of themselves and those that are not. But the formation of the class of all classes that are not members of themselves leads to paradox: if it is a member of itself, then it is not a member of itself, and if it is not a

---

[4] Frege's contribution to the philosophy of language is detailed in Ch. 5.

member of itself, then it is a member of itself. A system that leads to such a paradox cannot be logically sound.

The second volume of *Grundgesetze* was already in press when Russell's letter arrived. Utterly downcast, Frege described the paradox in an appendix, and attempted to patch the system by weakening the guilty axiom. But this revised system in its turn proved inconsistent. After retiring from Jena in 1918 Frege seems to have given up his belief that arithmetic can be derived from logic, and returned to the Kantian view that it is, like geometry, synthetic a priori.

We now know that the logicist programme can never be carried out. The path from the axioms of logic to the theorems of arithmetic is barred at two points. First, as Russell showed, the naive set theory that was part of Frege's logical basis was inconsistent in itself. Second, the notion of 'axioms of arithmetic' was itself called in question when it was later shown (by the Austrian mathematician Kurt Gödel in 1931) that it was impossible to give arithmetic a complete and consistent axiomatization.

Nonetheless, Frege's philosophical legacy was enormous. He often compared the mathematician to a geographer who maps new continents. His own career as a thinker resembled that of Christopher Columbus as an explorer. Just as Columbus failed to find a passage to India but made Europe acquainted with a whole new continent, so Frege failed to derive arithmetic from logic, but made innovations in logic and advances in philosophy that permanently changed the whole map of both subjects. Like Columbus, Frege succumbed to discouragement and depression; he was never to know that he was the founder of an influential philosophical movement. But he did not give up all hope that his work had value: leaving his papers to his son just before his death in 1925 he wrote, 'Do not despise the pieces I have written. Even if all is not gold, there is gold in them.'

Psychology and Pragmatism in William James

William James (1842–1910) was six years older than Frege, but he began his philosophical career quite late in life. He was born in New York, the son of a Swedenborgian theologian and the elder brother of the celebrated novelist Henry James. He was educated partly in America and partly in Europe, where he attended schools in France and Germany. For a while he hesitated between painting and medicine as a career, but in 1864 he enrolled in the Harvard Medical School. After taking his degree he suffered a period of ill health and depression, but after a recovery (which he attributed to reading the works of the French philosopher Charles Renouvier) he was appointed to the Harvard faculty in 1873 as an instructor in anatomy and physiology. His interests shifted towards empirical psychology, and in 1876 he established the first psychological laboratory in America. Among his pupils was the novelist Gertrude Stein. His two-volume *Principles of Psychology*, of 1890, was a racy survey of the results of the infant discipline. The task of psychology, as James saw it, was to link conditions of the brain with the varying phenomena of the stream of consciousness.

The book became a standard textbook, but by the time it was published James had left psychology and become a professor of philosophy—a subject that had fascinated him since his discussions with Peirce and others in the Metaphysical Club of 1872. Like his father, James was deeply concerned with religious issues, and was anxious to reconcile a scientific world-view with a belief in God, freedom, and immortality. His professional career as a philosophical writer was inaugurated in 1897 with the appearance of *The Will to Believe*, in which he discussed situations where we have to decide on issues in the absence of compelling theoretical evidence. In such cases, he argued, the duty to believe truth should be given equal weight with the duty to avoid error. He soon built up an international reputation, and in 1901–2 he gave the Gifford lectures in Edinburgh, which were later published as *Varieties of Religious Experience*. In that work he set himself to examine 'the feelings, acts and experiences of individual men in their solitude, so far as they apprehend themselves to stand in relation to whatever they may consider the divine.' He subjected the phenomena of mysticism and other forms of religious sentiment to empirical investigation in the hope of establishing their authenticity and validity.

It was the publication of *Pragmatism* in 1907 that established James's position as the doyen of American philosophy. Both the title and the main theme of the work were credited by James to Peirce, and in his formulation of his pragmatic principle, his debt is obvious.

To attain perfect clearness in our thoughts of an object, we need only consider what conceivable effects of a practical kind the object may involve—what sensations we are to expect from it, and what reactions we must prepare. Our conception of these effects, whether immediate or remote, is then for us the whole of our conception of the object, so far as that conception has positive significance at all. (*P* 47)

However, whereas Peirce's pragmatism was a theory of meaning, James's was a a theory of truth, and whereas Peirce's pragmatism was interpersonal and objective, James's was individualist and subjective. For this reason, Peirce disowned James's theory and renamed his own 'pragmaticism'.

According to James's pragmatism, an idea is true so long as to believe it is profitable to our lives: 'The true is the name of whatever proves itself to be good in the way of belief' (*P* 42). He and his followers sometimes summed this up in the slogan, 'What is true is what works'. Critics objected that belief in a falsehood might make people happier than belief in a truth, which meant that truth could not be identified with long-term satisfactoriness. Both believers and unbelievers were shocked by James's statement, 'if the hypothesis of God works satisfactorily in the widest sense of the word, it is true' (*P* 143).

James insisted that his theory did not involve any denial of objective reality. Reality and truth are different from each other. Things have reality; it is ideas and beliefs that are true. 'Realities are not *true*, they *are*; and beliefs are true *of* them' (*T* 196). It is not by discovering whether the consequences of a belief are good that we learn whether it is true or not; but it is the consequences that assign 'the only intelligible practical *meaning* to that difference in our beliefs which our habit of calling them true or false comports' (*T* 273).

It is often said that what makes a belief true is its correspondence with reality. James is willing to accept this, but asks what in the concrete the notion of correspondence amounts to. When we speak of an idea 'pointing to' reality, or 'fitting it', or 'corresponding', or 'agreeing' with it, what we are really talking about is the processes of validation or verification that lead us from the idea to the reality. Such mediating events, James says, *make* the idea true.

In a series of essays (collected in *The Meaning of Truth*, 1909) James defended, qualified, and refined his pragmatism. But it remained unclear whether in his system the actual existence of a reality is a necessary condition of a belief in it being satisfactory (in which case he is committed to correspondence as an element of truth) or whether a belief in an object may be satisfactory without that object actually existing (in which case he is open to the charge of preferring wishful thinking to genuine inquiry).

In the same year as he published *The Meaning of Truth* James published *A Pluralistic Universe*, in which he applied pragmatism in support of a religious world-view. He spoke of our awareness of a 'wider self from which saving experiences flow in' and of a 'mother sea of consciousness'. He believed, however, that the amount of suffering in the world prevents us from believing in an infinite, absolute divinity: the superhuman consciousness is limited either in power, or in knowledge, or in both. Even God cannot determine or predict the future; whether the world will become better or worse depends on the choices of human beings in cooperation with him.

In his old age James, a genial and affable personality and a great communicator, was revered by many inside and outside the United States. Peirce, on the other hand, was isolated and destitute, and in 1907 was discovered by one of James's students nearly dead from starvation in a Cambridge lodging house. James organized a fund which supplied Peirce's basic needs until his death from cancer in 1914. James himself died of heart disease in 1910; on his deathbed in Cambridge he asked his brother Henry to remain close for six weeks to receive any messages he could send to him from beyond the grave. No messages are recorded.

James died before completing his metaphysical system, but his pragmatist programme was continued by others after his death. John Dewey (1859–1952), in a long academic career at Ann Arbor, Chicago, and Columbia in New York, applied it most particularly in the area of American education, but he also wrote influential books on many social and political topics. His constant aim was to explore how far methods of inquiry that had been so successful in physical science and in technology could be extended into other areas of human endeavour.

In England F. C. S. Schiller (1864–1937) developed a version of pragmatism that he called 'humanism'. Schiller was a graduate of Balliol College, Oxford, and taught for a while at Cornell University in upstate New York, where he met James, before returning to a fellowship at Corpus Christi College. He was a lonely figure at Oxford because in the last years of the nineteenth century, philosophy departments in the major universities of the United Kingdom were dominated by a British version of Hegelian idealism.

British Idealism and its Critics

After the death of John Stuart Mill a reaction had set in against the tradition of British empiricism of which he had been such a distinguished exponent. In 1874, a year after Mill's death, a Balliol tutor, T. H. Green (1836–82), brought out an edition of David Hume's *Treatise of Human Nature* with a substantial introduction subjecting the presuppositions of empiricism to devastating criticism. In the same year there appeared the first of a long series of English translations of the works of Hegel, which had first been introduced to Oxford in the 1840s by Benjamin Jowett (1817–93), the Master of Green's college. Two years later F. H. Bradley of Merton published *Ethical Studies*, a founding classic of British Hegelianism. In 1893 Bradley completed *Appearance and Reality*, the fullest and most magisterial statement of British idealism. Shortly afterwards at Cambridge the methods and some of the doctrines of Hegel's *Logic* were expounded in a series of treatises by the Trinity College philosopher J. M. E. McTaggart.

Green's idealism, like James's pragmatism, was partly motivated by religious concerns. 'There is one spiritual and self-conscious being of which all that is real is the activity and expression,' he wrote in *Prolegomena to Ethics*, published the year after his death in 1882; 'we are all related to this spiritual being, not merely as parts of the world which is its expression, but as partakers in some inchoate measure of the self-consciousness through which it at once constitutes itself and distinguishes itself from the world.' This participation, he maintained, was the source of morality and religion. Bradley and McTaggart, however, evacuated idealism of any remotely Christian content, and the latter went so far as to deny that there was any Absolute other than a community of finite selves.

It was common ground among the British idealists, however, that reality was essentially spiritual in nature: they rejected the dualist idea that mind and matter were two equal and independent realms of being. But Bradley's 'monism' had another fundamental aspect: the claim that reality is to be considered as a totality. Truth belongs not to individual, atomistic propositions, but only to judgements about being as a whole. In *Appearance and Reality* Bradley sought to show that if we try to conceive the universe as a complex of independent substances distinct from their relations to each other we fall into contradiction. Every item in the universe is related—internally related, by its very essence—to every other item. The objects of everyday experience, the space and time that they inhabit, and indeed the very subject of experience, the individual self—all these are mere appearances, helpful for practical purposes, but quite misleading as to the true nature of reality.

The dominance of idealism was decisively called into question at the turn of the century by two young Cambridge philosophers, G. E. Moore (1873–1958) and Bertrand Russell (1872–1970). Both were pupils of McTaggart and took their first steps in philosophy as Hegelians. But Russell found Hegel himself much less impressive than McTaggart, and was disgusted by his woolly attitude to mathematics. Moore, in 'The Nature of Judgement' (1899), rejected the fundamental thesis that reality is a creation of the mind, and replaced it with a Platonic realism: concepts are objective, independent realities, and the world consists of such concepts combined with each other into true propositions. After this attack on metaphysical idealism, Moore four years later attacked empiricist idealism. In 'The Refutation of Idealism' he rejected the claim that *esse* is *percipi*; to exist is something quite different from being perceived, and the objects of our knowledge are independent of our knowledge of them. Moreover, material objects are something we directly perceive.

Moore's revolt against idealism had a great impact on Russell. 'It was an immense excitement', he later recalled, 'after having supposed the sensible world unreal, to be able to believe again that there really were such things as tables and chairs' (*A* 135). He received a great sense of liberation from the thought that, *pace* Locke and his successors, grass really was green. Like Moore, he combined his renunciation of idealism with the affirmation of a Platonic faith in universals: every word, particular or general, stood for an objective entity. In particular, in reaction against Bradley, he attached great importance to the independent reality of relations. In a brilliant study of the philosophy of Leibniz in 1899 he went so far as to maintain that the elaborate and incredible structure of the metaphysics of monads arises from the single error of thinking that all sentences must be of subject–predicate form, instead of realizing that relational sentences are irreducible to that pattern.

The hall of Trinity College Cambridge, home to G.E.Moore, Bertrand Russell, and Ludwig Wittgenstein

Russell on Mathematics, Logic, and Language

Relations were a matter of particular interest to Russell at this time because the focus of his thought was on the nature of mathematics, in which relational statements such as '*n* is the successor of *m*' play an important role. Independently of Frege, and initially without any knowledge of his work, Russell had undertaken a logicist project of deriving mathematics from pure logic. His endeavour was indeed more ambitious than Frege's since he hoped to show that not just arithmetic, but geometry and analysis also, were derived from general logical axioms. Between 1900 and 1903, influenced in part by the Italian mathematician Giuseppe Peano, he worked out his ideas for incorporation into a substantial volume, *The Principles of Mathematics*. It was in the course of this work that he encountered the paradox that bears his name, the paradox generated by the class of all classes that are not members of themselves. As we have seen, he communicated this discovery to Frege, to whom he had been directed by Peano. Russell introduced Frege's work to an English readership in an appendix to *The Principles*. In the light of the paradox, the two great logicists saw that their project, if it was to succeed, would need considerable modification.

Russell's attempt to avoid the paradox took the form of a Theory of Types. According to this theory, it was wrong to treat classes as randomly classifiable objects. Individuals and classes belonged to different logical types, and what could be asserted of elements of one type could not be significantly asserted of another. 'The class of dogs is not a dog' was not true or false but meaningless. Similarly, what can significantly be said of classes cannot be said of classes of classes, and so on through the hierarchy of logical types. To avoid the paradox, we must observe the difference of types between different levels of the hierarchy.

But now another difficulty arises. Recall that Frege had, in effect, defined the number two as the class of all pairs, and defined all the natural numbers in a similar manner. But a pair is just a two-membered class, so the number two, on this account, is a class of classes. If we put limitations on the formation of classes of classes, how can we define the series of natural numbers? Russell retained the definition of zero as the class whose only member is the null class, but he now treated the number one as the class of all classes equivalent to the class whose members are (*a*) the members of the null class, plus (*b*) any object not a member of that class.

The number two was treated in turn as the class of classes equivalent to the class whose members are (*a*) the members of the class used to define one, plus (*b*) any object not a member of that defining class. In this way the numbers can be defined one after the other, and each number is a class of classes of individuals.

However, the natural number series can be continued thus ad infinitum only if the number of objects in the universe is itself infinite. For if there are only *n* individuals then there will be no classes with *n* + 1 members, and so no cardinal number *n* + 1. Russell accepted this and therefore added to his axioms an axiom of infinity, i.e. the hypothesis that the number of objects in the universe is not finite. Whether or not this hypothesis is true, it is surely not a truth of pure logic, and so the need to postulate it appears to nullify the logicist project of deriving arithmetic from logic alone.

Russell's later philosophy of mathematics was presented to the world in two remarkable works. The first, more technical, presentation was written in collaboration with his former tutor A. N. Whitehead and appeared in three volumes between 1910 and 1913 under the title *Principia Mathematica*. The second, more popular work, *Introduction to Mathematical Philosophy*, was written while he was serving a prison sentence for his activities as an anti-war protester in 1917.

By this time, Russell had achieved distinction outside the philosophy of mathematics in areas that were later to become major preoccupations of British philosophers. His early work, along with that of Moore, is often said to have inaugurated a new era in British philosophy, the era of 'analytic philosophy'. Even though the impetus to the analytic style of thinking can be traced back, as Russell himself was happy to admit, to the work of Frege, it was Moore who first gave currency, in the twentieth century, to the term 'analysis' itself as the mark of a particular way of philosophizing.

'Analysis' was, first and foremost, an anti-idealist slogan: instead of accepting the necessity of understanding a whole before one could understand its parts, Moore and Russell insisted that the right road to understanding was to analyse wholes by taking them to pieces. But what was it that was to be taken to pieces—things or signs? Initially, both Moore and Russell saw themselves as analysing concepts, not language—concepts that were objective realities independent of the mind. 'Where the mind can distinguish elements', Russell wrote in 1903, 'there must *be* different elements to distinguish' (*PM* 466). Analysis would reveal the complexity of concepts, and exhibit their constituent elements. These constituents might be the subjects of further analysis, or they might be simple and unanalysable. In *Principia Ethica* (1903) Moore famously claimed that *good* was such a simple, unanalysable property.

Russell, at the time of *The Principles of Mathematics*, believed that in order to save the objectivity of concepts and judgements it was necessary to accept the existence of propositions that subsisted independently of their expression in sentences. Not only concepts, relations, and numbers had being, he believed, but also chimeras and the Homeric gods. If they had no being, it would be impossible to make propositions about them. 'Thus being is a general attribute of everything, and to mention anything is to show that it is' (*PM* 449).

It was Russell's seminal paper of 1905, 'On Denoting', that gave analysis a linguistic turn. In that paper he showed how to make sense of sentences containing expressions like 'the round square' and 'the present King of France' without maintaining that these expressions denoted some entity, however shadowy, in the world. The paper was for long regarded as a paradigm of analysis; but of course it contains no analysis of round squares or non-existent kings. Instead, it shows how to rewrite such sentences, preserving their meaning, but removing the apparent attribution of being to the non-existent. And Russell's method is explicitly linguistic: it rests on making a distinction between those symbols (such as proper names) that denote something and the world, and other symbols which he called 'incomplete symbols', of which definite descriptions such as 'the present King of France' are one instance. These symbols have no meaning on their own—they do not denote anything—but the sentences in which they occur do have a meaning, that is to say they express a proposition that is either true or false.[5]

Logical analysis, then, as practised in 'On Denoting' is a technique of substituting a logically clear form of words for another form of words which is in some way misleading. But in Russell's mind logical analysis was not only a linguistic device for the classification of sentences. He came to believe that once logic had been cast into a perspicuous form it would reveal the structure of the world.

---

[5] Russell's theory of definite descriptions is presented in detail in Ch. 5.

Logic contains individual variables and propositional functions: corresponding to this, Russell believed, the world contains particulars and universals. In logic complex propositions are built up as truth-functions of simple propositions. Similarly, Russell came to believe, there were in the world independent atomic facts corresponding to the simple propositions. Atomic facts consisted either in the possession by a particular of a characteristic, or else in a relation between two or more particulars. This theory of Russell's acquired the name 'logical atomism'.

The development of the theory can be followed in the books that Russell wrote in the years leading up to the First World War: *The Problems of Philosophy* (1912), a lastingly popular introduction to the subject, and the more professional *Our Knowledge of the External World* of 1914. The most vivid presentation was in a series of lectures in London in 1918, 'The Philosophy of Logical Atomism', published much later in *Logic and Knowledge* (1956). Russell came to believe that every proposition that we can understand must be composed wholly of items with which we are acquainted. 'Acquaintance' was his word for immediate presentation: we were acquainted, for instance, with our own sense-data, which were his equivalents of Hume's impressions or Descartes's thoughts. But direct acquaintance was also possible with the universals that lay behind the predicates of a reformed logical language; so much of Russell's early Platonism remained. Acquaintance, however, was not possible with objects distant in space and time: we could not be acquainted with Queen Victoria or even with our own past sense-data. The things that were not known by acquaintance were known by description; hence the importance of the theory of descriptions in the development of logical atomism.

Russell now applied the theory of descriptions not only to round squares and fictional objects but to many things that common sense would regard as perfectly real, such as Julius Caesar, tables, and cabbages. These, he now maintained, were logical constructions out of sense-data. In a sentence such as 'Caesar crossed the Rubicon', uttered in England now, we have a proposition in which there are no individual constituents with which we are acquainted. In order to explain how we can understand the sentence, Russell analysed the names 'Caesar' and 'Rubicon' as definite descriptions which, spelt out in full, would not include any terms referring to the objects apparently named in the sentence.

Ordinary proper names, therefore, were disguised descriptions. A fully analysed sentence would contain only logically proper names (words referring to particulars with which we are acquainted) and universal terms (words indicating characters and relations). Russell's account of what counted as logically proper names varied from time to time. In the most austere versions of the theory only pure demonstratives appeared to count as names, so that an atomic proposition would be something like '(this) red' or '(this) beside (that)'.

'The Philosophy of Logical Atomism' was far from being Russell's last word on philosophy. In 1921 he wrote *The Analysis of Mind*, which defended a version of William James's neutral monism, the theory that both mind and matter consist of a neutral material which is, for all practical purposes, nothing other than the data of internal and external senses. During the 1930s and 1940s Russell wrote many popular books on social and political topics, and he became famous for the unorthodox nature of his moral ideas and notorious for the breakdown of successive marriages. In 1940, having been appointed to a short-term professorship at the City College of New York, he was declared unfit to teach by the State Supreme Court. In 1945 he published a brilliantly written, if often inaccurate, *History of Western Philosophy*, which led to his being awarded the Nobel Prize for literature.

Russell's last philosophical book was *Human Knowledge: Its Scope and Limits*, published in 1948, in which he attempted to provide an empiricist justification of scientific method. To his disappointment, the book received little attention. Indeed, though he became very widely known in later life, especially after he inherited an earldom, as a campaigner on social and political topics, particularly on the issue of nuclear disarmament, his reputation among professional philosophers never recovered the level of respect accorded to his works prior to 1920. Logical atomism itself, as he was the first to admit, was in large part due to the ideas of one of his former pupils, Ludwig Wittgenstein, to whose history we now turn.

Wittgenstein's Tractatus

Wittgenstein was born in Vienna in 1889 into an Austrian family of Jewish descent. The family was large and wealthy, the father a prominent steel millionaire who had nine children by his Catholic wife, and had all of them baptized as Catholics. The family was also highly artistic; Johannes Brahms was a frequent guest, and Ludwig's brother Paul was a concert pianist who achieved international fame in spite of losing an arm in the 1914–18 war. Ludwig was educated at home until he was fourteen, after which he attended for three years the *Realschule* at Linz. Among his schoolboy contemporaries was Adolf Hitler.

At school Wittgenstein, partly under the influence of Schopenhauer, ceased to be a religious believer. He studied engineering in Berlin, and later at the University of Manchester, where he designed a jet-reaction engine for aircraft. He read Russell's *Principles of Mathematics* and through it became acquainted with the work of Frege, whom he visited at Jena in 1911. On Frege's advice he went to Cambridge, and spent five terms at Trinity College, studying under Russell, who quickly recognized and generously fostered his genius.

Wittgenstein left Cambridge in 1913 and went to live as a solitary in a hut he had built himself in Norway. The notes and letters he wrote at this period exhibit the germination of the view of philosophy he was to retain throughout his life. Philosophy, he wrote, was not a deductive discipline; it could not be placed on the same footing as the natural sciences. 'Philosophy gives no pictures of reality and can neither confirm nor confute scientific investigations' (*NB* 93).

When war broke out in 1914 Wittgenstein enlisted as a volunteer in the Austrian artillery, and served with conspicuous courage on the eastern and Italian fronts. He was captured by Italian soldiers in the southern Tyrol in November 1918 and sent to a prison camp near Monte Cassino. During his military service he had written philosophical thoughts into his diary, and during his imprisonment he turned them into the only philosophical book that he published in his lifetime, *Tractatus Logico-Philosophicus*. He sent this book from the prison camp to Russell, with whom he was later able to discuss it in Holland. It was published in German in 1921 and shortly afterwards in England with an English translation by C. K. Ogden and an introduction by Russell.

The *Tractatus* is short, beautiful, and cryptic. It consists of a series of numbered paragraphs, often very brief. The first is 'The world is all that is the case' and the last is 'Whereof one cannot speak, thereof one must be silent.' The key theme of the book is the picture theory of meaning. Language, we are told, consists of propositions that picture the world.

Propositions are the perceptible expressions of thoughts, and thoughts are logical pictures of facts, and the world is the totality of facts.

An English sentence, such as 'The London train leaves at 11.15' or 'Blood is thicker than water', does not look like a picture. But Wittgenstein believed that propositions and thoughts were pictures in a literal sense; if they did not look like pictures, that was because language throws a heavy disguise around thought. But even in ordinary language, he insisted, there is a perceptibly pictorial element. Take the sentence 'My fork is to the left of my knife'. This says something quite different from another sentence containing exactly the same words, namely 'My knife is to the left of my fork'. What makes the first sentence have the meaning it does is the fact that within it *the words* 'my fork' occur to the left of *the words* 'my knife', as they do not in the second sentence. So here a spatial relationship between words pictures a spatial relationship between things (*TLP* 4.102).

Few cases are as simple as this. If the sentence were spoken instead of written, it would be a temporal relation between sounds rather than a spatial relationship on the page that would represent the relationship between the items on the table. But this in turn is because the spoken sequence and the spatial array have a certain abstract structure in common. According to the *Tractatus* any picture must have something in common with what it depicts. This shared minimum Wittgenstein calls its logical form. Most propositions, unlike the untypical example above, do not have spatial form in common with the situation they depict; but any proposition must have logical form in common with what it depicts.

To reveal the pictorial structure of thought behind the disguise of ordinary language, Wittgenstein believed, we have to proceed by logical analysis along the lines suggested by Russell. In this analysis, he maintained, we will in the end come to symbols that denote entirely non-complex objects. A fully analysed proposition will consist of a combination of atomic propositions, each of which will contain names of simple objects, names related to each other in ways that will picture, truly or falsely, the relations between the objects they represent. Such an analysis may be beyond human powers, but the thought the proposition expresses already, in the mind, has the complexity of the fully analysed proposition. We express this thought in plain German or English by the unconscious operation of extremely complicated rules. The connection between language and the world is made by the correlation between the ultimate elements of these thoughts deep in the mind, and the atomic objects that constitute the essence of the world. How these correlations are made we are not told: it is a mysterious process which, it seems, each of us must manage for himself, creating as it were a private language.

Having expounded the picture theory of the proposition and the world-structure that goes with it, Wittgenstein shows how propositions of various kinds are to be analysed into combinations of atomic pictures. Science consists of propositions whose truth-value is determined by the truth-values of the atomic propositions from which they are built up. Logic consists of tautologies, that is to say, complex propositions that are true no matter what the truth-value of their constituent propositions. Not all propositions are capable of analysis into atomic propositions: there are some that reveal themselves as pseudo-propositions. Among these are propositions of ethics and theology. So too, it turns out, are the propositions of philosophy, including those of the *Tractatus* itself.

The *Tractatus*, like other metaphysical treatises, tries to describe the logical form of the world; but this is something that cannot be done. A picture must be independent of what it pictures; it must be capable of being a false picture no less than a true one. But since any proposition must contain the logical form of the world, it cannot picture it. What the metaphysician attempts to say cannot be said, but only shown. The paragraphs of the *Tractatus* are like a ladder that must be climbed and then kicked away if we are to see the world aright. Philosophy is not a theory, but an activity, the activity of clarifying non-philosophical propositions. Once clarified, the propositions will mirror the logical form of the world and thus show what the philosopher wishes to, but cannot, say.

Neither science nor philosophy can show us the meaning of life. But this does not mean that a problem is left unsolved.

Doubt can exist only where a question exists, a question only when an answer exists, and an answer only where something *can be said*. We feel that even when *all possible* scientific questions have been answered, the problems of life remain completely untouched. Of course there are then no questions left, and this itself is the answer. The solution of the problem of life is seen in the vanishing of this problem. (*TLP* 6.5–6.521)

Even if one could believe in immortality, it would not confer meaning on life; nothing is solved by surviving for ever. An eternal life would be as much a riddle as this one. 'God does not reveal himself *in* the world,' Wittgenstein wrote; 'it is not how things are in the world that is mystical, but *that* it exists' (*TLP* 6.432, 6.44).

Philosophy can do very little for us. What it can do, however, had been done once for all by the *Tractatus*—or so Wittgenstein believed. With perfect consistency, having published the book he gave up philosophy and took up a number of more humdrum jobs. On the death of Karl Wittgenstein in 1912 Ludwig like his siblings had inherited a large fortune, but on returning from the war he renounced his share, and supported himself instead as a gardener in a monastery or a schoolmaster in rural schools. In 1926 a charge of sadistic punishment was brought against him on behalf of one of his pupils, and though he was acquitted this brought his schoolteaching career to an end.

Logical Positivism

Wittgenstein returned to Vienna, and had a hand in designing the architecture of a new house for his sister. He was introduced by her to Moritz Schlick, since 1922 Professor of the Philosophy of Science at Vienna University, with whom he resumed his philosophical inquiries. The two met on Monday evenings in 1927 and 1928, and were joined by others, including Rudolf Carnap and Friedrich Waismann. In 1929 Wittgenstein went to Cambridge to work on a philosophical manuscript (published posthumously as *Philosophische Bemerkungen*). During his absence the discussion group developed into a self-conscious philosophical movement and issued a manifesto, the *Wissenschaftliche Weltauffassung der Wiener Kreis*, which launched a campaign against metaphysics as an outdated system that must give way to a scientific world-view.

The anti-metaphysical programme exploited some of the ideas of Wittgenstein's *Tractatus*, and proclaimed that necessary truths were necessary only because they were tautologies. This enabled them to accept that mathematical truths were necessary while denying that they told us anything about the world. Knowledge about the world could be gained only by experience, and propositions had meaning only if they could be either verified or falsified by experience. The thesis that the meaning of a proposition was its mode of its verification, the verification principle, was the great weapon in the attack on metaphysics. If two metaphysicians disputed over the nature of the Absolute, or the purpose of the universe, they could be silenced by the question, 'What possible experience would settle the issue between you?'

Disputes quickly broke out about the status and formulation of the verification principle. Was it itself a tautology? Was it verifiable by experience? Neither answer seemed satisfactory. Moreover, general laws of science, no less than metaphysical dogmas, seemed incapable of conclusive verification. Still, they were capable of falsification, and that would be sufficient to give them significance. Shall we then replace the verification principle with a falsification principle? But if we do, it is hard to see how assertions of existence are significant, since only an exhaustive tour of the universe could conclusively falsify them. It seemed prudent to reformulate the criterion of significance in a weaker form that laid down that a proposition was meaningful only if there were some observations that would be relevant to its truth or falsity. Wittgenstein gave only qualified assent to the verification principle, but at this time he frequently defended its a priori analogue that the sense of a mathematical proposition is the method of its proof.

The true task of philosophy, the positivists thought, was not so much to lay down universal philosophical propositions as to clarify non-philosophical statements, and in this they were at one with Wittgenstein. Their chosen method of such clarification was to show how empirical statements were built up truth-functionally from elementary, or 'protocol', statements that were direct records of experience. The words occurring in protocol statements derived their meaning from ostensive definition—that is to say, from a gesture that would point to the feature of experience for which the word stood.

This programme came up against a massive obstacle. The experiences recorded by protocols appear to be private to each individual. If meaning depends on verification, and each of us carries out verification by a process to which no one else has access, how can anyone ever understand anyone else's meaning? Schlick tried to answer this by a distinction between form and content. The content of my experience is what I enjoy or live through when, for example, I see something red or see something green. This is private and incommunicable. But the form, or structure, of experience may be common to many. When I see a tree or a sunset I cannot know whether other people have the same experiences—perhaps, when they look at a tree they see what I see when I look at a sunset. But as long as we all agree to call a tree green and a sunset red, we are able to communicate with each other and construct the language of science.

Wittgenstein was dissatisfied with this solution, and strove to give an account of meaning that would not present a threat of solipsism. He distanced himself from the Vienna Circle and returned permanently to Cambridge. Having submitted the *Tractatus* as a Ph.D. dissertation he became a Fellow of Trinity College. The Circle continued its anti-metaphysical programme, notably in a journal, *Erkenntnis*, edited by Schlick in conjunction with Hans Reichenbach of Berlin. Its ideas were given wide currency in Britain by the publication in 1936 of A. J. Ayer's *Language, Truth and Logic*. Later in the same year, however, Schlick was shot dead by a disgruntled student; and by 1939 the Circle ceased to exist, with some of its most prominent members forced into exile. The Circle's most distinguished legacy to posterity was its publication, in 1935, of *The Logic of Scientific Discovery* by Karl Popper, who was never a fully paid-up member of the group.

Wittgenstein's Later Philosophy

In the 1930s Wittgenstein became the most influential teacher of philosophy in Britain. During this period he turned epistemology and philosophy of mind upside down. Previous philosophers, from Descartes to Schlick, had striven to show how knowledge of the external public world—whether scientific or commonsensical—could be built up from the ultimate, immediate, private data of intuition or experience. Wittgenstein, in these years, showed that private experience, far from being the bedrock on which knowledge and belief is founded, was something that itself presupposed a shared public world. Even the words that we use to frame our most secret and inward thoughts derive the only sense they have from their use in our common external discourse. The problem of philosophy is not to construct the public from the private, but to do justice to the private in the context of the social.

After his return to philosophy Wittgenstein abandoned many of the theses of the *Tractatus*. He ceased to believe in logical atoms, and ceased to look for a logically articulate language cloaked in common speech. A defining doctrine of logical atomism had been that every elementary proposition is

A.J. Ayer, who popularised Logical Positivism in Britain in the 1930s

independent of every other elementary proposition. This was clearly not true of the positivists' protocol statements: the truth-value of 'This is a red patch' is not independent of the truth-value of 'This is a blue patch'. Reflection on this led Wittgenstein to question the distinction between elementary and non-elementary propositions and to give up the idea that the ultimate elements of language were names designating simple objects.

In the *Tractatus*, Wittgenstein came to believe, he had grossly oversimplified the relation between language and the world. The connection between the two was to consist in two features only: the linking of names to objects, and the match or mismatch of propositions to facts. This, he now thought, was a great mistake. Words look like each other, in the same way as a clutch looks very like a foot-brake; but words differ from each other in function as much as the mechanisms operated by the two pedals. Wittgenstein now emphasized that language was interwoven with the world in many different ways: and to refer to these tie-ups he coined the expression 'language-game'.

As examples of language-games Wittgenstein lists obeying and giving orders, describing the appearance of objects, expressing sensations, giving measurements, constructing an object from a description, reporting an event, speculating about the future, making up stories, acting plays, guessing riddles, telling jokes, asking, cursing, greeting, and praying. Each of these language-games, and many others, need to be examined if we are to understand language. We can say that the meaning of a word is its use in a language-game—but this is not a general theory of meaning, it is simply a reminder that if we wish to give an account of the meaning of a word we must look for the part it plays in our life. The use of the word 'game' is not meant to suggest that language is something trivial; the word was chosen because games exhibit the same kind of variety as linguistic activities do. There is no common feature that marks all games as games, and likewise there is no one feature that is essential to language—there are only family likenesses between the countless language-games.

Wittgenstein never abandoned his early view that philosophy is an activity, not a theory. Philosophy does not discover any new truths, and philosophical problems are solved not by the acquisition of new information, but by the rearrangement of what we already know. The function of philosophy, Wittgenstein once said, is to untie the knots in our thinking. This means that the philosopher's movements will be complicated, but his result will be as simple as a plain piece of string.

We need philosophy if we are to avoid being entrapped by our language. Embodied in the surface grammar of our language there is a philosophy that bewitches us, by disguising from us the variety of ways in which language functions as a social, interpersonal activity. Philosophical misunderstanding will not harm us if we restrict ourselves to everyday tasks, using words within the language-games that are their primitive homes. But if we start upon abstract studies—of mathematics, say, or of psychology, or of theology—then our thinking will be hampered and distorted unless we can free ourselves of philosophical confusion. Intellectual inquiry will be corrupted by mythical notions about the nature of numbers, or of the mind, or of the soul.

Like the positivists, Wittgenstein was hostile to metaphysics. But he attacked metaphysics not with a blunt instrument like the verification principle, but by the careful drawing of distinctions that enable him to disentangle the mixture of truism and nonsense within metaphysical systems. 'When philosophers use a word—"knowledge", "being", "object", "I", "proposition", "name"—and try to grasp the *essence* of the thing, one must always ask oneself: is the word ever actually used in this way in the language which is its original home? What *we* do is to bring words back from their metaphysical to their everyday use' (*PI* I, 116).[6]

While teaching at Cambridge between the wars, Wittgenstein published nothing. He wrote copiously, filling notebooks, drafting and redrafting manuscripts, and circulating substantial handouts among his pupils, who also took and preserved detailed notes of his lectures. But none of this material was published until after his death. His ideas circulated, often in garbled form, largely by word of mouth.

When Austria became part of Nazi Germany by the *Anschluss* of 1938, Wittgenstein became a British citizen. During the war he worked as a paramedic, and in 1947 he resigned his Cambridge chair, being succeeded by his Finnish pupil Georg Henrik von Wright. He continued to write philosophy and to communicate philosophical thoughts to close friends and disciples. After a period of solitary life in Ireland, he stayed in the houses of various friends in Oxford and Cambridge until his death in 1951 at the age of sixty-two.

Analytic Philosophy after Wittgenstein

In 1949 Gilbert Ryle, Professor of Metaphysics at Oxford, published a book called *The Concept of Mind*. The ideas presented in that book bore a strong resemblance to Wittgenstein's. Ryle was strongly anti-Cartesian, and indeed the first chapter of the book was entitled 'Descartes' Myth'. Ryle emphasized a distinction between 'knowing how' and 'knowing that', which may have owed something to Heidegger. His discussion of the will and the emotions annihilated the notion of internal impressions which many philosophers had inherited from the British empiricists. In a chapter on 'Dispositions and Occurrences' he brought to the attention of modern philosophers the importance of the Aristotelian distinctions between different forms of actuality and potentiality. His discussion of sensation, imagination, and intellect leaned too heavily in the direction

---

[6] Wittgenstein's attitude to metaphysics is treated at length in Ch. 7.

of behaviourism to win general acceptance. Nonetheless, the book remained a classic of analytic philosophy of mind.

However, when Wittgenstein's *Philosophical Investigations* appeared posthumously in 1953 it was possible to see ideas that Ryle had displayed vividly but crudely now presented with far greater subtlety and profundity. It was, and remains, a matter of controversy how far Ryle, in the development of his ideas, had drawn on conversations with Wittgenstein and hearsay accounts of his Cambridge lectures, and how far he had reached similar conclusions by independent reflection.

Wittgenstein left the copyright of his literary remains to three of his former pupils: Georg Henrik von Wright, Elizabeth Anscombe, and Rush Rhees. The three philosophers corresponded to different facets of Wittgenstein's own personality and work. Von Wright, who held Wittgenstein's Cambridge chair from 1948 to 1951 and then returned to a career in his native Finland, resembled Wittgenstein the logician of the *Tractatus*; the books that first made his reputation were on induction, probability, and modal logic. Anscombe, an Oxford tutor who in her turn held the Cambridge chair towards the end of the century, carried forward the work of the later Wittgenstein on philosophy of mind, and with her book *Intention* inaugurated extensive discussion of practical reasoning and the theory of action. Of the three Rhees was the most sympathetic to the mystical and fideistic side of Wittgenstein's temperament, and inspired in Wales a characteristic school of philosophy of religion.

During the later decades of the twentieth century the literary executors presided over the publication of Wittgenstein's extensive *Nachlass*. Many volumes appeared, of which the most significant were *Philosophical Grammar* (1974) and *Philosophical Remarks* (1975) from the pre-war manuscripts, and *Remarks on the Foundations of Mathematics* (1978), *Remarks on the Philosophy of Psychology* (1980), plus *On Certainty* (1969) from later notebooks up until the time of Wittgenstein's death. The entire *Nachlass* was published by Oxford University Press in 1998, in transcription and facsimile, in an electronic form prepared by the University of Bergen.

After Wittgenstein's death many people regarded W. V. O. Quine (1908–2000) as the doyen of Anglophone philosophy. Having early established a reputation as a formal logician, Quine spent time with the Vienna Circle, and in Prague and Warsaw. After his return to the United States in 1936 he joined the faculty at Harvard, where he remained for the rest of his professional life with the exception of years of war service in the navy. His most important books were *From a Logical Point of View* (1953), which contained two famous essays, 'On What there Is' and 'Two Dogmas of Empiricism', and *Word and Object* (1960), which was a magisterial exposition of his system, later supplemented by a number of less influential studies.

Quine's aim in philosophy was to provide a framework for a naturalistic explanation of the world in the terms of science and especially physical science. He offered to do so by an analysis of language that is both empiricist and behaviourist. All the theories by which we explain the world (whether informal or scientific) are based on the input to our sense-receptors. All the terms and sentences occurring in the theories are to be defined in terms of the behaviour of the speakers and hearers who use them. The basic form of the meaning of an utterance is stimulus meaning: the class of all stimulations that would prompt a language-user to assent to the utterance.

In spite of his pursuit of a radically empiricist programme, Quine made his first major impact on philosophy with 'Two Dogmas of Empiricism' (written in 1951). He stated in the following terms the two targets of his attack:

One is a belief in some fundamental cleavage between truths which are *analytic*, or grounded in meanings independently of matters of fact, and truths which are *synthetic*, or grounded in fact. The other dogma is *reductionism*: the belief that each meaningful statement is equivalent to some logical construct upon terms which refer to immediate experience. (*FLPV* 20)

Quine did not deny that there are logically true statements, statements that remain true under any interpretation of their non-logical terms—e.g. 'No unmarried man is married'. But we cannot move from such a logically true statement to the allegedly analytic statement 'No bachelor is married' because that depends on taking 'unmarried man' and 'bachelor' as synonymous. But what is synonymy? Shall we say that two expressions are synonymous if one can be substituted for the other in a sentence without affecting its truth-value? But 'creature with a heart' and 'creature with a kidney' are interchangeable in that manner, but no one supposes that 'All creatures who have hearts have kidneys' is analytic. Nor can we appeal to any notion of necessity in order to define analyticity; the explanation must go the other way round.

Shall we try, instead, to define what it is for a sentence to be synthetic, saying for instance that a sentence is synthetic if and only if it can be verified or falsified by experience? Quine argues that this move rests on a false conception of verification: it is not single sentences, but whole systems, that are verified or falsified. 'Our statements about the external world face the tribunal of sense experience not individually, but only as a corporate body' (*FLPV* 140).

> The totality of our so-called knowledge or beliefs, from the most casual matters of geography and history to the profoundest laws of atomic physics or even of pure mathematics and logic, is a man-made fabric which impinges on experience only at the edges. Or, to change the figure, total science is like a field of force whose boundary conditions are experience. A conflict with experience at the periphery occasions readjustments in the interior of the field. Truth values have to be redistributed over some of our statements. Reevaluation of some statements entails reevaluation of others, because of their logical interconnections—the logical laws being in turn simply certain further statements of the system, certain further elements in the field. (*FLPV* 140)

It follows from this that it is folly to single out a class of analytic statements, which remain true whatever happens. Any statement can be held true come what may, if we make drastic adjustments elsewhere in the system. On the other hand no statement—not even a law of logic—is totally immune to revision. Science as a whole does depend both on language and on experience—but this duality cannot be traced in individual sentences.

If no sense can be given to the notions of synonymy and analyticity, then the whole notion of meaning is suspect, because there can be no criteria of identity for meaning. Certainly, Quine insisted, there are no such things as meanings that have to be interpreted by appeal to intentional concepts such as belief or understanding. Meaning must be explained purely in extensionalist terms, by mapping sensory stimuli on to verbal behaviour. Quine imagines a field linguist endeavouring to translate from a wholly alien language, using as his only data 'the forces that he sees impinging on the native's surfaces and the observable behaviour, vocal and otherwise, of the native' (*WO* 28).

The upshot of Quine's thought experiment is to identify three levels of indeterminacy. First, there is indeterminacy of individual reference. The linguist may observe that the natives use the sound 'Gavagai' only in the presence of rabbits. But—even assuming that this is an observation state-ment—it may equally well refer to rabbit, rabbit stage, or rabbit part. Second, there is indeterminacy at the level of the entire language: the data may support equally well two different, incompatible translation manuals. This indeterminacy is a particular example of a more general phenom-enon, namely that theories, and not only theories of translation, are underdetermined by sensory inputs. More than one total scientific system, therefore, may be compatible with all the data ever available.

We must indeed give up the idea that there is any fixed furniture of the world. What exists depends upon what theory we adopt. In his early essay 'On What There Is', Quine famously said, 'To be is to be the value of a bound variable.' When he said this he was following in the footsteps of Frege and Russell, who insisted that in a scientific theory no names should be allowed that lacked a definite reference. When all dubious names have been eliminated with the aid of Russell's theory of description we are left with sentences of the form 'There is an x such that x is . . . ' followed by a set of predicates setting out the properties by which the putative individual is to be identified. What exists, according to the theory, will be the entities over which the quantifiers range. But because different theories may be equally supported, so may different ontologies. What can be said to exist is always relative to a theory.

Wittgenstein and Quine are often regarded, especially in continental Europe, as the two leading exponents of analytical philosophy. In fact, their philosophies are very different from each other.[7] In particular the two men disagreed about the nature of philosophy. Because of his disbelief in the analytic–synthetic distinction Quine saw no sharp boundary between philosophy and empirical science. Wittgenstein, throughout his life, con-tinued to believe what he wrote in the *Tractatus* (4.111), 'Philosophy is not one of the natural sciences. The word "philosophy" must mean something which stands above or below, but not beside the natural sciences.' Scien-tism, i.e. the attempt to see philosophy as a science, was his *bête noire*. In the *Blue Book* he wrote, 'Philosophers constantly see the methods of science before their eyes, and are irresistibly tempted to answer questions in the

---

[7] The differences have been luminously detailed by P. M. S. Hacker, *Wittgenstein's Place in Twentieth Century Analytic Philosophy* (Oxford: Blackwell, 1996), 183–227.

way science does. This tendency is the real source of metaphysics, and leads the philosopher into complete darkness' (*BB* 18).

In the United States, however, the scientism introduced by Quine had come to stay. One of its most eloquent exponents was Quine's Harvard pupil Donald Davidson (1917–2003), who taught at many universities in the United States, ending, for the last twenty-two years of his life, at Berkeley. Davidson's chosen method of publication was the short paper, but many of his essays have been collected into volumes, notably *Essays on Actions and Events* (1980) and *Inquiries into Truth and Interpretation* (1984). In the philosophy of mind and action, Davidson's scientism took the form of a denial that there was a divide between philosophy and psychology; in the philosophy of language it took the form of an empirical and extensional theory of meaning.

Davidson's 1967 paper 'Truth and Meaning' begins as follows:

It is conceded by most philosophers of language, and recently by some linguists, that a satisfactory theory of meaning must give an account of how the meanings of sentences depend upon the meanings of words. Unless such an account could be supplied for a particular language, it is argued, there would be no explaining the fact that, on mastering a finite vocabulary, and a finitely stated set of rules, we are prepared to produce and to understand any of a potential infinitude of sentences. (*ITI* 17)

Davidson's theory of meaning is built upon a theory of truth. A truth-theory for a language L sets out the truth-conditions for all the sentences of L. This is to be done, not by the impossible method of listing every sentence, but by showing how the component parts of sentences contribute to the truth-conditions of sentences in which they occur. Such a theory will contain a finite list of terms and a finite set of syntactical rules but it will entail as derived theses the potentially infinite set of truth-sentences of the form: ' "S" is true in L if and only if *p*'.

Like Quine, Davidson illustrates his theory by considering a case in which we encounter a community with a totally alien language. In order to interpret it, we have to build up a truth-theory for their language by seeing what sentences they assent to in what circumstances; but we avoid the threat of indeterminacy and scepticism by assuming that the natives have true and reasonable beliefs and draw conclusions and make decisions in a rational way. This is 'the principle of charity'.

The actual behaviour of people is determined by their reasons, that is to say their desires and beliefs, which Davidson construes as mental events. The relation between these mental events and the actions they 'rationalize' is a causal one: to say that an action is intentional is precisely to say it was caused by the appropriate beliefs and wants. But for Davidson the causation is oblique: we cannot form psychological laws connecting agents' beliefs and desires with the acts they cause. Instead, Davidson argues, every individual mental event is also an individual physical event, and this event is related by physical laws to the individual physical events that are identical with the actions. No psychophysiological laws can be stated, however, relating physiological events of certain kinds with psychological events of certain kinds.

Davidson's position is materialist, in that there are never any events that are not physical events. But he endeavours to take the sting out of this materialism by insisting on what he calls 'the anomalousness of the mental'. Any mental event is identical with a physical event, but different descriptions apply to the event qua mental and qua physical. As a mental event it is subject not to causal laws but to interpretation, because its identity as a mental event depends upon its position in a network of other mental events. As a mental event, but not as a physical event, it is subject to normative evaluation as rational or irrational. This makes the exact nature of mental–physical causation, as Davidson admits, deeply mysterious.

In England philosophers continued to believe that there was a gulf, and not just a fuzzy border, between science and philosophy. They maintained, like Ryle and Wittgenstein, that the goal of philosophy was not information but understanding. Peter Strawson (1919–2006) with his tutor Paul Grice, in a paper entitled 'In Defence of a Dogma', rebutted Quine's attack on the analytic–synthetic distinction. In his own philosophizing, Strawson was anything but dogmatic. At a time when Oxford philosophy was overconfident of its own value, and unwilling to learn from philosophers distant in space and time, Strawson reminded his colleagues of the value of other styles of philosophy by writing about, and to some extent modelling his work on, Kant's *Critique of Pure Reason*. At a time when 'metaphysics' was regarded by many as a dirty word, Strawson gave the subtitle 'An Essay in Descriptive Metaphysics' to his most important work, *Individuals* (1959).

Descriptive metaphysics aims to describe the actual structure of our thought about the world, with no pretension to improve that structure (such pretension is the mark of revisionary metaphysics). In *Individuals* Strawson sought to draw out the fundamental conditions for a language in which it is possible to refer to objects and reidentify them, and to make predications about them. He saw his task as one of conceptual analysis, but one of a wide and general scope. 'The structure the metaphysician seeks', Strawson wrote, 'does not readily display itself on the surface of language, but lies submerged' (*I* 10).

Strawson sought to establish that in our conceptual scheme material bodies and persons occupy a special position: particulars of these two kinds are the basic particulars. The two speech acts of referring and describing, corresponding to the subject–predicate structure of language, are only possible if we can identify and reidentify material objects, and this requires a unified spatio-temporal framework. (In a world of pure sounds, in which there is only pitch and temporal sequence, reidentification is hard to come by.) A structure of objects located in space and time and possessing properties is prior to, and presupposed by, any language that might simply record the distribution of features in various locations.

Persons, no less than material bodies, are for Strawson a fundamental logical category. A person must not be conceived in the terms of Cartesian dualism. If minds are Cartesian egos to which only private experiences can be ascribed, then the problem of how one ascribes states of consciousness to others becomes insoluble. 'It is a necessary condition of one's ascribing states of consciousness, experiences, to oneself, in the way that one does, that one should also ascribe them, or be prepared to ascribe them, to others who are not oneself' (*I* 99). One can ascribe such states to others only if one can identify other objects of experience. And one cannot identify others if one can identify them *only* as subjects of experience, possessors of states of consciousness. Hence, what is primitive is the concept not of a mind, but of a person:

What I mean by the concept of a person is the concept of a type of entity such that *both* predicates ascribing states of consciousness *and* predicates ascribing corporeal characteristics, a physical situation etc., are equally applicable to a single individual of that single type... The concept of a person is logically prior to that of an individual consciousness. The concept of a person is not to be analysed as that of an animated body or of an embodied anima. (*I* 102–3)

Nonetheless, Strawson believed, it was not impossible to conceive of one's own individual survival after bodily death. Such survival, however, would be the survival of an individual that was strictly solitary, unable to communicate with others, and unable to bring about effects in the world. In proportion as memories fade and impotence palls, the survivor's concept of himself as an individual becomes attenuated. 'At the limit of attenuation there is, *from the point of view of his survival as an individual,* no difference between the continuance of experience and its cessation. Disembodied survival, on such terms as these, may well seem unattractive. No doubt it is for this reason that the orthodox have wisely insisted on the resurrection of the body' (*I* 116).

Strawson's own death, early in 2006, marked the end of an era in English philosophy.

3

Freud to Derrida

In the nineteenth century there was a constant interchange of philosophical ideas between the countries of continental Europe and the English-speaking world. Kant and Hegel were massively influential in British universities, while the tradition of British empiricism was found attractive by many radical thinkers on the Continent. The career of William James illustrates the cosmopolitan nature of the philosophy of the time. Converted to philosophy by the reading of a French philosopher, he studied in Germany and lectured frequently in Britain, while based in the United States. Again, the young Bertrand Russell was not at all an insular philosopher: while working out his philosophy of mathematics he was in regular correspondence with the German Frege and the Italian Peano.

By the middle of the twentieth century all this had changed. Continental and Anglophone philosophers went their separate ways, hardly speaking the same language as each other. In Britain and America the analytic tradition in philosophy, which Russell had helped to found, had come to be dominant in academic circles, and had almost driven out alternative styles of philosophizing. In continental Europe existentialism was the fashionable school, led in France by Jean-Paul Sartre and in Germany by Martin Heidegger. Well-meaning attempts to bring together proponents of the different styles of philosophizing met with only limited success in the second half of the century.

Freud and Psychoanalysis

The Continental thinker who had the greatest influence on Anglo-American philosophical thought throughout the twentieth century was

A gathering of Anglophone and Continental philosophers, presided over by Gilbert Ryle, in Christ Church Oxford c. 1970.

not a philosopher at all, but a man who regarded himself as a scientist, and indeed as the inventor of a new science: Sigmund Freud. Very few philosophers described themselves as Freudians, but all who were engaged in teaching philosophy of mind, ethics, or philosophy of religion were forced to take account of Freud's novel and exciting proposals in these areas.

Freud was born in Moravia in 1856 into an Austrian family of non-observant Jews. In 1860 the family moved to Vienna, and Freud trained as a doctor in the university there, joining the staff of the General Hospital in 1882, where he specialized initially in brain anatomy. He also collaborated with the neurologist Joseph Breuer, treating hysterical patients under hypnosis. Three years later he moved to Paris to study under the neurologist Jean-Martin Charcot, and soon after his return, in 1886, went into private medical practice. In the same year he married Martha Bernays, by whom he had six children, three girls and three boys.

In 1895, in conjunction with Breuer, Freud published a work on hysteria which presented an original analysis of mental illness. Gradually he ceased to use hypnosis as a method of treatment and replaced it with a novel form of therapy which he called psychoanalysis, consisting, as he put it himself, in nothing more than an exchange of words between patient and doctor.

The premiss underlying the new method was that the hysterical symptoms were the result of memories of a psychological trauma which had been repressed by the patient, but which could be recovered by means of a process of free association. The patient, lying on a couch, was encouraged to talk about whatever came to mind. Freud became convinced, as a result of many such sessions, that the relevant psychological traumas dated back to infancy and had a sexual content. His theories of infantile sexuality led to a breach with Breuer.

In isolation from medical colleagues, Freud continued in practice in Vienna. In 1900 he published the most important of his works, *The Interpretation of Dreams*, in which he argued that dreams no less than neurotic symptoms were a coded expression of repressed sexual desires. The theory here presented, he maintained, was applicable to normal as well as neurotic persons, and he followed it up a year later with a study entitled *The Psychopathology of Everyday Life*. These were the first of a series of highly readable books constantly modifying and refining his psychoanalytic theories. In 1902 Freud was appointed to an extraordinary chair of neuropathology at Vienna University, and he began to acquire pupils and colleagues. Prominent among these were Alfred Adler and Carl Jung, both of whom eventually broke with him and founded their own schools.

In 1923 Freud published *The Ego and the Id*, in which he presented a new and elaborate anatomy of the unconscious mind. Never deterred by controversy, he presented a deflationary account of the origin of religion in *The Future of an Illusion* (1927). He was himself an atheist, but this did not prevent him from identifying with Jewish culture or from suffering the assaults of anti-Semitism. Psychoanalysis was banned by the Nazis and when Austria was annexed by Germany in 1938 he was forced to migrate to England. He was given a warm welcome in London, where his works had been translated and published by members of the Bloomsbury group. Having suffered for sixteen years from cancer of the jaw, Freud died on 23 September 1939 of a lethal injection of morphine administered by his physician at his own request. His psychoanalytic work was continued by his youngest daughter, Anna.

In a set of introductory lectures delivered between 1915 and 1917 Freud summed up psychoanalytic theory in two fundamental theses. The first is that the greater part of our mental life, whether of feeling, thought, or volition, is unconscious. The second is that sexual impulses, broadly defined, are supremely important not only as potential causes of mental illness but also as the motor of artistic and cultural creation. If the sexual element in the work of art and culture remains to a great extent unconscious, this is because socialization demands the sacrifice of basic instincts. Such instincts become sublimated, that is to say diverted from their original goals and channelled towards socially acceptable activities. But sublimation is an unstable state, and untamed and unsatisfied instincts may take their revenge through mental illness and disorder.

The existence of the unconscious, Freud believed, is manifested in three different ways: through everyday trivial mistakes, through reports of dreams, and through the symptoms of neurosis. Dreams and neurotic symptoms, it is true, do not on their face, or as interpreted by the unaided patient, reveal the beliefs, desires, and sentiments of which the unconscious is deemed by Freud to consist. But the exercise of free association in analysis, he believed, as interpreted by the analyst, reveals the underlying pattern of the unconscious mind.

It is sexual development that is the key to this pattern. Infantile sexuality, Freud explained, begins with an oral stage, in which pleasure is focused on the mouth. This is followed by an anal stage, between the ages of one and three, and a 'phallic' stage, in which the child focuses on its own penis or clitoris. At that time, Freud maintained, a boy is sexually attracted to his mother, and resents his father's possession of her. But his hostility to his father leads him to fear that his father will retaliate by castrating him. So the boy abandons his sexual designs on his mother, and gradually identifies with his father. This is the Oedipus complex, a crucial stage in the emotional development of every boy. Neurotic characters are people who have become fixated at an early stage of their development. The recovery of Oedipal wishes, and the history of their repression, was an important part of every analysis. Freud was in no doubt that *mutatis mutandis* there was a feminine equivalent of the Oedipus complex, but it was never fully worked out in a convincing manner.

Towards the end of his life, Freud replaced the earlier dichotomy of conscious and unconscious with a threefold scheme of the mind. 'The mental apparatus', he wrote in *The Ego and the Id*, 'is composed of an *id* which is the repository of the instinctual impulses, of an *ego* which is the most superficial portion of the id and one which has been modified by the influence of the external world, and of a superego which develops out of the id, dominates the ego, and represents the inhibitions of instinct that are characteristic of man' (*SE* xx. 266).

The whole endeavour of the ego, Freud says, is to effect a reconciliation between the parts of the soul. So long as the ego is in harmony with the id and the superego, all will be well. But in the absence of such harmony mental disorders will develop. Conflicts between the ego and the id lead to neuroses; conflicts between the id and the superego lead to melancholia and depression. When the ego comes into conflict with the external world, psychoses develop.

Freud would not thank us for including him in a history of philosophy, since he regarded himself as a scientist, dedicated to discovering the rigid determinisms that underlie human illusions of freedom. In fact, most of his detailed theories, when they have been made precise enough to admit of experimental testing, have been shown to lack foundation. Medical professionals disagree how far psychoanalytic techniques are effective forms of therapy, and if they are, whence they derive their efficacy. When they do achieve success it appears to be not by uncovering deterministic mechanisms, but by expanding the self-awareness and freedom of choice of the individual. But despite all the theoretical criticisms that can be made of his work, Freud has had an enormous influence on society—in relation to sexual mores, to our understanding of mental illness, to our appreciation of art and literature, and on interpersonal relationships of many kinds.

Freud was not the first thinker to assign to the sexual impulse a place of fundamental significance in the human psyche. He had been preceded by many generations of theologians who regarded our actual human condition as having been shaped by a sin of Adam which was sexual in origin, transmission, and effect. If nineteenth-century prudery strove to conceal the ubiquity of sex, the veil was always easy to tear away. Freud loved to quote a dictum of Schopenhauer that it was the joke of life that sex, man's chief concern, should be pursued in secret. Sex was, Schopenhauer said, the true hereditary lord of the world, treating with scorn all preparations made to bind it.

Freud's contemporaries were shocked by his emphasis on infantile sexuality. But Victorian sentimentality about children was an attitude of recent origin. It was not shared, for instance, by Augustine, who wrote in his *Confessions*: 'What is innocent is not the infant's mind, but the feebleness of his limbs. I have myself watched and studied a jealous baby. He could not yet speak, and pale with jealousy and bitterness, glared at his brother sharing his mother's milk. Who is unaware of this fact of experience?' The sexual permissiveness of many modern societies is due not only to the availability of contraceptives but to a whole climate of thought which Freud did much to create. It is not that he recommended sexual licence in his published writings, but that he gave currency to an influential metaphor: the vision of sexual desire as a psychic fluid that must find an outlet through one channel or another. In the light of that metaphor, sexual abstinence appears as a dangerous damming-up of forces that will eventually break through any restraining barriers with a disastrous effect on mental health.

The very concept of mental health, as developed in modern times, may be said to date from the time when Freud, Breuer, and Charcot began to treat hysterical patients as genuine invalids instead of malingerers. This, it is often said, was more of a moral decision than a medical discovery, but most people nowadays would regard it as the right moral decision. It can be claimed that Freud redrew the boundaries between morals and medicine. Forms of behaviour that previous to his time would have been regarded as transgressions worthy of punishment have now long been seen, in the courthouse no less than in the consulting room, as maladies fit for therapy. The difficulty in making a hard and fast distinction between clinical judgement and moral evaluation is strikingly illustrated by changing attitudes to homosexual behaviour. This, having been long regarded as heinously criminal, was for nearly a century regarded as symptomatic of a psychopathological disorder, and is now regarded by many as the key element of a rationally chosen alternative lifestyle.

Freud's influence on art and literature has been great, in spite of his unflattering view of artistic creation as closely similar to neurosis. Novelists make use of associative techniques similar to those of the analyst's couch, and critics delight to interpret works of literature in Oedipal terms. Historians enjoy writing psychobiography, analysing the actions of mature public figures on the basis of real or imagined episodes in their childhood. Painters and sculptors have taken Freudian symbols out of a dream world and given them concrete form.

All of us, in fact, directly or indirectly, have imbibed a great deal of psychoanalytic theory. In discussion of our relationships with our family and friends we talk unself-consciously of repression and sublimation, and we describe characters as anal or narcissistic. People who have never read a word of Freud can happily identify their own and others' Freudian slips. No philosopher since Aristotle has made a greater contribution to the everyday vocabulary of psychology and morality.

It is hard to fault the judgement of W. H. Auden, who mourned Freud's death in twenty-eight intricate quatrains:

> If often he was wrong, and, at times, absurd,
>   to us he is no more a person
>   now but a whole climate of opinion.

Husserl's Phenomenology

The life of Edmund Husserl resembles, at crucial points, that of Sigmund Freud. Husserl was three years younger than Freud. Like him he was born into a Jewish family in Moravia, and attended lectures in Vienna. Both men devoted the greater part of their lives to a personal project that was intended to be the first really scientific study of the human mind. At the end of their lives both men fell foul of Nazi anti-Semitism, with Freud driven out of Austria to die in exile, and Husserl's books burnt by German troops marching into Prague in 1939.

Husserl's professional life, however, was quite different from Freud's. His initial studies were in mathematics and astronomy, not in medicine. He went on to pursue an orthodox academic career in philosophy, holding posts in a succession of university departments. Though his doctorate was from Vienna, he went on for his habilitation degree to Halle, and the chairs to which he was later called were in German and not Austrian universities.

Husserl's interest in philosophy was first awakened by the lectures of Franz Brentano in Vienna between 1884 and 1886. Brentano (1838–1917) was an ex-priest, an erudite scholar who had sought to relate Aristotelian philosophy of mind to contemporary experimental inquiry in a book *Psychology from an Empirical Standpoint* (1874), which was to prove widely influential. The data of consciousness, the book explained, come in two kinds: physical and mental phenomena. Physical phenomena are such things as colours and smells; mental phenomena, such as thoughts, are characterized by having a content, or immanent object. This feature, for which Brentano reintroduced the scholastic term 'intentionality', was the key to the understanding of mental acts and life.

While influenced by Brentano's approach to psychology, Husserl continued initially to focus his attention on mathematics. His habilitation thesis at Halle was on the concept of number, and his first book, published in 1891, was the *Philosophy of Arithmetic*. This sought to explain our numerical concepts by identifying the mental acts that were their psychological origin. Our concept of plurality, for instance, was alleged to derive from a process of 'collective combination' that grouped items into aggregates. Because of his desire to find a basis for mathematics in empirical psychology, Husserl was forced into some unattractive conclusions. He denied, for instance, that zero and one were numbers, and he had to make a sharp distinction between the arithmetic of small numbers and the arithmetic of large numbers. With our mind's eye we can see only tiny groups, so only a small part of arithmetic can rest on an intuitive basis; once we deal with larger numbers, we move away from intuition into a merely symbolic realm.

Reviewers of Husserl's book, notably Frege, complained that it contained a confusion between imagination and thought. The mental events that were the subject matter of psychology, being private to the individual, could not be the foundation of a public science such as arithmetic. That must rest on thoughts that were the common property of the race. Husserl yielded to the criticism and abandoned his early psychologism. In his *Logical Investigations* of 1900–1 he argued that logic cannot be derived from psychology, and that any attempt to do so must involve a vicious circle since it will have to appeal to logic in the course of its deduction. Henceforth, like Frege, he maintained a sharp distinction between logic and psychology. But while Frege, followed by the analytic tradition, focused philosophy on the logical side of the divide, Husserl, followed by the Continental tradition, saw the psychological side as philosophy's rightful home. At this period, however, Frege and Husserl were at one in basing philosophy—whether logical or psychological—on an explicit Platonic realism.

The overall situation at the beginning of the twentieth century has been vividly, if not quite impartially, described by Gilbert Ryle:

Husserl at the turn of the century was under many of the same intellectual pressures as were Meinong, Frege, Bradley, Peirce, G. E. Moore and Bertrand Russell. All alike were in revolt against the idea-psychology of Hume and Mill;

all alike demanded the emancipation of logic from psychology; all alike found in the notion of meaning their escape-route from subjectivist theories of thinking; nearly all of them championed a Platonic theory of meanings, i.e. of concepts and propositions; all alike demarcated philosophy from natural science by allocating factual enquiries to the natural sciences and conceptual enquiries to philosophy; nearly all of them talked as if these conceptual enquiries of philosophy terminated in some super-inspections of some super-objects, as if conceptual enquiries were, after all, super-observational enquiries; all of them, however, in the actual practice of their conceptual enquiries necessarily diverged from the super-observations that their Platonising epistemology required. Husserl talked of intuiting essences somewhat as Moore talked of inspecting concepts, and as Russell talked of acquaintanceship with universals, but of course it was by their intellectual wrestlings, not by any intellectual intuitings, that they tackled their actual conceptual difficulties. (*CP* i. 180)

Ryle does well to emphasize the common starting point of the analytic and Continental traditions; but in the case of Husserl, the intellectual wrestlings were, in fact, more complicated than this brisk passage suggests.

Husserl took over from Brentano the notion of intentionality, that is to say, the idea that what is characteristic of mental, as opposed to physical, phenomena is that they are directed to objects. I think of Troy, perhaps, or I worry about my investments—intentionality is the feature indicated in the little words 'of' and 'about'. What is the relation between what is going on in my mind and a long defunct city or stock markets across the world? Husserl, and many after him, spent years wondering about the answer to that question.[1]

Two things are essential to a thought: that it should have a content and that it should have a possessor. Suppose that I think of a dragon. Two things make this the thought it is: first, that it is the thought of a dragon and not of an eagle or a horse; second, that it is my thought and not your thought or Napoleon's thought. Husserl would mark these features by saying that it was an *act* of mine with a particular *matter* (its intentional object). Other people, too, may think of dragons; in that case, for Husserl, we have several individual acts belonging to the same species. The concept

---

[1] Intentionality is nothing to do with 'intention' in the modern sense. Brentano took the word from medieval contexts, in which it was derived from the verb 'intendere', meaning to pull a bowstring in the course of aiming at a target. An intentional object is, as it were, the target of a thought.

dragon, in fact, is nothing other than the species to which all such acts belong.

Concepts are thus, in the *Logical Investigations*, defined on the basis of psychological items. How, then, is logic related to concepts thus understood? In the same way, Husserl now believed, as the theorems of geometry are related to empirical three-dimensional bodies. Thus he was able to disown his earlier psychologism, and make a clear distinction between psychology and logic. He now proceeded to go further, and draw a line between psychology and epistemology. He did so by a reinvention of psychology as a new discipline of 'phenomenology'.

Phenomenology was developed during the first decade of the twentieth century. In 1900 Husserl was appointed to an associate professorship at the University of Göttingen. There he had as a colleague the renowned mathematician David Hilbert, but his most enthusiastic collaborators in his new venture were a group of philosophers at Munich, who coined the phrase 'phenomenological movement'. By 1913 the movement was self-confident enough to publish a yearbook for phenomenological research. In the first issue of this appeared a book-length text of Husserl's, which was planned as the first volume of a work to be entitled *Ideas Pertaining to a Pure Phenomenology*.

The aim of phenomenology was the study of the immediate data of consciousness, without reference to anything that consciousness might tell us, or purport to tell us, about the extra-mental world. When I think of a phoenix, the intentionality of my thought is exactly the same whether or not there are any phoenixes in reality. Already, in 1901, Husserl had written, 'It makes no essential difference to an object presented and given to consciousness whether it exists, or is fictitious, or is perhaps completely absurd. I think of Jupiter as I think of Bismarck, of the tower of Babel as I think of Cologne Cathedral, of a regular thousand-sided polygon as of a regular thousand-faced solid' (*LI* ii. 99). So too, Husserl believed, when I see a table. The intentionality of my experience is just the same whether there is a real table there or if I am hallucinating. The phenomenologist should make a close study of the psychological phenomena, and place in brackets the world of extra-mental objects. His attitude to the existence of that world should be one of suspense of judgement, for which Husserl used the Greek word *epoche*. This was called 'the phenomenological reduction'. It was, as it were, philosophy drawing in its horns.

Phenomenology is not the same as phenomenalism. A phenomenalist believes that nothing exists except phenomena, and that statements about such things as material objects have to be translated into statements about appearances. Berkeley and Mill held versions of phenomenalism.[2] Husserl, on the other hand, did not assert in *Ideas* that there are no realities other than phenomena; he deliberately left open the possibility that there is a world of non-phenomenal objects. Only, such objects are no concern, or at least no initial concern, of the philosopher.

The reason for this is that, according to Husserl, we have infallible immediate knowledge of the objects of our own consciousness while we have only inferential and conjectural information about the external world. Husserl made a distinction between immanent perception, which was self-evident, and transcendent perception, which was fallible. Immanent perception is my immediate acquaintance with my own current mental acts and states. Transcendent perception is my perception of my own past acts and states, of physical things and events, and of the contents of other people's minds.

Immanent perception provides the subject matter of phenomenology. Immanent perception is more fundamental than transcendent perception not only because immanent perception is self-evident while transcendent perception is fallible, but because the inferences and conjectures that constitute transcendent perception are based, and have to be based, on the deliverances of immanent perception. Only consciousness has 'absolute being'; all other forms of being depend upon consciousness for their existence (*Ideas*, i. 49). Thus phenomenology is the most basic of all disciplines, because the items that are its subject matter provide the data for all other branches of philosophy and science.

Husserl projected *Ideas* as a three-volume work, but the last two volumes were published only after his death. In 1916 he moved to Freiburg and remained as a professor in the university there until he retired in 1928, having rejected in 1923 a call to the University of Berlin. At Freiburg his lectures attracted a wide international audience, and he had among his pupils some who were to become highly influential philosophers, such as Martin Heidegger and Edith Stein. In those years he developed in several

[2] See vol. II, p. 203, and p. 8 above.

directions the system presented in *Ideas I*. One the one hand he extended the phenomenological method in order to undercut some assumptions that Descartes had left unquestioned, so that his *epoche* became more radical than Cartesian doubt. On the other hand, he endeavoured to combine his methodological solipsism with a solution to the problem of intersubjectivity that would establish the existence of other minds. His final position was a transcendental idealism which he maintained was the inseparable conclusion of phenomenology (*CM* 42). Some of the results of his later reflections were published in two works that appeared in the year after his retirement: *Cartesian Meditations* and *Formal and Transcendental Logic*.

The Existentialism of Heidegger

Two years earlier one of Husserl's pupils had published a book that was to have a much greater impact on philosophy than either of these. The *Sein und Zeit* of Martin Heidegger (1889–1976) claimed that phenomenology, up to this point, had been too half-hearted. It purported to examine the data of consciousness, but it employed notions like 'subject', 'object', 'act', and 'content' which were not items that it had discovered in consciousness, but items inherited from earlier philosophy. Most importantly, Husserl had accepted the framework of Descartes in which there were the two correlative realms of consciousness and reality. Only one of these, consciousness, was the subject matter Husserl had adopted for phenomenology. But the first task of phenomenology, Heidegger maintained, was to study the concept of Being (*Sein*) which was prior to the cleavage between consciousness and reality. The experience that leads us to contrast these two as polar opposites is the primary phenomenon to be examined.

We must therefore go back behind Descartes in order to get clear about the nature of philosophy, and take as our starting point not consciousness but Being. But it will not suffice, Heidegger warns us, simply to return to the categories of Plato and Aristotle, which already have an element of artificial sophistication. The Presocratics provide the best examples for a thoroughgoing phenomenalist to imitate, because they pre-date the formation of a professional philosophical vocabulary with all the presuppositions such a vocabulary entails. Heidegger would set himself the task of

Martin Heidegger, doyen of continental existentialism

inventing a pristine vocabulary that would enable us, as it were, to philosophize in the nude.

The most important of Heidegger's coinages is *Dasein*. *Dasein* is the kind of being that is capable of asking philosophical questions, and as Heidegger expounds *Dasein* it sounds initially suspiciously like the Cartesian ego. But whereas Descartes's ego was essentially a thinking thing, a *res cogitans*, thinking is only one, and not the most fundamental, of the ways in which *Dasein* has its being. The primitive element of *Dasein* is 'being-in-the-world', and thinking is only one way of engaging with the world: acting upon it and reacting to it are at least as important elements. *Dasein* is prior to the distinction between thinking and willing or theory and practice. *Dasein* is caring about (*besorgen*). *Dasein* is not a *res cogitans*, but a *res curans*: not a thinking thing, but a caring thing. Only if I have some care about, or interest in, the world will I go on to ask questions about it and give answers to those questions in the form of knowledge-claims.

Concepts and judgements can be thought of as instruments for coping with the world. But there are more primitive such instruments, things that are tools in a literal sense. A carpenter relates to the world by using a hammer. He does not need to be thinking about the hammer to be using it well; consciousness of the hammer may indeed get in the way of the concentration on his project that is his true engagement with reality. Entities that we cope with in this transparent mode are called by Heidegger 'ready-to-hand'. The distinction between what is and what is not ready-to-hand underlies our construction of the spatiality of the world.

Heidegger emphasizes the temporal nature of *Dasein*: we should think of it not as a substance but as the unfolding of a life. Our life is not a self-contained, self-developing entity: from the outset we find ourselves thrown into a physical, cultural, and historical context. This 'thrownness' (*geworfenheit*) is called by Heidegger the 'facticity' of *Dasein*. Nor is my life exhausted by what I am now and have hitherto been: I *can* be what I have not yet been, and my potentialities are as essential to my being as my achievements are. Indeed, according to Heidegger, in defining what I am the future has priority over the past and the present. *Dasein*, says Heidegger, is 'an ability to be' and what I am aiming at in my life determines the significance of my present situation and capacities. But whatever my achievements and potentialities are, they all terminate in death—but though death *terminates* them, it does not *complete* them. Any view of my life as a whole must take account of the difference between what I will be and what I might have been: hence comes guilt and anxiety.

If Heidegger is right, there is something absurd in the attempts of philosophers, from Descartes to Russell, to prove the existence of an external world. We are not observers trying, through the medium of experience, to gain knowledge of a reality from which we are detached. From the outset we are ourselves elements of the world, 'always already being-in-the-world'. We are beings among other beings, acting upon and reacting to them. And our actions and reactions need not at all be guided by consciousness. It is, in fact, only when our spontaneous actions misfire in some way that we become conscious of what we are doing. This is when the 'ready-to-hand' becomes 'unready-to-hand'.

The activity of *Dasein*, for Heidegger, has three fundamental aspects. First, there is what he calls 'attunement': the situations into which we are thrown manifest themselves as attractive, or alarming, or boring, and so on, and we respond to them with moods of various kinds. Second, *Dasein* is discursive: that is to say, it operates within a world of discourses, among entities that are articulated and interpreted for us by the language and culture that we share with others. Third, *Dasein* is 'understanding' in a special sense—that is to say, its activities are directed (not necessarily consciously) towards some goal, some 'for-the-sake-of' which will make sense of a whole life within its cultural context. These three aspects of *Dasein* correspond to the past, present, and future of time: the time that gives *Sein und Zeit* the second part of its title.

Though *Dasein* operates within a biological, social, and cultural context, there is no such thing as a human nature that gives rise to the activities of the human individual. The essence of *Dasein*, says Heidegger, is its existence. In saying this, he became the father of 'existentialism', the school of philosophy that emphasizes that individuals are not mere members of a species and are not determined by universal laws. What I essentially am is what I freely take myself to be. The ungroundedness of such a choice is alarming, and I may well take refuge in unthinking conformity. But that is an inauthentic decision, a betrayal of my *Dasein*. To be authentic I must make my own life in full awareness that there is no ground, either in human nature or in divine command, for the choices I make, and that no choice is going to bring any transcendent meaningfulness to my life.

Being and Time is a difficult book to read, and any interpreter who wishes to make its ideas seem readily intelligible has to write in a style very different from Heidegger's own. It is a matter of dispute whether Heidegger's idiosyncratic vocabulary and convoluted syntax were essential to his project or were an unnecessary piece of self-indulgence. But there is no doubt that his work was not just original but important. One of Heidegger's most pungent opponents, Gilbert Ryle, admitted at the end of a critical review of the book that he had nothing but admiration for his 'phenomenological analysis of the root workings of the human soul'.

As a work of phenomenology, *Sein und Zeit* enjoyed a greater éclat than any of the works of phenomenology's founder, Husserl. The relationship between the disciple and his master had an unhappy ending. In 1929 Heidegger succeeded Husserl as Professor of Philosophy at Freiburg and in 1933 he became Rector of the university. In a notorious inaugural address in May of that year he welcomed Nazism as the vehicle through which the German people would at last carry out its historic spiritual mission. One of his first acts as Rector was to exclude from the University Library all Jewish faculty members, including Emeritus Professor Husserl, who still had five years to live. After the war Heidegger had to do penance for his support of Hitler and was himself prevented from teaching in the university from 1945 to 1950. However, his thought remained influential up to and beyond his death in 1976.

The Existentialism of Sartre

In contrast to the right-wing existentialism of Heidegger, in France Jean-Paul Sartre, once briefly a student under him, developed a form of existentialism that moved steadily towards the political left. Born in Paris in 1905, Sartre studied at the École Normale Supérieure from 1924 to 1928 and for some years supported himself by teaching philosophy in high schools. It was, however, in Berlin and Freiburg from 1933 to 1935 that he began to develop his own philosophy, which found its first expression in two philosophical monographs published in 1936, *The Transcendence of the Ego* and *Imagination: A Psychological Critique*. These were followed by a novel, *Nausea*, in 1938 and *Sketch for a Theory of the Emotions* in 1939.

Sartre's pre-war essays are detailed studies in the philosophy of mind in the phenomenological mould. Sartre, like Heidegger, complained that Husserl had not taken the phenomenological reduction far enough. Husserl had accepted the Cartesian ego, the thinking subject, as a datum of consciousness, but in fact it is no such thing: when I am absorbed in what I am seeing or hearing I have no thought of myself. It is only by reflection that we make the self into an object, so if we are to be thorough phenomenologists we must start from pre-reflexive consciousness. The self, the thinking subject, lies outside consciousness and therefore belongs, no less than other minds, to the transcendent world.

In *Imagination* Sartre attacks the notion, widespread among philosophers but particularly explicit in Hume, that in imagination we are surveying the contents of an interior mental world. It is a mistake, Sartre showed, to think that perception and imagination both consisted in the mental presence of pictures or simulacra, the only difference between them being that in perception the images are more intense or vivid than they are in imagination. In fact, Sartre maintained, imagining relates us to extra-mental objects, not to internal images. It does so no less than perception, but in a different mode. This is most easily made out in the case where we imagine a real, but absent, person; in the cases where what we imagine does not in fact exist, what we are doing is creating an object in the world.

Emotions, too, according to Sartre, are misconceived if we think of them as passive internal sensations. Emotion is a certain manner of apprehending the world: to feel hatred towards someone, for instance, is to perceive him as hateful. But obviously emotion is not an impartial, unbiased awareness of our environment; on the contrary, Sartre goes so far as to describe it as 'a magical transformation' of the situations in which we find ourselves. When we are depressed, for instance, we as it were cast a spell over the world such as to make all efforts to cope with it appear pointless.

When war broke out in 1939 Sartre was conscripted, and in 1940 he fought in the army until captured by the Germans. Released after the armistice, he returned to Paris as a philosophy teacher, but also took part in the resistance to Nazi occupation. In 1943 he published his *magnum opus, Being and Nothingness*. While his pre-war essays had been Husserlian in inspiration, this work owes a great debt to Heidegger, which is acknowledged by the form of its title. Parts of *Being and Nothingness* are as difficult as anything in *Sein und Zeit*. But, as befits a novelist and playwright, Sartre had a gift, which Heidegger lacked, for illustrating philosophical points with detailed and convincing narratives. After the war Sartre returned to present the main themes of his work in a briefer and more popular manner in *Existentialism and Humanism* (1946).

Being (*l'être*), for Sartre, is what precedes and underlies all the different kinds and aspects of things that we encounter in consciousness. We sort things into kinds and classes in accordance with our interests and as instruments for our purposes. If we strip off all the distinctions that consciousness has made, we are left with pure being, being in itself, *l'en-soi*. This is opaque, massive, simple, and above all contingent. It is 'without reason, without cause, without necessity' (*BN* 619). To say that it is without cause is not to say that it is its own cause, *causa sui*; it is just simply there— 'gratuitous' Sartre calls it, and sometimes 'de trop'.

The *en-soi* is one of the two key concepts of *Being and Nothingness*. The other is *le pour-soi*, the for-itself, that is to say human consciousness. How is this related to the nothingness of the title? Sartre's answer is that man is the being through whom nothingness comes into the world. Negation is the element that makes the difference between *le pour-soi* and *l'en-soi*.

Sartre is here expanding a theme of Heidegger's. While English philosophers took Heidegger's dictum 'nothing noths' (*Das Nichts nichtet*) as the quintessence of absurdity, Sartre accepts the objectification of *nothing*, and attempts to give it an important significance. When consciousness articulates the world, it does so by means of negation. If I have a concept of *red*, I divide the world into the red and the not-red. If I distinguish between chairs and tables, then I must consider chairs as not-tables and tables as not-chairs. If I want to make a distinction between consciousness and being, I must say that consciousness is not-being: 'the being by which nothingness comes into the world must be its own nothingness' (*BN* 23).

To the historian, it looks as if Sartre is reintroducing into philosophy a conundrum devised by Parmenides and solved long ago by Plato.[3] A. J. Ayer, in 1945, compared Sartre's treatment of *le néant* with the response of the King in *Alice in Wonderland* when Alice says that she sees nobody on the road: 'I only wish I had such eyes... To be able to see Nobody! And at that distance too!' Fortunately, *Being and Nothingness*, despite its title, contains much that is of importance quite independently of Sartre's account of 'nihilification'. The most interesting idea is again taken from Heidegger. Whereas for most objects essence precedes existence, 'there is at least one being whose existence comes before his essence, a being which exists before it can be defined by any conception of it. That being is man' (*EH* 66). Human freedom precedes the essence of man and makes it possible. Whereas an oak tree has to follow a particular life pattern because that is the kind of thing it is, human beings do not belong to a kind in this way: it is for each person to decide what kind of thing to be. Human freedom creates a fissure in the world of objects.

The life of a human individual, according to Sartre, is not determined in advance, neither by a creator, nor by necessitating causes, nor by absolute moral laws. The one necessity I cannot escape is the necessity to choose. Human freedom is absolute but it is also alarming, and we try to hide it from ourselves, and adopt some predetermined role offered by morality, society, or religion. But our efforts at concealment are bound to fail, and we end up double-minded, tacitly aware of our freedom while striving to reduce ourselves to mere objects. This is the condition that Sartre calls 'bad faith'.

[3] See vol. I, pp. 200 and 214.

The alternative attitude is to accept and affirm one's freedom and accept the responsibility for one's own acts and life, unsustained by any pre-existing moral order and unconstrained by any contingent circumstances. To be sure, there will be physical limits to my possible actions, but by the adjustment of my own desires and projects it is I who confer significance on the situation in which I find myself. I must make a total choice of myself. 'I emerge alone and in dread in the face of the unique and first project which constitutes my being: all the barriers, all the railings, collapse, annihilated by the consciousness of my liberty; I have not, nor can I have, recourse to any value against the fact that it is I who maintain values in being' (*EH* 66).

In the years after the war Sartre, with Simone de Beauvoir, became the centre of the cultural and intellectual life of the left bank of Paris. He founded and edited an avant-garde monthly, *Les Temps Modernes*, and wrote a number of successful novels and plays, of which perhaps the best known was *Huis clos* ('In Camera'), which contains the often-quoted line 'Hell is other people'. In *Being and Nothingness*, in addition to the *en-soi* and the *pour-soi*, Sartre had introduced the notion of being-for-others. This is essentially the way in which I am presented to others and observed by them, becoming nothing more than an object for them, the object perhaps of their envy or contempt. The original meaning of being-for-others, he had written, is conflict. In his later work Sartre developed this theme and gave it greater importance.

On social and political views he took up positions close to those of the Communist Party, though Marxist determinism was not easy to reconcile with the absolute libertarianism that was the keynote of existentialism. In an effort to resolve this tension he wrote a *Critique of Dialectical Reason* in 1960. In 1964 he declined the Nobel Prize for literature and in 1968 he supported the student rebellions that threatened the de Gaulle government. He died in 1980.

Jacques Derrida

For a brief period in the 1960s it looked as if there might be a rapprochement between Continental and Anglophone philosophy. In 1962 a thirty-two-year-old philosopher, of Algerian Jewish parentage, called Jacques

Derrida published a doctoral thesis on Husserl and geometry. In the same year there was posthumously published a set of lectures by the Oxford philosopher J. L. Austin (1911–60), entitled *How to Do Things with Words*, which contained a theory of the different kinds of speech acts. In 1967 Derrida published three highly original works (*Writing and Difference*, *Speech and Phenomena*, and *Of Grammatology*) which bore clear marks of Austin's influence.

The two philosophers, however, treated the same topic in very different ways. Austin started, as early as 1946, from a distinction between two kinds of speech, constative and performative. A constative sentence is used to state how things are as a matter of fact: 'It is raining', 'The train is approaching'. Performative utterances, however, were not statements that could be judged and found true or false by comparison with the facts; they were speech acts that changed things rather than reported on them. Examples are 'I name this ship the *Queen Elizabeth*', 'I promise to meet you at ten o'clock', 'I bequeath my watch to my brother'.

Austin went on to classify many different kinds of performative utterances, such as bets, appointments, vetoes, apologies, and curses, and to identify concealed performative elements in apparently straightforward statements. In its developed stage his theory made room, in speech acts, for three elements: the locutionary, the illocutionary, and the perlocutionary force. Suppose someone says to me 'Shoot her!' The locutionary act is defined by specifying the sense of 'shoot' and the reference of 'her'. The illocutionary act is one of ordering, or urging, etc. The perlocutionary act (which takes place only if the illocutionary act achieves its goal) would be described by, for example, 'He made me shoot her'.

Austin introduced many new technical terms to bring out distinctions between different kinds of speech acts and elements within them. Each term, as introduced, is defined in lucid terms and is illuminated by examples. The overall effect is to bring clarity, at a microscopic level, into a vast and important field of the philosophy of language.

Derrida's method is quite different. He, too, introduces technical terms in great profusion: for instance, 'gram', 'reserve', 'incision', 'trace', 'spacing', 'blank', 'supplement', 'pharmakon', and many others. But he is much less willing to offer definitions of them, and often seems to reject the very request for a definition as somehow improper. The relevance of his illustrative examples is rarely clear, so that even banal features of language take on an air of mystery.

In treating of speech acts, Austin was not particularly interested in the distinction between what is spoken (as in an oral promise) and what is written (as in a will); the philosophical points he makes apply in general to both kinds of language use. Derrida, on the other hand, attached great important to the distinction, attacking what he calls 'phonocentrism', the alleged overemphasis in Western civilization on the spoken word. Given the emphasis placed by both law and business on getting things in writing, and the enormous efforts modern societies have put into making their citizens literate, Derrida's charge of phonocentrism has to be based on a number of eccentric texts starting with an ironic passage in Plato's *Phaedrus*.

Among performative speech acts promising is a paradigm case that interested both Austin and Derrida. Austin listed, in an instructive way, the different kinds of infelicity that may affect a promise, from insincerity to incapacity. Derrida was principally impressed by the fact that one may die before fulfilling a promise, a circumstance which he expresses by saying that every performative is haunted by death. But, *pace* Derrida, since we are all, always, mortal, the possibility of death tells us nothing about performatives in particular. Cycling to work, no less than making a promise, is something that may be interrupted by death. Of course, in a promise death may actually be mentioned, as when bride and groom vow fidelity 'till death do us part'. But in that case, a promise is not in fact broken, or left unfulfilled, when one of the spouses dies.

Derrida's hostility to phonocentrism was part of an attack on what he called 'the metaphysics of presence', the notion that the basis of claims to meaning and truth is something intimate given in consciousness. The prime target of his attack was Husserl, but the empiricist notion of sense-data lies open to similar criticism. Speech was given primacy over writing in Western tradition, he claims, because speech is closer than writing to the thinking that is idealized as the ultimate, transcendental object of signification. Derrida 'deconstructs' the opposition between speech and writing and gives the privileged position to the written text, the one furthest from the control of its author, the one most capable of diverse and superseding interpretations. Some have seen Derrida's attack on the metaphysics of presence as an enterprise, in a very different key, parallel to Wittgenstein's demolition of the notion of a private language.

Derrida in his early works showed evidence of great philosophical acumen; but after 1967 his thinking and writing moved further and further away from that of Austin and Wittgenstein. As his career developed, his style of operation moved far away not only from current analytic philosophy, but from philosophy as understood by the great philosophers from Aristotle to Husserl. It has always been seen as a task of philosophers to draw distinctions between concepts that may be confused with each other, and if necessary to invent or adapt terms to mark these distinctions. Derrida, by contrast, introduced new terms whose effect was to confuse ideas that are perfectly distinct.

Consider the notion of 'deferrence' (*différance*), in which Derrida took great pride.[4] Deferrence is supposed to combine the notions of deferring (putting off) and difference (being distinct). 'Deferrence', he tells us, 'is to be conceived prior to the separation between deferring as delay and differing as the actual work of difference' (*SP* 88). It is not clear how these two contrasting notions can be combined in this way, and the explications and paraphrases offered by Derrida are not altogether helpful:

Deferrence is what makes the movement of signification possible only if each so-called present element, each element appearing on the scene of presence, is related to something other than itself, thereby keeping within itself the mark of a past element, and already letting itself be vitiated by the mark of its relation to a future element, this trace being related no less to what is called the future than to what is called the past, and constituting what is called the present by means of this very relation to what it is not, to what it absolutely is not: that is, not even to a past or a future as a modified present. (*Diff.* 13)

One can see what he means. If I say to the breakfast waiter 'bacon and eggs', the meaning of what I say depends on the fact that at the moment when I utter the word 'and' the word 'bacon' is in the past, but remains related to it; moreover the 'and' is also related to the word 'eggs' that has not yet been uttered, but is about to be related to it. Very true. And if that is what deferrence means, then what Derrida says of it is perfectly correct: 'it is not the name of an *object*, not the name of some "being" that could be present. And for that reason it is not a concept either.' But that cannot be all 'deferrence' means, because we know that some of Derrida's readers have

---

[4] The word 'différance' is often translated by 'differance', but my translation corresponds more exactly to the construction of the French word. I must, however, ask the reader to pronounce it exactly like 'difference', out of deference to Derrida, who attached importance to the equivalent French words sounding alike.

taken it to be a name of God—though Derrida reassures us that it 'blocks every relationship to theology' (P 40). The various paraphrases we find of 'deferrence' in his texts are perhaps themselves an instance of deferrence: IOUs that are quite distinct from a definition and which put off to an indefinite future an actual conferment of sense.

Derrida devised a method of dealing with authors, a technique that can be nicknamed the nosegay method. To assemble a nosegay, one collects a number of texts that contain the same word (or often just the same phoneme). One then snips them out of context and date, discards utterer or voice, and modifies the natural sense by italicization, omission, or truncation. One gathers them together and presents them as a nosegay with some striking or provocative thesis tied around it. The nosegay technique became popular in some departments of literature, since it demands considerably less effort than more traditional methods of literary criticism.

The later Derrida maintains the reader's attention by the deft deployment of rhetoric. A particularly successful device might be named 'the irrefutable paradox'. One of the most often quoted lines in *Grammatology*— underlined by the author himself—is 'There is nothing outside the text.' An arresting, even shocking, remark! Surely the Black Death and the Holocaust were not textual events in the way that a new edition of Johnson's *Lives of the Poets* is a textual event. But later Derrida kindly explains that by text he does not mean a corpus of writing, but something that overruns the limits of the world, of the real, of history.[5] Well, if what we are being told is simply that there is nothing outside the universe, it would be rash to contradict. And an injunction to try to see things in context is surely sound advice.

Like the skilful rhetorician that he is, Derrida keeps his readers awake by bringing in sex and death. We have already met death haunting the performatives; we meet sex in equally irrelevant places. Talking to oneself, we are told, stands in the same relation to talking aloud as masturbation stands to copulation. No doubt it does. A no less apt comparison would have been with solitaire vs. whist; but that would not have tickled the reader in quite the same way. Again, at the end of the book of Revelation,

---

[5] 'Living On', in Harold Bloomfield (ed.), *Deconstruction and Criticism* (New York: Seabury Press, 1979).

Jacques Derrida, photographed after he had achieved iconic status in many circles

we read: 'And the Spirit and the bride say Come! And let him that heareth say Come!' (22: 17). Derrida has written at length on this text, making great play with the double entendre that attaches, in French as in English, to the word 'come'. If one were churlish enough to point out that the Greek word translated 'come' cannot possibly have the sense of 'achieve orgasm', one would no doubt be told that one had missed the whole thrust of the exercise.

It may appear unseemly to criticize Derrida in the manner just illustrated. The reason for doing so is that such a parody of fair comment is precisely the method he adopted in his own later work: his philosophical weapons are the pun, the bawdy, the sneer, and the snigger. Normally, the historian tries to identify some of the major doctrines of a philosopher, present them as clearly as he can, and then perhaps add a word of evaluation. In the later Derrida there are no doctrines to present. It is not just that an unsympathetic reader may fail to identify or understand them; Derrida himself rejects the idea that his work can be encapsulated in theses. Indeed, sometimes he even disclaims the ambition to be a philosopher.

Is it not unfair, then, to include Derrida, whether for blame or praise, in a history such as this? I think not. Whatever he himself may say, he has been taken by many people to be a serious philosopher, and he should be evaluated as such. But it is unsurprising that his fame has been less in philosophy departments than in departments of literature, whose members have had less practice in discerning genuine from counterfeit philosophy.

4

Logic

Mill's Empiricist Logic

John Stuart Mill's *System of Logic* falls into two principal parts. The first two books present a system of formal logic; the remainder of the work deals with the methodology of the natural and social sciences. He begins the first part with an analysis of language, and in particular with a theory of naming.

Mill was the first British empiricist to take formal logic seriously, and from the start he is anxious to dissociate himself from the nominalism that had been associated with empiricism since the time of Hobbes. By 'nominalism' he means the two-name theory of the proposition: the theory that a proposition is true if and only if subject and predicate are names of the same thing. The Hobbesian account, Mill says, fits only those propositions where both predicate and subject are proper names, such as 'Tully is Cicero'. But it is a sadly inadequate theory of any other propositions.

Mill uses the word 'name' very broadly. Not only proper names like 'Socrates' and pronouns like 'this', but also definite descriptions like 'the king who succeeded William the Conqueror', count as names for him. So too do general terms like 'man' and 'wise', and abstract nouns like 'wisdom'. All names, whether particular or general, whether abstract or concrete, denote things; proper names denote the things they name and general terms denote the things they are true of: thus not only 'Socrates' but also 'man' and 'wise' denote Socrates. General terms, in addition to having a denotation in this way, also have a connotation: there are items they connote as well as items they denote. What they connote are the attributes they signify, that is to say, what would be specified in a dictionary definition of them. In logic, connotation is prior to denotation: 'when mankind fixed the word wise they were not thinking of Socrates' (*SL* 1.2.5.2).

Since 'name' covers such a multitude of terms, Mill can accept the nominalist view that every proposition is a conjunction of names. But this does not commit him to the Hobbesian view since, unlike Hobbes, he can appeal to connotation in setting out the truth-conditions of propositions. A sentence joining two connotative terms, such as 'all men are mortal', tells us that certain attributes (those, say, of animality and rationality) are always accompanied by the attribute of mortality.

In his second book, Mill discusses inference, of which he distinguished two kinds, real and verbal. Verbal inference brings us no new knowledge about the world; knowledge of the language alone is sufficient to enable us to derive the conclusion from the premiss. As an example of a verbal inference, Mill gives the inference from 'No great general is a rash man' to 'No rash man is a great general': both premiss and conclusion, he tells us, say the same thing. There is real inference when we infer to a truth, in the conclusion, which is not contained in the premisses.

Mill found it very difficult to explain how new truths could be discovered by general reasoning. He accepted that all reasoning was syllogistic, and he claimed that in every syllogism the conclusion is actually contained and implied in the premisses. Take the argument from the premisses 'All men are mortal, and Socrates is a man' to the conclusion 'Socrates is mortal'. If this syllogism is to be deductively valid, then surely the proposition 'Socrates is mortal' must be presupposed in the more general assumption 'All men are mortal'. On the other hand if we substitute for 'Socrates' the name of someone not yet dead (Mill's example was 'the Duke of Wellington') then the conclusion does give us new information, but it is not justified by the evidence summarized in the first premiss. Hence the syllogism is not a genuine inference:

All inference is from particulars to particulars. General propositions are merely registers of such inferences already made, and short formulae for making more. The major premise of a syllogism, consequently, is a formula of this description; and the conclusion is not an inference drawn *from* the formula, but an inference drawn *according to* the formula; the real logical antecedent or premise being the particular facts from which the general proposition was collected by induction. (*SL* 3.3.4)

'Induction' was a name that had long been given by logicians to the process of deriving a general truth from particular instances. But there is more than one kind of induction. Suppose I state 'Peter is a Jew, James is a Jew, John is a Jew...' and then go on to enumerate all the Apostles. I may go on to conclude 'All the Apostles are Jews', but if I do so, Mill says, I am not really moving from particular to general: the conclusion is merely an abridged notation for the particular facts enunciated in the premiss. Matters are very different when we make a generalization on the basis only of an incomplete survey of the items to which it applies—as when we conclude from previous human deaths that all humans of all times will die.

Mill's criticism of deductive argument involves a confusion between logic and epistemology. An inference may be, as he says, deductively valid without being informative: validity is a necessary but not a sufficient condition for an argument to produce true information. But syllogism is not the only form of inference, and there are many valid non-syllogistic arguments (e.g. arguments of the form 'A = B', 'B = C', therefore 'A = C') which are quite capable of conveying information. Even in the case of syllogism, it is possible to give an account that makes it a real inference if we interpret 'All men are mortal' not as saying that 'mortal' is a name of every member of the class of men but—in accordance with Mill's own account of naming—as saying that there is a connection between the attributes connoted by 'man' and by 'mortal'.

Mill would no doubt respond by asking how we could ever know such a connection, if not by induction; and the most interesting part of his Logic is his attempt to set out the rules of inductive discovery. He set out five rules, or canons, of experimental inquiry to guide researchers in the inductive discovery of causes and effects. We may consider as illustrations the first two of these canons.

The first is called the method of agreement. It states that if a phenomenon F appears in the conjunction of the circumstances A, B, and C, and also in the conjunction of the circumstances C, D, and E, then we are to conclude that C, the only common feature, is causally related to F.

The second, the method of disagreement, states that if F occurs in the presence of A, B, and C, but not in the presence of A, B and D, then we are to conclude that C, the only feature differentiating the two cases, is causally related to F.

Mill maintains that we are always, though not necessarily consciously, applying his canons in daily life and in the courts of law. Thus, to illustrate the second canon he says, 'When a man is shot through the heart, it is by this method we know that it was the gunshot which killed him: for he was in the fullness of life immediately before, all circumstances being the same, except the wound.'

Mill's methods of agreement and disagreement are a sophistication of Bacon's tables of presence and absence.[1] Like Bacon's, Mill's methods seem to assume the constancy of general laws. Mill says explicitly, 'The proposition that the course of Nature is uniform, is the fundamental principle, or general axiom, of Induction.' But where does this general axiom come from? As a thoroughgoing empiricist, Mill treats it as being itself a generalization from experience: it would be rash, he says, to assume that the law of causation applied on distant stars. But if this very general principle is the basis of induction, it is difficult to see how it can itself be established by induction. But then Mill was prepared to affirm that not only the fundamental laws of physics, but those of arithmetic and logic, including the very principle of non-contradiction itself, were nothing more than very well-confirmed generalizations from experience.[2]

Frege's Refoundation of Logic

On these matters Frege occupied the opposite pole from Mill. While for Mill propositions of every kind were known a posteriori, for Frege arithmetic no less than logic was not only a priori but also analytic. In order to establish this, Frege had to investigate and systematize logic to a degree that neither Mill nor any of his predecessors had achieved. He organized logic in a wholly new way, and became in effect the second founder of the discipline first established by Aristotle.

One way to define logic is to say that it is the discipline that sorts out good inferences from bad. In the centuries preceding Frege the most important part of logic had been the study of the validity and invalidity of a particular form of inference, namely the syllogism. Elaborate rules had been drawn up to distinguish between valid inferences such as

---

[1] See vol. III, p. 31.   [2] See Ch. 6 below.

	All Germans are Europeans.
	Some Germans are blonde.
Therefore,	Some Europeans are blonde.

and invalid inferences such as

	All cows are mammals.
	Some mammals are quadrupeds.
Therefore,	All cows are quadrupeds.

Though both these inferences have true conclusions, only the first is valid, that is to say, only the first is an inference of a form that will never lead from true premises to a false conclusion.

Syllogistic, in fact, covers only a small proportion of the forms of valid reasoning. In Anthony Trollope's *The Prime Minister* the Duchess of Omnium is anxious to place a favourite of hers as Member of Parliament for the borough of Silverbridge, which has traditionally been in the gift of the Dukes of Omnium. He tells us that she 'had a little syllogism in her head as to the Duke ruling the borough, the Duke's wife ruling the Duke, and therefore the Duke's wife ruling the borough'. The Duchess's reasoning is perfectly valid, but it is not a syllogism, and cannot be formulated as one. This is because her reasoning depends on the fact that 'rules' is a transitive relation (if A rules B and B rules C, then A does indeed rule C), while syllogistic is a system designed to deal only with subject–predicate sentences, and not rich enough to cope with relational statements.

A further weakness of syllogistic was that it could not cope with inferences in which words like 'all' or 'some' occurred not in the subject place but somewhere in the grammatical predicate. The rules would not determine the validity of inferences that contained premises such as 'All politicians tell some lies' or 'Nobody can speak every language' in cases where the inference turned on the word 'some' in the first sentence or the word 'every' in the second.

Frege devised a system to overcome these difficulties, which he expounded first in his *Begriffsschrift*. The first step was to replace the grammatical notions of *subject* and *predicate* with new logical notions, which Frege called 'argument' and 'function'. In the sentence 'Wellington defeated Napoleon' grammarians would say (or used to say) that 'Wellington' was the subject and 'defeated Napoleon' the predicate. Frege's introduction of

Trollope's Lady Glencora Palliser ruled not just one but two Dukes of Omnium. Here, in Millais' illustration to *Phineas Finn*, she establishes her dominion over the elder Duke by presenting him with a grandson.

the notions of *argument* and *function* offers a more flexible method of analysing the sentence.

This is how it works. Suppose that we take our sentence 'Wellington defeated Napoleon' and put into it, in place of the name 'Napoleon', the name 'Nelson'. Clearly this alters the content of the sentence, and indeed it turns it from a true sentence into a false sentence. We can think of the sentence as in this way consisting of a constant component, 'Wellington defeated . . .', and a replaceable element, 'Napoleon'. Frege calls the first, fixed component a function, and the second component the argument of the function. The sentence 'Wellington defeated Napoleon' is, as Frege would put it, the value of the function 'Wellington defeated . . .' for the argument 'Napoleon' and the sentence 'Wellington defeated Nelson' is the value of the same function for the argument 'Nelson'.

We could also analyse the sentence in a different way. 'Wellington defeated Napoleon' is also the value of the function ' . . . defeated Napoleon' for the argument 'Wellington'. We can go further, and say that the sentence is the value of the function ' . . . defeated . . .' for the arguments 'Wellington' and 'Napoleon' (taken in that order). In Frege's terminology, 'Wellington defeated . . .' and ' . . . defeated Napoleon' are functions of a single argument; ' . . . defeated . . .' is a function of two arguments.[3]

It will be seen that in comparison with the subject–predicate distinction the function–argument dichotomy provides a much more flexible method of bringing out logically relevant similarities between sentences. Subject–predicate analysis is sufficient to mark the similarity between 'Caesar conquered Gaul' and 'Caesar defeated Pompey', but it is blind to the similarity between 'Caesar conquered Gaul' and 'Pompey avoided Gaul'. This becomes a matter of logical importance when we deal with sentences such as those occurring in syllogisms that contain not proper names like 'Caesar' and 'Gaul', but quantified expressions such as 'all Romans' or 'some province'.

Having introduced these notions of function and argument, Frege's next step is to introduce a new notation to express the kind of generality expressed by a word like 'all' no matter where it occurs in a sentence. If 'Socrates is

[3] As I have explained them above, following *Begriffsschrift*, functions and arguments and their values are all bits of language: names and sentences, with or without gaps. In his later writings Frege applied the notions more often not to linguistic items, but to the items that language is used to express and talk about. I will discuss this in the chapter on metaphysics (Ch. 7).

mortal' is a true sentence, we can say that the function '... is mortal' holds true for the argument 'Socrates'. To express generality we need a symbol to indicate that a certain function holds true no matter what its argument is. Adapting the notation that Frege introduced, logicians write

(x)(x is mortal)

to signify that no matter what name is attached as an argument to the function '... is mortal', the function holds true. The notation can be read as 'For all x, x is mortal' and it is equivalent to the statement that everything whatever is mortal.

This notation for generality can be applied in all the different ways in which sentences can be analysed into function and argument. Thus '(x)(God is greater than x)' is equivalent to 'God is greater than everything'. It can be combined with a sign for negation ('∼') to produce notations equivalent to sentences containing 'no' and 'none'. Thus '(x)∼(x is immortal)' = 'For all x, it is not the case that x is immortal' = 'Nothing is immortal'. To render a sentence containing expressions like 'some' Frege exploited the equivalence, long accepted by logicians, between (for example) 'Some Romans were cowards' and 'Not all Romans were not cowards'. Thus 'Some things are mortal' = 'It is not the case that nothing is mortal' = '∼(x)∼(x is mortal)'. For convenience his followers used, for 'some', a sign '(Ex)' as equivalent to '∼(x)∼'. Frege's notation, and its abbreviation, can be used to make statements about the existence of things of different kinds. '(Ex)(x is a horse)', for instance, is tantamount to 'There are horses' (provided, as Frege notes, that this sentence is understood as covering also the case where there is only one horse).

Frege believed that objects of all kinds were nameable—numbers, for instance, were named by numerals—and the argument places in his logical notation can be filled with the name of anything whatever. Consequently '(x)(x is mortal)' means not just that everyone is mortal, but that everything whatever is mortal. So understood, it is a false proposition, because, for instance, the number ten is not mortal.

It is rare, in fact, for us to want to make statements of such unrestricted generality. It is much more common for us to want to say that everything *of a certain kind* has a certain property, or that everything that has a certain given property also has a certain other property. 'All men are mortal' or 'What goes up must come down' are examples of typical universal

sentences of ordinary language. In order to express such sentences in
Frege's system one must graft his predicate calculus (the theory of quantifiers such as 'some' and 'all') on to a propositional calculus (the theory of
connectives between sentences, such as 'if' and 'and').

In Frege's system of propositional logic the most important element
is a sign for conditionality, roughly corresponding to 'if' in ordinary
language. The Stoic logician Philo, in ancient times, had defined 'If p
then q' by saying that it was a proposition that was false in the case in
which p was true and q false, and true in the three other possible cases.[4]
Frege defined his sign for conditionality (which we may render '$\rightarrow$') in a
similar manner. He warned that it did not altogether correspond to
'if...then' in ordinary language. If we take '$p \rightarrow q$' as equivalent to 'If p
then q' then propositions such as 'If the sun is shining, $3 \times 7 = 21$' and 'If
perpetual motion is possible, then pigs can fly' turn out true—simply
because the consequent of the first proposition is true, and the antecedent
of the second proposition is false. 'If' behaves differently in ordinary
language; the use of it that is closest to '$\rightarrow$' is in sentences such as 'If
those curtains match that sofa, then I'm a Dutchman'. Frege's sign can be
looked on as a stripped-down version of the word 'if', designed to capture
just that aspect of its meaning that is necessary for the formulation of
rigorous proofs containing it.

In Frege's terminology, '$\ldots \rightarrow \ldots$' is a function that takes sentences as
its arguments: its values, too, are sentences. Whether the sentences that are
its values (sentences of the form '$p \rightarrow q$') are true or false will depend only
on whether the sentences that are its arguments ('p' and 'q') are true or
false. We may call functions of this kind 'truth-functions'. The conditional
is not the only truth-function in Frege's system. So too is negation,
represented by the sign '$\sim$', since a negated sentence is true just in case
the sentence negated is false, and vice versa.

With the aid of these two symbols Frege built up a complete system of
propositional logic, deriving all the truths of that logic from a limited set of
primitive truths or axioms, such as '$(q \rightarrow p) \rightarrow (\sim p \rightarrow \sim q)$' and
'$\sim \sim p \rightarrow p$'. Connectives other than 'if', such as 'and' and 'or', are defined
in terms of conditionality and negation. Thus, '$\sim q \rightarrow p$' rules out the case
in which p is false and $\sim q$ is true: it means that p and q are not both false,

---

[4] See vol. I, p. 138.

and therefore is equivalent to '*p* or *q*' (in modern symbols, '*p* V *q*'). '*p* and *q*' ('*p* & *q*'), on the other hand, is rendered by Frege as '$\sim (q \rightarrow \sim p)$'. As Frege realized, a different system would be possible in which conjunction was primitive, and conditionality was defined in terms of conjunction and negation. But in logic, he maintained, deduction is more important than conjunction, and that is why 'if' and not 'and' is taken as primitive.

Earlier logicians had drawn up a number of rules of inference, rules for passing from one proposition to another. One of the best known was called *modus ponens*: 'From "*p*" and "If *p* then *q*" infer "*q*"'. In his system Frege claims to prove all the laws of logic using this as a single rule of inference. The other rules are either axioms of his system or theorems proved from them. Thus the rule traditionally called contraposition, which allows the inference from

> If John is snoring, John is asleep

to

> If John is not asleep, John is not snoring,

is justified by the first of the axioms quoted above.

When we put together Frege's propositional calculus and his predicate calculus we can symbolize the universal sentences of ordinary language, making use of both the sign of generality and the sign of conditionality. The expression

> $(x)(Fx \rightarrow Gx)$

can be read

> For all *x*, if *Fx* then *Gx*,

which means that whatever *x* may be, if '*Fx*' is true then '*Gx*' is true.

If we substitute 'is a man' for '*F*' and 'is mortal' for '*G*' then we obtain 'For all *x*, if *x* is a man, *x* is mortal', which is what Frege offers as the translation of 'All men are mortal'. The contradictory of this, 'Some men are not mortal', comes out as '$\sim(x)(x$ is a man $\rightarrow x$ is mortal)' and its contrary, 'No man is mortal', comes out as '$(x)(x$ is a man $\rightarrow \sim x$ is mortal)'. By the use of these translations, Frege is able to prove as part of his system theorems corresponding to the entire corpus of Aristotelian syllogistic.

Frege's logical calculus is not just more systematic than Aristotle's; it is also more comprehensive. His symbolism is able, for instance, to mark the difference between

Every boy loves some girl = $(x)(x$ is a boy $\rightarrow Ey(y$ is a girl $\&\ x$ loves $y))$

and the apparently similar (but much less plausible) passive version of the sentence

Some girl is loved by every boy = $(Ey(y$ is a girl $\&\ (x)(x$ is a boy $\rightarrow x$ loves $y))$.

Aristotelian logicians in earlier ages had sought in vain to find a simple and conspicuous way of bringing out such differences of meaning in ambiguous sentences of ordinary language. A final subtlety of Frege's system must be mentioned. The sentence 'Socrates is mortal', as we have seen, can be analysed as having 'Socrates' for argument, and '... is mortal' as function. But the function '... is mortal' can itself be regarded as an argument of a different function, a function operating at a higher level. This is what happens when we complete the function '... is mortal' not with a determinate argument, but with a quantifier, as in '$(x)(x$ is mortal)'. The quantifier '$(x)(x...)$' can then be regarded as a second-level function of the first-level function '... is mortal'. The initial function, Frege always emphasizes, is incomplete; but it may be completed in two ways, either by having an argument inserted in its argument place, or by itself becoming the argument of a second-level function. This is what happens when the ellipsis in '... is mortal' is filled with a quantifier such as 'Everything'.

Induction and Abduction in Peirce

A number of Frege's innovations in logic occurred, quite independently, to C. S. Peirce; but Peirce was never able to incorporate his results into a rigorous system, much less to publish them in a definitive form. Peirce's importance in the history of logic derives rather from his investigations into the structure of scientific inquiry. Deductive logic assists us in organizing our knowledge; but the kind of reasoning that extends our knowledge ('ampliative inference' as Peirce calls it) is of three kinds: induction, hypothesis, and analogy. All of these inferences, Peirce claimed,

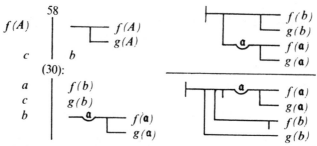

Modern symbolic logic no longer uses the actual symbol system of its founder Frege, which was difficult to print. The illustration shows the pattern, in his notation, for deriving results such as "If this ostrich is a bird and cannot fly, it follows that some birds cannot fly".

depend essentially on sampling. Any account, therefore, of non-deductive inference must be related to the mathematical theory of probability (*EWP* 177).

Scientists frame hypotheses, make predictions on the bases of these hypotheses, and then make observations with a view to confirming or refuting their hypotheses. These three stages of inquiry are called by Peirce abduction, deduction, and induction. In the abductive phase the inquirer selects a theory for consideration. In the deductive phase he formulates a method to test it. In the inductive phase he evaluates the results of the test.

How does a scientist decide which hypotheses are worth inductive testing? Indefinitely many different theories might explain the phenomena he wishes to investigate. If he is not to waste his time, his energy, and his research funding, the scientist needs some guidance about which theories to explore. This guidance is given by the rules of the logic of abduction. The theory must, if true, be genuinely explanatory; it must be empirically testable; it should be simple and natural and cohere with existing knowledge, though not necessarily with our subjective opinions about antecedent likelihood. (*P* 7.220–1)

Rules of abduction, however, do not by themselves explain the success of scientists in their choice of hypotheses. We have to believe that in their investigation of nature they are assisted by nature herself.

Science presupposes that we have a capacity for 'guessing' right. We shall do better to abandon the whole attempt to learn the truth ... unless we can trust to the human mind's having such a power of guessing right that before very many hypotheses shall have been tried, intelligent guessing may be expected to lead us to the one which will support all tests. (*P* 6.530)

This trust has to be presupposed at the outset, even though it may rest on no evidence. But in fact the history of science shows such trust to be well founded: 'it has seldom been necessary to try more than two or three hypotheses made by clear genius before the right one was found' (*P* 7.220)

Once the theory has been chosen, abduction is succeeded by deduction. Consequences are derived from the hypothesis, experimental predictions that is, which will come out true if the hypothesis is correct. In deduction, Peirce maintained, the mind is under the dominion of habit: a general idea will suggest a particular case. It is by verifying or falsifying the predictions of the particular instantiations that the scientist will confirm, or as the case may be refute, the hypothesis under test.

It is induction that is the all-important element in the testing, and induction is essentially a matter of sampling.

Suppose a ship arrives in Liverpool laden with wheat in bulk. Suppose that by some machinery the whole cargo be stirred up with great thoroughness. Suppose that twenty-seven thimblefuls be taken equally from the forward, midships, and aft parts, from the starboard, center and larboard parts, and from the top, half depth and lower parts of her hold, and that these being mixed and the grains counted, four-fifths of the latter are found to be of quality A. Then we infer, experientially and provisionally, that approximately four fifths of all the grain in the cargo is of the same quality. (*EWP* 177)

By saying that we draw the inference provisionally, Peirce means that if our experience be indefinitely extended, and every correction that presents itself be duly applied, then our approximation will become indefinitely close in the long run. Inference of this kind, Peirce claims, rests on no postulation of matter of fact, but only on the mathematics of probability.

Induction thus described is quantitative induction: an inference from the proportion of a sample to the proportion of a population. But there is another kind of induction that is important not only in science but in everyday life. That is qualitative induction, when we infer from one or more observed qualities of an individual to other, unobserved qualities. To illustrate this Peirce introduces us to the concept of the *mugwump*. A mugwump, he tells us, has certain characteristics:

He has a high self-respect and places great value upon social distinction. He laments the great part that rowdyism and unrefined good-fellowship play in the dealings of American politicians with their constituency.... He holds that monetary considerations should usually be the decisive ones in questions of public policy. He respects the principle of individualism and of *laissez-faire* as the greatest agency of civilisation. These views, among others, I know to be the obtrusive marks of a 'mugwump'. Now, suppose I casually meet a man in a railway train and falling into conversation find that he holds opinions of this sort; I am naturally led to suppose that he is 'mugwump'. That is hypothetic inference. That is to say, a number of readily verifiable a marks of a mugwump being selected, I find this man has these, and infer that he has all the other characters that go to make a thinker of that stripe. (*EWP* 210)

This homespun example illustrates the three stages of scientific inquiry as described by Peirce. My fellow passenger deplores the plebeian vulgarity of his congressman. I frame the hypothesis that he is a mugwump. I conclude that he is likely to oppose government regulation of business. I ask him his opinion on a recent measure in restraint of trade, and my hypothesis is confirmed by his vehement denunciation. It remains, however, no more than probable, in spite of further conversation, for the train journey is, mercifully, only finitely long.

The Saga of Principia Mathematica

Peirce's logical investigations left little mark on the development of logic in the early twentieth century. It was rather the work of Frege that was carried forward, in particular by the work of Russell and Whitehead, his successors in the quest for the logicist grail. The three volumes of *Principia Mathematica* contain a systematization of logic that soon became much better known than that presented in Frege's own works.

One reason for the greater popularity of *Principia* is that it replaces Frege's ingenious but cumbersome symbolism with a much more convenient notation, which Russell and Whitehead took over from its inventor, the Italian mathematician Giuseppe Peano. Whereas Frege's system was two-dimensional, and called for complicated typesetting, the Peano system is linear, and calls only for a few special signs in addition to letters of the alphabet. Thus the tilde sign '∼' was used for negation, the sign 'V' for disjunction, and the horseshoe sign '⊃' for the truth-functional 'if'. These signs for logical connectives are still in common use, though we use in this text instead of the horseshoe the sign '$\rightarrow$', which is nowadays preferred. For conjunction Russell and Whitehead used a simple point, as in 'p.q'; nowadays the ampersand, as in 'p & q', is commonly used instead. Russell and Whitehead expressed universal quantification thus: '$(x)F(x)$'; and existential quantification thus: '$(Ex)F(x)$'. These symbols, too, are now in common use; the 'E' in existential quantification is sometimes printed in reverse.

The system of *Principia* is, like Frege's, an axiomatic system in which logical truths are derived by rule from a handful of axioms. The initial set of axioms, however, differs from Frege's set, and whereas Frege had taken 'if' and 'not' as primitive connectives from which the others could be defined, Russell and Whitehead took 'or' and 'not' (which they called 'logical constants') as basic. In fact many other sets of axioms are possible, with different primitive constants, and they were studied by logicians in the next decades.

But it soon came to be realized that axiomatic systems were not the only way, or even necessarily the best way, to give logic a rigorous form. This was shown by Wittgenstein, who invented a formal device which, like many of those of Frege, passed into the logic textbooks, namely the truth-table.

It is possible to define the propositional connectives by setting out in a table the truth-conditions of propositions containing them. Thus the table

p	q	p & q
T	T	T
F	T	F
T	F	F
F	F	F

represents that 'p & q' is true in the case in which 'p' and 'q' are both true, and false in the three other possible cases, namely (*a*) when 'p' is false and 'q' is true, (*b*) when 'p' is true and 'q' is false, (*c*) when 'p' and 'q' are both false. The truth-value of 'p & q', as the table brings out, is determined by the truth-values of the component propositions 'p' and 'q'; the compound proposition, we may say, is a *truth-function* of its constituents, and the possible combinations of the truth-values of the constituents set out the *truth-conditions* for the compound proposition.

Similar tables can be set out for the other logical constants, such as 'or' and 'if'. 'If p then q' is written as '$p \rightarrow q$' and is interpreted as a truth-functional condition that is true in all cases except where 'p' is true and 'q' is false. The simplest truth-table is the one for 'not':

p	$\sim p$
T	F
F	T

This shows that a proposition is true when its negation is false, and vice versa.

Propositions of great length and complexity may be built up by repeated use of the logical constants, but however complex they are their truth-value can always be determined from the truth-values of the simple propositions that make them up (Wittgenstein, *TLP* 5.31). Consider the following proposition:

If p and q, then not-p and q.

This is a truth-function of 'p' and 'q' as shown in the following table:

p	q	p & q	$\rightarrow$	$\sim p$ & q
T	T	T T T	F	F T F T
F	T	F F T	T	T F T T
T	F	T F F	T	F T F F
F	F	F F F	T	T F F F

This table is constructed in the following manner. First the columns under each occurrence of the single propositional variables are filled in by copying out the values given in the two left-hand columns, which represent a conventional arrangement to ensure that all possible combinations of truth-values are covered (*TLP* 4.31). Then in the fourth column from the right the truth-value of 'not-p' is filled in under the '$\sim$' sign by reversing the truth-value of 'p'. Then the columns under the '&s' are filled in by deriving the truth-value of the conjunct propositions via the table given earlier. Finally the '$\rightarrow$' column is computed, the truth-values being derived from the truth-functional definition of 'if... then'. This column shows the value of the whole complex formula for every possible combination of truth-values of its constituents. It turns out to be false if 'p & q' is true, and to be true in all other cases.

When we construct truth-tables for complex propositions in this manner, we sometimes find that they take the same truth-value for every possible truth-value of the elementary propositions. Thus, the proposition '*p* or not *p*' is true whether '*p*' is true or false, as we see thus:

p	*p* V ~*p*
T	T T FT
F	F T TF

On the other hand, the proposition '*p* and not-*p*' is false whatever '*p*' may be:

p	*p* & ~*p*
T	T F FT
F	F F TF

A proposition that is true for all truth-possibilities of its elementary propositions is called a *tautology*; a proposition that is false for all truth-possibilities is called a *contradiction* (*TLP* 4.46). The tautology set out above corresponds to the law of excluded middle. The tautology that is the negation of the contradiction set out above corresponds to the law of non-contradiction. These two laws were two of the three traditional laws of thought.

In this way the study of tautologies links with old-fashioned logics, but it also marks an advance on Frege's handling of propositional logic. It can be shown that all formulae that are tautologous by Wittgenstein's test are either axioms or theorems of Frege's system, and conversely that anything that can be proved from Frege's axioms will be a tautology. The truth-table method and the axiomatic system thus turn out to be two devices for handling the same material, namely the logical truisms of the propositional calculus. But the truth-table method has several advantages over the axiomatic method.

First, it represents all logical truths as on a level with each other, whereas Frege's system and the system of *Principia* privilege an arbitrarily chosen set of them as axioms. Second, there is no need to appeal to any self-evidence in logic: the truth-table method is entirely mechanical, in the sense that it can be carried out by a machine. Finally, given a formula of the propositional calculus we can always settle, by the use of a truth-table, whether or not it is a tautology. An axiomatic system offers nothing comparable. To be sure, if we discover a proof we know the formula is a theorem; but if we fail to discover a proof this may exhibit nothing more than the limits of our own ingenuity. If we are asked 'Is p a tautology or not?', Wittgenstein's method gives us a foolproof method of answering the question not only with a 'yes' but with a 'no'. The axiomatic method does not offer a similar *decision procedure* (to use the term that became standard among logicians).

The classical propositional calculus, as formulated in different ways by Frege, Russell, and Wittgenstein, was criticized by a school of logicians, founded by L. E. J. Brouwer, who deplored the use in mathematics of the principle of excluded middle. These logicians, called 'intuitionists', conceived mathematics as a construction of the human mind, and therefore they assigned truth only to such mathematical propositions as were capable of demonstration. On this basis it would be wrong to affirm 'p' without independent proof, simply because one had refuted 'not-p'. Intuitionists devised systems of logic that lacked not only '$p \lor \sim p$' but other familiar theorems such as '$\sim\sim p \to p$'.

Logicians in the 1920s and 1930s showed that there were many different ways in which the propositional and predicate calculus could be formalized. Besides axiomatic systems containing one or other set of axioms plus a number of rules of inference, one could have a system with no rules but an infinite set of axioms, or a system with no axioms and a limited number of rules. A system of the latter kind was devised by Georg Gentzen in 1934: it consisted of seven rules for the introduction of the logical constants and quantifiers, and eight rules for their elimination. Formal logic, if presented in this manner, resembles non-formal arguments in everyday life more closely than any axiomatic system does. Systems of this kind, accordingly, were called systems of 'natural deduction'. They were appropriate not only for classical but also for intuitionist logic.

Besides devising a variety of methods of systematizing logic, logicians interested themselves in establishing second-order truths about the properties of various systems. One property that it is desirable, indeed essential, for a system of logic to possess is the property of consistency. Given a set of axioms and rules, for instance, we need to show that from those axioms, by those rules, it will never be possible to derive two propositions that contradict each other. Another property, which is desirable but not essential, is that of independence: we wish to show that no axiom of the system is derivable by the rules from the remaining axioms of the system. The logician Paul Bernays in 1926 showed that the propositional system of *Principia Mathematica* was consistent, and that four of its axioms were independent of each other, but the fifth was deducible as a thesis from the remaining four.

The method of proving consistency and independence depends upon treating the axioms and theorems of a deductive system simply as abstract formulae, and treating the rules of the system simply as mechanical procedures for obtaining one formula from another. The properties of the system are then explored by offering a set of objects as a model, or interpretation, of the abstract calculus. The elements of the system are mapped on to the objects and their relations in such a way as to satisfy, or bring out true, the formulae of the system. A formula P will entail a formula Q if and only if all interpretations that satisfy P also satisfy Q. This model-theoretic approach to logic gradually assumed an importance equal to that of the earlier approach that had focused on the notion of proof.

A third property of deductive systems that was explored by logicians in the inter-war years was that of completeness. An axiomatic presentation of the propositional calculus is complete if and only if every truth-table tautology is provable within the system. Hilbert and Ackermann in 1928 offered a proof that the propositional calculus of *Principia Mathematica* was in this sense complete. Indeed, it was complete also in the stronger sense that if we add any non-tautologous formula as an axiom, we reach a contradiction. In 1930 Kurt Gödel proved that first-order predicate calculus, the logic of quantification, was complete in the weaker, but not the stronger, sense.

The question now arose: was arithmetic, like general logic, a complete system? Frege, Russell, and Whitehead had hoped that they had established that arithmetic was a branch of logic. Russell wrote, 'If there are still those who do not admit the identity of logic and mathematics, we may challenge them to indicate at what point, in the successive definitions and deductions of *Principia Mathematica*, they consider that logic ends and mathematics begins' (*IMP* 194–5). If arithmetic was a branch of logic, and if logic was complete, then arithmetic should be a complete system too.

Gödel, in an epoch-making paper of 1931, showed that it was not, and could not be turned into one. By an ingenious device he constructed a formula within the system of *Principia* that can be shown to be true and yet is not provable within the system: a formula that in effect says of itself that it is unprovable. He did this by showing how to turn formulae of the logical system into statements of arithmetic by associating the signs of *Principia* with natural numbers, in such a way that every relationship between two formulae of the logical system corresponds to a relation between the numbers thus associated. In particular, if a set of formulae A, B, C is a proof of a formula D, then there will be a specific numerical relationship between the Gödel numbers of the four formulae. He then went on to construct a formula that could only have a proof in the system if the relevant Gödel numbers violated the laws of arithmetic. The formula must therefore be unprovable; yet Gödel could show, from outside the system, that it was a true formula. We might think to remedy this problem by adding the unprovable formula as an axiom to the system; but this will enable another, different, unprovable formula to be constructed, and so on ad infinitum. We have to conclude that arithmetic is incomplete and incompletable.

Even if a system is complete, it does not follow that there will always be a way of deciding whether or not a particular formula is valid. Production of a proof will of course prove that it is; but failure to produce a proof does not prove that it is invalid. For propositional calculus, there is such a decision procedure: the truth-table method will show whether something is or is not a tautology. Arithmetic, being incompletable, a fortiori is undecidable. But between propositional logic and arithmetic, what of first-order predicate logic, which Gödel had shown to be complete: is there a decision procedure there? The painstaking work of logicians showed that parts of the system were decidable, but that there can be no decision procedure for the entire calculus, nor can we give a satisfactory rubric to determine which parts are decidable and which are not.

Modern Modal Logic

Meanwhile, other logicians were studying a branch of logic that had been neglected since the Middle Ages, modal logic. Modal logic is the logic of the notions of necessity and possibility. Its study in modern times dates from the work of C. I. Lewis in 1918, who approached it via the theory of implication. What is it for a proposition p to imply a proposition q? Russell and Whitehead treated their horseshoe sign (the truth-functional 'if') as a sign of implication, on the grounds that 'If p and $p \to q$ then q' was a valid inference. But they realized that it was an odd form of implication—it entails, for instance, that any false proposition implies every proposition—and so they gave it the name of 'material implication'. Lewis insisted that the only genuine implication was strict implication: *p* implies *q* only if it is *impossible* that *p* should be true and *q* false. '*p* strictly implies *q*', he maintained, was equivalent to '*q* follows logically from *p*'. He drew up axiomatic systems in which the sign for material implication was replaced by a new sign to represent strict implication, and these systems were the first formal systems of modal logic. Strict implication struck many critics as being hardly less paradoxical than material implication, since an impossible proposition strictly implies every proposition, so that 'If cats are dogs then pigs can fly' comes out true.

Lewis's modal researches, however, were interesting in their own right. He offered five different axiom systems, which he numbered S1 to S5, and showed that each of the axiom sets was consistent and independent. They vary in strength. S1, for instance, does not allow a proof of 'If *p&q* is possible, then *p* is possible and *q* is possible' (which seems very plausible), while S5 contains 'If *p* is possible, then *p* is necessarily possible' (which seems rather dubious). In some ways the most interesting system is S4, which Gödel showed was equivalent to the logic of *Principia Mathematica* with the following additional axioms (reading 'if' as material, not strict, implication):

(1) If necessarily *p*, then *p*.
(2) If necessarily *p*, then (if necessarily [if *p* then *q*] then necessarily *q*).
(3) If necessarily *p*, then necessarily necessarily *p*.

He added also a rule, that if '*p*' was any thesis of the system, we can add also 'necessarily *p*'. The system exploits the interdefinability of necessity (which he represented by the symbol □) and possibility (represented by ◇). As was well known in antiquity and the Middle Ages, 'necessarily' can be defined as 'not possibly not' and 'possibly' as 'not necessarily not'.

There are many statements that can be formulated within modal logic about whose truth-value there is no consensus among logicians. The most contentious ones are those in which modal operators are iterated. The system that Gödel axiomatized, S4, contains as derivable theses the two following formulae:

If possibly possibly *p*, then possibly *p*
If necessarily *p*, then necessarily necessarily *p*

It does not, however, contain these two:

If possibly *p*, then necessarily possibly *p*

If possibly necessarily *p*, then necessarily *p*

which are provable in S5 and are characteristic features of that system. The relative merits of S4 and S5 as systems of modal logic remain a matter of debate today, and not only among logicians. Some philosophers of religion, for instance, have argued that if it is possible that a necessary being (i.e. God) exists, then a necessary being does exist. This involves a tacit appeal to the second of the S5 theses listed above.

There are a number of parallels between modal operators and the quantifiers of predicate logic. The interdefinability of 'necessary' and 'possible' parallels the interdefinability of 'all' and 'some'. Just as 'For all *x*, *Fx*' entails '*Fa*', so 'Necessarily *p*' entails '*p*', and just as '*Fa*' entails 'For some *x*, *Fx*', so '*p*' entails 'possibly *p*'. There are laws of distribution in modal logic that are the analogues of those in quantification theory: thus it is necessary that *p* and *q* if and only if it is both necessary that *p* and necessary that *q*, and it is possible that *p* or *q* if and only if it is either possible that *p* or it is possible that *q*. Because of this, if we introduce quantification into modal logic, and use modal operators and quantifiers together, we have a system that resembles double quantification.

In quantified modal logic it is important to mark the order in which the operators and quantifiers are placed. It is easily seen that 'For all *x*, *x* is possibly *F*' is not the same as 'It is possible that for all *x*, *x* is *F*': in a fair lottery, everyone has a chance of being the winner, but there is no chance that everyone is the winner. Likewise we must distinguish between 'There is something that necessarily *Φ*s' and 'Necessarily, there is something that *Φ*s'. It is true that of necessity there is someone than whom no one is more obese. However, that person is not necessarily so obese: it is perfectly possible for him to slim and cease to be a champion fatty. Sentences in which the modal operator precedes the quantifier (as in the second of each of the two pairs above) were called in the Middle Ages modals *de dicto*, and sentences in which the quantifier comes earlier (as in the first of each of the two pairs above) were called modals *de re*. These terms have been revived by modern modal logicians to make very similar distinctions.

Despite the parallels between modal logic and quantification theory there is also an important difference, once we introduce into the system the notion of identity. In the technical term introduced by Quine, modal logics are referentially opaque, whereas quantificational contexts are not. Referential opacity is defined as follows. Let E be a sentence of the form A = B (where A and B are referring expressions). Then if P is a sentence containing A, and Q is a sentence resembling P in all respects except that it contains B where P contains A, then P is referentially opaque if P and E do not together imply Q.

Modal contexts are easily seen to be opaque in this way. When Quine wrote, the number of planets was nine, but whereas 'Necessarily, 9 is greater than 7' is true, 'Necessarily, the number of planets is greater than 7' is not. Because of this opacity some logicians, notably Quine, rejected modal logic altogether. But the work of a number of logicians in the early 1960s—notably Føllesdal, Kripke, and Hintikka—made modal logic respectable.

The key idea of modern modal logic is to exploit the similarities between quantification and modality by defining necessity as truth in all possible worlds, and possibility as truth in some possible world. Plain truth is then thought of as truth in the actual world, which is one among all possible worlds. Talk of possible worlds need not involve any metaphysical implications: for the purposes of modal semantics any model with the appropriate formal structure will suffice.

To illustrate how the semantics is set out, consider a universe in which there are just two objects, a and b, and three predicates, F, G, and H, and let us suppose that there are three possible worlds in that universe of which world 2 is the actual one, which we may call alpha.

World 1	Fa	$\sim Ga$	$\sim Ha$	$\sim Fb$	Gb	Hb
World 2	Fa	$\sim Ga$	Ha	$\sim Fb$	Gb	$\sim Hb$
World 3	Fa	Ga	$\sim Ha$	Fb	Gb	Hb

If necessity is truth in all possible worlds, we have in this universe 'Necessarily Fa' and 'Necessarily Gb'. The thesis 'If necessarily p, then p' is exemplified by the truth of Fa and Gb in alpha, the actual world. If possibility is truth in some possible world we have, for example, 'Possibly Fb' and 'Possibly Ga', even though 'Fb' and 'Ga' are false in alpha.

The iteration of modalities, which as we saw gave rise to problems, is now explained in terms of a relationship to be defined between different possible worlds. One possible world may or may not be *accessible* from another. When we use a single operator, as in 'possibly p', we can be taken to be saying 'In some world beta, accessible from alpha, p is the case'. If we iterate, and say 'possibly possibly p', we mean 'In some world gamma, accessible from beta, which is accessible from alpha, p is the case'. It cannot be taken for granted that every world accessible from beta is also accessible from alpha: whether this is the case will depend on how the accessibility relation is defined. This, in turn, will determine which system—which, for instance, of Lewis's S1–S5—is the appropriate one for our purposes.

If the notions that we wish to capture in our modal logic are those of logical necessity and possibility, then every possible world will be accessible from every other possible world, since logic is universal and transcendent. But there are other forms of necessity and possibility. There is, for instance, epistemic necessity and possibility, where 'possibly p' means 'For all I know to the contrary, p'. Philosophers have also extended the notion of modality into many different contexts, where there are pairs of operators that behave in ways that resemble the paradigmatic modal operators. In the logic of time, for instance, 'always' corresponds to 'necessary' and 'sometimes' to 'possible', both pairs of operators being interdefinable with the aid of negation. In deontic logic, the logic of obligation, 'obligatory' is the necessity operator, and 'permitted' is the possibility operator. In these and other cases the accessibility relationship will need careful definition: in a logic of tenses, for instance, future worlds, but not past worlds, will be accessible from the actual (i.e. the present) world.[5]

The problem of referential opacity arises in all these broadly modal contexts. It can be dealt with by making a distinction between two different kinds of reference. To be a genuine name, a term must be, in the terminology of Kripke, a rigid designator: that is to say, it must have the same reference in every possible world. There are other expressions whose reference is determined by their sense (e.g. 'the discoverer of oxygen') and therefore may change from one possible world to another. Once this distinction has been made, it is easy to accept that a statement such as '9 = the number of the planets' is not a genuine identity statement linking two names. '9' is indeed a rigid designator that keeps its reference across possible worlds; but 'the number of the planets' is a description that in different worlds may refer to different numbers.

---

[5] The logic of time and tense was first studied systematically by A. N. Prior in *Time and Modality* (Oxford: Oxford University Press, 1957) and deontic logic by G. H. von Wright in *An Essay on Deontic Logic* (Amsterdam: North-Holland, 1968).

5

Language

In the course of the nineteenth century, philosophers turned their attention ever more intensely on the topic of meaning. What do words and sentences signify? How do they signify and do they all signify in the same way? What is the relationship between meaning and truth? These questions were now asked with an urgency that had not been felt since the Middle Ages.[1]

Frege on Sense and Reference

A seminal work in the theory of meaning was Frege's paper of 1892, 'Sense and Reference'. That paper starts from a question about statements of identity. Is identity a relation? If it is a relation, is it a relation between signs or between what signs stand for? It seems that it cannot be a relation between objects that signs stand for, because if so, when '$a = b$' is true then '$a = a$' cannot differ from '$a = b$'. On the other hand, it seems that it cannot be a relationship between signs, because names are arbitrary, and if a sentence of the form '$a = b$' expressed a relationship between symbols it could not express any fact about the extra-linguistic world. Yet a sentence such as 'The morning star is identical with the evening star' expresses not a linguistic tautology, but an astronomical discovery.

Frege solved this problem by distinguishing between two different kinds of signification. Where other philosophers talk of meaning, Frege

---

[1] For medieval theories of meaning, see vol. II, pp. 130–1, 146–7.

introduces a distinction between the *reference* of an expression (the object to which it refers, as the planet Venus is the reference of 'the morning star') and the *sense* of an expression (the particular mode in which a sign presents what it designates). 'The evening star' differs in sense from 'the morning star' even though it has been discovered that both expressions refer to Venus. Frege says, in general, that an identity statement will be true and informative if the sign of identity is flanked by two names with the same reference but different senses. The word 'name' is, as the example shows, used by Frege in a broad sense to include complex designations of objects. He is prepared to call all such designations 'proper names' (*CP* 157–8).

Frege applies the distinction between sense and reference to sentences of all kinds. In his account of meaning there are items at three levels: signs, their senses, and their references. By using signs we express a sense and denote a reference (*CP* 161). In a well-regulated language, Frege believed, every sign would have a sense and only one sense. In natural languages words like 'bank' and 'port' are ambiguous, and a name like 'Aristotle' can be paraphrased in many different ways; we have to be content if the same word has the same sense in the same context. On the other hand, there is no requirement, even in an ideal language, that every sense should have only one sign. The same sense may be expressed by different signs in different languages or even in the same language. In a good translation, the sense of the original text is preserved. What is lost in translation is what Frege calls 'the colour' of the text. Colour is important for poetry but not for logic; it is not objective in the way that sense is.

The sense of a word is what we grasp when we understand the word. It is quite different from a mental image, even though, if a sign refers to a tangible object, I may well have a mental image associated with it. Images are subjective and vary from person to person; an image is *my* image or *your* image. The sense of a sign, on the other hand, is something that is the common property of all users of the language. It is because senses are public in this way that thoughts can be passed on from one generation to another.

For Frege, it is not only proper names—simple or complex—that have senses and references. What of entire sentences, which express thoughts? Is the thought, that is to say the content of the sentence, its sense or its reference?

122

Let us assume for the time being that the sentence has reference. If we now replace one word of the sentence by another having the same reference, but a different sense, this can have no bearing upon the reference of the sentence. Yet we can see that in such a case the thought changes; since e.g. the thought in the sentence 'The morning star is a body illuminated by the Sun' differs from that in the sentence 'The evening star is a body illuminated by the Sun'. Anybody who did not know that the evening star is the morning star might hold the one thought to be true, the other false. The thought, accordingly, cannot be the reference of the sentence, but must rather be considered as the sense. (*CP* 162)

If the thought expressed by a sentence is not its reference, does the sentence have a reference at all? Frege agrees that there can be sentences lacking reference: sentences occurring in works of fiction such as the *Odyssey*. But the reason these sentences lack a reference is that they contain names that lack a reference, such as 'Odysseus'. Other sentences do have a reference; and consideration of fictional sentences will enable us to determine just what that reference is.

We must expect that the reference of a sentence is determined by the reference of the parts of a sentence. Let us inquire, therefore, what is missing from a sentence if one of its parts lacks a reference. If a name lacks a reference, that does not affect the thought, since that is determined only by the sense of its constituent parts, not by their reference. It is only if we treat the *Odyssey* as science rather than myth, if we want seriously to take the sentences it contains as true or false, that we need to ascribe a reference to 'Odysseus'. 'Why do we want every proper name to have not only a sense, but also a reference? Why is the thought not enough for us? Because, and to the extent that, we are concerned with its truth-value' (*CP* 163). We are, Frege says, driven into accepting as the reference of a sentence its truth-value, the True, or as the case may be, the False. Every seriously propounded indicative sentence is a name of one or other of these objects. All true sentences have the same reference as each other, and so do all false sentences.

The relation, then, between a sentence and its truth-value is the same as that between a name and its reference. This is a surprising conclusion: surely, to assert that pigs have wings is to do something quite different from naming anything. Frege would agree; but that is because asserting a sentence is something quite different from putting a sentence together out of subject and predicate. 'Subject and predicate (understood in the logical sense) are indeed elements of thought; they stand on the same level as items for comprehension. By combining subject and predicate one reaches only a thought, never passes from sense to reference, never from a thought to its truth value' (*CP* 164). Sentences can occur unasserted, perhaps as a clause in a conditional, such as 'If pigs have wings, then pigs can fly'. Though every serious sentence names a truth-value (in this case the False) the mere use of a sentence does not commit the user to specifying its truth-value. Only if we assert a sentence do we *say that* it is a name of the True.

Many philosophers since Frege have made use of his distinction between sense and reference, and have accepted that there is an important difference between predication and assertion; but almost all have rejected the notion that complete sentences have a reference of any kind. Indeed, in his own later writings Frege himself seems to have given up the idea that there were two grand objects, the True and the False; instead, he came to accept that truth was not an object but a property, albeit one of an indefinable, *sui generis* kind (*CP* 353).

Towards the end of his life Frege became more interested in aspects of language that were not captured by his system of logic—the 'colouring' in the expression of thoughts. Scientific language as it were presents thoughts in black and white; but in humane disciplines sentences may clothe thoughts in colourful garb, with expressions of feeling. We interject words and phrases like 'Alas!' or 'Thank God!' and we use charged words like 'cur' instead of plain words like 'dog'. Such features of sentences are not concerns of logic because they do not affect their truth-value. A statement containing the word 'cur' in place of 'dog' does not become false merely because the person uttering it does not feel the hostility that the word expresses (*PW* 140).

In his paper 'The Thought' Frege considered the features of language represented by the tenses of verbs, and by indexical expressions such as 'today', 'here', and 'I'. If a sentence contains a present-tense verb, as in 'It is snowing', then in order to grasp the thought expressed you need to know when the sentence was uttered. Something similar happens with the use of the first-person pronoun. 'I am hungry' said by Peter expresses a different thought than is expressed by 'I am hungry' said by Paul. One thought may be true and the other false. So one and the same sentence may, in different contexts, express a different thought. The opposite may also happen, according to Frege. If on 9 December I say 'It was snowing yesterday'

A letter from Frege to Husserl, explaining his distinction between sense and reference.

I express the same thought as if on 8 December I say 'It is snowing today'. It was left to logicians of a later generation to try to incorporate such complications into formal systems.

The Pragmatists on Language and Truth

Charles Sanders Peirce, who had developed quantificational theory independently of Frege, likewise expressed, in a different terminology, many of Frege's insights into philosophy of language. Both philosophers rejected the traditional way of distinguishing between subject and predicate, and analysed propositions into elements of two kinds, one a complete symbol (the *arguments* in Frege's *Begriffsschrift*) and the other an incomplete, or unsaturated, symbol (the *functions* of *Begriffsschrift*). The proper names that Frege called 'arguments' Peirce called 'indices', and Frege's concept expressions or functions were called by Peirce 'icons'. For Peirce a particularly important class of icons was expressions for relations. 'In the statement of a relationship,' he wrote, 'the designations of the correlates ought to be considered as so many logical subjects and the relative itself as the predicate.' In his treatment of sentences concerning two-place relationships such as 'John loves Mary' Peirce differed little from Frege. However, he extended the notion of relationship in two directions, by considering what he called the 'valency' (i.e. the number of arguments) of different relations. He was interested in particular in three-place relationships (such as 'John gave Fido to Mary'); and in addition to 'polyadic' relationships with two or more subjects, he introduced the term 'monadic relationship' for ordinary one-place predicates such as ' ... is wise'. He was even willing to call a complete proposition a 'medadic relation'—that is, a relative proposition with zero (in Greek *meden*) unsaturated places.

Peirce's logic and theory of language was embedded in a general theory of signs, which he called 'semiotics', and to which he attached great importance. A sign stands for an object by being understood or interpreted by an intelligent being; the interpretation is itself a further sign. Peirce calls the external sign a 'representamen' and the sign as understood 'the interpretant'. The semiotic function of signs is a triadic relation between representamen, object, and interpretant.

Peirce classified signs into three classes. There are natural signs: clouds, for instance, are a natural sign of rain, and stripped bark on a tree may be a sign of the presence of deer. Next, there are iconic signs, which signify by resembling their objects. Naturalistic paintings and sculptures are the most obvious examples, but there are others such as maps. Two features are essential to an iconic sign: (1) it should share with its object some feature that each could have if the other did not exist; (2) the method of interpreting this feature should be fixed by convention. Finally, there are symbols, of which words are the most important example, but which include such things as uniforms and traffic signals. These, like iconic signs, are determined by convention, but unlike iconic signs they do not operate by exploiting any resemblance to their objects.

Since Peirce, theorists have divided semiotics into three disciplines: syntactics, the study of grammar and whatever may underlie grammatical structure; semantics, the study of the relationship between language and reality; and pragmatics, the study of the social context and the purposes and consequences of communication. Peirce's own work operated at the interface of all three disciplines; but in the work of his followers, despite their school title of 'pragmatists', discussion focused upon two key concepts of semantics, namely meaning and truth.

Peirce and James explained meaning in similar ways: in order to discover what an utterance meant you had to explore what would be the practical consequences of its being true, and if there was no difference between the consequences of two different beliefs then they were in effect the same belief. But James maintained that the truth of a belief, and not just its meaning, depended on its consequences, or rather on the consequences of believing it. If my believing that p is something that pays in the long run, something whose overall consequence is profitable for my life, then p is true for me. The pragmatist's claim, he tells us, is this:

Truth, concretely considered, is an attribute of our beliefs, and these are attitudes that follow satisfactions. The ideas around which the satisfactions cluster are primarily only hypotheses that challenge or summon a belief to come and take its stand upon them. The pragmatist's idea of truth is just such a challenge. He finds it ultra-satisfactory to accept it, and takes his own stand accordingly. (T 199)

Pragmatism, he claimed, was not at all inconsistent with realism. Truth and reality are not the same as each other; truth is something known, thought, or said about the reality. Indeed, the notion of a reality independent of any believer, James said, was at the base of the pragmatist definition of truth. Any statement, to be counted true, must agree with some such reality.

Pragmatism defines 'agreeing' to mean certain ways of 'working', be they actual or potential. Thus, for my statement 'the desk exists' to be true of a desk recognized as real by you, it must be able to lead me to shake your desk, to explain myself by words that suggest that desk to your mind, to make a drawing that is like the desk you see, etc. Only in such ways as this is there sense in saying it agrees with *that* reality, only thus does it gain for me the satisfaction of hearing you corroborate me. (*T* 218)

Passages like this suggest that pragmatism adds to, rather than subtracts from, the common-sense notion of truth. For '*p*' to be true, it appears, not only must it be the case that *p*, but it must actually have been verified, or at least verifiable, that *p* is the case. To an objector who protested that when a belief is true, its object does exist, James retorted, 'it is *bound* to exist, on sound pragmatic principles'. How is the world made different for me, he asked, by my conceiving an opinion of mine as true? 'First, an object must be findable there (or sure signs of such an object must be found) which shall agree with the opinion. Second, such an opinion must not be contradicted by anything else I am aware of' (*T* 275).

But in spite of his bluff, sleeves-rolled-up, manner of speech, James was rather a slippery writer, and it is quite difficult to pin him down on the question whether a proposition can be true without any fact to correspond to it. He tries to avoid the question by making the notion of truth a relative one. In human life, he tells us, the word 'truth' can only be used 'relatively to some particular trower'. Critics objected that there were some truths (say, about the pre-human past) that nobody would ever know; to which James replied that these, though never actual objects of knowledge, were always possible objects of knowledge, and in defining truth we should surely give priority to the real over the merely virtual. But there is another, more serious, objection to his claim that truth is relative to the truth-claimer. Surely if I hold that *p* is true, and you hold that not-*p* is true, it is a genuine question which of us is in the right.

128

Russell's Theory of Descriptions

One of James's earliest and most trenchant critics was Bertrand Russell, who attacked the pragmatist account of truth in an article of 1908 entitled 'Transatlantic Truth'. 'According to the pragmatists', he wrote, 'to say "it is true that other people exist" means "it is useful to believe that other people exist". But if so, then these two phrases are merely different words for the same proposition; therefore when I believe the one I believe the other' (James, *T* 278). But, Russell claimed, one proposition could be true and the other false; and in general it was often much easier in practice to find out whether *p* was true than whether it was good to believe that *p*. 'It is far easier', Russell wrote, 'to settle the plain question of fact "Have popes always been infallible?" than to settle the question whether the effects of thinking them infallible are on the whole good' (James, *T* 273).

In the years leading up to *Principia Mathematica*, however, Russell's philosophical interests were focused less on the nature of truth than on the different kinds of meaning that words and phrases might have, and also the possible ways in which they might turn out to lack meaning. When he wrote *The Principles of Mathematics* he had a very simple view of meaning which led to a very catholic view of being, reminiscent of Parmenides.[2]

Being is that which belongs to every conceivable term, to every possible object of thought—in short to everything that can possibly occur in any proposition, true or false, and to all such propositions themselves.... 'A is not' must always be either false or meaningless. For if A were nothing it could not be said not to be; 'A is not' implies that there is a term A whose being is denied, and hence that A is. Thus, unless 'A is not' be an empty sound, it must be false—whatever A may be, it certainly is. Numbers, the Homeric gods, relations, chimeras and four-dimensional spaces all have being, for if they were not entities of a kind, we could make no propositions about them. Thus being is a general attribute of everything, and to mention anything is to show that it is. (*PM* 449)

It was not long before he began to believe that a system that made distinctions between different ways in which signs might signify was more credible than one in which the world contained a profusion of different kinds of object all related to symbols by a single simple relation of denotation. He soon, for instance, adopted Frege's method of dealing

---

[2] See vol. I, pp. 200–4.

with assertions and denials of existence. As he was to put it in *Principia Mathematica*:

Suppose we say 'The round square does not exist'. It seems plain that this is a true proposition, yet we cannot regard it as denying the existence of a certain object called 'the round square'. For if there were such an object, it would exist: we cannot first assume that there is a certain object, and then proceed to deny that there is such an object. Whenever the grammatical subject of a proposition can be supposed not to exist without rendering the proposition meaningless, it is plain that the grammatical subject is not a proper name, i.e. not a name directly representing some object. Thus in all such cases the proposition must be capable of being so analysed that what was the grammatical subject shall have disappeared. Thus when we say 'The round square does not exist' we may, as a first attempt at such analysis, substitute 'it is false that there is an object x which is both round and square'. (*PM*, 2nd edn., 66)

Russell continued to believe that any genuine proper name must stand for something, must 'directly represent some object'. But he thought that not all apparent names were genuine names. For instance, he thought that Frege was wrong to treat 'Aristotle' and 'the tutor of Alexander' as being the same kind of symbol, each a name with a sense and a reference. If 'Aristotle' was a genuine proper name, he maintained, it did not have a sense, but had meaning solely by having a reference. On the other hand an expression like 'the tutor of Alexander' was not a name at all, because unlike a genuine name it had parts that were symbols in their own right. Russell's positive account of such expressions is called his *theory of definite descriptions*; it was first put forward in his paper 'On Denoting' of 1905.

   Consider the sentence 'The author of *Hamlet* was a genius'. For this to be true, it must be the case that one and only one individual wrote *Hamlet* (otherwise no one has the right to be called '*the* author of *Hamlet*'). So Russell proposed to analyse the sentence into three elements, thus:

   For some x, (1) x wrote *Hamlet*
            and (2) For all y, if y wrote *Hamlet*, y is identical with x
            and (3) x was a genius.

The first element says that at least one individual wrote *Hamlet*, and the second that at most one individual wrote *Hamlet*. Having thus established that exactly one individual wrote *Hamlet*, the analysed sentence uses the third element to go on to say that that unique individual was a genius.

In the unanalysed sentence 'the author of *Hamlet*' looks like a complex name, and would have been treated as one in Frege's system. As analysed by Russell no such nominal expression appears, and instead we have a combination of predicates and quantifiers. The analysis is meant to apply not only when—as in this case—there actually is an object that answers to the definite description, but also when the description is a vacuous one, such as 'the present King of France'. A sentence such as 'The King of France is bald', when analysed along Russellian lines, turns out to be false. Consider the following two sentences:

(1) The sovereign of the United Kingdom is male.
(2) The sovereign of the United States is male.

Neither of these sentences is true, but the reason differs in the two cases. The first sentence is plain false, because though there is a sovereign of the United Kingdom she is female; the second fails to be true because the United States has no sovereign ruler. On Russell's analysis this sentence is not just untrue but positively false, and accordingly its negation, 'It is not the case that the sovereign of the United States is male', is true. (On the other hand 'The sovereign of the United States is not male' comes out, like the second sentence above, positively false.)

What is the point of this complicated analysis? It is natural to think that since there is no sovereign of the United States, sentence (2) is not so much false as misleading; the question of its truth-value does not arise. This is no doubt true of our use of such definite descriptions in ordinary language, but Frege and Russell aimed to construct a language that would be a more precise instrument than ordinary language for the purposes of logic and mathematics. They both regarded it as essential that such a language should contain only expressions with a definite sense, by which they meant that all sentences containing the expressions should have a truth-value. If we allow into our system sentences lacking a truth-value, then inference and deduction become impossible.

Frege proposed to avoid truth-value gaps by various arbitrary stipulations. Russell's analysis, whereby 'the sovereign of X' is in no case a referring expression at all, achieves the definiteness that he and Frege both sought, and does so by far less artificial means. It is easy enough to recognize that 'the round square' denotes nothing, because it is an obviously self-contradictory expression. But prior to investigation it may not be at all so clear whether some complicated mathematical formula contains a hidden contradiction. And if it does so, we shall not be able to discover this by logical investigation (e.g. by deriving a *reductio ad absurdum*) unless sentences containing it are assured of a truth-value.

The Picture Theory of the Proposition

In the *Tractatus Logico-Philosophicus* Wittgenstein built upon Russell's theory of descriptions in order to analyse the descriptions of complex objects. 'Every statement about complexes', he wrote, 'can be resolved into a statement about their constituents and into the propositions that describe the complexes completely.' Consider the following sentence (not one of Wittgenstein's own examples):

Austria-Hungary is allied to Russia.

That sentence was untrue when Wittgenstein wrote the *Tractatus* because Austria-Hungary was at war with Russia. It is not true now for a quite different reason, because the political unit called 'Austria-Hungary' no longer exists. If we follow the lead of Russell, we will say that in both cases the sentence is meaningful but false. The two possibilities of falsehood are clearly parallel to those for 'The sovereign of X is male'. 'Austria-Hungary' can be looked on as a definite description, roughly, 'the union of Austria and Hungary'.

If we follow Wittgenstein and analyse the sentence on the lines of Russell's theory, we get:

For some x and some y, $x =$ Austria
and $y =$ Hungary
and x is united to y
and x is allied to Russia
and y is allied to Russia.

Or more simply we can say that 'Austria-Hungary is allied to Russia' means 'Austria is allied to Russia and Hungary is allied to Russia, and Austria is united to Hungary'. In the *Tractatus* Wittgenstein built a great deal of metaphysics on the possibility of analysis of this kind. But in philosophy of language, he wrote, 'Russell's merit is to have shown that the apparent logical form of a proposition need not be its real form.'

When he wrote the *Tractatus* Wittgenstein believed that language disguised the structure of thought beyond recognition. It was the task of philosophy to uncover, by analysis, the naked form of thought beneath the drapery of ordinary language. Complex propositions were to be reduced to elementary propositions, and elementary propositions would be revealed as pictures of reality. Wittgenstein recorded in his diary on 29 September 1914 how the idea first dawned on him that propositions were essentially pictorial in nature:

The general concept of the proposition carries with it a quite general concept of the coordination of proposition and situation. The solution to all my questions must be extremely simple. In a proposition a world is as it were put together experimentally. (As when in the law-court in Paris a motor-car accident is represented by means of dolls, etc.) This must yield the nature of truth straight away. (*NB* 7)

The thesis that a proposition is a picture is not so implausible when we realize that Wittgenstein counted as pictures not only paintings, drawings, and photographs, and not only three-dimensional models, but also such things as maps, musical scores, and gramophone records. His picture theory is perhaps best regarded as a theory of representation in general.

In any representation there are two things to consider: (*a*) what it is a representation *of*; (*b*) whether it represents it correctly or incorrectly. The distinction between these two features of a representation, in the case of a proposition, is the distinction between what the proposition *means*, and whether what it means is true or false—the distinction between sense and truth-value.

If, in a law court, a toy lorry and a toy pram are to represent a collision between a lorry and a pram, several things are necessary. First, the toy lorry must go proxy for the real lorry, and the toy pram for the real pram: the elements of the model must stand in for the elements of the situation to be represented. This is called by Wittgenstein the pictorial relationship that makes the picture a picture (*TLP* 2.1514). Second, the elements of the model must be related to each other in a particular way. The positioning of the toy lorry and the toy pram represents the spatial relationship at the time of the accident, in a way in which it would not if the toys had simply been stowed away together in a cupboard. This, for Wittgenstein, is the *structure* of the picture (*TLP* 2.15). Every picture, then, consists of structure plus pictorial relationship.

133

The relationship between the toys in court is a fact, and this led Wittgenstein to say that a picture, a proposition, is a fact and not a mere collection of objects or names. It is a fact that could have been otherwise. The possibility of structure—in the case of the toys in court, their three-dimensionality—is called by Wittgenstein pictorial form. Pictorial form is what pictures have in common with what they picture, the common element that enables one to be a picture of the other at all. Thus, a picture represents a possibility in the real world (*TLP* 2.161).

How does the picture connect with the reality it represents? This is done by the choice of an object qua object with a certain pictorial form. If I select a set of toys as three-dimensional proxies for three-dimensional objects, I at the same time make their three-dimensional properties the pictorial form of the picture. I make the connection with reality by making the correlation between the elements of the picture and the elements of the situation it is to represent. How do I make this correlation? When he wrote the *Tractatus* Wittgenstein thought this was an empirical matter of no importance to philosophy.

Pictures can be more or less abstract, more or less like what they picture: their pictorial form can be more or less rich. The minimum that is necessary if a picture is to be able to portray a situation is called by Wittgenstein logical form (*TLP* 2.18). The elements of the picture must be capable of combining with each other in a pattern corresponding to the relationship of the elements of what is pictured. Thus, for instance, in a musical score the ordering of the notes on the page from left to right represents the ordering of the sounds in time. The spatial arrangements of the notes is not part of the pictorial form, since the sounds are not in space; but the ordering is common to both, and that is what is logical form.

Wittgenstein applied his general theory of representation to thoughts and to propositions. A logical picture of a fact, he said, is a thought, and in the proposition a thought is expressed in a manner perceptible to the senses (*TLP* 3, 3.1). Though, in the *Tractatus*, thoughts are prior to propositions and give life to propositions, Wittgenstein has much less to tell us about thoughts than about propositions, and in order to understand him it is better to focus on propositions as pictures than on thoughts as pictures. If we ask what are the elements of thoughts, for instance, we are given no clear answer; but if we ask what are the elements of propositions an answer immediately presents itself: names.

Indeed the picture theory of the propositions grew out of Wittgenstein's reflections on the difference between propositions and names. For Frege names and propositions alike had both sense and reference, the reference of a proposition being a truth-value. But, as Wittgenstein came to see, there is an important contrast between the relation between names and what they refer to, on the one hand, and propositions and what they refer to, on the other. To understand a proper name, like 'Bismarck', I must know to whom or what it refers; but I can understand a proposition without knowing whether it is true or false. What we understand, when we understand a proposition, is not its reference but its sense. A name can have only one relationship to reality: it either names something or it is not a significant symbol at all. But a proposition has a two-way relation: it does not cease to have a meaning when it ceases to be true (*TLP* 3.144).

So, to understand a name is to grasp its reference; to understand a proposition is to grasp its sense. There is a further difference between names and propositions consequent on this first difference. The reference of a name has to be explained to one; but to understand the sense of a proposition no explanation is necessary. A proposition can communicate a new sense with old words: we can understand a proposition that we have never heard before and whose truth-value we do not know. It is this fact to which Wittgenstein appeals when he asserts that a proposition is a picture.

What Wittgenstein meant by calling a proposition a picture can be summed up in nine theses:

(1) A proposition, unlike a name, is essentially composite. (*TLP* 4.032)
(2) The elements of a proposition are correlated by human decision with elements of reality. (*TLP* 3.315)
(3) The combination of these elements into a proposition presents— without further human intervention—a possible situation or state of affairs. (*TLP* 4.026)
(4) A proposition stands in an essential relation to the possible situation it represents: it shares its logical structure. (*TLP* 4.03)
(5) This relationship can only be shown, but not said, because logical form can only be mirrored, not represented. (*TLP* 4.022)
(6) Every proposition is bipolar: it is either true or false. (*TLP* 3.144)

(7) A proposition is true or false by agreeing or disagreeing with reality: it is true if the possible situation it depicts obtains in fact, and false if it does not. (*TLP* 4.023)

(8) A proposition must be independent of the actual situation, which, if it obtains, makes it true; otherwise it could never be false. (*TLP* 3.13)

(9) No proposition is a priori true. (*TLP* 3.05)

In stating these theses I have not used the word 'picture', because the theory is interesting and important whether or not it is misleading to encapsulate it in the slogan 'A proposition is a picture'. Wittgenstein did in fact believe that all the theorems remain true if for 'proposition' one substitutes the word 'picture'. He was also well aware that propositions do not look like pictures. But he believed that if a proposition were fully articulated and written out in an ideal language, then to each element of the propositional sign would correspond a single object in the world. Thus its pictorial nature would leap to the eye (*TLP* 3.2).

We should not think, however, that there is anything wrong with the unanalysed sentences we utter in ordinary life. Wittgenstein insists that all the propositions of our everyday language, just as they stand, are in perfect logical order (*TLP* 5.5563). That is because the full analysis of them is already present in the thought of any of us who understand them, although of course we are no more conscious of how our words symbolize than we are of how our sounds are produced (*TLP* 4.002).

Not all sentences produced by English speakers, however, are genuine propositions: many are only pseudo-propositions which analysis would reveal to lack sense. The last seventeen pages of the *Tractatus* are devoted to a brisk demonstration of how the propositions of logic (6.1 ff.), mathematics (6.2 ff.), a priori science (6.3 ff.), ethics and aesthetics (6.4 ff.), and finally philosophy (6.5 ff.) are all in different ways pseudo-propositions.

The only propositions that deserve a place in logic books are tautologies, which say nothing themselves but simply exhibit the logical properties of genuine propositions, which do say things (*TLP* 6.121). Mathematics consists of equations, but equations are concerned not with reality but only with the substitutability of signs. In real life we make use of mathematical propositions only in passing from one non-mathematical proposition to another (*TLP* 6.2–3). In science, propositions such as the axioms of Newtonian mechanics are not really propositions; rather, they are expressions of insights into the forms in which genuine scientific proposi-tions can be cast (*TLP* 6.32 ff.).

In ethics and aesthetics, likewise, there are no genuine propositions. No proposition can express the meaning of the world or of life, because all propositions are contingent—they have true–false poles—and no genuine value can be a contingent matter (*TLP* 6.41). Finally, the propositions of philosophy itself fall under the axe. Philosophy is not a corpus of proposi-tions but an activity, the activity of analysis. Applied to the propositions of everyday life, philosophy gives them a clear meaning; applied to pseudo-propositions it reveals them as nonsensical. The propositions of the *Tractatus* itself are meaningless because they are attempts to say what can only be shown. This, however, does not make them useless, because their very failure is instructive.

My propositions serve as elucidations in the following way: anyone who under-stands me eventually recognizes them as nonsensical, when he has used them as steps to climb up beyond them. (He must, so to speak, throw away the ladder after he has climbed up it.)
He must transcend these propositions, and then he will see the world aright. (*TLP* 6.54)

Language-Games and Private Languages

When he returned to philosophy in the 1920s and 1930s, Wittgenstein retained the idea that philosophy was an activity, not a theory, and that philosophical pronouncements were not propositions in the same sense as statements of everyday language. But he came to have a very different view of how ordinary propositions had meaning. Early and late, he believed that ordinary language was in order just as it stood. At the time of the *Tractatus*, however, he believed this because he thought ordinary language was underpinned by a perfect language articulated into logical atoms. From the *Philosophische Grammatik* onwards he believed this because he thought ordinary language was embedded in the social activities and structures that he called 'language-games'.

What is it, he asked in the *Grammatik*, that gives significance to the sounds and marks on paper that make up language? By themselves the symbols

The house in Vienna that Wittgenstein designed in the 1920s for his sister. It has the same austere and intimidating beauty as the *Tractatus*.

seem inert and dead; what is it that gives them life (*PG* 40, 107; *PI* I. 430)? The obvious answer is that they become alive by being meant by speakers and writers and understood by hearers and readers. This obvious answer is the true one; but we must get clear what meaning and understanding are. They are not, as one might think, mental processes that accompany spoken sentences. If you are tempted to think this, try to perform that process without the speaking. 'Make the following experiment,' says Wittgenstein; '*say* "It's cold here" and *mean* "it's warm here". Can you do it? and what are you doing as you do it?' (*PI* I. 332, 510).

If you try to perform an act of meaning without uttering the appropriate sentence, you are likely to find yourself reciting the sentence itself under your breath. But of course it would be absurd to suggest that simultaneously with every public utterance of a sentence there is also a *sotto voce* one. It would take skill to ensure that the two processes were exactly in synchrony—and how disastrous it would be if they got out of step so that the meaning of a word got wrongly attached to its neighbour!

It is true that when we hear a sentence in a language we know, there are mental events—feelings, images, etc.—that differ from those that occur when we hear a sentence in a language we do not know. But these experiences will vary from case to case, and cannot be regarded as themselves constituting the understanding. Understanding cannot really be thought of as a process at all. Wittgenstein asks:

When do we understand a sentence? When we have uttered the whole of it? Or while we are uttering it? Is the understanding an articulated process like the speaking of the sentence; and does its articulation correspond to the articulation of the sentence? Or is it non-articulated, accompanying the sentence in the way in which a pedal point accompanies a melody? (*PG* 50)

Understanding language, like knowing how to play chess, is a state rather than a process; but we should not think of it as a state of some hidden mental mechanism.

Sometimes we are tempted to think that the conscious operations of our mind are the outcome of a mental process at a level lower than that of introspection. Perhaps, we think, our mental mechanism operates too swiftly for us to be able to follow all its movements, like the pistons of a steam engine or the blades of a lawn mower. If only we could sharpen our faculty for introspection, or get the machinery to run in slow motion, we might then be able actually to observe the processes of meaning and understanding.

According to one version of the mental-mechanism doctrine, to understand the meaning of a word is to call up an appropriate image in connection with it. I am told 'Bring me a red flower' and according to this story I have to have a red image in my mind, and ascertain what colour flower to bring by comparing it with this image. But that cannot be right: otherwise how could one obey the order 'Imagine a red patch'? The theory sets us off on an endless regress (*BB* 3; *PG* 96).

Suppose we replace the alleged inspection of an image with the actual inspection of a red bit of paper. Surely, the greater vividness of the sample will make it even more explanatory! But no: if it is to be explained how someone knows what 'red' means it is equally to be explained how he knows that his sample—whether mental or physical—is red. 'As soon as you think', Wittgenstein says, 'of replacing the mental image by, say, a painted one, and as soon as the image thereby loses its occult character, it ceases to seem to impart any life to the sentence at all' (*BB* 5). Of course, it is true that often as we talk mental images pass through our minds. But it is not they that confer meanings on the words we use. It is rather the other way round: the images are like the pictures illuminating a written text in a book.

One of the most important versions of the mistaken theory that meaning is a mental process is the thesis that naming is a mental act. This idea is the target of one of the most important sections of the *Philosophical Investigations*: the attack on the notion of a private language, or more precisely, of the notion of private ostensive definition.

In the epistemology of Russell and the logical positivists, ostensive definition played a crucial role: it was where language linked up with knowledge by acquaintance. But Wittgenstein insists that acquaintance with the object for which a word stands is not the same thing as knowledge of the word's meaning. Acquaintance with the object will not suffice without a grasp of the role in language of the word to be defined. Suppose I explain the word 'tove' by pointing to a pencil and saying 'This is called "tove"'. The explanation would be quite inadequate, because I may be taken to mean 'This is a pencil' or 'This is round' or 'This is wood' and so on (*PG* 60; *BB* 2). To name something it is not sufficient to confront it and to utter a sound: the asking and giving of names is something that can be done only in the context of a language-game.

This is so even in the relatively simple case of naming a colour or a material object; matters are much more complicated when we consider the names of mental events and states, such as sensations and thoughts. Consider the way in which the word 'pain' functions as the name of a sensation. We are tempted to think that for each person 'pain' acquires its meaning by being correlated by him with his own private, incommunicable sensation. But Wittgenstein showed that no word could acquire meaning in this way. One of his arguments runs as follows.

Suppose that I want to keep a diary about the occurrence of a certain sensation, and that I associate the sensation with the sign 'S'. It is essential to the supposition that no definition of the sign can be given in terms of our ordinary language, because otherwise the language would not be a private one. The sign must be defined for me alone, and this by a private ostensive definition. 'I speak, or write the sign down and at the same time I concentrate my attention on the sensation . . . in this way I impress on myself the connection between the sign and the sensation' (*PI* I. 258).

Wittgenstein argues that no such ceremony could establish an appropriate connection. When next I call something 'S', how will I know what I mean by 'S'? The problem is not that I may misremember and call something 'S' which is not S; the trouble goes deeper. Even to think *falsely* that something is S, I must know the meaning of 'S', and this, Wittgenstein argues, is impossible in a private language. But can I not appeal to memory to settle the meaning? No, for to do so I must call up the right memory, the memory of S, and in order to do that I must already know what 'S' means. There is in the end no way of making out a difference between correct and incorrect use of 'S', and that means that talk of 'correctness' is out of place. The private definition I have given to myself is no real definition.

The upshot of Wittgenstein's argument is that there cannot be a language whose words refer to what can only be known to the individual speaker of the language. The English word 'pain' is not a word in a private language because, whatever philosophers may say, other people can very often know when a person is in pain. It is not by private ostensive definition that 'pain' becomes the name of a sensation; pain-language is grafted on to the pre-linguistic expression of pain when the parents teach a baby to replace her initial cries with a conventional, learned expression through language.

141

What is the point of the private language argument, and who is it directed against? Wittgenstein once wrote that philosophical therapy is directed against the philosopher in each of us. It is quite plausible to propose that each of us, when we begin to philosophize, implicitly believe in a private language. Certainly, many first-year students are tempted by the sceptical suggestion. 'For all we know, what I call "red" you call "green" and vice versa.' This suggestion was at the root of Schlick's distinction between form and content in protocol sentences, and the whole edifice of logical positivism tumbles down if a private language is impossible. So too do the epistemologies of Russell and of the earlier Wittgenstein himself.

But the scope of the private language argument extends much further back in the history of philosophy. Descartes, in expressing his philosophical doubt, assumes that my language has meaning while the existence of my own and other bodies remains uncertain. Hume thought it possible for thoughts and experiences to be recognized and classified while the existence of the external world is held in suspense. Mill and Schopenhauer, in different ways, thought that a man could express the contents of his mind in language while questioning the existence of other minds. All of these suppositions are essential to the structure of the philosophy in question, and all of them require the possibility of a private language.

Both empiricism and idealism entail that the mind has no direct knowledge of anything but its own contents. The history of both movements shows that they lead in the direction of solipsism, the doctrine 'Only I exist'. Wittgenstein's attack on private definition undercuts solipsism by showing that the possibility of the very language in which it is expressed depends on the existence of the public and social world. The destruction of solipsism carries over into a refutation of the empiricism and idealism that inexorably involve it.

Wittgenstein's demolition of the notion of a private language was the most significant event in the philosophy of language in the twentieth century. After his death, philosophy of language took a different turn because of differing conceptions of the nature of philosophy itself. Wittgenstein had made a sharp distinction between science, which is concerned with the acquisition of new information, and philosophy, which sought to provide understanding of what we already know. But Quine's attack on the traditional distinction between analytic and synthetic propositions led many philosophers, particularly in the United States, to question whether there was a sharp boundary between philosophy and empirical science.

In particular, there was a drive to amalgamate the philosophy of language with psychology and linguistics. This was spearheaded from the philosophical side by Donald Davidson in the quest of a systematic theory of meaning for natural languages, and from the side of linguistics by Noam Chomsky with successive theories postulating hidden mechanisms underlying the acquisition of everyday grammar. In my view, Wittgenstein was correct in seeing the task of philosophy as completely different from that of empirical science, and many developments in the philosophy of language in the latter part of the twentieth century served to obscure, rather than to enrich, the insights that had been gained in its earlier decades.

6

Epistemology

Two Eloquent Empiricists

Mill described his *System of Logic* as a textbook of the doctrine that derives all knowledge from experience. He was, therefore, a proponent of empiricism, though he did not like the term. Indeed, in an important respect, he was one of the most resolute empiricists there have ever been. He went beyond his predecessors in claiming that not only all science, but also all mathematics, derived from experience. The axioms of geometry and the first principles of mathematics are, he says, 'notwithstanding all appearances to the contrary, results of observations and experiences, founded, in short, on the evidence of the senses' (*SL* 2.3.24.4).

The definition of each number, Mill maintained, involves the assertion of a physical fact.

Each of the numbers two, three, four &c., denotes physical phenomena, and connotes a physical property of those phenomena. Two, for instance, denotes all pairs of things, and twelve all dozens of things, connoting what makes them pairs or dozens; and that which makes them so is something physical; since it cannot be denied that two apples are physically distinguishable from three apples, two horses from one horse, and so forth: that they are a different visible and tangible phenomenon. (*SL* 3.24.5)

He does not make clear exactly what the property is that is connoted by the name of a number, and he admits that the senses find some difficulty in distinguishing between 102 horses and 103 horses, however easy it may be to tell two horses from three. Nonetheless, there is a property connoted by numbers, namely, the characteristic manner in which the agglomeration is made up, and may be separated into parts. For instance, collections of objects exist, which while they impress the senses thus ∴ may be separated into two parts thus . . . 'This proposition being granted, we term all such parcels Threes' (*SL* 2.6.2).

Critics of Mill were to observe that it was a mercy that not everything in the world is nailed down; for if it were, we should not be able to separate parts, and two and one would not be three. It does not, on sober reflection, seem that there is any physical fact that is asserted in the definition of a number like 777,864. But Mill's thesis that arithmetic is essentially an empirical science does not stand or fall with his account of the definition of numbers.

He claims, for instance, that a principle such as 'The sums of equals are equals' is an inductive truth or law of nature of the highest order. Inductive truths are generalizations based on individual experiences. Assertions of such truths must always be to some extent tentative or hypothetical; and so it is in this case. The principle 'is never accurately true, for one actual pound weight is not exactly equal to another, nor one measured mile's length to another; a nice balance, or more accurate measuring instruments, would always detect some difference' (*SL* 2.6.3).

Here critics said that Mill was confusing arithmetic with its applications. But it was important for Mill to maintain that arithmetic was an empirical science, because the alternative, that it was an a priori discipline, was the source of infinite harm. 'The notion that truths external to the mind may be known by intuition or consciousness, independently of observation and experience is, I am persuaded, in these times the great intellectual support of false doctrines and bad institutions' (*A* 134). To avoid this mischief Mill was willing to pay a high price, and entertain the possibility that at some future time, in some distant galaxy, it might turn out that two and two made not four but five.

Considered as a philosopher, John Henry Newman belonged to the same empiricist tradition as John Stuart Mill. He disliked the German metaphysics that was beginning to infiltrate Oxford during his time there. 'What a vain system of words without ideas such men seem to be piling up,' he remarked. After his conversion to Rome he was equally ill at ease with the scholastic philosophy favoured by his Catholic confrères. The only direct acquaintance we have with things outside ourselves, he asserted, comes through our senses; to think that we have faculties for direct knowledge of immaterial things is mere superstition. Even our senses convey us but a

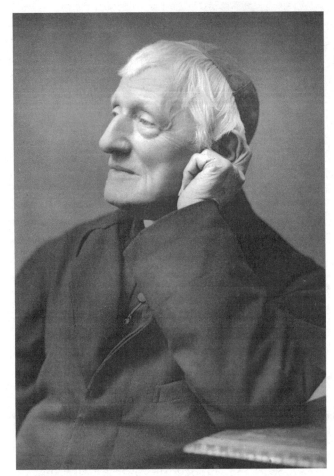

John Henry Newman, whose *Grammar of Assent*, though written to a religious agenda, is a classic of epistemology in its own right.

little way out of ourselves: we have to be near things to touch them; we can neither see nor hear nor touch things past or future. But though a staunch empiricist, Newman gives a more exalted role to reason than it was granted by the idealist Kant:

Now reason is that faculty of mind by which this deficiency [of the senses] is supplied: by which knowledge of things external to us, of beings, facts, and events, is attained beyond the range of sense. It ascertains for us not natural things only, or immaterial only, or present only, or past or future; but even if limited in its power, it is unlimited in its range . . . It reaches to the ends of the universe, and to the throne of God beyond them; it brings us knowledge, whether real or uncertain, still knowledge, in whatever degree of perfection, from every side;

but at the same time, with this characteristic that it obtains it indirectly, not directly. (*US* 199)

Reason does not actually perceive anything: it is a faculty for proceeding from things that are perceived to things that are not. The exercise of reason is to assert one thing on the grounds of some other thing.

Newman identifies two different operations of the intellect that are exercised when we reason: inference (from premisses) and assent (to a conclusion). It is important to keep in mind that these two are quite distinct from each other. We often assent to a proposition when we have forgotten the reasons for assent; on the other hand assent may be given without argument, or on the basis of bad arguments. Arguments may be better or worse, but assent either exists or not. It is true that some arguments are so compelling that assent immediately follows inference. But even in the cases of mathematical proof there is a distinction between the two intellectual operations. A mathematician who has just hit upon a complex proof would not assent to its conclusion without going over his work and seeking corroboration from others.

Assent, as has been said, may be given without adequate evidence or argument. This often leads to error; but is it always wrong? Locke maintained that it was: he gave, as a mark of the love of truth, the not entertaining any proposition with greater assurance than the proofs it is built on will warrant. 'Whoever goes beyond this measure of assent, it is plain receives not truth in the love of it, loves not truth for truth-sake, but for some other by-end' (*Essay concerning Human Understanding*, IV. xvi). Locke maintained that there can be no demonstrable truth in concrete matters, and therefore assent to a concrete proposition must be conditional and fall short of certitude. Absolute assent has no legitimate exercise except as ratifying acts of intuition or demonstration.

Newman disagrees. There are no such things as degrees of assent, he maintains, though there is room for opinion without the assent that is necessary for knowledge.

Every day, as it comes, brings with it opportunities for us to enlarge our circle of assents. We read the newspapers; we look through debates in Parliament, pleadings in the law courts, leading articles, letters of correspondents, reviews of books, criticisms in the fine arts, and we either form no opinion at all upon the subjects discussed, as lying out of our line, or at most we have only an opinion about them ... we never say that we give [a proposition] a degree of assent. We might as well talk of degrees of truth as degrees of assent. (*GA* 115)

Nonetheless, Newman argues, assent on evidence short of intuition or demonstration may well be legitimate, and frequently is so.

We are sure beyond all hazard of a mistake, that our own self is not the only being existing; that there is an external world; that it is a system with parts and a whole, a universe carried on by laws; and that the future is affected by the past. We accept and hold with an unqualified assent, that the earth, considered as a phenomenon, is a globe; that all its regions see the sun by turns; that there are vast tracts on it of land and water; that there are really existing cities on definite sites, which go by the names of London, Paris, Florence and Madrid. We are sure that Paris or London, unless suddenly swallowed up by an earthquake or burned to the ground, is today just what it was yesterday, when we left it. (*GA* 117)

Each of us is certain that we shall all one day die. But if we are asked for evidence of this, all that we can offer is circuitous argument or *reductio ad absurdum*.

We laugh to scorn the idea that we had no parents though we have no memory of our birth; that we shall never depart this life, though we can have no experience of the future; that we are able to live without food, though we have never tried; that a world of men did not live before our time, or that that world has no history: that there has been no rise and fall of states, no great men, no wars, no revolutions, no art, no science, no literature, no religion. (*GA* 117)

On all these truths, Newman sums up, we have an immediate and unhesitating hold, and we do not think ourselves guilty of not loving truth for truth's sake because we cannot reach them by a proof consisting of a series of intuitive propositions. None of us can think or act without accepting some truths 'not intuitive, not demonstrated, yet sovereign'.

Though he denies that there are degrees of assent, Newman makes a distinction between simple assent and complex assent or certitude. Simple assent may be unconscious, it may be rash, it may be no more than a fancy. Complex assent involves three elements: it must follow on proof, it must be accompanied by a specific sense of intellectual contentment, and it must be irreversible. The feeling of satisfaction and self-gratulation characteristic of certitude attaches not to knowledge itself, but to the consciousness of possessing knowledge.

One difference between knowledge and certitude that is commonly agreed among philosophers is this: If I know *p*, then *p* is true; but I may be certain that *p* and *p* be false. Newman is not quite consistent on this issue. Sometimes he talks as if there is such a thing as false certitude; at other times he suggests that a conviction can only be a certitude if the proposition in question is objectively true (*GA* 128). But whether or not certitude entails truth, it is undeniable that to be certain of something involves believing in its truth. It follows that if I am certain of a thing, I believe it will remain what I now hold it to be, even if my mind should have the bad fortune to let my belief drop. If we are certain of a belief, we resolve to maintain it and we spontaneously reject as idle any objections to it. If someone is sure of something, if he has such a conviction, say, that Ireland is to the west of England, if he would be consistent, he has no alternative but to adopt 'magisterial intolerance of any contrary assertion'. Of course, despite one's initial resolution, one may in the event give up one's conviction. Newman maintains that anyone who loses his conviction on any point is thereby proved never to have been certain of it.

How do we tell, then, at any given moment, what our certitudes are? No line, Newman thinks, can be drawn between such real certitudes as have truth for their object, and merely apparent certitudes. What looks like a certitude always is exposed to the chance of turning out to be a mistake. There is no interior, immediate test sufficient to distinguish genuine from false certitudes (*GA* 145).

Newman correctly distinguishes certainty from infallibility. My memory is not infallible: I remember for certain what I did yesterday but that does not mean that I never misremember. I am quite clear that two and two make four, but I often make mistakes in long additions. Certitude concerns a particular proposition, infallibility is a faculty or gift. It was possible for Newman to be certain that Victoria was queen without claiming to possess any general infallibility.

But how can I rest in certainty when I know that in the past I have thought myself certain of an untruth? Surely what happened once may happen again.

Suppose I am walking out in the moonlight, and see dimly the outlines of some figure among the trees;—it is a man. I draw nearer, it is still a man; nearer still, and all hesitation is at an end.—I am certain it is a man. But he neither moves nor speaks when I address him; and then I ask myself what can be his purpose in hiding among the trees at such an hour. I come quite close to him and put out my arm. Then I find for certain that what I took for a man is but a singular shadow, formed by the falling of the moonlight on the interstices of some branches or their foliage. Am I not to indulge my second certitude, because I was wrong in my first? Does not any objection, which lies against my second from the failure of my first, fade away before the evidence on which my second is founded? (*GA* 151)

The sense of certitude is, as it were, the bell of the intellect, and sometimes it strikes when it should not. But we do not dispense with clocks because on occasions they tell the wrong time.

No general rules can be set out that will prevent us from ever going wrong in a specific piece of concrete reasoning. Aristotle in his *Ethics* told us that no code of laws, or moral treatise, could map out in advance the path of individual virtue: we need a virtue of practical wisdom (*phronesis*) to determine what to do from moment to moment. So too with theoretical reasoning, Newman says: the logic of language will take us only so far, and we need a special intellectual virtue, which he calls 'the illative sense', to tell us the appropriate conclusion to draw in the particular case.

In no class of concrete reasonings, whether in experimental science, historical research, or theology, is there any ultimate test of truth and error in our inferences besides the trustworthiness of the Illative Sense that gives them its sanction; just as there is no sufficient test of poetical excellence, heroic action, or gentleman-like conduct, other than the particular mental sense, be it genius, taste, sense of propriety, or the moral sense, to which those subject matters are severally committed. (*GA* 231–2)

Newman's epistemology has not been much studied by subsequent philosophers because of the religious purpose that was his overarching aim in developing it. But the treatment of belief, knowledge, and certainty in *The Grammar of Assent* has merits that are quite independent of the theological context, and which bear comparison with classical texts of the empiricist tradition from Locke to Russell.

Peirce on the Methods of Science

Within the decade after the publication of Newman's *Grammar*, C. S. Peirce, in America, was endeavouring to devise an epistemology appropriate to an age of scientific inquiry. He presented it in a series of articles in the *Popular Science Monthly* entitled 'Illustrations of the Logic of Science'. The most famous of the series are the two first articles, 'The Fixation of Belief' and 'How to Make our Ideas Clear' (*CP* 5.358 ff., 388 ff.).

In the first essay Peirce observes that inquiry always originates in doubt, and ends in belief.

The irritation of doubt is the only immediate motive for the struggle to obtain belief. It is certainly best for us that our beliefs should be such as may truly guide our actions so as to satisfy our desires; and this reflection will make us reject any belief that does not seem to have been so formed as to insure this result. But it will only do so by creating a doubt in the place of that belief. With the doubt, therefore, the struggle begins, and with the cessation of doubt it ends. Hence, the sole object of inquiry is the settlement of opinion. (*EWP* 126)

In order to settle our opinions and fix our beliefs, Peirce says, four different methods are commonly used. They are, he tells us, the method of tenacity, the method of authority, the a priori method, and the scientific method.

We may take a proposition and repeat it to ourselves, dwelling on all that supports it and turning away from anything that might disturb it. Thus, some people read only newspapers that confirm their political beliefs, and a religious person may say 'Oh, I could not believe so-and-so, because I should be wretched if I did'. This is the method of tenacity, and it has the advantage of providing comfort and peace of mind. It may be true, Peirce says, that death is annihilation, but a man who believes he will go straight to heaven when he dies 'has a cheap pleasure that will not be followed by the least disappointment'.

The problem you meet if you adopt the method of tenacity is that you may find your beliefs in conflict with those of other equally tenacious believers. The remedy for this is provided by the second method, that of authority. 'Let an institution be created that shall have for its object to keep correct doctrines before the attention of the people, to reiterate them perpetually, and to teach them to the young; having at the same time power to prevent contrary doctrines from being taught, advocated, or expressed.' This method had been most perfectly practised in Rome, from the days of Numa Pompilius to Pio Nono, but throughout the world, from Egypt to Siam, it has left majestic relics in stone of a sublimity comparable to the greatest works of nature.

There are two disadvantages to the method of authority. First, it is always accompanied by cruelty. If the burning and massacre of heretics is frowned

"The method of authority" that Peirce condemned reached a high point when Pius IX's Vatican Council declared Popes to be infallible. The right method in epistemology, according to Peirce, should be called, by contrast, "fallibilism".

upon in modern states, nonetheless a kind of moral terrorism enforces uniformity of opinion. 'Let it be known that you seriously hold a tabooed belief and you may be perfectly sure of being treated with a cruelty less brutal but more refined than hunting you like a wolf.' Second, no institution can regulate opinion on every subject, and there will always be some independent thinkers who, by comparing their own culture with others, will see that the doctrines inculcated by authority arise only from accident and custom.

Such thinkers may adopt a third method, attempting, by a priori meditation, to produce a universally valid metaphysics. This is more intellectually respectable than the other two methods, but it has manifestly failed to produce a fixation of beliefs. From earliest times to latest, the pendulum has swung between idealist and materialist metaphysics without ever coming to rest.

We must therefore adopt the fourth method, the method of science. The first postulate of this method is the existence of a reality independent of our minds.

There are real things, whose characters are entirely independent of our opinions about them; those realities affect our senses according to regular laws, and, though our sensations are as different as our relations to the objects, yet, by taking advantage of the laws of perception, we can ascertain by reasoning how things really are, and any man, if he has sufficient experience and reason enough about it, will be led to the one true conclusion. (*EWP* 133)

The task of logic is to provide us with guiding principles to enable us to find out, on the basis of what we know, something we do not know, and thus to approximate ever more closely to this ultimate reality.

Though Peirce insisted that doubt was the origin of inquiry, he rejected Descartes's principle that true philosophy must begin from universal, methodical scepticism. Genuine doubt must be doubt of a particular proposition, for a particular reason. Cartesian doubt was no more than a futile pretence, and the Cartesian endeavour to regain certainty by private meditation was even more pernicious. 'We individually cannot reasonably hope to attain the ultimate philosophy we pursue; we can only seek it, therefore, for the *community* of philosophers' (*EWP* 87).

Descartes was right that the first task in philosophy is to clarify our ideas; but he failed to give an adequate account of what he meant by clear and distinct ideas. If an idea is to be distinct, it must sustain the test of dialectical examination. Processes of investigation, if pushed far enough, will give one certain solution to every question to which they can be applied. Scientists may study a problem—e.g. that of the velocity of light—by many different methods. They may at first obtain different results, but as each perfects his method and his processes, the results will move steadily together towards a destined centre. It is at that centre that truth is to be found.

Does this conflict with the thesis that reality is independent of thought? Peirce's answer to this is complex and subtle.

On the one hand, reality is independent, not necessarily of thought in general, but only of what you or I or any finite number of men may think about it ... on the other hand, though the object of the final opinion depends on what that opinion is, yet what that opinion is does not depend on what you or I or any man thinks. Our perversity and that of others may indefinitely postpone the settlement of opinion; it might even conceivably cause an arbitrary proposition to be universally accepted as long as the human race should last. (*EWP* 155)

It is possible, therefore, that *p* should be true even though every human being believes it to be false. Peirce offers two ways of making room for this possibility. On the one hand, he says, another race might succeed the extinction of ours, and the true opinion would be the one they ultimately came to. But he also says that 'the catholic consent that constitutes the truth is by no means to be limited to men in this earthly life or to the human race, but extends to the whole communion of minds to which we belong' (*EWP* 60).

It is important to be clear about the content of the beliefs that we attain in the course of this communal, unceasing pursuit of truth. Belief, Peirce says, has three properties: first, it is something we are aware of; second, it appeases the irritation of doubt; third, it involves the establishment in our nature of a rule of action, that is to say, a habit. Different beliefs are distinguished by the different modes of action to which they give rise. 'If beliefs do not differ in this respect, if they appease the same doubt by producing the same rule of action, then no more differences in the manner of consciousness of them can make them different beliefs.'

To illustrate this point Peirce uses a religious example. Protestants say that after the words of consecration have been said the offerings on the altar are bread and wine; Catholics say they are not. But members of the two sects do not differ from each other in the expectations they have of the sensible effects of the sacrament. 'We can mean nothing by wine but what has certain effects, direct or indirect, upon our senses; and to talk of something as having all the sensible characters of wine, yet being in reality blood, is senseless jargon' (*EWP* 146).

It is in this context that Peirce first put forward his principle of pragmatism, which he presents as the rule for attaining the maximum clearness about our ideas. 'Consider what effects, that might conceivably have practical bearings, we conceive the object of our conception to have. Then, our conception of these effects is the whole of our conception of the object' (*EWP* 146). It is important to note that Peirce's pragmatism is a theory not of truth, but of meaning; and as such it anticipates the verification theory of meaning later put forward by the logical positivists. He applies the principle to the concepts of hardness, weight, freedom, and force, and concludes, in the latter case, 'if we know what the effects of force are, we are acquainted with every fact that is implied in saying that a force exists, and there is nothing more to know' (*EWP* 151).

In Peirce's writing it is not always clear how he sees the relationship between logic and psychology. At the beginning of his essays to illustrate the logic of science he writes thus:

The object of reasoning is to find out, from the consideration of what we already know, something else that we do not know. Consequently, reasoning is good if it be such as to give a true conclusion from true premises and not otherwise. Thus the question of its validity is purely one of fact and not of thinking. (*EWP* 122)

On the other hand, Peirce sometimes writes as if logical truths were laws of mental behaviour. Thus, having told us that the three main classes of logical inference are deduction, induction, and hypothesis, he goes on to say, 'In deduction the mind is under the dominion of a habit or association by virtue of which a general idea suggests in each case a corresponding reaction' (*EWP* 209). Perhaps the two statements are to be reconciled in this way: reasoning, whether good or bad, is a matter of habit; but it is a matter of fact, not of thought, whether a particular piece of reasoning is valid or not.

Frege on Logic, Psychology, and Epistemology

In the writings of Frege, there is no lack of explicit discrimination between logic and psychology. While he was writing his logicist works, from *Begriffsschrift* onwards, Frege was not interested in epistemology for its own sake, but he was concerned to set out the relationship between epistemology and other related disciplines. In the tradition of Descartes, Frege believed, epistemology had been given a fundamental role in philosophy that should really be assigned to logic. On the other hand, philosophers in the empiricist tradition had confused logic with psychology. In working out his logical system Frege was anxious to show the difference in nature and role between logic and these two other branches of study.

Frege took over, and adapted for his own purposes, Kant's distinction between a priori and a posteriori knowledge. To ensure that talk of a priori knowledge involves no confusion between psychology and logic, he reminds us that it is possible to discover the content of a proposition before we hit on a proof of it. We must distinguish, therefore, between how we first come to believe a proposition, and how we would eventually justify it. There must *be* a justification, if we are to talk of knowledge at all, for knowledge is belief that is both true and justified. It is absurd to talk of an a priori mistake, because one can only know what is true.

When a proposition is called *a posteriori* or analytic in my sense, this is not a judgement about the conditions, psychological, physiological and physical, which have made it possible to represent the content of the proposition in consciousness. Nor is it a judgement about the possibly defective method by which some other person has come to believe it true. Rather, it is a judgement about the fundamental ground which provides the justification for believing it to be true. (*FA* 3)

If the proposition is a mathematical one, its justification must be mathematical; it cannot be a psychological matter of processes in the mathematician's mind. To be sure, mathematicians have sensations and mental images, and these may play a part in the thoughts of someone who is calculating. But these images and thoughts are not what arithmetic is about. Different mathematicians associate different images with the same number: in operating with the number one hundred, one person may think of '100' and another of 'C'. Even if psychology could give a causal explanation of the occurrence of the thought that ten squared is one hundred, it would still be totally different from arithmetic, for arithmetic is concerned with the truth of such propositions, psychology with their occurrence in thought. A proposition may be thought of without being true, and a proposition may be true without being thought of.

Psychology is interested in the cause of our thinking, mathematics in the proof of our thoughts. Cause and proof are quite different things. Without an appropriate ration of phosphorus in his brain, no doubt, Pythagoras would have been unable to prove his famous theorem; but that does not mean that a statement of the phosphorus content of his brain should occur as a line in the proof. If humans have evolved, no doubt there has been evolution in human consciousness; so if mathematics was a matter of sensations and ideas, we would need to warn astronomers against drawing conclusions about events in the distant past. Frege brings out the absurdity of this position in an ironic passage:

You reckon that $2 \times 2 = 4$; but the idea of number has a history, an evolution. It may be doubted whether it had yet progressed so far. How do you know that in that distant past that proposition already existed? Might not the creatures then alive have held the proposition $2 \times 2 = 5$? Perhaps it was only later that natural selection, in the struggle for existence, evolved the proposition $2 \times 2 = 4$, and perhaps that in its turn is destined to develop into $2 \times 2 = 3$. (*FA*, pp. vi–vii)

Throughout his life, Frege continued to maintain a sharp distinction between logic and psychology. In his late essay 'Thoughts' he warned against the ambiguity inherent in the statement that logic deals with the laws of thought. If, by 'laws of thought', we mean psychological laws that relate mental events to their causes, then they are not laws of logic because they would make no distinction between true and false thoughts, since error and superstition have causes no less than sound belief. Logical laws are 'laws of thought' only in the same sense as moral laws are laws of behaviour. Actual thinking does not always obey the laws of logic any more than actual behaviour always obeys the moral law.

However, in his late 'Thoughts' Frege ventures into epistemology in a manner that tends to blur the distinctions he had so resolutely defended. He inquires about the sense, or mode of presentation, of the first-person pronoun 'I', which he treats as a proper name that has its user as its reference. Everyone, Frege says, 'is presented to himself in a special and primary way, in which he is presented to no one else'. Suppose that Horatio has the thought that he has been wounded. Only he can grasp the sense of that thought, since it is only to himself that he is presented in this special way.

He cannot communicate a thought he alone can grasp. Therefore, if he now says 'I have been wounded' he must use 'I' in a sense which can be grasped by others, perhaps in the sense of 'the person who is now speaking to you'. In doing so he makes the circumstances of his utterance serve the expression of the thought. (*CP* 360)

This seems to contradict Frege's hitherto consistent claim that whereas mental images might be private, thoughts were the common property of us all. On his own principles an incommunicable thought about a private ego would not be a thought at all. But instead of rejecting the idea that 'I' is a proper name and discarding the whole notion of the Cartesian ego, Frege went on to present in highly Cartesian terms a full-blown doctrine of two separate worlds, one interior and private and the other exterior and public. Perceptible things of the physical world, he said, are accessible to us all: we can all see the same houses and touch the same trees. But in addition, he claimed, there is an inner world of sense-impressions, images and feelings, of desires and wishes—items which, for present purposes, we may call 'ideas'.

Anyone who maintains, as Frege did in this essay, that our mental life takes place within an inner private world must at some time face the question: what reason is there for believing that there is any such thing as an outer world? Descartes, in his *Meditations*, used sceptical arguments to purify the reader, temporarily, from belief in anything beyond the private realm; he then endeavoured to restore the reader's faith in the external world by appealing to the truthfulness of God. Frege here accepts the Cartesian distinction between matter (the world of things) and mind (the world of ideas). Like Descartes, he accepted the need to provide an answer to idealist scepticism, the thesis that nothing exists except ideas.

What if everything were only a dream, a play performed upon the stage of my consciousness (*CP* 363)? I seem to be walking in a green field with a companion; but perhaps the realm of things is empty, and all I have is ideas of which I myself am the owner. If only what is my idea can be the object of my awareness, then for all I know there is no green field (for a field is not an idea, and there are no green ideas) and no companion (for human beings are not ideas). For all I know there are not even any ideas other than my own (for I can know of no one else to own them). Frege concludes: 'Either the thesis that only what is my idea can be the object of my awareness is false, or all my knowledge and perception is restricted to the range of my ideas, to the stage of my self-consciousness. In this case I should have only an inner world and I should know nothing of other people' (*CP* 364). Indeed, does not this train of sceptical reasoning lead to the conclusion that I am myself an idea? Lying in a deckchair, I have a range of visual impressions, from the toes of my shoes to the blurred outline of my nose. By what right do I pick out one of my ideas and set it up as owner of the others? Why have an owner for ideas at all?

Here we come to a full stop. If there is no owner of ideas, there are no ideas either; there cannot be an experience without someone to experience. A pain is necessarily *felt*, and what is felt must have someone feeling it. If so, there *is* something that is not yet my idea, and yet can be an object of my thought, namely myself. Frege, like Descartes, brings scepticism to an end with a *cogito, ergo sum*. But whereas Descartes's ego was a non-ideal *subject* of thinking, Frege's ego is a non-ideal *object* of thought. Its existence refutes the thesis that only what is part of the content of my consciousness can be the object of my thought.

If there is to be such a thing as science, Frege maintained, 'a third realm must be recognized'—a world in addition to the world of things and the world of ideas. The ego, as the owner of ideas, is the first citizen of this third realm. The third realm is the realm of objective thought. The denizens of this realm share with ideas the property of being imperceptible by the senses, and share with physical objects the property of being independent of an owner. Pythagoras' theorem is timelessly true and needs no owner; it does not begin to be true when it is first thought of or proved (*CP* 362).

Other people, Frege says, can grasp thoughts no less than I; we are not owners of our thoughts as we are owners of our ideas. We do not *have* thoughts; thoughts are what we *grasp*. What is grasped is already there and all we do is take possession of it. Our grasping a thought has no more effect on the thought itself than our observing it affects the new moon. Thoughts do not change or come and go; they are not causally active or passive in the way in which objects are in the physical world. In that world, one thing acts on another and changes it; it is itself acted upon and itself changes. This is not so in the timeless world that Pythagoras' theorem inhabits (*PW* 138).

Few who have followed Frege down the path of Cartesian scepticism will follow him in the route he offers out of the maze. His response to the challenge is no more convincing than Descartes's own. Both philosophers, having accepted a division between a public world of physical things and a private world of human consciousness, seek to rejoin what they have separated by appealing to a third world: the divine mind in the case of

Descartes, and the world of thoughts in the case of Frege. In each case the fatal mistake was the acceptance of the initial dichotomy. There are not two worlds, but a single one to which there belong not just inert physical objects but also conscious rational animals. Frege was wrong, and sinned against his own cardinal principle of separating thoughts from ideas, in accepting that consciousness provides us with incommunicable contents and unshareable certainties.

Knowledge by Acquaintance and Knowledge by Description

Six years before Frege published his articles on the nature of thought, Bertrand Russell had written his brief *Problems of Philosophy*, a book that was to give many generations of philosophy students their first introduction to epistemology. Russell was a godson of John Stuart Mill, and for a great part of his life he endeavoured to be faithful to the British empiricist tradition of which Mill had been such an intrepid exponent. But Russell could not accept Mill's view of mathematics as an empirical science, and so his empiricism was always blended with an element of the Platonism that he shared with Frege. His starting point in *Problems* is the systematic doubt of Descartes.

It seems to me that I am now sitting in a chair, at a table of a certain shape, on which I see sheets of paper with writing or print. By turning my head I see out of the window buildings and clouds and the sun. I believe that the sun is about ninety-three million miles from the earth; that it is a hot globe many times bigger than the earth; that, owing to the earth's rotation, it rises every morning, and will continue to do so for an indefinite time in the future. (*PP* 7–8)

However evident this seems, Russell tells us, it may all be reasonably doubted. The table looks different and feels different from different angles and to different people in different circumstances. The real table is not what we immediately experience, but is an inference from what is immediately known. What is immediately known in sensation is something quite different from any real table.

Let us give the name of 'sense data' to the things that are immediately known in sensation: such things as colours, sounds, smells, hardnesses, roughnesses, and so on. We shall give the name 'sensation' to the experience of being immediately aware of these things. Thus, whenever we see a colour, we have a sensation *of* the colour, but the colour itself is a sense-datum, not a sensation. The colour is that *of* which we are immediately aware, and the awareness itself is the sensation. (*PP* 12)

Sense-data are the only things of which we can be really certain. Descartes brought his own doubt to an end with the *cogito*, 'I think, therefore I am'. But this, Russell warns us, says something more than what is certain: sense-data bring no assurance of an abiding self, and what is really certain is not 'I am seeing a brown colour' but 'a brown colour is being seen'. Sense-data are private and personal: is there any reason to believe in public neutral objects such as we imagine tables to be? If there is not, then a fortiori there is no reason to believe in persons other than myself, since it is only through their bodies that I have any access to others' minds.

Russell concedes that there is no actual proof that the whole of life is not just a dream. Our belief in an independent external world is instinctive rather than reflective, but this does not mean that there is any good reason to reject it. If we agree provisionally that there are physical objects as well as sense-data, should we say that these objects are the causes of the sense-data? If we do, we must immediately add that there is no reason to think that these causes are *like* sense-data—e.g. that they are coloured. Common sense leaves us quite in the dark about their true nature.

In order to clarify the relationship between sense-data and the objects that cause them, Russell introduces his celebrated distinction between knowledge by acquaintance and knowledge by description.

We shall say that we have *acquaintance* with anything of which we are directly aware, without the intermediary of any process of inference or any knowledge of truths. Thus in the presence of my table I am acquainted with the sense-data that make up the appearance of my table—its colour, shape, hardness, smoothness, etc. . . . My knowledge of the table as a physical object, on the contrary, is not direct knowledge. Such as it is, it is obtained through acquaintance with the sense-data that make up the appearance of the table. We have seen that it is possible, without absurdity, to doubt whether there is a table at all, whereas it is not possible to doubt the sense-data. My knowledge of the table is of the kind which we shall call 'knowledge by description'. The table is 'the physical object which causes such-and-such sense-data'. This *describes* the table by means of the sense-data. (*PP* 46–7)

Sense-data are not the only things with which we have acquaintance. Introspection gives us acquaintance with our own thoughts, feelings, and desires. Memory gives us acquaintance with past data of the inner or outer senses. We may even, though this is a matter of doubt, have acquaintance with our own selves. We do not have acquaintance with physical objects or other minds. But we do have acquaintance with rather more rarefied entities: namely, universal concepts, such as *whiteness*, *brotherhood*, and so on.

Like Plato, Russell thought that universals belonged to a supra-sensible world, the world of being. The world of being was unchangeable, rigid, perfect, and dead. It was the world of existence that contained thoughts, feelings, and sense-data. By temperament some people preferred one world, and others preferred the other. But 'both are real, and both are important to the metaphysician' (*PP* 100).

Every proposition that we can understand, Russell maintained, must be composed wholly of constituents with which we are acquainted. How then can we make statements about Bismarck, whom we have never seen, or Europe, which is far too big to be taken in by a sense-datum? Russell's answer is that any judgement about Bismarck or Europe really contains a nested series of definite descriptions, and all knowledge about them is ultimately reducible to knowledge of what is known by acquaintance. Only in this way can we have any knowledge of things that we have never experienced.

When he came to write *Our Knowledge of the External World* (1914) Russell described the relationship between physical objects and sense-data by saying that the former were logical constructions out of the latter. Whereas in *Problems* he though that objects *caused* sense-data, but were distinct from them, he now came to believe that statements about the objects of everyday life, and scientific statements also, were reducible by analysis into statements about sensory experiences. But this too turned out to be a temporary phase in his thinking, and in his last philosophical work, *Human Knowledge: Its Scope and Limits* (1948), he returned to a causal theory of perception. In the meantime much had happened to call in question the whole basis and method of his epistemology.

Husserl's Epoche

Husserl was the last great philosopher in the Cartesian tradition. He saw the phenomenological reduction, and in particular the programme of *epoche*, or suspension of judgement about the existence of extra-mental reality, as a refinement of Descartes's methodological doubt. In several ways he sought to be more radical than Descartes in cutting away from the foundations of philosophy whatever it is possible to doubt. First of all, he denied the indubitability of the *cogito* if that is supposed to affirm the existence of an enduring self rather than just the subject of my present sensations. Second, he thought that Descartes took the data of consciousness at their face value, without distinguishing within them between what was actually given in sensation, and what in them was the result of a metaphysical interpretation that tacitly presupposed the existence of an external world, spread out in space and time and subject to a principle of causality (*LI* 16).

The differences that separate Husserl from Descartes are, however, unimportant in comparison with the similarities that bind the two together. Both philosophers saw epistemology as the basic discipline, which is prior to all other parts of philosophy and to all empirical sciences. Husserl, like Descartes, never doubted two things: the certainty of his own mental states and processes, and the language that he uses to report these phenomena. These certainties, they both believe, can survive any doubt about the external world.

Descartes believed that God could have created my mind, just as it is, without there being any such thing as matter. Husserl argued that our awareness of external objects consists in our partial glimpses and contacts with them—our 'adumbrations' of them, as he puts it. But unless these adumbrations exhibited the order they do, we could not in any way construct objects out of them. However, it is perfectly conceivable that this order might be shattered, leaving only a chaotic series of sensations. If so, we would cease to perceive physical objects, and our world would be destroyed. But consciousness, Husserl argued, would survive such a destruction of the world (*Ideas*, 49).

If my own consciousness is indubitably certain, while the world of matter is essentially dubious, nothing could seem more judicious than to suspend judgement about the latter while concentrating on the accurate description and analysis of the former. But Husserl's *epoche*, or suspension of judgement, is not the neutral starting point that it appears to be between realism and idealism. For the assumption that consciousness can be given expression in a purely private world begs the question against realism from the start. Because they separate the content of consciousness from any non-contingent link with its expression in language and its objects in the external world, both Husserl and Descartes find themselves trapped into a form of solipsism, from which Descartes tries to escape by appeal to the veracity of God, and Husserl, in his later years, by postulating a transcendental consciousness.

The line of argument that drove Husserl to become a transcendental idealist went as follows. His starting point was the natural one that consciousness is part of the world, with physical causes. But if one is to avoid having to postulate, like Kant, a *Ding an Sich* which is unattainable by experience, one must say that the physical world is itself a creation of consciousness. But if the consciousness that creates it is our own ordinary psychological consciousness, then we are confronted by paradox: the world as a whole is constituted by one of its elements, human consciousness. The only way to avoid the paradox is to say that the consciousness that constitutes the world is no part of the world but is transcendental.[1]

The world that consciousness creates, however, is shaped not only by our own experiences but by the culture and fundamental assumptions in which we live: what Husserl calls 'the life-world'. The life-world is not a set of judgements based on evidence, but rather an unexamined substrate underlying all evidence and all judgement. However, it is not something ultimate and immutable. Our life-world is affected by developments in science just as science is rooted in our life-world. Hypotheses get their meaning through their connection with the life-world, but in their turn they gradually change it. In a paper first published in 1939, *Experience and Judgement*, Husserl wrote:

everything which contemporary natural science has furnished as determinations of what exists also belongs to us, to the world, as this world is pregiven to the adults of our time. And even if we are not personally interested in natural science, and even if we know nothing of its results, still, what exists is pregiven to us in advance as determined in such a way that we at least grasp it as being in principle scientifically determinable.

It is not easy to see how to reconcile these late thoughts with the earlier stages of Husserl's thinking. Similarly, readers of Wittgenstein's latest

---

[1] Here I am indebted to Herman Philipse's article 'Transcendental Idealism' in *CCH* 239–319.

writings find him exploring new and disquieting ideas on the nature of the ultimate justification of knowledge and belief.[2]

Wittgenstein on Certainty

Descartes's scepticism has had a more enduring effect than his rationalism: philosophers have been more impressed by the difficulties raised in his First and Third Meditations than by the replies to those difficulties in the Fourth and Sixth Meditations. Husserl's transcendental idealism is only the last of a long series of unsuccessful attempts to respond to Cartesian scepticism about the external world while accepting the Cartesian picture of the internal world. Wittgenstein's private language argument, which showed that there was no way of identifying items of consciousness without reference to the public world, cut the ground beneath the whole notion of Cartesian consciousness. But it was only in the last years of his life, in the epistemological writings published posthumously as *On Certainty*, that Wittgenstein addressed Cartesian scepticism head-on.

In response to sceptical doubt of the kind presented in the First Meditation, Wittgenstein makes two initial points. First, doubt needs grounds (*OC* 323, 458). Second, a genuine doubt must make a difference in someone's behaviour: someone is not really doubting whether he has a pair of hands if he uses his hands as we all do (*OC* 428). In reply, Descartes could agree with the first point; that is why he invented the evil genius, to provide a ground for suspicion of our intuitions. The second point he would answer with a distinction: the doubt he is recommending is a theoretical, methodological doubt, not a practical one.

Wittgenstein's next criticism is much more substantial. A doubt, he claims, presupposes the mastery of a language-game. In order to express the doubt that *p* one must understand what is meant by saying *p*. Radical Cartesian doubt destroys itself because it is bound to call in question the meaning of the words used to express it (*OC* 369, 456). If the evil genius is

---

[2] The similarity between the two is pointed out by Dagfinn Føllesdal in his paper 'Ultimate Justification in Husserl and Wittgenstein', in M. E. Reicher and J. C. Marek (eds.), *Experience and Analysis* (Vienna: ÖBT & HPT, 2005), to which I am indebted for the quotation in the above paragraph.

deceiving me totally, then he is deceiving me about the meaning of the word 'deceive'. So 'The evil genius is deceiving me totally' does not express the total doubt that it was intended to.

Even within the language-game, there must be some propositions that cannot be doubted. 'Our doubts depend on the fact that some propositions are exempt from doubt, are as it were the hinges on which those turn' (*OC* 341). But if there are propositions about which we cannot doubt, are these also propositions about which we cannot be mistaken? Wittgenstein distinguished between mistake and other forms of false belief. If someone were to imagine that he had just been living for a long time somewhere other than where he had in fact been living, this would not be a mistake, but a mental disturbance; it was something one would try to cure him of, not to reason him out of. The difference between madness and mistake is that whereas mistake involves false judgement, in madness no real judgement is made at all, true or false. So too with dreaming: the argument 'I may be dreaming' is senseless, because if I am dreaming this remark is being dreamt as well, and indeed it is also being dreamt that these words have any meaning (*OC* 383).

Wittgenstein's purpose in *On Certainty* is not just to establish the reality of the external world against Cartesian scepticism. His concern, as he acknowledged, was much closer to that of Newman in *The Grammar of Assent*: he wanted to inquire how it was possible to have unshakeable certainty that is not based on evidence. The existence of external objects was certain, but it was not something that could be proved, or that was an object of knowledge. Its location in our world-picture (*Weltbild*) was far deeper than that.

In the last months of his life Wittgenstein sought to clarify the status of a set of propositions that have a special position in the structure of our epistemology, propositions which, as he put it, 'stand fast' for us (*OC* 116). Propositions such as 'Mont Blanc has existed for a long time' and 'One cannot fly to the moon by flapping one's arms' look like empirical propositions. But they are 'empirical' propositions in a special way: they are not the results of inquiry, but the foundations of research; they are fossilized empirical propositions that form channels for the ordinary, fluid propositions. They are propositions that make up our world-picture, and a world-picture is not learnt by experience; it is the inherited background against

"Motor cars don't grow out of the earth" was one of Wittgenstein's examples of propositions that build up our world picture. It was by calling such propositions in question that surrealists like Joan Miró achieved their effects.

which I distinguish between true and false. Children do not learn them; they as it were swallow them down with what they do learn (*OC* 94, 476).

It is quite sure that motor cars don't grow out of the earth. We feel that if someone could believe the contrary he could believe *everything* we say is untrue, and could question everything that we hold to be sure.

But how does this *one* belief hang together with all the rest? We would like to say that someone who could believe that does not accept our whole system of verification. The system is something that a human being acquires by means of observation and instruction. I intentionally do not say 'learns'. (*OC* 279)

When we first begin to believe anything, we believe not a single proposition but a whole system: light dawns gradually over the whole.

Though these propositions give the foundations of our language-games, they do not provide grounds, or premises for language-games. 'Giving grounds', Wittgenstein said, 'justifying the evidence, comes to an end; but the end is not certain propositions striking us immediately as true, i.e. it is not a kind of *seeing* in our part; it is our acting, which lies at the bottom of the language game.' (*OC* 204).

Epistemology in the twentieth century went through parallel stages of development in different climates of thought. In each case from an initial concentration on the individual consciousness epistemologists moved towards an appreciation of the role of social communities in the build-up of the web of belief. Likewise, they moved from a concentration on the purely cognitive aspect of experience to an emphasis on its affective and practical element. This development took place both within different schools of philosophy (Continental and analytic) and also within the thought of individual philosophers such as Husserl and Wittgenstein. In each case the development brought enrichment to a field of philosophy that had initially been cramped by excessive individualism.

7

Metaphysics

Varieties of Idealism

In the first part of the nineteenth century the most significant philosophers were all idealists of one kind or another. The period was the heyday of transcendental idealism in Germany, with Fichte, Schelling, and Hegel working towards a theory of the universe as the developing history of an absolute consciousness. But even those who were most critical of absolute idealism owed allegiance to a different form of idealism, the empiricist idealism of Berkeley according to which to be is to be perceived. John Stuart Mill in England and Arthur Schopenhauer in Germany both take as their starting point Berkeley's thesis that the world of experience consists of nothing but ideas, and both try to detach Berkeley's theory of matter from its theological underpinning.[1]

According to Mill, our belief that physical objects persist in existence when they are not perceived amounts to no more than our continuing expectation of further perceptions in the future. He defines matter as 'a permanent possibility of sensation'; he tells us that the external world is the world of possible sensations succeeding one another in a lawful manner.

Right at the start of his *World as Will and Idea* Schopenhauer tells us, 'The world is my idea.' Everything in the world exists only as an object for a subject, exists only in relation to consciousness. To achieve philosophical wisdom a man must accept that 'he has no knowledge of a sun and of an earth, but only of an eye that sees the sun and a hand that feels the earth' (*WWI* 3). The subject, Schopenhauer says, is that which knows all things and is known by none; it is therefore the bearer of the world.

---

[1] See vol. III, pp. 76, 315.

Schopenhauer accepts from Kant that space, time, and causality are necessary and universal forms of every object, intuited in our consciousness prior to any experience. Space and time are a priori forms of sensibility, and causality is an a priori form of understanding. Understanding (*Verstand*) is not peculiar to humans, because other animals are aware of relations between cause and effect. Understanding is what turns raw sensation into perception, just as the rising sun brings colour into the landscape. The faculty that is peculiar to humans is reason (*Vernunft*), that is to say the ability to form abstract concepts and link them to each other. Reason confers on humans the possibility of speech, deliberation, and science; but it does not increase knowledge, it only transforms it. All our knowledge comes from our perceptions, which are what constitute the world.

The thesis that the world exists only for a subject leads to paradox. Schopenhauer accepted an evolutionary account of history: animals existed before men, fishes before land animals, and plants before fishes. A long series of changes took place before the first eye ever opened. Yet, according to the thesis that the world is idea, the existence of this whole world is forever dependent on that first eye, even if it was only that of an insect.

Thus we see, on the one hand, the existence of the whole world necessarily dependent on the first knowing [conscious] being, however imperfect it be; on the other hand, this first knowing animal just as necessarily dependent on a long chain of causes and effects which has preceded it, and in which it itself appears as a small link. (*WWI* 30)

This antinomy can be resolved only if we move from consideration of the world as idea to the world as will.

The second book of *The World as Will and Idea* begins with a consideration of the natural sciences. Some of these, such as botany and zoology, deal with the permanent forms of individuals; others, such as mechanics and physics, promise explanations of change. These offer laws of nature, such as those of inertia and gravitation, which determine the position of phenomena in time and space. But these laws offer no information about the inner nature of the forces of nature—matter, weight, inertia, and so on—that are invoked in order to account for their constancy. 'The force on account of which a stone falls to the ground or one body repels another is, in its inner nature, not less strange and mysterious than that which produces the movements and the growth of an animal' (*WWI* 97).

Scientific inquiry, so long as it restricts its concern to ideas, leaves us unsatisfied. 'We wish to know the significance of these ideas; we ask whether this world is merely idea; in which case it would pass by us like an empty dream or a baseless vision, not worth our notice; or whether it is also something else, something more than idea, and if so what' (*WWI* 99). We would never be able to get any further if we were mere knowing subjects— winged cherubs without a body. But each of us is rooted in the world because of our embodiment. My knowledge of the world is given me through my body, but my body is not just a medium of information, one object among others; it is an active agent of whose power I am directly conscious. It is my will that gives me the key to my own existence and shows me the inner mechanism of my actions.

The movements of my body are not effects of which my will is the cause: the act and the will are identical. 'Every true act of a man's will is also at once and without exception a movement of his body.' Conversely, impressions upon the body are also impacts on the will—pleasant, if in accordance with the will, painful if contrary to the will. Each of us knows himself both as an object and as a will; and this is the key to the understanding of the essence of every phenomenon in nature.

[We shall] judge of all objects which are not our own bodies, and are consequently not given to our consciousness in a double way but only as ideas, according to the analogy of our own bodies, and shall therefore assume that as in one aspect they are idea, just like our bodies, and in this respect are analogous to them, so in another aspect, what remains of objects when we set aside their existence as idea of the subject must in its inner nature be the same as that in us which we call *will*. For what other kind of existence or reality should we attribute to the rest of the material world? Whence should we take the elements out of which we construct such a world? Besides will and idea nothing is known to us or thinkable. (*WWI* 105)

The force by which the crystal is formed, the force by which the magnet turns to the pole, the force which germinates and vegetates in the plant— all these forces, so different in their phenomenal existence, are identical in their inner nature with that which in us is the will. Phenomenal existence is mere idea, but the will is a thing in itself. The word 'will' is like a magic spell that discloses to us the inmost being of everything in nature.

This does not mean—Schopenhauer quickly insists—that a falling stone has consciousness or desires. Deliberation about motives is only the form that will takes in human beings; it is not part of the essence of will, which comes in many different grades, only the higher of which are accompanied by knowledge and self-determination. Why, we may wonder, should we say that natural forces are lower grades of will, rather than saying that the human will is the highest grade of force? Schopenhauer's reply to this is that our concept of force is an abstraction from the phenomenal world of cause and effect, whereas will is something of which we have immediate consciousness. To explain will in terms of force would be to explain the better known by the less known, and to renounce the only immediate knowledge we have of the world's inner nature.

Will is groundless: it is outside the realm of cause and effect. It is wrong, therefore, to ask for the cause of original forces such as gravity or electricity. To be sure, the expressions of these forces take place in accordance with the laws of cause and effect; but it is not gravity that causes a stone to fall, but rather the proximity of the earth. The force of gravity itself is no part of the causal chain, because it lies outside time. So do all other forces.

Through thousands of years chemical forces slumber in matter till the contact with the reagents sets them free; then they appear; but time exists only for the phenomena, not for the forces themselves. For thousands of years galvanism slumbered in copper and zinc, and they lay quietly beside silver, which will inevitably be consumed in flame as soon as all three are brought together under the required conditions. (*WWI* 136)

This account of the operation of causality in the world has some features in common with the occasionalism of Malebranche, and Schopenhauer draws attention to the resemblance.[2] 'Malebranche is right: every natural cause is only an occasional cause.' But whereas for Malebranche God was the true cause of every natural effect, for Schopenhauer the true cause is the universal will. A natural cause, he tells us,

only gives opportunity or occasion for the manifestation of the one indivisible will which is the 'in-itself' of all things, and whose graduated objectification is the whole visible world. Only the appearance, the becoming visible in this place, at this time, is brought about by the cause and is so far dependent on it, but not the whole of the phenomenon, nor its inner nature. (*WWI* 138)

---

[2] See vol. III, p. 59.

The universal will is objectified at many different levels. The principal difference between the higher and lower grades of will lies in the role of individuality. In the higher grades individuality is prominent: no two humans are alike, and there are marked differences between individual animals of higher species. But the further down we go, the more completely individual character is lost in the common character of the species. Plants have hardly any individual qualities, and in the inorganic world all individuality disappears. A force like electricity must show itself in precisely the same way in all its million phenomena. This is the reason why it is easier to predict the phenomena the further down we go in the hierarchy of will.

Throughout the world of nature will is expressed in conflict. There is conflict between different grades of will, as when a magnet lifts a piece of iron, which is the victory of a higher form of will (electricity) over a lower (gravitation). When a person raises an arm, that is a triumph of human will over gravity, and in every healthy animal we see the conscious organism winning a victory over the physical and chemical laws that operate on the constituents of the body. It is this perpetual conflict that makes physical life burdensome and brings the necessity of sleep and eventually of death. 'At last these subdued forces of nature, assisted by circumstances, win back from the organism, wearied even by the constant victory, the matter it took from them, and attain to an unimpeded expression of their being' (*WWI* 146). At the bottom end of the scale, similarly, we see the universal essential conflict that manifests will. The earth's revolution around the sun is kept going by the constant tension between centrifugal and centripetal force. Matter itself is kept in being by attractive and repulsive forces, gravitation and impenetrability. This constant pressure and resistance is the objectivity of will in its very lowest grade, and even there, as a mere blind urge, it expresses its character as will.

The will, in Schopenhauer's system, occupies the same position as the thing-in-itself in Kant's. Considered apart from its phenomenal activities, it is outside time and space. Since time and space are the necessary conditions for multiplicity, the will must be single; it remains indivisible, in spite of the plurality of things in space and time. The will is objectified in a higher way in a human than in a stone; but this does not mean that there is a larger part of will in the human and a smaller part in the stone, because the relation of part and whole belongs only to space. So too does plurality: 'the will reveals itself just as completely in one oak as in millions' (*WWI* 128).

The different grades of objectification of the will are identified by Schopenhauer with the Ideas of Plato. These too, like the will itself, are outside space and time.

Those different grades of the will's objectification, expressed in innumerable individuals, exist as the unattained patterns of these, or as the eternal forms of things. Not themselves entering into time and space, the medium of individuals, they remain fixed, subject to no change, always being, never having become. The particular things, however, arise and pass away; they are always becoming and never are. (*WWI* 129)

The combination of Platonic idealism with Indian mysticism gives Schopenhauer's system a uniquely metaphysical quality. However much they admired his style, or admitted his influence, few philosophers felt able to follow him all the way. There has never been a school of Schopenhauerians as there have been schools of Kantians and Hegelians. The one person who was willing to declare himself a disciple of Schopenhauer was the Wagner of *Tristan und Isolde*.

Metaphysics and Teleology

It is a far cry from Schopenhauer's mystical idealism to Darwin's evolutionary naturalism, and indeed it may seem odd to mention a biologist at all in a chapter on metaphysics. But Darwin's theories had implications, which went beyond his immediate interests, for the general theory of causation. Aristotle, who was the first to systematize metaphysics, did so in terms of four kinds of causes: material, formal, efficient, and final. The final cause was the goal or end of a structure or activity. Explanations in terms of final causes were called 'teleological' after the Greek word for end, *telos*. For Aristotle teleological explanations were operative at every level, from the burrowing of an earthworm to the rotation of the heavens. Since Darwin, many thinkers have claimed, there is no longer any room at all for teleological explanation in any scientific discipline.

Aristotelian teleological explanations of activities and structures have two features: they explain things in terms of their ends, not their beginnings, and they invoke the notion of goodness. Thus, an activity will be explained by reference not to its starting point but to its terminus; and

A lithograph of F. Stassen illustrates the moment in Wagner's opera in which Isolde hands the fateful potion to Tristan.

arrival at the terminus will be exhibited as some kind of good for the agent whose activity is to be explained. Thus, the downward motion of heavy bodies on earth was explained by Aristotle as a movement towards their natural place, the place where it was best for them to be, and the circular motion of the heavens was to be explained by love of a supreme being. Similarly, teleological explanation of the development of organic structures showed how the organ, in its perfected state, conferred a benefit

175

on the complete organism. Thus, ducks grow webbed feet so that they can swim.

Descartes rejected the use of teleological explanation in physics or biology. Final causation, he maintained, implied in the agent a knowledge of the end to be pursued; but such knowledge could only exist in minds. The explanation of every physical movement and activity must be mechanistic; that is, it must be given in terms of initial, not final, conditions, and those conditions must be stated in descriptive, not evaluative, terms. Descartes offered no good argument for his contention, and his thesis ruled out straightforward gravitational attraction no less than the Aristotelian cosmic ballet. Moreover, Descartes was wrong to think that teleological explanation must involve conscious purpose: whatever Aristotle may have thought about the heavenly bodies, he never believed that an earthworm, let alone a falling pebble, was in possession of a mind.

It was not Descartes, but Newton and Darwin, who dealt the serious blows to Aristotelian teleology, by undermining, in different ways, its two constituent elements. Newtonian gravity, no less than Aristotelian motion, provides an explanation by reference to a terminus: gravity is a centripetal force, a force 'by which bodies are drawn, or impelled, or in any way tend, towards a point as to a centre'. But Newton's explanation is fundamentally different from Aristotle's in that it involves no suggestion that it is in any way good for a body to arrive at the centre to which it tends.

Darwinian explanations in terms of natural selection, on the other hand, resemble Aristotle's in demanding that the terminus of the process to be explained, or the complexity of the structure to be accounted for, shall be something that is beneficial to the relevant organism. But unlike Aristotle, Darwin explains the processes and the structures, not in terms of a pull by the final state or perfected structure, but in terms of the pressure of the initial conditions of the system and its environment. The red teeth and red claws involved in the struggle for existence were, of course, in pursuit of a good, namely the survival of the individual organism to which they belonged; but they were not in pursuit of the ultimate good that is to be explained by selection, namely, the survival of the fittest species. It is thus that the emergence of particular species in the course of evolution could be explained not only without appeal to a conscious designer, but without evoking teleology at all.

It is, of course, only at one particular level that Darwin's system offers to render teleology superfluous. Human beings, such as husbandmen, act for the sake of goals not only in breeding improved stock, but in human life and business in general. Others among the higher animals not only act on instinct, but pursue goals learnt by experience. Moreover, Darwinian scientists have not given up the search for final causes. Indeed, contemporary biologists are much more adept at discerning the function of structures and behaviours than their predecessors in the period between Descartes and Darwin. What Darwin did was to make teleological explanation respectable by offering a general recipe for translating it into an explanation of a mechanistic form. His successors thus feel able freely to use such explanations, without offering more than a promissory note about how they are to be reduced to mechanism in any particular case. Once they have identified the benefit, G, that an activity or structure confers on an organism, they feel entitled to say without further ado that 'the organism evolved in such a way that G'.

Two great questions about teleology are left unanswered by the work of Darwin. First, are the free and conscious decisions of human beings irreducibly teleological, or can they be given an explanation in mechanistic terms? There are those who believe that when more is known about the human brain it will be possible to show that every human thought and action is the outcome of mechanistic physical processes. This belief, however, is an act of faith; it is not the result of any scientific discovery or of any philosophical analysis.

Second, if we assume that broadly Darwinian explanations can be found for the existence of the teleological organisms we see around us, does our investigation rest there? Or can the universe itself be regarded as a system that operates, through mechanistic means, to the goal of producing species of organisms, in the way that a refrigerator works through mechanistic means to the goal of a uniform temperature? Is the universe itself one huge machine, a goal-directed system?

Biologists are divided whether evolution itself has a direction. Some believe that it has an inbuilt tendency to produce organisms of ever greater complexity and ever higher consciousness. Others claim that there is no scientific evidence that evolution has any kind of privileged axis. Either way, the question remains whether it is teleological explanation or mechanistic explanation that is the one that operates at a fundamental level of the universe. If God created the world, then mechanistic explanation is underpinned by teleological explanation; the fundamental explanation of the existence and operation of any creature is the purpose of the creator. If there is no God, but the universe is due to the operation of necessary laws upon blind chance, then it is the mechanistic level of explanation that is fundamental. So far as I know, no one, whether scientist or philosopher, has provided a definitive answer to this question.

Realism vs. Nominalism

Throughout the history of philosophy one metaphysical problem recurs again and again, presented in different terms. This is the question whether, if we are to make sense of the world we live in, there must exist, outside the mind, entities of a quite different kind from the fleeting individuals that we meet in everyday existence. In the ancient world, Plato and Aristotle discussed whether or not there were Ideas or Forms existing independently of matter and material objects. Throughout the Middle Ages, realist and nominalist philosophers disputed whether universals were realities or mere symbols. In the modern era philosophers of mathematics have conducted a parallel debate about the nature of mathematical objects, with formalists identifying numbers with numerals, and realists asserting that numbers have an independent reality, constituting a third world separate from the world of mind and the world of matter.

The most vociferous defender of realism in modern times is Frege. In a lecture entitled 'Formal Theories of Arithmetic' (*CP* 112–21) he attacks the idea that signs for numbers, like '$\frac{1}{2}$' and 'π', are merely empty signs designating nothing. Even calling them 'signs', he says, already suggests that they do signify something. A resolute formalist should call them 'shapes'. If we took seriously the contention that '$\frac{1}{2}$' does not designate anything, then it is merely a splash of printer's ink or a splurge of chalk, with various physical and chemical properties. How can it possibly have the property that if added to itself it yields 1? Shall we say that it is given this property by definition? A definition serves to connect a sense with a word; but this sign was supposed to have no content. Sure, it is up to us to give a signification to a sign, and therefore it is partly dependent on human choice what properties the content of a sign has. But these properties are properties of the content, not of the sign itself, and hence, according to the formalist, they will not be properties of the number. What we cannot do is to give things properties merely by definition.

In the *Grundgesetze* Frege uses against the formalists the kind of argument that Wyclif used against the nominalists of the Middle Ages.[3]

One cannot by pure definition magically conjure into a thing a property that in fact it does not possess—save that of now being called by the name with which one has named it. That an oval figure produced on paper with ink should by a definition acquire the property of yielding one when added to one, I can only regard as a scientific superstition. One could just as well by a pure definition make a lazy pupil diligent. (*BLA* 11)

For Frege, not only numbers but functions too were mind-independent realities. Consider an expression such as '$2x^2 + x$'. This expression splits into two parts, a sign for an argument and an expression for a function. In the expressions

$$(2 \times 1^2) + 1$$
$$(2 \times 4^2) + 4$$
$$(2 \times 5^2) + 5$$

we can recognize the same function occurring over and over again, but with different arguments, namely 1, 4, and 5. The content that is common to these expressions is what the function is. It can be represented by '$2(\ )^2 + (\ )$', that is, by what is left of '$2x^2 + x$' if we leave the xs out. The argument is not part of the function, rather it combines with the function to make a complete whole. A function must be distinguished from its value for a particular argument: the value of a mathematical function is always a number, as the number 3 is the value of our function for the argument 1, so that '$(2 \times 1^2) + 1$' names the number 3. A function itself, unlike the numbers that are its arguments and its values, is something incomplete, or 'unsaturated' as Frege calls it. That is why it is best represented, symbolically, by a sign containing gaps. In itself, it is not a sign but a reality lying behind the sign.

It was not only in mathematics that Frege was a resolute realist. He extended the notion of function in such a way that all concepts of any kind

[3] See vol. II, pp. 152–3.

turn out to be functions. The link between mathematical functions and predicates such as '...killed...' or '...is lighter than...' is made in a striking passage of 'Function and Concept' where we are invited to consider the function '$x^2 = 1$'.

The first question that arises here is what the values of this function are for different arguments. Now if we replace x successively by -1, 0, 1, 2 we get:

$$(-1)^2 = 1$$
$$0^2 = 1$$
$$1^2 = 1$$
$$2^2 = 1$$

Of these equations the first and third are true, the others false. I say 'the value of our function is a truth-value' and distinguish between the truth-values of what is true and what is false. (*CP* 144)

Once this move has been made, it is possible for Frege to define a concept as a function whose value for every argument is a truth-value. A concept will then be the extra-linguistic counterpart of a predicate in language: what is represented, for instance, by the predicate '...is a horse.' Concepts, like numbers, are quite independent of mind or matter: we do not create them, we discover them; but we do not discover them by the operation of our senses. They are objective, though they do not have the kind of reality (*Wirklichkeit*) that belongs to the physical world of cause and effect.

Frege's realism is often called Platonism, but there is a significant difference between Plato's Ideas and Frege's concepts. For Plato, the Ideal Horse was itself a horse: only by being itself a horse could it impart horsiness to the non-ideal horses of the everyday world.[4] Frege's concept *horse*, by contrast, is something very unlike a horse. Any actual horse is an object, and between objects and concepts there is, for Frege, a great gulf fixed. Not only is the concept *horse* not a horse, it is, Frege tells us, not a concept. This remark at first hearing brings us up short; but there is nothing really untoward about it. Prefacing '*horse*' with 'the concept' has the effect of turning a sign for a concept into a sign for an object, just as putting quotation marks round the word 'swims' turns the sign for a verb into a noun which, unlike a verb, can be the subject of a sentence. We can

[4] See vol. I, p. 208.

say truly ' "swims" is a verb', but also ' " "swims" " is a noun'. That is the clue to understanding Frege's claim that the concept *horse* is not a concept.

First, Second, and Third in Peirce

In the English-speaking world, the most original system of metaphysics devised in the nineteenth century was that of C. S. Peirce. It is true that Peirce's principle of pragmatism resembles the verification principle of the logical positivists, and that from time to time he was willing to denounce metaphysics as 'meaningless gibberish'; nonetheless, he himself constructed a system that was as abstruse and elaborate as anything to be found in the writings of German idealists.

Like Hegel, Pierce was fascinated by triads. He wrote in *The Monist* in 1891:

Three conceptions are perpetually turning up at every point in every theory of logic, and in the most rounded systems they occur in connection with one another. They are conceptions so very broad and consequently indefinite that they are hard to seize and may be easily overlooked. I call them the conceptions of First, Second, Third. First is the conception of being or existing independent of anything else. Second is the conception of being relative to, the conception of reaction with, something else. Third is the conception of mediation, whereby a first and second are brought into relation. (*EWP* 173)

This triadic system was inspired by Peirce's research into the logic of relations. He classified predicates according to the number of items to which they relate. ' ... is blue' is a monadic or one-place predicate, ' ... is the son of ... ', with two places, is dyadic, and ' ... gives ... to ... ' is triadic. A sense-impression of a quality is an example of a 'firstness', heredity is an example of a 'secondness'. The third class of items can be exemplified by the relationship whereby a sign signifies ('mediates') an object to an interpreting mind. Universal ideas are a paradigm case of thirdness, and so are laws of nature. If a spark falls into a barrel of gunpowder (first) it causes an explosion (second) and does so according to a law that mediates between the two (third).

Peirce was willing to apply this triadic classification very widely, to psychology and to biology as well as to physics and chemistry. He even employed it on a cosmic scale: in one place he wrote 'Mind is First, Matter is Second, Evolution is Third' (*EWP* 173). Moreover, he offered an elaborate proof that while a scientific language must contain monadic, dyadic, and triadic predicates, there are no phenomena that require four-place predicates for their expression. Expressions containing such predicates can always be translated into expressions containing only predicates of the three basic kinds.

Thirdness, however, Peirce sees as an irreducible element of the universe, neglected by nominalist philosophers, who refused to accept the reality of universals. The aim of all scientific inquiry is to find the thirdness in the variety of our experience—to discover the patterns, regularities, and laws in the world we live in. But we should not be looking for universal, exceptionless laws that determine all that happens. The doctrine of necessity, indeed, was one of Peirce's chief targets in his criticism of the *Weltanschauung* of nineteenth-century science. He states it thus:

> The proposition in question is that the state of things existing at any time, together with certain immutable laws, completely determine the state of things at every other time (for a limitation to *future* time is indefensible). Thus, given the state of the universe in the original nebula, and given the laws of mechanics, a sufficiently powerful mind could deduce from these data the precise form of every curlicue of every letter I am now writing. (*EWP* 176)

This proposition, Peirce thought, was quite indefensible. It could be put forward neither as a postulate of reasoning nor as the outcome of observation. 'Try to verify any law of nature and you will find that the more precise your observations, the more certain they will be to show irregular departures from the law' (*EWP* 182). Peirce maintained that there was an irreducible element of chance in the universe: a thesis which he called 'tychism' from the Greek word for chance, τυχη. In support of tychism he enlisted both Aristotle and Darwin. The inclusion of chance as a possible cause, he said, was of the utmost essence of Aristotelianism; and the only way of accounting for the laws of nature was to suppose them results of evolution. 'This supposes them not to be absolute, not to be obeyed precisely. It makes an element of indeterminacy, spontaneity, or absolute chance in nature' (*EWP* 163). Thus, there was ample room for belief in the autonomy and freedom of the human will.

There were, Peirce thought, three ways of explaining the relationship between physical and psychical laws. The first was neutralism, which

A lecture manuscript of Peirce, which illustrates the curlicues that he believed to be unpredictable by deterministic laws.

placed them on a par as independent of each other. The second was materialism, which regarded psychical laws as derived from physical ones. The third was idealism, which regarded psychical laws as primordial and physical laws as derivative. Neutralism, he thought, was ruled out by Ockham's razor: never look for two explanatory factors where one will do. Materialism involved the repugnant idea that a machine could feel. 'The one intelligible theory of the universe is that of objective idealism, that matter is effete mind, inveterate habits becoming physical laws' (*EWP* 168).

Peirce offered to explain the course of the universe in terms of firstness, secondness, and thirdness. 'Three elements are active in the world', he wrote; 'first, chance; second, law; and third, habit-taking' (*CP* i. 409). In the infinitely remote beginning, there was nothing but unpersonalized feeling, without any connection of regularity. Then, the germ of a generalizing tendency would arise as a sport, and would be dominant over other sports. 'Thus, the tendency to habit would be started; and from this with the other principles of evolution all the regularities of the universe would be evolved' (*EWP* 174).

Peirce's theory of cosmic evolution differs from Darwinism in several ways. First of all, he states its principle in utterly general terms, with no reference to animal or plant species:

Wherever there are large numbers of objects, having a tendency to retain certain characters unaltered, this tendency, however, not being absolute but giving room for chance variations, then, if the amount of variation is absolutely limited in certain directions by the destruction of everything that reaches these limits, there will be a gradual tendency to change in directions of departures from them. (*EWP* 164)

Second, while Darwin's doctrine of the survival of the fittest sought to eliminate the need to explain the course of nature in terms of Aristotelian final causes, Peirce, like Aristotle, saw the pursuit of an ultimate goal as the dynamic that rules the universe. Surprising as it may seem, it is love that is the driving force of cosmic history. The original slimy protoplasm has the power of growth and reproduction; it is capable of feeling and it has the property of taking habits. 'Love, recognizing germs of loveliness in the hateful, gradually warms it into life and makes it lovely.' That, for Peirce, is the secret of evolution.

Peirce distinguished three modes of evolution: evolution by fortuitous variation, evolution by mechanical necessity, and evolution by creative love. In accordance with his passion for fashioning English terms from Greek roots, he called these types of evolution tychastic, anancastic, and agapastic, from the Greek words respectively for chance, necessity, and love. Darwin's evolutionary theory was tychastic: there was, Peirce thought, little positive evidence for it, and its popularity was due to the nineteenth century's passion for heartless laissez-faire economics. 'It makes the felicity of the lambs just the damnation of the goats, transposed to the other side of the equation.' The principle of necessity that underpinned anancastic evolution had already, Peirce believed, been disposed of by his arguments. We are left with the third form of evolution, agapastic evolution. Such a form of evolution had been proposed by Lamarck: the endeavours of parents produce beneficial modifications that are inherited by their offspring. 'A genuine evolutionary philosophy,' Peirce tells us in conclusion, 'that is, one that makes the principle of growth a primordial element of the universe, is so far from being antagonistic to the idea of a personal creator, that it is really inseparable from that idea' (*EWP* 214). We have come some distance from the empiricist verificationism that seemed to be the kernel of Peirce's pragmatism.

The Metaphysics of Logical Atomism

Metaphysics goes hand in hand with logic also in Wittgenstein's *Tractatus*. Though most of the book is devoted to the nature of language, its earliest pages consist of a series of pronouncements about the nature of the world. Both historically and logically the theses about the world are dependent upon Wittgenstein's thesis about language; but they amount to a metaphysical system that merits consideration in its own right.

According to the *Tractatus*, to each pair of contradictory propositions there corresponds one and only one fact: the fact that makes one of them true and the other false. The totality of such facts is the world. Facts may be positive or negative: a positive fact is the existence of a state of affairs, a negative fact is the non-existence of a state of affairs. A state of affairs, or situation (*Sachverhalt*), is a combination of objects. An object is essentially a possible constituent of a state of affairs, and its possibility of occurring in combination with other objects in states of affairs is its nature. Since every object contains within its nature all the possibilities of its combination with other objects, it follows that if any object is given all objects are given (*TLP* 1.1–2.011).

Objects are simple and lack parts, but they can combine into complexes. They are ungenerable and indestructible, because any possible world must contain the same objects as this one; change is only an alteration in the configuration of objects. Objects may differ from each other by nature, or in external properties, or they may be merely numerically distinct, indiscernible but not identical (*TLP* 2.022–2.02331). The objects make up the unalterable and subsistent form, substance, and content of the world.

Objects combine into states of affairs: the way in which they are connected gives the state of affairs its structure. The possibility of a structure is the form of the state of affairs. States of affairs are independent of one another: from the existence or non-existence of one of them it is impossible to infer the existence or non-existence of another. Since facts are the existence and non-existence of states of affairs, it follows that facts too are independent of each other. The totality of facts is the world.

These dense pages of the *Tractatus* are difficult to understand. No examples are given of objects that are the bedrock of the universe. Commentators have offered widely varying interpretations: for some, objects are sense-data; for others, they are universals. Possibly, both of these items would have been recognized by Wittgenstein as objects: after all, they are the same as the items that, according to Russell, were known to us by acquaintance. But the lack of examples in the *Tractatus* is not accidental. Wittgenstein believed in the existence of simple objects and atomic states of affairs not because he thought he could give instances of them, but because he thought that they must exist as the correlates in the world for the names and elementary propositions of a fully analysed language.

His reasoning to that conclusion is based on three premises. First, whether a sentence has meaning or not is a matter of logic. Second, what particular things exist is a matter of experience. Third, logic is prior to all experience. Therefore, whether a sentence has meaning or not can never depend on whether particular things exists. This conclusion lays down a condition that any system of logic must meet. To meet it, Wittgenstein thought, one must lay down that names could signify only simple objects. If 'N' is the name of a complex, then 'N' would have no meaning if the complex were broken up, and sentences containing it would be senseless. So when any such sentence is fully analysed, the name 'N' must disappear and its place be taken by names that name simples (*TLP* 3.23, 3.24; *PI* i. 39).

Simple objects, in the world of the *Tractatus*, are concatenated into atomic states of affairs, which correspond to elementary propositions that are concatenations of names. The world can be completely described by listing all elementary propositions, and listing which of them are true and which are false (*TLP* 4.26). For the true elementary propositions will record all the positive facts, and the false elementary propositions will correspond to all the negative facts, and the totality of facts is the world (*TLP* 2.06).

Bad and Good Metaphysics

The *Tractatus* is one of the most metaphysical works ever written: its likeness to Spinoza's *Ethics* is no coincidence. Yet it was taken as a bible by one of the most anti-metaphysical groups of philosophers, the Vienna Circle. The logical positivists seized on the idea that necessary truths were necessary only because they were tautologies: this enabled them, they believed, to reconcile the necessity of mathematics with a thoroughgoing empiricism. They then employed the verification principle as a weapon that enabled them to dismiss all metaphysical statements as meaningless.

Wittgenstein, throughout his life, shared the positivists' view that the removal, the dissolution, of metaphysics was one of the tasks of the philosopher. He described the task of the philosopher as 'bringing words back from their metaphysical to their everyday use'. He condemned the metaphysics that was a search for the hidden essence of language or of the world. Yet he was himself a metaphysician in his own right—and not just at the time of the *Tractatus*, whose propositions he condemned as nonsensical, but throughout his later philosophy. He recognized that there could be a legitimate attempt to understand essences, in which he was himself engaged. In our investigations, he said, 'we try to understand the essence of language, its function and construction'. What was wrong, on his view, was to consider the essence not as something that lies open to view and must merely be given a perspicuous description, but as something interior and hidden: a kind of metaphysical ectoplasm or hardware that explains the functioning of mind and language. There were in particular three kinds of metaphysics against which Wittgenstein set his face: spiritualistic metaphysics, scientistic metaphysics, and foundationalist metaphysics.

When we consider human thought, the metaphysical impulse may lead us to postulate spiritual substances, or spiritual processes. We are misled by grammar. When grammar makes us expect a physical substance, but there is not one, we invent a metaphysical substance; where it makes us expect an empirical process, but we cannot find one, we postulate an incorporeal process. This is the origin of Cartesian dualism; the Cartesian mind is a metaphysical substance and its operation upon the body is a metaphysical process. Cartesianism is metaphysical in the sense of isolating statements about mental life from any possibility of conclusive verification or falsification in the public world.

Besides dualist metaphysics, there is materialist metaphysics. 'The characteristic of a metaphysical question', he wrote, 'is that we express an unclarity about the grammar of words in the form of a scientific question' (*BB* 35). Metaphysics is philosophy masquerading as natural science, and this is the form of metaphysics particularly beloved of materialists. It is a metaphysical error to think, for instance, that exploration of the brain will help us to understand what is going on in our minds when we think and understand.

The great metaphysicians of the past have often thought of their subject as having primacy over all other parts of philosophy: Aristotle called metaphysics 'first philosophy' and Descartes thought metaphysics was the root of the tree of knowledge. Wittgenstein denied that any part of philosophy should be privileged in this way. One could start philosophizing at any point, and leave off the treatment of one philosophical problem to take up the treatment of another. Philosophy had no foundations, and did not provide foundations for other disciplines. Philosophy was not a house, nor a tree, but a web.

The real discovery is the one that makes me capable of stopping doing philosophy when I want to.
The one that gives philosophy peace, so that it is no longer tormented by questions which bring *itself* in question.
Instead, we now demonstrate a method, by examples; and the series of examples can be broken off.
Problems are solved (difficulties eliminated), not a *single* problem. (*PI* I. 133)

But while Wittgenstein, throughout his life, was hostile to scientistic and foundational metaphysics, in his later work he did in fact make substantial contributions to areas of philosophy that would traditionally have been regarded as metaphysical. Much of Aristotle's *Metaphysics* is devoted to philosophical activities that resemble quite closely Wittgenstein's own method.

The distinction between actuality and potentiality, and the classification of different kinds of potentiality, is universally recognized (by both friend and foe) as being one of Aristotle's most characteristic contributions to philosophy and in particular to the philosophy of mind. His distinctions were later systematized by scholastic philosophers in the Middle Ages. Wittgenstein undertook a prolonged investigation of the nature of potentiality in the

Brown Book, where sections 58–67 are devoted to various language-games with the word 'can'. The distinctions that he draws between processes and states, and between different kinds of states, correspond to the Aristotelian distinctions between *kinesis*, *hexis*, and *energeia*. The criteria by which the two philosophers make the distinctions often coincide. The example that Wittgenstein discusses at length, to illustrate the relation between a power and its exercise, namely learning to read (*PI* i. 156 ff.), is close to the standard Aristotelian example of a mental *hexis*, namely, knowledge of grammar. We may call the systematic study of actuality and potentiality *dynamic metaphysics*, and if we do so we must say that Wittgenstein was one of the most consummate practitioners of that particular form of metaphysics.

It was not an Aristotelian type, however, but a Leibnizian one, that turned out to be the most flourishing version of metaphysics in the latter half of the twentieth century. The development of modal semantics in terms of possible worlds[5] need not, in itself, have had metaphysical implications, but a number of philosophers interpreted it in a metaphysical sense and were prepared to countenance the idea that there were identifiable individuals that had only possible and not actual existence.

In my view, this was a mistaken development. There is a difficulty in providing a criterion of identity for merely possible objects. If something is to be a subject of which we can make predications, it is essential that it shall be possible to tell in what circumstances two predications are made of *that same subject*. Otherwise we shall never be able to apply the principle that contradictory predications should not be made of the same subject. We have various complicated criteria by which we decide whether two statements are being made about the same actual man; by what criteria can we decide whether two statements are being made about the same *possible* man? These difficulties were entertainingly brought out by Quine in his famous paper 'On What There Is' of 1961:

Take, for instance, the possible fat man in that doorway; and again, the possible bald man in that doorway. Are they the same possible man, or two possible men? How do we decide? How many possible men are there in that doorway? Are there more possible thin ones than fat ones? How many of them are alike? Are no *two* possible things alike? Is this the same as saying that it is impossible for two things to

---

[5] See p. 119 above.

be alike? Or, finally, is the concept of identity simply inapplicable to unactualised possibles? But what sense can be found in talking of entities which cannot meaningfully be said to be identical with themselves and distinct from one another? (*FLPV* 666)

The questions asked by Quine seem to me unanswerable, and thus to expose the incoherence of the notion of unactualized possible individuals. But in the last decades of the century philosophers of great talent exercised themselves to answer Quine's questions and thus to solve what was called 'the problem of transworld identity'. In the light of the history recorded in these volumes it

W.V.O. Quine, the great enemy of the metaphysics of possible worlds. How many possible men, he would have asked, are sharing the room with him here?

seems to me more prudent to adhere to the grand Aristotelian principle that there is no individuation without actualization—the counterpart of the cardinal anti-Platonic principle that there is no actualization without individuation.

In the English-speaking world metaphysics was flourishing at the beginning of the twentieth century, with Peirce in America extolling the principle of cosmic love, and the neo-Hegelians in Britain tracing the lineaments of the Absolute. As the century progressed philosophers became more and more hostile to metaphysics; this hostility climaxed with the positivism of the 1930s, but continued influential well into the second half of the century. With the approach of the twenty-first century, metaphysics once more became respectable, but with a difference. The place once occupied by the monistic metaphysics of the British idealists is now taken by the pluralistic, indeed exuberant, metaphysics of the explorers of possible worlds. It will be interesting to see whether the twenty-first century exhibits a similar cycle of metaphysical thought.

8

Philosophy of Mind

Bentham on Intention and Motive

B entham's *Principles of Morals and Legislation* contained a detailed analysis of human action. It devoted substantial chapters to such topics as intention and motive. Not since the Middle Ages had a great philosopher devoted such minute attention to the different cognitive and affective elements whose presence or absence may contribute to the moral character of individual actions. Bentham's approach to the topic resembles that of Aquinas, but he is much more generous in providing concrete examples to illustrate his points. More importantly, there is a significant difference between the two philosophers both in terminology and in moral evaluation.[1]

For Aquinas, an action was intentional if it was chosen as a means to an end; if an action was only an unavoidable accompaniment or consequence of such a choice it was not intentional, but only voluntary. Bentham disliked the word 'voluntary'; it was misleading, he said, because it sometimes meant *uncoerced* and sometimes meant *spontaneous*. He preferred to use the word 'intentional'. However, he made the same distinction as Aquinas, but marked it as a distinction between two kinds of intention. A consequence, he said, may be either directly intentional ('when the prospect of producing it constituted one of the links in the chain of causes by which the person was determined to act') or obliquely intentional ('when the consequence was foreseen as likely, but the prospect of producing it formed no link in the determining chain'). For Bentham, an incident that is directly

---

[1] See vol. II, p. 263.

intentional may be either ultimately or mediately intentional, according to whether the prospect of producing it would or would not have operated as a motive if not viewed as productive of a further event. This distinction between ultimate and mediate intention corresponds to the scholastic distinction between ends and means.

Bentham illustrated his panoply of distinctions by referring to the story of the death of King William II of England, who died while stag hunting from a wound inflicted by one Sir Walter Tyrell. He rang the changes on the possible degrees of consciousness and intentionality in the mind of Tyrell, and assigned the appropriate classification to each imagined case: unintentional, obliquely intentional, directly intentional, mediately intentional, ultimately intentional.

The effect of Bentham's terminology was to define intention itself in purely cognitive terms: to find out what a person intended you need to ascertain what she knew, not what she wanted. What she wanted is relevant only to the subclass of intentionality involved. An act is unintentional only if its upshot was quite unforeseen; it is thus that 'you may intend to touch a man without intending to hurt him; and yet, as the consequences turn out, you may chance to hurt him'. The cognitive slant that Bentham gives to intention is of great importance, since for him intention is a key criterion for the moral and legal evaluation of actions.

We should not think, however, Bentham tells us, that intentions are good and bad in themselves. 'If [an intention] be deemed good or bad in any sense, it must be either because it is deemed to be productive of good or of bad consequences or because it is deemed to originate from a good or from a bad motive' (P 8. 13). Now consequences depend on circumstances, and circumstances are simply either known or unknown to the agent. So whatever is to be said of the goodness or badness of a person's intention as resulting from the consequences of his act depends on his knowledge ('consciousness') of the circumstances.

In the ninth chapter of the *Principles* Bentham classifies the different possible degrees of such consciousness. If a man is aware of a circumstance when he acts, then his act is said to have been an *advised* act, with respect to that circumstance; otherwise an *unadvised* act. Besides being unaware of circumstances that actually obtain, an agent may suppose that circumstances do obtain which in fact do not obtain; this is *missupposal* and makes an act *misadvised*. If an act is intentional, and is advised with respect to all circumstances relevant to a particular consequence, and there is no missupposal of preventive circumstances, then the consequence is intentional. 'Advisedness, with respect to the circumstances, if clear from the missupposal of any preventive circumstance, extends the intentionality from the act to the consequences' (P 9. 10).

Bentham makes a distinction between intentions and motives: a man's intentions may be good and his motives bad. Suppose that 'out of malice a man prosecutes you for a crime of which he believes you to be guilty, but of which in fact you are not guilty'. Here the motive is evil, and the actual consequences are mischievous; nonetheless, the intention is good, because the consequences of the man's action would have been good if they had turned out as he foresaw.

In discussing motives Bentham stresses the evaluative overtones of words such as 'lust', 'avarice', and 'cruelty'. In itself, he says, no motive is either good or bad; these words denote bad motives only in the sense that they are never properly applied except where the motives they signify happen to be bad. 'Lust', for instance, 'is the name given to sexual desire when the effects of it are regarded as bad.' It is only in individual cases that motives can be good or bad. 'A motive is good, when the intention it gives birth to is a good one; bad, when the intention is a bad one; and an emotion is good or bad according to the material consequences that are the objects of it' (P 10. 33).

By 'motive' Bentham means what, described in neutral terms, he would call an ultimately and directly intentional consequence. From his explanation it is clear that it does not supply a separate title of moral qualification of an act; the only mental state primarily relevant to the morality of a voluntary act is the cognitive state with regard to the consequences.

Bentham's account of motive is in accord with the general utilitarian position that moral goodness and badness in actions is to be judged in terms of their consequences with respect to pleasure and pain. His cognitive conception of intention brought his followers into conflict with the doctrine of double effect according to which there may be a moral difference between doing something on purpose and merely foreseeing it as an unwanted consequence of one's choices. These moral issues will be discussed in detail in Chapter 9.

In his *Groundwork* Kant exalted the importance of motive more than any other moral philosopher had ever done. Bentham's position stands at the opposite extreme of ethical theory. As J. S. Mill was to put it, the utilitarians 'have gone beyond almost all others in affirming that the motive has nothing to do with the morality of the action'. Not only motive, but also intention as commonly understood, is irrelevant to utilitarian moral judgement of behaviour. It is an agreeable paradox that the founder of utilitarianism should have offered a fuller analysis of the concepts of intention and motive than any previous writer had achieved.

Reason, Understanding, and Will

In continental Europe the analysis of mental concepts took a different course. The absolute idealism of a philosopher such as Hegel makes it difficult to distinguish in his work between philosophy of mind and metaphysics. Schopenhauer, however, starting from Kant's distinction between understanding (*Verstand*) and reason (*Vernunft*), offers a detailed study of the differences that mark off human from animal cognitive faculties.

Understanding, as well as sensation, is something that animals share with humans, because understanding is the capacity to grasp causal relations, which is something that animals can clearly do. Indeed, the sagacity of animals like foxes and elephants sometimes surpasses human understanding. But human beings alone possess reason, that is to say, abstract knowledge embodied in concepts. Reason is the capacity for reflection, which places humans far above animals, both in power and in suffering. Animals live in the present alone; man lives at the same time in the future and the past (*WWI* 36).

Reason confers three great gifts on humans: language, freedom, and science. The first and most essential is language.

Only by the aid of language does reason bring about its most important achievements, namely the harmonious and consistent action of several individuals, the planned cooperation of many thousands, civilization, the State; and then, science, the storing up of previous experience, the summarizing into one concept of what is common, the communication of truth, the spreading of error, thoughts and poems, dogmas and superstitions. (*WWI* 37)

The importance of abstract knowledge is that it can be retained and shared. Understanding can grasp the mode of operation of a lever, or the support of an arch; but more than understanding is needed for the construction of machines and buildings. For practical purposes, mere understanding may sometimes be preferable: 'it is of no use to me to know in the abstract the exact angle, in degrees and minutes, at which I must apply a razor, if I do not know it intuitively, that is, if I have not got the feel of it'. But when long-term planning is necessary, or when the help of others is required, abstract knowledge is essential.

Animals and humans, according to Schopenhauer, both have wills, but only humans can deliberate. It is only in the abstract that different motives can be simultaneously presented in consciousness as objects of choice. Ethical conduct must be based on principles; but principles are abstract. However, reason, though necessary for virtue, is not sufficient for virtue. 'Reason is found with great wickedness no less than with great kindness, and by its assistance gives great effectiveness to the one as to the other' (*WWI* 86).

The will, for Schopenhauer, is present and active throughout the universe, but we grasp its nature only through the human willing of which we are ourselves directly aware. All willing, Schopenhauer tells us, arises from a want, a deficiency, and therefore from suffering. A wish may be granted, but for one wish that is satisfied there are ten that are denied. Desire lasts long; fulfilment is only momentary. 'No attained object of desire can give lasting satisfaction, but merely a fleeting gratification; it is like the alms thrown to the beggar, that keeps him alive today that his misery may be prolonged till the morrow' (*WWI* 196).

As a general rule, knowledge is at the service of the will, engaged in the satisfaction of its desires. This is always the case in animals, and is symbolized by the way in which the head of a lower animal is directed towards the ground. In humans, too, for the most part knowledge is the slave of will; but humans can rise above the consideration of objects as mere instruments for the satisfaction of desire. The human stands erect, and like the Apollo Belvedere he can look into the far distance, adopting an attitude of contemplation, oblivious to the body's needs.

In this state the human mind encounters a new class of objects: not just the Lockean ideas of perception, nor just the abstract ideas of reason, but the universal Ideas that Plato described. The way to grasp the Ideas is this: let your whole consciousness be filled with the quiet contemplation of a landscape or a building, and forget your own individuality, your own needs and desires. What you will then know will no longer be an individual, but an eternal form, a particular degree of objectification of the universal will. And you will lose yourself and become a pure, will-less, painless, timeless subject of knowledge, seeing things *sub specie aeternitatis*. 'In such contemplation the particular thing becomes at once the *Idea* of its species, and the perceiving individual becomes *pure subject of knowledge*. The individual, as such, knows only particular things; the pure subject of knowledge knows only Ideas' (*WWI* i 179). In contemplation free from the servitude of the will, we lose our concern with happiness and unhappiness. Indeed, we cease to be individual: we become 'that *one* eye of the world which looks out from all knowing creatures, but which can become perfectly free from the service of will in man alone'.

Every human being has it within his power to know the Ideas in things, but a specially favoured individual may possess this knowledge more intensely and more continuously than ordinary mortals. Such a person is what we mean by a genius.

Schopenhauer spells out for us the characteristics of the genius: the genius is imaginative and restless, he dislikes mathematics, and he lives on the borderline of madness. His gift finds expression above all in works of art, and it is through works of art that those of us who are not geniuses can be introduced to the liberating effect of contemplation. Schopenhauer spells this out in a detailed consideration of the various arts. The deliverance from the tyranny of the will that is offered by art is, however, a limited and temporary one. The only way to a complete liberation is by renouncing altogether the will to live.[2]

What, in Schopenhauer's system, is the relationship between soul and body? First of all, there is a complete rejection of the dualistic idea that there are causal relations between the inner and the outer. The will and the movements of the body are not two different events linked by causality: the actions of the body are the acts of the will made perceptible. The whole body, with all its parts, Schopenhauer says, is nothing but the objectification of the will and its desires:

Teeth, throat and bowels are objectified hunger; the organs of generation are objectified sexual desire; the grasping hand, the hurrying feet, correspond to the more indirect desires of the will which they express. As the human form in

---

[2] Schopenhauer's aesthetic theory is considered in Ch. 10 and his ethical theory in Ch. 9 below.

general corresponds to the human will in general, so the individual bodily structure corresponds to the individually modified will, the character of the individual, and therefore it is throughout and in all its parts characteristic and full of expression. (*WWI* 108)

Schopenhauer here anticipates a famous remark of Wittgenstein's, 'The human body is the best picture of the human soul' (*PI* II. 178).

The body is intimately involved in knowledge as well as in desire; my own body is the starting point of my perception of the world, and my knowledge of other perceptible objects depends on their effects on my body. But even when we rise above knowledge of ideas to knowledge of Ideas, the body still has a role, as Schopenhauer rather surprisingly tells us. 'Man is at once impetuous and blind striving of will (whose pole or focus lies in the genitals) and eternal, free, serene subject of pure knowledge (whose pole is the brain)' (*WWI* 203).

Is there any part of a human being that survives the death of the body, or does total extinction await us? On the one hand Schopenhauer says, 'Before us there is indeed only nothingness'; on the other hand, he can say, 'if, *per impossibile*, a single being, even the most insignificant, were entirely annihilated, the whole world would inevitably be destroyed with it' (*WWI* 129). The latter claim is derived from the metaphysical principle that the will which is the inner reality of every individual is itself single and indivisible. Interpreters have sought to reconcile the two pronouncements by suggesting that at death the human person is absorbed into the single will: it continues, therefore, to exist, but it loses all individuality.

Experimental vs. Philosophical Psychology

As the nineteenth century progressed, psychologists endeavoured to launch a new science of the mind, which would study mental phenomena by empirical and experimental methods. In Europe the first psychological laboratory was set up in 1879 at the University of Leipzig by Wilhelm Wundt, a professor of physiology, specializing in the nervous system, who five years earlier had published an influential text entitled 'Principles of Physiological Psychology'. William James, who had gone to Germany to study in this field, anticipated Wundt by setting up a psychology laboratory in Harvard, and in 1878 the first ever doctorate in psychology was awarded.

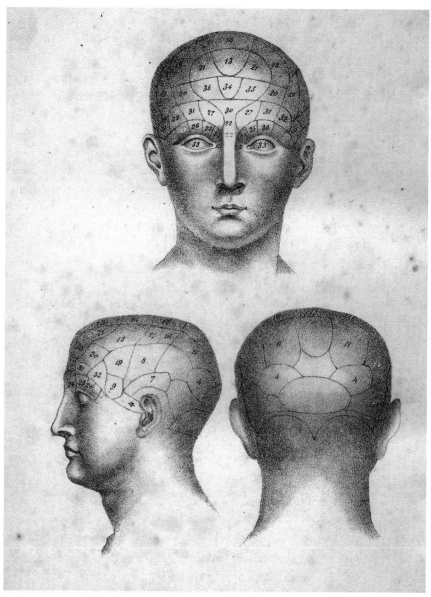

Phrenology was an early attempt to make psychology scientific. This illustration from an 1825 textbook attempts to relate bumps in the skull to traits of character.

James summed up the findings of the new science in his volumes *Principles of Psychology* (1890), a work described by Bertrand Russell as possessing 'the highest possible excellence'.

The task of the new psychology was to relate mental events and states to processes in the brain and nervous system. James's textbook introduced the student to the relevant physiology and reported the work of European psychologists on the reaction times of experimental subjects. It ranged widely, from the instinctive behaviour of animals to the phenomena of hypnotism. For most of the time, James was surveying the work of others; but from time to time he made his own original contribution to the subject.

James's most famous innovation in philosophical psychology was his theory of the emotions. While his contemporaries strove to find the exact relation between emotional feelings and their concomitant bodily processes, James proposed that the emotions were nothing more than the perception of these processes. In *The Principles of Psychology* he wrote:

Our natural way of thinking about coarser emotions is that the mental perception of some fact excites the mental affection called the emotion, and that this latter state of mind gives rise to the bodily expression. My theory, on the contrary, is that the bodily changes follow directly the perception of the exciting fact, and that our feeling of the same changes as they occur IS the emotion. Commonsense says, we lose our fortune, are sorry and weep; we meet a bear, are frightened and run; we are insulted by a rival, are angry and strike. The hypothesis here to be defended says that this order of sequence is incorrect, that the one mental state is not immediately induced by the other, that the bodily manifestations must first be interposed between, and that the more rational statement is that we feel sorry because we cry, angry because we strike, afraid because we tremble. (ii. 250)

In order to account for the great variety of emotional states, James insisted that there was hardly any limit to the permutations and combinations of possible minute bodily changes, and each one of these, he claimed, was felt, acutely or obscurely, the moment it occurred. But he was not able to give any independent criterion for the occurrence of such feelings.

James's theory of the emotions had been anticipated by Descartes. The influence of Descartes is, in fact, all-pervasive in his account of the human mind. Nineteenth-century psychologists were anxious to emancipate themselves from the thrall of philosophy; but while their investigations of physiological phenomena produced genuine scientific discoveries, their notion of the conscious mind was taken over, lock, stock, and barrel, from the Cartesian tradition in philosophy. This is abundantly clear in James's *Principles*, but is perhaps most candidly expressed in his early paper of 1884, 'The Function of Cognition' (*T* 1–42).

All states of consciousness, James there says, can be called 'feelings'; and by 'feeling' he means the same as Locke meant by 'idea' and Descartes meant by 'thought'. Some feelings are cognitive and some are not. In order to determine what makes the difference between cognitive and non-cognitive states, James invites us to consider a feeling of the most basic possible kind:

Let us suppose it attached to no matter, nor localized at any point in space, but left swinging *in vacuo*, as it were, by the direct creative *fiat* of a god. And let us also, to escape entanglement with difficulties about the physical or psychical nature of its 'object', not call it a feeling of fragrance or of any other determinate sort, but limit ourselves to assuming that it is a feeling of *q*. (*T* 3)

We are further invited to consider this as a feeling that constitutes the entire universe, and lasts only an infinitesimal part of a second.

James inquires what addition to this primal feeling would be needed to make it into a cognitive state. He replies (*a*) that there must be in the world another entity resembling the feeling in its quality *q*, and (*b*) the feeling must either directly or indirectly operate upon this other entity. James's account of knowledge does not appear very plausible, but it is not his conclusion but his starting point that it is important to notice. He envisages consciousness as consisting fundamentally of a series of solitary atoms devoid of any context or relation to any behaviour or to any body.

Later in his life James took a less atomistic view of the nature of feeling, believing that as a matter of empirical fact consciousness flowed in a continuous stream without sharp breaks between one item and the next. But he retained the idea of consciousness as an essentially private internal phenomenon, connected only contingently with any external manifestation in speech and behaviour, and capable in principle of existing in isolation from any body. This, of course, was precisely how Descartes had conceived of consciousness.

Physiological psychologists saw themselves as liberating themselves from philosophy by substituting experiment for introspection as the method of studying the mind. But in this they were mistaken in two ways. First, a thinker like James retains the picture of consciousness as an object of introspection: something we can *see* when we look *within*; something to which we have ourselves direct access, but which others can learn of only indirectly, by accepting our verbal testimony or making causal inferences from our physical behaviour. Second, whatever Locke and Hume may have thought, the philosophy of mind does not operate by scrupulous observation of internal phenomena but by the examination of the concepts that we make use of in expressing our experience.

The hollowness of Descartes's notion of consciousness was exposed, later in the twentieth century, by the work of Wittgenstein (who admired James as a particularly honest and candid exponent of the Cartesian tradition). But in James's own lifetime, what appeared to be the most serious challenge to the work of the experimental psychologists came from a different quarter: from the picture of the mind presented by Freudian psychoanalysis.

The Freudian Unconscious

In his *Introductory Lectures on Psychoanalysis* Freud states as one of the two main foundations of his theory that the greater part of our mental life, whether of feeling, thought, or volition, is unconscious. Before deciding whether we should accept this principle we need to look closely at what is meant by 'unconscious'. There are several possible senses of the word, and depending on which sense we take, Freud's thesis may turn out a truism or a piece of hardy speculation.

It is obvious that at any given moment only a tiny fraction of what we know and believe is present to consciousness in the sense of being an object of our immediate attention. For more than sixty years I have known the nursery rhyme 'Three Blind Mice' and have believed that the battle of Waterloo took place in 1815; but the occasions on which I have recited the rhyme or adverted to the date have been few and far between. The distinction between knowledge and its exercise was already made by Aristotle as a distinction between first and second actuality. Knowing Greek, he said, was an actuality in comparison with the simple ability to learn languages with which all humans are endowed. But knowledge of Greek was only a first actuality, an ability that is exercised only when I am speaking, hearing, reading, or thinking in Greek. That was the second actuality. A parallel distinction can be made with regard to one's wishes, plans, and intentions. You no doubt wish to have an adequate provision for your pension. But the thought of your pension does not occupy your mind all the time: only when you are worrying about it, or engaged in taking steps to make such provision, are you conscious of this wish of yours.

If this is the way in which we make the distinction between the conscious and the unconscious then Freud's statement that most of our mental life is unconscious is nothing more than a philosophical commonplace. But of course, Freud meant more than that. Knowledge, thoughts, and feelings of the kind I have described can, in appropriate circumstances, easily be brought to mind. If someone asks me the date of the battle of Waterloo I can give it; if a financial adviser asks you about your pension provision you have no difficulty in admitting that it is a matter of concern. The unconscious that Freud postulated, in contrast, is not at all so easy to bring to consciousness.

There are in fact three levels of the Freudian unconscious. To disentangle these we must recall that according to Freud there are three sets of phenomena that reveal the existence of the unconscious, namely, trivial everyday mistakes, reports of dreams, and neurotic symptoms.

We all frequently make slips of the tongue, fail to recall names, and mislay useful objects. Freud believed that such 'parapraxes', as he called them, are not as accidental as they seem and may have hidden motives. He quotes the case of a Viennese professor who in his inaugural lecture, instead of saying, according to his script, 'I have no intention of underrating the achievements of my illustrious predecessor' said 'I have every intention of underrating the achievements of my illustrious predecessor.' Freud regards the professor's slip of the tongue as a better guide to his intentions that the words he had written in his notes. But of course the professor was perfectly well aware of his true attitude to his predecessor's work: his intention was only 'unconscious' in the sense that he did not mean to *express* it so publicly. Something similar can happen in writing as well as in speech. Freud tells of a husband who, writing to his estranged wife some years after the sinking of the *Lusitania*, urged her to join him across the Atlantic with the words 'Sail on the *Lusitania*' when he meant to write 'Sail on the *Mauretania*'. Dramatists, Freud maintained, have long been aware of the significance of such parapraxes. In *The Merchant of Venice*, when Portia is struggling between her public obligation to be neutral between her suitors and her private love for Bassanio, Shakespeare makes her say to him:

> One half of me is yours, the other half yours—
> Mine own, I would say.

That such 'Freudian slips' can be revelatory of states of mind that the utterer would prefer to conceal is now very widely accepted. But note that the mental state in question is something that can be verified in a perfectly straightforward way, by seeking a truthful confession from the person guilty of the slip. Such states are, for Freud, the superficial level of the unconscious; he sometimes called this level 'the preconscious' (*NIL* 96).

Matters are rather different when we come to the second method of tapping into the unconscious: the analysis of dream reports. The interpretation of dreams, Freud maintained, 'is the royal road to a knowledge of the unconscious activities of the mind'. But the interpretation is not something that the dreamer can casually undertake for herself; it calls for long and perhaps painful sessions with the psychoanalyst.

Dreams, Freud claimed, are almost always the fulfilment, in fantasy, of a repressed wish. True, few dreams are obvious representations of a satisfaction, and some dreams such as nightmares seem to be just the opposite. But this, according to Freud, is because we dream in code. The true, latent content of the dream is given a symbolic form by the dreamer; this is the 'dream-work', which produces the innocuous manifest content reported by the dreamer. Once stripped of its symbolic form the latent content of the dream can commonly be revealed as sexual, and indeed Oedipal. However, Freud warns us, 'the straightforward dream of sexual relations with one's mother which Jocasta alludes to in the *Oedipus Rex* is a rarity in comparison with the multiplicity of dreams which psychoanalysis must interpret in the same sense' (*SE* xix. 131 ff.).

How is a dream to be decoded and the dream-work undone? Every dream can easily be given a sexual significance if one takes every pointed object like an umbrella to represent a penis, and every capacious object like a handbag to represent the female genitals. But Freud's method was nothing like as crude as that. He did not believe that it was possible to create a universal dictionary linking symbols to what they signified. The significance of a dream item for a particular dreamer could only be discovered by finding out what the dreamer herself associated with that item. Only after such an exploration could one discover the nature of the unconscious wish whose fulfilment was fantasized in the dream.

The third (though chronologically the first) method by which Freud purported to explore the unconscious was by the examination of neurotic symptoms. A typical case is the following. One of his patients, an Austrian undergraduate, was staying at a holiday resort during the vacation. He was suddenly obsessed with the thought that he was too fat: he said to himself 'Ich bin zu dick'. Consequently, he gave up all heavy foods, and used to leap up from the table before the pudding arrived in order to run up mountains in the August heat. 'Our patient could think of no explanation of this senseless obsessional behaviour until it suddenly occurred to him that at this time his fiancée had also been stopping at the same resort in company with an attractive English cousin called Dick.' His purpose in slimming, Freud suggests, had been to get rid of this Dick (*SE* x. 183).

There is a certain circularity in Freud's procedure for discovering the deeper levels of the unconscious. The existence of these deeper levels is held to be proved by the evidence of dreams and neuroses. But dreams and neurotic symptoms do not, either on their face or as interpreted by the unaided patient, reveal the beliefs, desires, and sentiments of which the unconscious is supposed to consist. For a cure to be effective, the patient has to acknowledge the alleged latent desire. But the analyst's decoding is often rejected by the patient, and the criterion of success in decipherment is that the decoded message should accord with the analyst's notion of what the unconscious is like. But that notion was supposed to derive from, and not to precede, the exploration of dreams and symptoms.

Towards the end of his life Freud replaced the dichotomy of conscious and unconscious with a threefold scheme. 'Superego, ego and id', he said in *New Introductory Lectures* (1933), 'are the three realms, regions, or provinces into which we divide the mental apparatus of the individual' (*NIL* 97). The id is the unconscious locus of hunger and love and instinctual drives. It is ruled by the pleasure principle, and it is both more extensive and more obscure than the other parts of the soul. 'The logical laws of thought', Freud tells us, 'do not apply in the id, and this is true above all of the law of contradiction. Contrary impulses exist side, by side, without cancelling each other out or diminishing each other' (*SE* xxii. 73).

The ego, by contrast, represents reason and common sense, and it is devoted to the reality principle. It is the part of the soul most in touch with the external world perceived by the senses. The ego is the rider and the id the horse. 'The horse supplies the locomotive energy, while the rider has the privilege of deciding on the goal and of guiding the powerful animal's movement' (SE xx. 201). But the ego's control is not absolute: the ego is more like a constitutional monarch who has to think long and hard before vetoing any proposal of parliament. Psychoanalysis, however, can strengthen the ego's hold on the id, and assist it in its task of controlling instinctual desires, choosing harmless moments for their satisfaction or diverting their expression. Varying his metaphor, Freud speaks in hydraulic terms of the operation of the id as a flow of energy that can find a normal discharge, be channelled into alternative outlets, or be dammed up with catastrophic results.

The superego, finally, is an agency that observes, judges, and punishes the behaviour of the ego. One form of its manifestations is the utterances of conscience, forbidding actions in advance and reproaching the ego for them after the event (NIL 82). The superego is not present from birth; in early childhood its place is taken by parental authority. As the child develops, the superego takes over one half of the function of parents—not their loving and caring activities, but only their harshness and severity, their preventive and punitive functions. The superego is also 'the vehicle of the ego ideal by which the ego measures itself, which it emulates and whose demand for ever greater perfection it is always striving to fulfil' (SE xxii. 65).

Freud claimed that the modification of his earlier theory had been forced on him by the observation of the patients on his couch. Yet the mind, in this later form, closely resembles the tripartite soul of Plato's Republic.[3] The id corresponds to what Plato calls appetite (epithumetikon), the source of the desires for food and sex. The ego has much in common with Plato's reasoning power (logistikon): it is the part of the soul most in touch with reality and has the task of controlling instinctual desire. Finally, the superego resembles Plato's temper (thumoeides); both are non-rational punitive forces in the service of morality, the source of shame and self-directed anger.

The ego, as depicted by Freud, has to try to satisfy three tyrannical masters: the external world, the superego, and the id.

Goaded on by the id, hemmed in by the super-ego, and rebuffed by reality, the ego struggles to cope with its economic task of reducing the forces and influences which

---

[3] See vol. I, pp. 237–9, and A. Kenny, *The Anatomy of the Soul* (Oxford: Blackwell, 1974), 10–14.

work in it and upon it to some kind of harmony; and we may well understand how it is that we so often cannot repress the cry 'Life is not easy'. (*NIL* 104)

Like Plato, Freud regards mental health as harmony between the parts of the soul, and mental illness as unresolved discord between them. 'So long as the ego and its relations to the id fulfil these ideal conditions (of harmonious control) there will be no neurotic disturbance' (*SE* xx. 201). The ego's whole endeavour is 'a reconciliation between its various dependent relationships' (xix. 149). In the absence of such reconciliation mental disorders develop, and Freud details the symptoms of different kinds of internal conflict.

Philosophical Psychology in the Tractatus

While Freud, in the Austrian capital, was giving his Introductory Lectures on Psychoanalysis, Wittgenstein, in the Austrian army, was constructing, in his notebooks, a different model of the mind. Wittgenstein accepted that psychology was a genuine empirical science, and he saw philosophy of mind as standing in the same relation to psychology as philosophy in general stood to the natural sciences: its task was to clarify its propositions and draw limits to its competence (*TLP* 4.112, 4.113). It would do this by analysing sentences reporting beliefs, judgements, perception, and the like; and above all by casting the light of logic on the nature of thought.

The first thing the *Tractatus* tells us about a thought is that it is a logical picture of facts. A logical picture is a picture whose pictorial form—that which it has in common with what it depicts—is logical form. Ordinary pictures may have more than logical form in common with what they depict, as a painting has spatial form in common with a landscape; but a thought is a picture in the mind that has in common with what it depicts nothing other than logical form.

Sometimes Wittgenstein identifies thoughts with propositions (*TLP* 4). But if we examine his use of 'proposition' closely, it is clear that there are two different elements involved. There is the propositional sign or sentence, which is the holding of a relation between written or spoken words. There is also what is expressed by this propositional sign, namely the thought, which is itself the holding of a relation between psychic elements, about whose precise nature Wittgenstein refused to commit himself, since that was a matter for empirical psychology (*TLP* 3.1, 3.11–12). A propositional sign can only be a proposition if projected by a thought on to the world, and conversely a relationship between mental elements can only be a thought if it is a projection on to the world of a propositional sign (*TLP* 3.5).

'In a proposition', Wittgenstein says at 3.2, 'a thought can be expressed in such a way that elements of the propositional sign correspond to the objects of the thought.' The 'objects of the thought' are the psychic elements whose relation to each other constitutes the thought. A proposition is fully analysed when the elements of the propositional sign correspond to the elements of the thought. An unanalysed proposition of ordinary language does not bear this relation to the thought; on the contrary, it disguises the thought. We can understand ordinary language and grasp the thought beneath its folds only because of enormously complicated tacit conventions. Wittgenstein in the *Tractatus* resembles Freud in attaching great weight to unconscious operations of the mind; the structure of the thoughts that lie behind our utterances are something of which we have not the faintest awareness.

Among our thoughts there appear to be some that are thoughts about thoughts: propositions reporting beliefs and judgements, for example. These are apparent counter-examples to the general thesis of the *Tractatus* that one proposition could occur within another only truth-functionally, because a sentence like 'A believes that p' is not a truth-function of p. Wittgenstein deals with the problem in drastic fashion: such sentences are not genuine propositions at all.

'It is clear,' we are told at 5.542, 'that "A believes that p", "A has the thought that p", and "A says p" are of the form " 'p' says p", and this does not involve a correlation of a fact with an object, but rather the correlation of facts by means of the correlation of their objects.' ' "p" says p' is a pseudo-proposition: it is an attempt to say what can only be shown; a proposition can only show its sense and cannot state it. We may think that, according to the *Tractatus*, the fact that, say, in 'London is bigger than Paris' 'London' is to the left of 'is bigger than' and 'Paris' is to the right of 'is bigger than' that *says* that London is bigger than Paris. But it is only this fact *plus the conventions of the English language* that says any such thing. What does the saying in the sentence is what the propositional sign has in common with all other propositional signs which could achieve the same purpose; and what *this* is could only be described by—*per impossibile*—specifying and making explicit the tacit conventions of English.

Suppose I think a certain thought; my thinking that thought will consist in certain psychic elements—mental images, or internal impressions, perhaps—standing in a relation to each other. That these elements stand in such and such a relation will be a psychological fact within the purview of science. But the fact that these elements have the meaning they have will not be a fact of science. Meaning is conferred on signs by *us*, by our conventions. But where are the acts of will that confer the meaning by setting up the conventions? They cannot be in the empirical soul studied by superficial psychology: any relation between *that* will and any pair of objects would be a scientific fact and therefore incapable of the ineffable activity of conferring meaning. When I confer meaning on the symbols I use, the I that does so must be a metaphysical I, not the self that is studied by introspective psychology. Thought, unlike language, will have the appropriate complexity to depict the facts of the world. But its complexity gives it only the *possibility* of depicting. That a thought actually does depict, truly or falsely, depends on the meaning of its elements, and that is given by the extra-psychological will that gives those elements an application and a use (*TLP* 5.631 ff.).

Intentionality

The philosophy of mind presented in the *Tractatus* is jejune and incredible. This is something that Wittgenstein was himself later to realize; but many who read the work when it first appeared must have observed that it ignored what many contemporaries regarded as the central aspect of mental acts and processes, namely intentionality. The concept of intentionality, medieval in origin, had been reintroduced to philosophy by Brentano in the nineteenth century, and given prominence in Husserl's *Logical Investigations* (1901–2) and *Ideas* (1913).

In his book *Psychology from an Empirical Standpoint* (1874) Brentano had sought to find a property that would mark off psychical from physical phenomena. He considered and rejected the suggestion that the peculiarity of psychical phenomena was that they lacked extension. He then proposed a different criterion of distinction:

Every psychical phenomenon is characterized by what the medieval scholastics called the intentional (or mental) existence of an object, and what we, not quite unambiguously, would call 'relation to a content' 'object-directedness' or 'immanent objectivity'. ('Object' here does not mean reality.) Each such phenomenon contains in itself something as an object, though not each in the same manner. In imagination something is imagined, in judgement something is accepted or rejected, in love something is loved, in hatred something is hated, in desire something is desired and so forth.

This intentional existence is a property only of psychical phenomena; no physical phenomenon displays anything similar. And so we can define psychical phenomena by saying that they are those phenomena that contain an object intentionally. (*PES* ii. 1. 5)

This famous passage is not altogether clear. It is true that where there is love something is loved, and where there is hatred something is hated—but is it not equally true that if heating takes place something is heated? Yet 'heat' is not a psychological verb. How can Brentano say that object-directedness is peculiar to psychological phenomena, when it seems to be a feature common to all grammatically transitive verbs, verbs that 'take an accusative'?

The answer becomes clear if we look to Brentano's scholastic sources, who made a distinction between two kinds of action, immanent and transient. Transient actions are actions that change their objects (heating is a transient action, which makes its object hot). Immanent actions do not change their objects, but their agents. To find out whether the doctor has cured his patient, we examine the patient; to find out whether he has fallen in love with his patient, we must observe the doctor. Brentano's distinction between psychical and physical phenomena corresponds to the distinction between immanent and transient actions.[4]

Husserl took over from Brentano the scholastic concept of intentionality and made it a centrepiece of his system, from 1901 onwards. In the fifth of the *Logical Investigations* he tells us that consciousness consists of intentional experiences or acts, and he makes a series of distinctions between different elements to be found in consciousness. The intentionality of an act is what it is *about*; it is also called the act-matter, the sense, and in later works, the *noema*.

---

[4] See e.g. Aquinas, *Summa Theologiae*, 1a 18. 3 ad 1.

A mental item is given its intentionality by an act of meaning (*Meinen*). There are two kinds of meaning: one kind is that which gives significance to a word, and the other kind is that which gives sense to a proposition. 'Each meaning is ... either a nominal meaning or a propositional meaning, or, still more precisely, either the meaning of a complete sentence or a possible part of such a meaning' (*LI* vi. 1).

Every mental act will be an act of a certain kind, belonging to a particular species, which will be determined by its matter. Every thought of a horse, whoever's thought it is, belongs to the same species; and the concept *horse* is precisely the species to which all these thoughts belong. Similarly, whenever anyone makes the judgement that blood is thicker than water, the meaning of that judgement, the proposition *blood is thicker than water*, is precisely the species to which all such acts of judgement belong. If A agrees with the judgement of B, then while A's judgement and B's judgement are distinct individual mental events, they are, because they have the same matter, instances of the same species. In his later writing Husserl called the individual act the *noesis* and the specific content the *noema*.

In addition to having matter, acts have qualities. It is not only words and sentences that have meaning, and not only the corresponding mental acts and states, such as knowing and believing. So too do perception, imagination, emotion, and volition. My seeing Rome and my imagining Rome are acts that have the same matter, or intentional object, but because seeing is different from imagining, they are acts of different quality (*LI* vi. 22).

Husserl's theory of intentionality was a fertile one, and his account of it contains many shrewd observations and valuable distinctions. But the nature of the act of meaning, which underpins the universe of mental phenomena, remains deeply mysterious. In the 1920s and 1930s some philosophers attempted to present a philosophy of mind that would dispense altogether with intentionality. Bertrand Russell, in his *Analysis of Mind*, presented an account of desire that made it definable in terms of the events that brought it to an end. 'A mental occurrence of any kind— sensation, image, belief or emotion,' he wrote,

may be a cause of a series of actions continuing, unless interrupted, until some more or less definite state of affairs is realized. Such a series of actions we call a 'behaviour cycle'.... The property of causing such a cycle of occurrences is called 'discomfort'... the cycle ends in a condition of quiescence, or of such action as tends to preserve the *status quo*. The state of affairs in which this condition of quiescence is achieved is called the 'purpose' of the cycle, and the initial mental occurrence involving discomfort is called a 'desire' for the state of affairs that brings quiescence. A desire is called 'conscious' when it is accompanied by a true belief as to the state of affairs that will bring quiescence; otherwise it is called 'unconscious'. (*AM* 75)

Behaviour cycles, according to Russell, are causally initiated by mental events possessing the characteristic of discomfort. The nature of these events is left unclear in his system. But other philosophers and psychologists, in their accounts of desire and emotion, dispensed altogether with mental events. For the behaviourist school, particularly after Pavlov had in 1927 presented his theory of conditioned reflexes, the relation between mental and bodily events was no longer a causal one. Behaviour cycles were not the effect of mental events, they were the actual constituents of such things as desire and satisfaction. Behaviourists regarded reports of mental acts and states as disguised reports of pieces of bodily behaviour, or at best of tendencies to behave bodily in certain ways. Intentionality thus vanished from psychology.

Wittgenstein's Later Philosophy of Mind

It was in reaction to Russell's account of desire and expectation that Wittgenstein began to develop his later philosophy of mind. What was wrong with Russell's account, he said, was precisely that it ignored intentionality; and he agreed with Husserl that intentionality was all-important if we were to understand language and thought. To give a correct account of it was one of the major problems of philosophy.

That's *him* (this picture represents *him*)—that contains the whole problem of representation.

What is the criterion, how is it to be verified, that this picture is the portrait of that object, i.e. that it is *meant* to represent it? It is not similarity that makes the picture a portrait (it might be a striking resemblance of one person, and yet be a portrait of someone else it resembles less) . . .

When I remember my friend and see him 'in my mind's eye' what is the connection between the memory image and its subject? The likeness between them? (*PG* 102)

Wittgenstein's achievement in philosophy of mind was to give an account that preserved the intentionality that the behaviourists had denied with-

A photograph of Wittgenstein taken in the period when he was working out his final philosophy of mind.

out accepting the Cartesian picture of consciousness in which Husserl's account was embedded.

One way to describe Wittgenstein's contribution to philosophy of mind is to say that he exhibited, with unparalleled sensitivity, that the human mind is not a spirit, not even an incarnate spirit. First and foremost, there is no such thing as the Cartesian ego, a self, or *moi*, that is referred to in first-person utterances. This is not because the word 'I' refers to something other than a self; it is because 'I' is not a referring expression at all. The self is a piece of philosopher's nonsense produced by misunderstanding of the reflexive pronoun.

When Descartes argued that he could doubt whether he had a body, but he could not doubt whether he existed, it was essential to his argument that it should be possible for him to use 'I' to refer to something of which his body was no part. But that was a great misunderstanding. My 'self' is not a part of myself, not even a very central part of myself; it is, obviously enough, myself. We talk of 'my body', but the possessive pronoun does not mean that there is an 'I' which is the possessor of a body that is other than myself. My body is not the body that I have, but the body that I am, just as the city of Rome is not a city that Rome has but the city that Rome is.

The second thing that is meant by saying that the mind is not a spirit is that it is not some ghostly medium or locus of mental events and processes that is accessible only by introspection. Wittgenstein frequently attacked a mythology about the nature of the mind that we are all prone to accept. We imagine a mechanism in our minds, a strange mechanism that works very well in its own mysterious medium but which, if understood as a mechanism in the ordinary sense, is quite unintelligible. Wittgenstein thought that this was a piece of hidden or latent nonsense. The way to turn latent nonsense into patent nonsense was to imagine that the mechanism really existed.

There is a temptation to think, for instance, that when you recognize somebody what you do is to consult a mental picture of her and check whether what you now see matches the picture. Wittgenstein suggests that if we have this nonsensical idea in our mind we can make ourselves see that it is nonsense, and that it in no way explains recognition. If we suppose the process to happen in the real world, with the picture as a real and not just a mental picture, our initial problem just returns. How do we recognize that this is a picture of a particular person in order to use it to recognize her? The only thing that gave the illusion of explanation in this case was the fuzzy nature of the original supposition; the fact that the process was supposed to take place in the ghostly medium of the mind.

The task of a scientific theory of the mind, according to some philosophers and psychologists, is to establish a principle of correlation between the occurrence of mental states and processes and the occurrence of states and processes in the brain. This correlation would only be a possibility if mental events (e.g. thoughts, or flashes of understanding) were themselves measurable in the way in which physical events are measurable. But thought and understanding are not processes in a psychic medium in the way in which electrolysis and oxidization are processes in a physical medium. Thought and understanding are not processes at all, as Wittgenstein showed by a painstaking analysis of uses of the words 'think' and 'understand'. The criteria by which we decide whether someone understands a sentence, for instance, are quite different from the criteria by which we decide what mental processes are going on while he is uttering or writing the sentence (*PG* 148).

Those who think of the mind as a ghostly medium, and thought and understanding as processes occurring there, regard the medium as accessible by introspection, and only by introspection. The mind, on this view, is an inner space that deserves exploration at least as much as outer space. But whereas—given enough time, money, and energy—everyone can explore the same outer space, each of us can only explore our own inner space. We do so by looking within at something to which we ourselves have direct access, but which others can learn of only indirectly, by accepting our verbal testimony or making inferences from our physical behaviour. The connection between consciousness on the one hand, and speech and behaviour on the other, is on this view a purely contingent one.

To demolish this conception was one of Wittgenstein's great merits. If the connection between consciousness and expression is merely contingent, then for all we know everything in the universe may be conscious. It is perfectly consistent with the idea that consciousness is something private, with which we make contact only in our own case, that the chair on which I am now sitting may be conscious. For all we know, may it not be in excruciating pain? Of course, if it is, we have to add the hypothesis that it is also exhibiting stoical fortitude. But why not?

If consciousness really is merely contingently connected with its expression in behaviour, can we be confident in our ascription of it to other human beings? Our only evidence that humans are conscious is that each of us, if he looks within *himself*, sees consciousness *there*. But how can a man generalize his own case so irresponsibly? He cannot look within others: it is the essence of introspection that it should be something that we all have to do for ourselves. Nor can he make a causal deduction from other people's behaviour. A correlation between other people's consciousness and their behaviour could never be established when the first term of the correlation is in principle unobservable.

'Only of a human being', Wittgenstein wrote, 'and what resembles (behaves like) a human being can one say: it has sensations; it sees; is blind; hears; is deaf; is conscious or unconscious' (*PI* 1. 281). This does not mean that he is a behaviourist; he is not identifying experience with behaviour, or even with dispositions to behave. The point is that what experiences one can have depends on how one *can* behave. Only someone who can play chess can feel the desire to castle; only someone who can talk can be overcome by an impulse to swear. Only a being that can eat can be hungry, and only a being that can discriminate between light and darkness can have visual experiences.

The relation between experiences of certain kinds, and the capacity to behave in certain ways, is not a merely contingent connection. Wittgenstein made a distinction between two kinds of evidence that we may have for the obtaining of states of affairs, namely *symptoms* and *criteria*. Where the connection between a certain kind of evidence and the conclusion drawn from it is a matter of empirical discovery, through theory and induction, the evidence may be called a *symptom* of the state of affairs; where the relation between evidence and conclusion is not something discovered by empirical investigation, but is something that must be grasped by anyone who possesses the concept of the state of affairs in question, then the evidence is not a mere symptom, but a *criterion* of the event in question. A red sky at night may be a symptom of good weather the following morning, but the absence of clouds, the shining of the sun, etc. tomorrow morning are not just symptoms but criteria for the good weather. Similarly, scratching is a criterion for itching, and reciting 'Three Blind Mice' is a criterion for knowing it—though of course not everyone who itches scratches, and one can know the rhyme for years and years without ever reciting it.

Exploiting the notion of *criterion* enabled Wittgenstein to steer between the Scylla of dualism and the Charybdis of behaviourism. He agreed with dualists that particular mental events could occur without accompanying bodily behaviour; on the other hand he agreed with behaviourists that the possibility of ascribing mental acts to people depends on such acts having, in general, a behavioural expression.

If it is wrong to identify the mind with behaviour, it is even more mistaken, according to Wittgenstein, to identify the mind with the brain. Such materialism is in fact a grosser philosophical error than behaviourism because the connection between mind and behaviour is a more intimate one than that between mind and brain. The relation between mind and behaviour is a criterial one, something prior to experience; the connection between mind and brain is a contingent one, discoverable by empirical science. Any discovery of links between mind and brain must take as its starting point the everyday concepts we use in describing the mind, concepts that are grafted on to behavioural criteria.

Oddly enough, developments in the philosophy of mind since Wittgenstein have shown that it is possible to combine the errors of materialism with those of dualism. One of the most ubiquitous misunderstandings of the nature of the mind is the picture of mind's relation to body as that between a little person or homunculus on the one hand, and a tool or instrument or machine on the other. We smile when medieval painters represent the death of the Virgin Mary by showing a small-scale model virgin emerging from her mouth; but basically the same idea can be found in the most unlikely places, including the writings of cognitive scientists.

Descartes, when first he reported the occurrence of retinal images, warned us not to be misled by the resemblance between images and their objects into thinking that when we saw the object we had another pair of eyes, inside our

A mosaic from S. Marco in Venice shows God infusing a soul into Adam – the soul being a homunculus with wings.

brain, to see the images. But he himself believed that seeing was to be explained by saying that the soul encountered an image in the pineal gland. This was a particularly striking version of what has been nicknamed 'the homunculus fallacy'—the attempt to explain human experience and behaviour by postulating a little human within an ordinary human.

What is wrong with the homunculus fallacy? In itself there is nothing misguided in speaking of images in the brain, if one means patterns in the brain, observable to a neurophysiologist, that can be mapped on to features of the visible environment. What is misleading is to take these mappings as representations, to regard them as visible to the mind, and to say that seeing consists in the mind's perception of these images.

The misleading aspect is that such an account pretends to explain seeing, but the explanation reproduces exactly the puzzling features it was supposed to explain. For it is only if we think of the relation between a mind and an image in the pineal gland as being just like the relation between a human being and pictures seen in the environment that we will think that talk of an encounter between the mind and the image has any illuminating power at all. But whatever needs explaining in the human turns up grinning and unexplained in the shape of the manikin.

At the present time, when energetic efforts are being made to construct a new cognitive science of the mind, it is the brain, or parts of the brain, that are usually assigned the role of the homunculus. We may be told that our brains ask questions, solve problems, decode signals, and construct hypotheses. Those who ascribe human capabilities to parts of human beings are unmindful of Wittgenstein's warning, 'Only of a human being and what resembles (behaves like) a human being can one say: it has sensations; it sees; is blind; hears; is deaf; is conscious or unconscious.' But the same point had been made millennia ago by Aristotle, who wrote, 'To say that the soul gets angry is as if one were to say that the soul weaves or builds a house. Probably it is better not to say that the soul pities, or learns, or thinks, but that the human being does these things with its soul' (de Anima 408^{b}12–15).

Wittgenstein's philosophy of mind was in fact closer to that of Aristotle than it is to contemporary materialist psychology. At one point he countenanced the possibility that there may be mental activities that lack any correlate in the brain:

No supposition seems to me more natural than that there is no process in the brain correlated with associating or with thinking; so that it would be impossible to read off thought-processes from brain processes.... It is perfectly possible that certain psychological phenomena *cannot* be investigated physiologically, because physiologically nothing corresponds to them. I saw this man years ago: now I have seen him again, I recognize him, I remember his name. And why does there have to be a cause of this remembering in my nervous system?... Why should there not be a psychological regularity to which *no* physiological regularity corresponds? If this upsets our concept of causality, then it is high time it was upset. (Z 608–10)

This frontal attack on the idea that there must be physical counterparts of mental phenomena was not intended as a defence of any kind of dualism. The entity that does the associating, thinking, and remembering is not a spiritual substance, but a corporeal human being. But Wittgenstein did seem to be envisaging as a possibility an Aristotelian soul or entelechy, which operates with no material vehicle—a formal and final cause to which there corresponds no mechanistic efficient cause.

9

Ethics

The Greatest Happiness of the Greatest Number

In most systems of morality, happiness is a concept of great importance. A long series of moral philosophers, tracing their ancestry back to Plato and Aristotle, had treated happiness as the supreme good, and some ethicists went so far as to affirm that human beings seek happiness in all their choices.[1] In challenging the primacy of happiness, Kant was unusual. In his *Groundwork* he proclaimed that duty, not happiness, was the supreme ethical motive. At first sight, therefore, when Bentham declared that every action should be evaluated in accordance with the tendency it appears to have to augment or diminish happiness, he was just reaffirming a long-standing consensus. But on closer inspection Bentham's greatest happiness principle is very different from traditional eudaimonism.

In the first place, Bentham identifies happiness with pleasure: it is pleasure that is the supreme spring of action. The *Introduction to the Principles of Morals and Legislation* famously begins:

Nature has placed mankind under the governance of two sovereign masters, pain and pleasure. It is for them alone to point out what we ought to do, as well as to determine what we shall do. On the one hand, the standard of right and wrong, on the other the chain of causes and effects, are fastened to their throne. They govern us in all we do, in all we say, in all we think: every effort we can make to throw off our subjection, will serve but to demonstrate and confirm it. (*P* 1. 1)

To maximize happiness, therefore, for Bentham, is the same thing as to maximize pleasure. Utilitarians could cite Plato as a forebear, since in his

---

[1] See vol. I, p. 81; vol. II, p. 272.

Protagoras he had offered for discussion the thesis that virtue consists in the correct choice of pleasure and pain.[2] Aristotle, on the other hand, made a distinction between happiness and pleasure, and in particular refused to identify happiness with the pleasures of the senses. Bentham by contrast not only treated happiness as equivalent to pleasure, but regarded pleasure itself as simply a sensation. 'In this matter we want no refinement, no metaphysics. It is not necessary to consult Plato, nor Aristotle. Pain and pleasure are what everybody feels to be such.'

Bentham was careful to point out that pleasure was a sensation that could be caused not only by eating and drinking and sex, but also by a multitude of other things, as varied as the acquisition of wealth, kindness to animals, or belief in the favour of a Supreme Being. So critics who regarded Bentham's hedonism as a call to sensuality were quite mistaken. However, whereas for a thinker like Aristotle pleasure was to be identified with the activity enjoyed, for Bentham the relation between an activity and its pleasure was one of cause and effect. Whereas for Aristotle the value of a pleasure was the same as the value of the activity enjoyed, for Bentham the value of each and every pleasure was the same, no matter how it was caused. 'Quantity of pleasure being equal', he wrote, 'push-pin is as good as poetry.' What went for pleasure went for pain, too: the quantity of pain, and not its cause, is the measure of its disvalue.

It is the quantification of pleasure and pain, therefore, that is of prime importance for a utilitarian: in deciding on an action or a policy we need to estimate the amount of pleasure and the amount of pain likely to ensue. Bentham was aware that such quantification was no trivial task, and he offered recipes for the measurement of pleasures and pains. Pleasure A counts more than pleasure B if it is more intense, or if it lasts longer, or if it is more certain, or if it is more immediate. In the 'felicific calculus' these different factors must be taken into account and weighed against each other. In judging pleasure-producing actions we must also consider fecundity and purity: a pleasurable action is fecund if it is likely to produce a subsequent series of pleasures, and it is pure if it is unlikely to produce a subsequent series of pains. All these factors are to be taken into account when we are operating the calculus with respect to our own affairs; if we are considering public policy, we must further consider another factor,

---

[2] See vol. I, p. 263.

which Bentham calls 'extension'—that is, how widely the pains and pleasures will be spread across the population.

Bentham offered a mnemonic rhyme to aid in operating the calculus:

> Intense, long, certain, speedy, fruitful, pure—
> Such marks in pleasures and in pains endure.
> Such pleasures seek if private be thy end;
> If it be public, wide let them extend.
> Such pains avoid, whichever be thy view
> If pains must come, let them extend to few.   (P 4. 2)

In using the felicific calculus for purposes of determining public policy, extension is the crucial factor. 'The greatest happiness of the greatest number' is an impressive slogan; but when probed it turns out to be riddled with ambiguity.

The first question to be raised is 'greatest number of *what*?' Should we add 'voters' or 'citizens' or 'males' or 'human beings' or 'sentient beings'? It makes a huge difference which answer we give. Throughout the two centuries of utilitarianism's history most of its devotees would probably give the answer 'human beings', and this is most likely the answer that Bentham would have given. He did not advocate women's suffrage, but only because he thought that to do so would provoke outrage; in principle he thought that on the basis of the greatest happiness principle 'the claim of [the female] sex is, if not still better, at least altogether as good as that of the other' (B ix. 108–9).

In recent years many utilitarians have extended the happiness principle beyond humankind to other sentient beings, claiming that animals have equal claims with human beings. Though a great lover of animals (especially cats) Bentham himself did not go as far as this, and he would have rejected the idea that animals have rights, because he did not believe in natural rights of any kind. But by making the supreme moral criterion a matter of sensation he made it appropriate to consider animals as belonging to the same moral community as ourselves since animals as well as humans feel pleasure and pain. This, in the long term, proved to be one of the most significant consequences of Bentham's break with the classical and Christian moral tradition, which placed supreme moral value in activities not of the sense but of the reason, and regarded non-rational animals as standing outside the moral community.

A second question about the principle of utility is this: should individuals, or politicians, in following the greatest happiness principle attempt to control the number of candidates for happiness (however these are defined)? Does the extension of happiness to a greater number mean that we should try to bring more people (or animals) into existence? What answer we give to this is linked to a third, even more difficult, question: when we are measuring the happiness of a population, do we consider only total happiness, or should we also consider average happiness? Should we take account of the distribution of happiness as well as of its quantity? If so, then we have to strike a difficult balance between quantity of happiness and quantity of people.

This issue is a problem rather for political philosophy than for moral philosophy. But even if we restrict our consideration to matters of individual morality, there remains a problem raised by the initial passage of the *Introduction* quoted above. The hedonism there proclaimed is twofold: there is a psychological hedonism (pleasure determines all our actions) and an ethical hedonism (pleasure is the standard of right and wrong). But the pleasure cited in psychological hedonism is the pleasure of the individual person; the pleasure invoked in ethical hedonism is the pleasure (however quantified) of the total moral community. If I am, in fact, predetermined in every action to aim at maximizing my own pleasure, what point is there in telling me that I am obliged to maximize the common good? This was a problem that was to exercise some of Bentham's successors in the utilitarian tradition.

Bentham commended utilitarianism by contrasting it with other ethical systems. The second chapter of the *Introduction* is entitled 'Of Principles Adverse to that of Utility'. He lists two such principles, the first being the principle of asceticism, and the second the principle of sympathy and antipathy. The principle of asceticism is the mirror image of the principle of utility, approving of actions to the extent that they tend to diminish the quantity of happiness. A man who accepts the principle of sympathy and antipathy, on the other hand, judges actions as good or bad to the extent that they accord or not with his own feelings (*P* 2. 2).

Bentham's principle of asceticism set up a straw man. Religious traditions have indeed set a high value on self-denial and mortification of the flesh; but even among religious teachers it is rare to find one who makes the infliction of suffering upon oneself the overarching principle of every action.[3] No one, religious or secular, had ever proposed a policy of pursuing the greatest misery of the greatest number. Bentham himself admits, 'The principle of asceticism never was, nor ever can be, consistently pursued by any living creature' (P 2. 10).

The principle of sympathy and antipathy is a catch-all that includes moral systems of very different kinds. Sympathy and antipathy, Bentham says, may be given various fancy names: moral sense, common sense, understanding, rule of right, fitness of things, law of nature, right reason, and so on. Moral systems that present themselves under such banners, Bentham believes, are all simply placing a grandiose screen in front of an appeal to individual subjective feeling. 'They consist all of them in so many contrivances for avoiding the obligation of appealing to any external standard, and for prevailing upon the reader to accept of the author's sentiment or opinion as a reason for itself' (P 2. 14). We cannot appeal to the will of God to settle whether something is right; we have to know first whether it is right in order to decide whether it is conformable to God's will. 'What is called the pleasure of God is, and must necessarily be (revelation apart) neither more nor less than the good pleasure of the person, whoever he be, who is pronouncing what he believes, or pretends, to be God's pleasure' (P 2. 18).

Bentham does not bring out what is the really significant difference between utilitarianism and other moral systems. We may divide moral philosophers into absolutists and consequentialists. Absolutists believe that there are some kinds of action that are intrinsically wrong, and should never be done, irrespective of any consideration of the consequences. Consequentialists believe that the morality of actions should be judged by their consequences, and that there is no category of act that may not, in special circumstances, be justified by its consequences. Prior to Bentham most philosophers were absolutists, because they believed in a natural law, or natural rights. If there are natural rights and a natural law, then some kinds of action, actions that violate those rights or conflict with that law, are wrong, no matter what the consequences.

Bentham rejected the notion of natural law, on the grounds that no two people could agree what it was. He was scornful of natural rights, believing

---

[3] One such is St John of the Cross, but even he sees this as a means to eventual superabundant happiness; see vol. III, p. 251.

that real rights could only be conferred by positive law; and his greatest scorn was directed to the idea that natural rights could not be overridden. 'Natural rights is simple nonsense: natural and imprescriptible rights, rhetorical nonsense—nonsense upon stilts' (*B* ii. 501). If there is no natural law and no natural rights, then no class of actions can be ruled out in advance of the consideration of the consequences of such an action in a particular case.

This difference between Bentham and previous moralists is highly significant, as can be easily illustrated. Aristotle, Aquinas, and almost all Christian moralists believed that adultery was always wrong. Not so for Bentham: the consequences foreseen by a particular adulterer must be taken into account before making a moral judgement. A believer in natural law, told that some Herod or Nero has killed 5,000 citizens guilty of no crime, will say without further ado, 'That was a wicked act'. A thoroughgoing consequentialist, before making such a judgement, must ask further questions. What were the consequences of the massacre? What did the monarch foresee? What would have happened if he had allowed the 5,000 to live?

Modifications of Utilitarianism

John Stuart Mill was, like Bentham, a consequentialist. But in other ways he toned down aspects of Bentham's teaching that had been found most offensive. In his treatise *Utilitarianism*, written in his late fifties, he acknowledges that many people have thought that the idea that life has no higher end than pleasure was a doctrine worthy only of swine. He replies that it is foolish to deny that humans have faculties that are higher than the ones they share with animals. This allows us to make distinctions between different pleasures not only in quantity but also in quality. 'It is quite compatible with the principle of utility to recognise the fact that some *kinds* of pleasure are more desirable and more valuable than others' (*U* 258).

How then do we grade the different kinds of pleasure? 'Of two pleasures', Mill tells us, 'if there be one to which all or almost all who have experience of both give a decided preference, irrespective of any feeling of moral obligation to prefer it, that is the more desirable pleasure.' Armed with this distinction a utilitarian can put a distance between himself and the swine. Few humans would wish to be changed into a lower animal even if promised a cornucopia of bestial pleasures. 'It is better to be a human being dissatisfied than a pig satisfied.' Again, no intelligent, educated person would wish, at any price, to become a foolish ignoramus. It is 'better to be Socrates dissatisfied than a fool satisfied' (*U* 260).

Happiness, according to Mill, involves not just contentment, but also a sense of dignity; any amount of the lower pleasures, without this, would not amount to happiness. Accordingly, the greatest happiness principle needs to be restated:

The ultimate end, with reference to and for the sake of which all other things are desirable (whether we are considering our own good or that of other people), is an existence exempt as far as possible from pain, and as rich as possible in enjoyments, both in point of quantity and quality; the test of quality, and the rule for measuring it against quantity, being the preference felt by those who in their opportunities of experience, to which must be added their habits of self-consciousness and self-observation, are best furnished with the means of comparison. (*U* 262)

Suppose, then, that a critic grants to Mill that utilitarianism need not be swinish. Still, he may insist, it does not appeal to the best in human nature. Virtue is more important than happiness, and acts of renunciation and self-sacrifice are the most splendid of human deeds. Mill agrees that it is noble to be capable of resigning one's own happiness for the sake of others—but would the hero or martyr's sacrifice be made if he did not believe that it would increase the amount of happiness in the world? A person who denies himself the enjoyment of life for any other purpose 'is no more deserving of admiration than the ascetic mounted on his pillar'.

Objections to utilitarianism come in two different forms. As a moral code, it may be thought to be too strict, or it may be thought to be too lax. Those who complain that it is too strict say that to insist that in every single action one should take account not just of one's own but of universal happiness is to demand a degree of altruism beyond the range of all but saints. Indeed, even to work out what is the most felicific of the choices available at any given moment calls for superhuman powers of calculation. Those who regard utilitarianism as too lax say that its abolition of absolute prohibitions on kinds of action opens a door for moral agents to persuade themselves whenever they feel like it that they are in the special circumstances that would justify an otherwise outrageous act. They could quote words that Mill himself wrote to Harriet Taylor soon after they met:

Where there exists a genuine and strong desire to do that which is most for the happiness of all, general rules are merely aids to prudence, in the choice of means; not peremptory obligations. Let but the desires be right, and the 'imagination lofty and refined'; & provided there be disdain of all false seeming, 'to the pure all things are pure'.[4]

In *Utilitarianism* Mill offers a defence on both fronts. Against the allegation of excessive rigour, he urges us to distinguish between a moral standard and a motive of action: utilitarianism, while offering universal happiness as the ultimate moral standard, does not require it to be the aim of every action. Moreover, there is no need to run through a felicific calculus in every case: it is absurd to talk 'as if, at the moment when some man feels tempted to meddle with the property or life of another, he had to begin considering for the first time whether murder and theft are injurious to human happiness' (*U* 275). To those who allege laxity, he responds with a *tu quoque*: all moral systems have to make room for conflicting obligations, and utility is not the only creed 'which is able to furnish us with excuses for evil doing, and means of cheating our own conscience' (*U* 277).

The difficulty about utilitarianism that Mill himself takes most seriously is the allegation that it is a recipe for preferring expedience to justice. Mill responds that the dictates of justice do indeed form part of the field of general expediency, but that nonetheless there is a difference between what is expedient, what is moral, and what is just. If something is expedient (in the sense of conducing to the general happiness) then, on utilitarian grounds, it should be done, but there need not be any question of duty involved. If something is not just expedient but also moral, then a duty arises; and it is part of the notion of a duty that a person may be rightly compelled to fulfil it. Not all duties, however, create correlative rights in other persons, and it is this extra element that makes the difference between morality in general and justice in particular: 'Justice implies something which is not only right to do, and wrong not to do, but which some individual person can claim from us as his moral right' (*U* 301). It is important, for Mill, to mark the connection between justice and *moral* rights: because he emphasizes that there can be legal rights that are unjust, and just claims that conflict with law.

---

[4] F. A. Hayek, *John Stuart Mill and Harriet Taylor* (London: Routledge, 1957), 59.

Mill explains how various notions connected with justice—desert, impartiality, equality—are to be reconciled with the utilitarian principle of expediency. With regard to quality, he cites a maxim of Bentham's, 'everybody to count for one, nobody for more than one'—each person's happiness is counted for exactly as much as another's. But he does not really address the problem inherent in the greatest happiness principle, that it leaves room for the misery of an individual to be discounted in order to increase the overall total of happiness in the community.

Indeed, in *Utilitarianism* Mill has little to say about distributive justice other than to note that those forms on offer vary from system to system:

Some Communists consider it unjust that the produce of the labour of the community should be shared on any other principle than that of exact equality; others think it just that those should receive most whose wants are greatest; while others hold that those who work harder, or who produce more, or whose services are more valuable to the community, may justly claim a larger quota in the division of the produce. And the sense of natural justice may be plausibly appealed to in behalf of every one of these opinions. (*U* 301)

Schopenhauer on Renunciation

The ethical teaching of Schopenhauer is closely linked to his metaphysics, and in particular to the theses that the world of experience is illusory and that the true reality, the thing-in-itself, is the universal will. We see individuals rising out of nothing, receiving their lives as a gift, and then suffering the loss of this gift in death, returning again to nothing. But if we consider life philosophically we find that the will, the thing-in-itself in all phenomena, is not at all affected by birth and death.

It is not the individual, but only the species, that Nature cares for, and for the preservation of which she so earnestly strives, providing for it with the utmost prodigality.... The individual, on the contrary, neither has nor can have any value for Nature, for her kingdom is infinite time and infinite space, and within these infinite multiplicity of possible individuals. Therefore she is always ready to let the individual fall, and hence it is not only exposed to destruction in a thousand ways by the most insignificant accident, but originally destined for it, and conducted towards it by Nature herself from the moment it has served its end of maintaining the species. (*WWI* 276)

We should be no more troubled by the thought that at death our individuality will be replaced by other individuals than we are troubled by the fact that in life every time we take in new food we excrete waste. Death is just a sleep in which individuality is forgotten. It is only as phenomenon that one individual is distinct from another. 'As thing-in-itself he is the will which appears in everything, and death destroys the illusion which separates his consciousness from that of the rest: this is afterlife or immortality' (*WWI* 282).

Morality is a matter of the training of character; but what this consists in can only be understood, according to Schopenhauer, if we accept Kant's

A portrait photograph of Schopenhauer taken about 1850

reconciliation of freedom with necessity. The will, which is the thing-in-itself, is free from eternity to eternity; but everything in nature, including human nature, is determined by necessity. Just as inanimate nature acts in accordance with laws and forces, so each human being has a character, from which different motives call forth his actions necessarily. If we had a complete knowledge of a person's character and the motives that are presented to him, we would be able to calculate his future conduct just as we can predict an eclipse of the sun or moon. We believe we are free to choose between alternatives, because prior to the choice we have no knowledge of how the will is going to decide; but the belief in liberty of indifference is an illusion.

If all our ethical conduct is determined by one's character, it might seem that it is a waste of trouble to try to improve oneself, and it is better simply to gratify every inclination that presents itself. In rejecting this, Schopenhauer makes a distinction between several kinds of character. There is what he calls the intelligible character, which is the underlying reality, outside time, that determines our response to the situations presented to us in the world. There is also the empirical character; that is to say, what we and others learn, through the course of experience, of the nature of our own intelligible character. Finally, there is the acquired character, which is achieved by those who have learnt the nature and limitations of their own individual character. These are persons of character in the best sense: people who recognize their own strengths and weaknesses, and tailor their projects and ambitions accordingly.

Our wills can never change, but many degrees are possible of awareness of will. Humans, unlike other animals, possess abstract and rational knowledge. This does not exempt them from the control of conflicting motives, but it makes them aware of the conflict, and this is what constitutes choice. Repentance, for instance, never proceeds from a change of will, which is impossible, but from a change of knowledge, from greater self-awareness. 'Knowledge of our own mind and its capacities of every kind, and their unalterable limits, is the surest way to the attainment of the greatest possible contentment with ourselves' (*WWI* 306).

Even to the best of humans, Schopenhauer holds out no great hope of contentment. We are all creatures of will, and will of its nature is insatiable. The basis of all willing is need and pain, and we suffer until our needs are satisfied. But if the will, once satisfied, lacks objects of desire, then life

230

becomes a burden of boredom. 'Thus life swings like a pendulum backwards and forwards between pain and ennui' (*WWI* 312). Walking is only constantly prevented falling; the life of our body is only ever-postponed death; the life of our mind is constantly deferred boredom. Want of food is the scourge of the working class, want of entertainment that of the world of fashion. All happiness is really and essentially negative, never positive.

The only sure way to escape the tyranny of the will is by complete renunciation. What the will wills is always life; so if we are to renounce the will we must renounce the will to live. This sounds like a recommendation to suicide; but in fact Schopenhauer condemned suicide as a false way of escape from the miseries of the world. Suicide could only be inspired by an overestimate of the individual life; it was motivated by concealed will to live.

Renunciation is renunciation of the self, and moral progress consists in the reduction of egoism, that is to say, the tendency of the individual to make itself the centre of the world and to sacrifice everything else to its own existence and well-being. All bad persons are egoists: they assert their own will to live, and deny the presence of that will in others, damaging, and perhaps destroying, the existence of others if they get in their way. There are people who are not only bad, but really wicked; they go beyond egoism, taking delight in the sufferings of others not just as a means to their own ends, but as an end in itself. Schopenhauer names Nero and Robespierre as examples of this level of cruelty.

A common or garden bad person, however, while regarding his own person as separated by a great gulf from others, nonetheless retains a dim awareness that his own will is just the phenomenal appearance of the single will to live that is active in all. He dimly sees that he is himself this whole will, and consequently he is not only the inflicter but the endurer of pain, a pain from which he is separated only by the illusive dream of space and time. This awareness finds its expression in remorse. Remorse in the bad man is the counterpart of resignation, which is the mark of the good man.

Between the bad man and the good man, there is an intermediate character: the just man. Unlike the bad man, the just man does not see individuality as being an absolute wall of partition between himself and others. Other persons, for him, are not mere masks, whose nature is quite different from his own. He is willing to recognize the will to live in others on the same level as his own, up to the point of abstaining from injury to his fellow humans.

In the really good man, the barrier of individuality is penetrated to a far greater degree, and the principle of individuation is no longer an absolute wall of partition. The good man sees that the distinction between himself and others, which to the bad man is so great a gulf, only belongs to a fleeting and illusive phenomenon. 'He is just as little likely to allow others to starve, while he himself has enough and to spare, as any one would be to suffer hunger one day in order to have more the next day than he could enjoy' (*WWI* 373).

But well doing and benevolence is not the highest ethical state, and the good man will soon be taken beyond it.

If he takes as much interest in the sufferings of other individuals as his own, and therefore is not only benevolent in the highest degree, but even ready to sacrifice his own individuality whenever such a sacrifice will save a number of other persons, then it clearly follows that such a man, who recognizes in all beings his own inmost and true self, must also regard the infinite suffering of all suffering beings as his own, and take on himself the pain of the whole world. (*WWI* 379)

This will lead him beyond virtue to asceticism. It will no longer be enough to love others as himself: he will experience a horror of the whole nature of which his own phenomenal existence is an expression. He will abandon the will to live, which is the kernel of this miserable world. He will do all he can to disown the nature of the world as expressed in his own body: he will practise complete chastity, adopt voluntary poverty, and take up fasting and self-chastisement. Schopenhauer's ideal man does indeed adopt the ascetic principle denounced by Bentham: 'he compels himself to refrain from doing all that he would like to do, and to do all that he would like not to do, even if this has no further end than that of serving to mortify his will' (*WWI* 382). Such asceticism, he says, is no vain ideal; it can be learned through suffering and it has been practised by many Christian, and still more by Hindu and Buddhist, saints.

It is true that the life of many saints has been full of the most absurd superstition. Religious systems, Schopenhauer believed, are the mythical clothing of truths which in their naked form are inaccessible to the uneducated multitude. But, he says, 'it is just as little needful that a saint should be a philosopher as that a philosopher should be a saint' (*WWI* 383)

The power of Schopenhauer's prose, and the enchantment of his metaphors, give the impress of grandeur to his ethical system. But it rests on a false metaphysic, and it leads to a self-stultifying conclusion. There is no reason to believe that the world is nothing but an illusory idea, or to accept that insatiable will is the ultimate reality. From the alternation between desire and satisfaction, Schopenhauer decided that life was a history of suffering and boredom; from the same premiss he might with equal justification have concluded that it was a history of excitement and contentment. In order to distinguish the world of will from the world of idea, and to reach a thing-in-itself, he has to persuade each of us that our own individuality is the fundamental reality; in order to persuade us to ascend the path through virtue to asceticism, he must get us to accept that our individuality is nothing but illusion.

Schopenhauer provides no convincing reason, other than a prejudice in favour of pessimism, why we should adopt the ascetic programme with which he concludes. To be sure, the more philanthropic a person is, the more she will identify with the lives of others; but why should she identify only with their sufferings and not also with their joys? St Francis of Assisi mortified his flesh as severely as any Indian mystic, and yet his prayer was that he would replace despair, darkness, and sadness with hope, light, and rejoicing.

The complete renunciation of the will to which we are called by Schopenhauer appears to be a contradiction in terms; for if the renunciation is voluntary, it is itself an act of the will, and if it is necessary it is not a real renunciation. Schopenhauer tries to escape by appealing to the Kantian distinction between a phenomenon that is necessary and a thing-in-itself that is free. But the will that is free is outside time, while the history of any self-denying saint belongs in the world of phenomena. One and the same act of self-denial cannot be both inside and outside time.

The Moral Ascent in Kierkegaard

Kierkegaard's moral system resembles Schopenhauer's in several ways. Both philosophers take a deeply pessimistic view of the ethical condition of the average human being, and both philosophers hold out a spiritual career that leads to renunciation. But whereas Schopenhauer's system was built on an atheistic metaphysic, Kierkegaard's evolves against a background of Protestant Christianity. For him the renunciation that is the high point of the ethical life is only a preliminary to an ultimate leap of faith. Whereas Schopenhauer's programme is designed to lead to the erasure of individuality, Kierkegaard's aims to put the individual in full possession of his own personality as a unique creature of God.

The final stage of the Kierkegaardian spiritual journey will be considered in Chapter 12; our present concern is with the previous stage—the ethical, which comes between the aesthetic and the religious. Kierkegaard's aesthetic person is governed by his feelings, and blind to spiritual values; but we must not think of him as a sensual boor, a philistine glutton, or a sexual deviant. As he is portrayed as one of the two protagonists in *Either/Or* he is a cultured, law-abiding person, popular in society and not without consideration for others. What distinguishes him from a serious moral agent is that he avoids entering into any engagements that would limit his capacity for the pursuit of whatever is immediately attractive. To preserve his freedom of choice he refuses to take any public or private office; he avoids any deep friendship, and marriage above all.

The aesthetic person, Kierkegaard argues, is deluded when he thinks of his existence as one of freedom; in fact it is extremely limited.

In case one were to think of a house, consisting of cellar, ground floor, and *premier étage*, so tenanted, or rather so arranged, that it was planned for a distinction of rank between the dwellers on the several floors; and in case one were to make a comparison between such a house and what it is to be a man—then unfortunately this is the sorry and ludicrous condition of the majority of men, that in their own house they prefer to live in the cellar. The soulish–bodily synthesis in every man is planned with a view to being spirit, such is the building; but the man prefers to dwell in the cellar, that is, in the determinants of sensuousness. And not only does he prefer to dwell in the cellar; no, he loves that to such a degree that he becomes furious if anyone would propose to him to occupy the *piano nobile* which stands empty at his disposition—for in fact he is dwelling in his own house. (*SD* 176)

Such a person, Kierkegaard says, is in a state of despair. 'Despair', as used in *Sickness unto Death* and other works, does not mean a state of gloom or despondency; the aesthetic person, in fact, may well believe that he is happy. A despairing person, in Kierkegaard's terms, is a person who has no hope of anything higher than his present life. To despair is to lack awareness of the possibility of achieving a higher, spiritual self. Despair, so understood, is not a rare, but a well-nigh universal phenomenon. Most men, in Kierkegaard's expressive phrase, 'pawn themselves to the world'. 'They use their talents, accumulate money, carry on worldly affairs, calculate shrewdly etc., etc., are perhaps mentioned in history, but themselves they are not; spiritually understood they have no self, no self for whose sake they could venture everything' (*SD* 168).

The first step towards a cure is the realization that one is in despair. Already, in the hidden recesses of the aesthetic person's happiness, there dwells an anxious dread. Gradually, he may come to realize that his dissipation is a dispersal of himself. He will be faced with the choice of abandoning himself to despair, or of moving upward by committing himself to an ethical existence.

The nature of such an existence, and the necessity for undertaking it, is spelt out most fully in the correspondence of Judge Vilhelm, the fictional author of the second part of *Either/Or*. Vilhelm is himself a fully paid-up member of ethical society: he is happily married, the father of four children, and a civil court judge. Unhappily for the reader, he also has a ponderous and repetitious manner of writing style, quite different from the witty and novelettish style with which Kierkegaard endowed the aesthetic author of *Either/Or*'s first part, who is now the recipient of the edifying letters.

Vilhelm goes to great lengths to express the contrast between the aesthetic and the ethical character, and sums it up in the following terms:

We said that every aesthetic life-view was despair; this was because it was built upon what may or may not be. That is not the case with the ethical life-view, for this builds life upon what has being as its essential property. The aesthetic, we said, is that in which a person is immediately what he is; the ethical is that whereby a person becomes what he becomes. (*E/O* 525)

Kierkegaard attaches great importance to the concept of the self. People often wish to have the talents or virtues of others; but they never seriously wish to be another person, to have a self other than their own (*E/O* 517). In the aesthetic stage, the self is undeveloped and undifferentiated; a morass of unrealized and conflicting possibilities: life is a hysterical series of experiments with no outcome. The aesthete is in a state of permanent pregnancy: always in travail and never giving birth to a self. To enter the ethical stage is to undertake the formation of one's true self, where 'self' means something like a freely chosen character. Instead of merely developing one's talents one follows a vocation. The ethical life is a life of duty; of duty, however, not externally imposed but internally realized. The proper development of the individual involves the internalization of universal law.

> Only when the individual himself is the universal, only then can the ethical be realised. This is the secret of conscience; it is the secret the individual life shares with itself, that is at one and the same time an individual life and also the universal.... The person who regards life ethically sees the universal, and the person who lives ethically expresses his life in the universal; he makes himself into the universal man, not by divesting himself of his concretion, for then he would be nothing at all, but by clothing himself in it and permeating it with the universal. (E/O 547)

In grammars of foreign languages, some particular word is chosen as a paradigm to illustrate the way that nouns decline and verbs conjugate. The words chosen have no particular priority over any other noun and verb, but they teach us something about every noun and verb. In a similar sense, Vilhelm says, 'Everyone can, if he wants, become a paradigm man, not by wiping out his contingency but by remaining in it and ennobling it. But he ennobles it by choosing it' (E/O 552). The pattern that he lays out to be followed leads through the acquisition of personal virtues, through the civic virtues, and ends finally with the religious virtues. The man whom Kierkegaard most often chooses as a paradigm of the ethical person is Socrates. His life illustrates the fact that the ethical stage may make strict demands on the individual, and call for heroic self-sacrifice.

Judge Vilhelm does not offer us Kierkegaard's last word on morality, because in his system the ethical is not the highest category. Kierkegaard himself neither took a job nor got married, which are the two marks of the ethical life. Because of his own and his family's history he felt incapable of the total sharing of all secrets which he thought was essential to a good marriage. Faced with the demands made by the ethical life, Kierkegaard tells us, the individual becomes vividly conscious of human weakness; he may try to overcome it by strength of will, but find himself unable to do so. He becomes aware that his own powers are insufficient to meet the demands of the moral law. This brings him to a sense of guilt and a consciousness of sinfulness. If he is to escape from this, he must rise from the ethical sphere to this religious sphere: he must make 'the leap of faith'.[5]

Nietzsche and the Transvaluation of Values

Nietzsche agreed with Kierkegaard that a call to the Christian life was something that could not be justified by reason. But whereas Kierkegaard concluded, 'So much the worse for mere reason', Nietzsche concluded, 'So much the worse for the call of Christianity'. Not that Nietzsche spent much time in demonstrating that Christianity was irrational: his main complaint against it was rather that it was base and degrading. In works like *The Genealogy of Morals* he seeks not so much to refute the claims of Christian morality as to trace its ignoble pedigree.

History, Nietzsche says, exhibits two different kinds of morality. In the earliest times, strong, privileged aristocrats, feeling themselves to belong to a higher order than their fellows, described their own qualities—noble birth, bravery, candour, blondness, and the like—as 'good'. They regarded the characteristics of the plebeians—vulgarity, cowardice, untruthfulness, and swarthiness—as 'bad'. That is master-morality. The poor and weak, resenting the power and riches of the aristocrats, turned this system on its head. They set up their own contrasting system of values, a morality for the herd that puts a premium on traits such as humility, sympathy, and benevolence, which benefit the underdog. They saw the aristocratic type of person not just as bad (*schlecht*) but as positively evil (*böse*). The erection of this new system Nietzsche called 'a transvaluation of values', and he blamed it on the Jews.

It was the Jews who, reversing the aristocratic equation (good = noble = beautiful = happy = loved by the gods), dared with a frightening consistency to suggest the contrary equation, and to hold on to it with the teeth of the most profound hatred (the hatred of the powerless). It is they who have declared 'the wretched alone are the good; the poor, the weak, the lowly are alone good; the suffering, the needy, the sick, the hideous, are the only ones who are pious, the only ones who are blessed, for them alone is salvation. You, on the other hand, you noblemen, you men of power, you are to all eternity the evil, the cruel, the covetous, the

---

[5] Kierkegaard's teaching on faith and religion is discussed in Ch. 12 below.

insatiate, and the godless ones. You will be forever unblessed, accursed, and damned.' (*GM* 19)

The revolt of the slaves, begun by the Jews, achieved its triumph with the rise of Christianity. In Rome itself, once the fatherland of aristocratic virtue, men now bow down to four Jews: Jesus, Mary, Peter, and Paul (*GM* 36).

Christianity puts itself forward as a religion of love, but in fact, according to Nietzsche, it is rooted in weakness, fear, and malice. Its dominant motive is what he calls *ressentiment*, the desire of the weak for revenge on the strong, which disguises itself as a wish to punish the sinner. Christians pose as the executors of divine commands, but this is only to cloak their own bad conscience. Christians exalt compassion as a virtue, but when they assist the afflicted it is commonly because they enjoy exercising power over them. Even when philanthropy is not hypocritical it does more harm than good, by humiliating the sufferer. Pity is a poison that infects a compassionate person with the sufferings of others (*Z* 112).

The success of Christianity has led to the degeneration of the human race. Systematic tenderness for the weak lowers the general health and strength of mankind. Modern man, as a result, is a mere dwarf, who has lost the will to be truly human. Vulgarity and mediocrity become the norm; only rarely there still flashes out an embodiment of the noble ideal.

The herd-man in Europe nowadays puts on airs as if he were the only acceptable type of human being. He glorifies the qualities that make him tame, docile, and useful to the herd as if they were the true human virtues: public spirit, benevolence, considerateness, industriousness, moderation, modesty, tolerance, compassion. But there are cases where a leader or bell-wether is felt to be indispensable; in such cases people keep trying to set up an aggregation of clever herd-men in place of real commanders: that is the origin, for instance, of all parliamentary constitutions. But what a blessing, in spite of everything, what a release from an increasingly unbearable burden is the appearance of an absolute commander for these herd-Europeans! This was demonstrated most recently by the effect of Napoleon when he appeared on the scene. The history of the impact of Napoleon can be said to be the history of the highest happiness this entire century has achieved in its most valuable men and moments. (*BGE* 86)

If the human race is to be saved from decadence, the first step must be to reverse the values of Christianity, introducing a second transvaluation of values. 'The weak and the failures shall perish: that is the first principle of *our* love of mankind,' Nietzsche wrote on the first page of his *Antichrist*.

Human beings fell into two types: 'ascending' people and 'descending' people, that is to say, people who represented the upward and downward track of human evolution. It was not always easy to tell which was which—only Nietzsche himself had a perfect nose to discriminate between the two—but once detected, the descending creatures had to make way for the well-constituted, taking away from them as little space, energy, and sunshine as possible (*WP* 373).

However, it is not just Christian morality that must be overturned. We must go beyond the opposition between good and evil that is the feature of any slave morality. It is not only Christians, for instance, who regard truth as a fundamental value. But we should not, Nietzsche argues, object to judgements just because they are false.

The question is rather to what extent the judgement promotes life, preserves life, preserves the species, perhaps even enhances the species. We are in principle inclined to claim that judgements that are most false—including synthetic a priori judgements—are the ones most indispensable to us. Human beings could not live without accepting logical fictions ... To give up false judgements would be to give up life, to deny life. Recognizing untruth as a condition of life? What a dangerous rejection of traditional values! A philosophy that dares to do this has already placed itself beyond good and evil. (*BGE* 7)

Truth is that kind of error without which a particular living being could not survive. Life is the supreme value by which all others are to be judged. 'Whenever we speak of values', Nietzsche wrote, 'we speak under the inspiration of life and from the perspective of life. Life itself forces us to establish values; it is life that does the evaluation by means of us whenever we posit values' (*TI* 24). Human life is the highest form of life that has so far emerged, but in the contemporary world it has sunk to the level of some of the forms that preceded it. We must affirm life and bring it to a new level, a synthesis transcending the thesis and antithesis of master and slave, the Superman (*Ubermensch*).

The proclamation of the Superman is the prophetic message of Nietzsche's oracular spokesman Zarathustra. The Superman will be the highest form of life, the ultimate affirmation of the will to live. But our will to live must not be, like Schopenhauer's, one that favours the weak; it must be a will to power. The will to power is the secret of all life; every living thing seeks to discharge its force, to give full scope to its ability. Pleasure is merely the consciousness of power's exercise. Knowledge—to

Supermen as represented on the jacket of a Nietzschean book.

the extent that there can be knowledge when there is no absolute truth—
is merely an instrument of power. The greatest realization of human
power will be the creation of Superman.

Humanity is merely a stage on the way to Superman, who is what gives
meaning to the world. 'Humanity is something that must be surpassed: man
is a bridge and not a goal' (Z 44). Superman, however, will not come into
existence through the forces of evolution, but only through the exercise of
will. 'Let your will say "Superman *is to be* the meaning of the earth." '

Zarathustra says: 'You could surely create the Superman! Perhaps not
you yourselves, my brothers! But you could transform yourselves into
forefathers and ancestors of the Superman: and let this be your finest
creation!' The arrival of Superman will be the perfection of the world and
give it meaning. But because of the eternal recurrence, it will not be the
end of history. Superman will have a second, and a third, and an infinite
number of comings.

What will Superman be like? This is something we need to know if his
character is to present any standard by which to make a judgement of
human virtue and vice. But Zarathustra has very little to tell us about him,
and in his later philosophical works Nietzsche no longer employed the
concept. He does, however, continue to talk of 'higher human beings', and
we get the impression that his ideal would be a combination of Goethe and
Napoleon, each of whom, in different ways, developed a variety of talents
to their maximum degree. The combination is a more plausible one than
another that he once scribbled in a notebook, 'Roman Caesar with the soul
of Christ'.

240

It is difficult to make a critical judgement about Nietzsche's ethics, since his writing is often wilfully chaotic, and it is unsurprising that scholars vary widely in their interpretation and evaluation. It is not easy, for instance, to find out where Nietzsche stands on an issue such as the morality of cruelty. When denouncing the role played by guilt in slave morality, he describes with eloquent outrage the tortures inflicted by persecuting bigots. But he is tender to the excesses of his aristocratic 'blond beasts' who 'perhaps come from a ghastly bout of murder, arson, rape, and torture, with bravado and a moral equanimity, as though some wild student's prank had been played'.

Certainly Nietzsche is an enthusiast where war is concerned. 'Renouncing war', he wrote, 'means renouncing the *great* life' (*TI* 23). War is an education in freedom, and freedom means that the manly instincts that delight in victory triumph over any other instinct, including the desire for happiness. 'The *liberated* man, and even more the liberated *spirit*, tramples underfoot the despicable kind of well-being that shopkeepers, Christians, cows, women, Englishmen, and other democrats, dream of' (*TI* 65).

Suicide, too, in certain circumstances engages Nietzsche's admiration. Physicians should remind their patients that sick persons are parasites on society, and that a time comes when it is indecent to live longer.

Die proudly if it is no longer possible to live proudly. Death freely chosen, death at the right time, brought about cheerfully and joyfully among children and witnesses—so that a real leave-taking is still possible, when the one who is taking his leave *is still there*; a true assessment of one's achievements and ambitions, a summing up of one's life—all this in contrast to the ghastly and pitiful comedy that Christianity has made of the hour of death. (*TI* 61)

If you do away with yourself, Nietzsche concludes, you are doing what is most admirable: it almost earns you the right to live.

But is Nietzsche an ethicist at all? Is he a genuine moralist with highly unconventional views of virtue and vice, or is he a completely amoral person with no concern for right and wrong? On the one hand, he is clearly operating in the same field as some great past moralists: his ideal human being bears a resemblance to the great-souled man of Aristotle's *Nicomachean Ethics*. On the other hand, he himself professes not just to be presenting novel views of good and evil, but to be transcending those categories altogether. He calls himself an immoralist, and tells us that there are no moral facts, and he does his best to devalue two of the key concepts of most moral systems, namely justice and guilt.

The answer, I think, is that Nietzsche shares with traditional morality an ultimate concern with human flourishing, and the reason that he condemns many conventional virtues is precisely because he believes that they hinder rather than help the achievement of a worthwhile life. But in his preference for the great over the good, and for the nobleman over the gentleman, he shows himself to have a fundamentally aesthetic, rather than ethical, criterion of the good life. His ideal human being not only does not love his neighbour: he *has* no neighbour.

Analytic Ethics

As an ethicist, G. E. Moore stands at the opposite pole from Nietzsche. He placed goodness at the apex of the pyramid of moral concepts, and he was not at all interested in genealogical questions of the origin and development of the concept. In his *Principia Ethica* (1903) he sees himself as giving an answer to the question 'How is goodness to be defined?' simply by inspection of the object or idea that the word 'good' stands for. The question, he maintained, is fundamental and must be faced before we ask what kinds of actions we ought to perform. For the actions we ought to perform are those that will cause more good to exist in the universe than any possible kind of alternative.

So before we ask what things are good, we must ask what kind of property goodness itself is. The question, he maintained, could not be answered by giving any definition of goodness, because goodness was a simple, indefinable notion, like the notion of yellow. But unlike yellowness, which was a natural property of things, goodness, Moore maintained, was a non-natural quality. If we consider goodness, and any other property akin to it, such as pleasantness, we will see that 'we have two different notions before our minds'. Even if everything good were in fact pleasant, it does not follow that 'good' and 'pleasant' mean the same. To identify goodness with any property such as pleasantness was to commit a fallacy: the naturalistic fallacy, of confusing a non-natural property with a natural one.

Though Moore maintained that goodness was not a natural property, he did not deny that it could be a property of natural things. Indeed, it was a principal task of moral philosophy to determine what things possessed this non-natural property. After lengthy investigation Moore came to the conclusion that the only things that have intrinsic goodness are friendship and aesthetic experience.

The arguments in *Principia Ethica* are extraordinarily flimsy, and Moore himself was later to admit that 'I did not give any tenable explanation of what I meant by saying that "good" was not a natural property.'[6] Yet the book was remarkably influential, especially through two significant groups of admirers. The Bloomsbury group, in particular J. M. Keynes, Lytton Strachey, and E. M. Forster, held up the book as a charter for a lifestyle that threw overboard conventional notions of respectability and rectitude. In addition, professional philosophers who could not swallow the notion of goodness as a non-natural property nonetheless used the expression 'naturalistic fallacy' as a mantra to dispose of moral theories of which they disapproved.

Under the influence of logical positivism, however, some philosophers began to deny that goodness was any sort of property, natural or non-natural, and to claim that ethical utterances were not statements of fact at all. Thus A. J. Ayer maintained that if I say 'Stealing money is wrong',

I produce a sentence which has no factual meaning—that is, expresses no proposition which can be either true or false. It is as if I had written 'Stealing money!!'—where the shape and thickness of the exclamation marks show, by a suitable convention, that a special sort of moral disapproval is the feeling which is being expressed. It is clear that there is nothing said here which can be true or false. Another man may disagree with me about the wrongness of stealing, in the sense that he may not have the same feelings about stealing as I have, and he may quarrel with me on account of my moral sentiments. But he cannot, strictly speaking, contradict me. (*LTL* 107)

This view of ethical utterances was called 'emotivism'. While Ayer laid stress on the expression of one's own emotion, other emotivists saw as the function of moral language the encouragement of feelings and attitudes in other people. But no emotivist was able to give a convincing account of the particular character of the sentiments in question, or to show in what way logic enters into moral reasoning when we use words like 'because' and 'therefore'.

[6] P. A. Schilpp (ed.), *The Philosophy of G. E. Moore* (Chicago: Open Court, 1942).

R. M. Hare (1919–2002), an Oxford tutor who later became White's Professor of Moral Philosophy, was anxious to make room in ethics for logic. In *The Language of Morals* (1952) and in *Freedom and Reason* (1963) Hare pointed out that there is a logic of imperatives no less than a logic of assertion, and he drew on this to expound a theory of moral reasoning. He distinguished between prescriptive and descriptive meaning. A descriptive statement is one whose meaning is defined by the factual conditions for its truth. A prescriptive sentence is one that entails, perhaps in conjunction with descriptive statements, at least one imperative. To assent to an imperative is to prescribe action, to tell oneself or others to do this or do that. Prescriptive language comes in two forms: there are straightforward imperatives, and there are value judgements.

Value judgements may contain a word like 'good' or a word like 'ought'. To call something 'good' is to commend it; to call something a good X is to say that it is the kind of X that should be chosen by anyone who wants an X. There will be different criteria for the goodness of Xs and the goodness of Ys, but this does not amount to a difference in the meaning of the word 'good', which is exhausted by its commendatory function. 'Ought' statements—which Hare, following Hume, thought could never be derived from 'is' statements—entail imperatives. 'A ought to Φ' entails an order to Φ addressed not only to A but to anyone else in a relevantly similar situation, and the addressees include the utterer of the sentence himself. The utterer's willingness to obey the order, if the occasion arises, is the criterion of his sincerity in uttering the sentence. Ought-sentences are not just prescriptive, but unlike common or garden commands they are universalizable.

Hare distinguished between ethics and morals. Ethics is the study of the general features of moral language, of which prescriptivity and universal-izability are the most important; moral judgements are prescriptions and prohibitions of specific actions. In principle, ethics is neutral between different and conflicting moral systems. But this does not mean that ethics is practically vacuous: once an understanding of ethics is combined with the desires and beliefs of an actual moral agent, it can lead to concrete and important moral judgements.

The way in which prescriptivity and universalizability enter into actual moral argument is explained thus by Hare. Though nothing other than my own choices gives authority to my moral judgements, my choices in addition to the logical properties of moral language give rise to something like a Golden Rule. Let us suppose that A owes money to B, B owes money to C, and neither is in a position to repay the debt on the due date. B may judge 'A ought to go to prison'. But since this judgement is univerzalisable, and B is in the same position as A, the judgement entails for B 'I ought to go to prison'—a judgement that is unlikely to command his assent. Hare maintained that considerations of this sort would lead to the adoption of a roughly utilitarian system of moral judgements, since he believed, implausibly, that only a small minority of fanatics would be content to be done by as they had done to others.

In the late 1950s Hare's prescriptivism was subjected to devastating criticism by a number of colleagues living in Oxford, notably Foot, Geach, and Anscombe.

Philippa Foot (b. 1920) in 'Moral Beliefs' (1958) and 'Goodness and Choice' (1961) attacked the distinction between descriptive and evaluative predicates by concentrating attention on the names of particular virtues and vices. She invites us to consider words like 'rude' and 'courageous'. It is not difficult to describe in purely factual terms behaviour that would merit these epithets; yet calling someone rude or courageous is clearly a matter of evaluation.

A judgement cannot be treated as moral judgement, Foot argued, simply on the basis of formal characteristics such as universalizability and prescriptivity. Merely by making the appropriate choices one cannot make clasping the hands three times in an hour into a good action, or determine that what makes a man a good man is having red hair. Moral beliefs must concern traits and actions that are beneficial or harmful to human beings. Since it is not a matter of human decision which traits and actions promote or diminish human flourishing, moral judgements likewise cannot depend simply on human choice.

In the ancient and medieval world the analysis of virtues and vices, and the investigation of their relationship to happiness, was a very substantial part of moral philosophy. It is largely due to Philippa Foot that in recent decades virtue theory, after centuries of neglect, has come to occupy a prominent part in moral philosophy.

Peter Geach (b. 1919) in 'Good and Evil' (1956) attacked the descriptive–evaluative distinction in the case also of the most general terms, such as 'good'. The important distinction, he claimed, is that between attributive and predicative terms. In the case of a predicative term like 'red' one can know what it is for an X to be red without knowing what an X is. The case is not the same with attributive terms like 'large' or 'false'. 'Good' and 'bad', Geach says, are always attributive, not predicative. If we say of an individual A that he is good *simpliciter*, we really mean that he is a good man, and if we call some behaviour good, we mean that it is a good human action. It is therefore folly to look for some property called goodness, or some activity called commending, which is always present when we call something good.

In 'Assertion' (1965) Geach showed that the meaning of 'good' could not be explained in terms of commendation, because in many contexts we use it without any intention of commending. 'Good' can be predicated, for instance, in if-clauses. Someone who says 'If contraception is a good thing, then free distribution of condoms is a good thing' need not be commending either contraception or the free distribution of condoms. Of course, 'good' may on occasion be used to commend, but this does not mean that its primary meaning is not descriptive.

Geach's wife, Elizabeth Anscombe, wrote an influential paper in 1958, 'Modern Moral Philosophy'. This was a frontal attack not only on Hare but on the whole of Anglophone moral philosophy since the time of Sidgwick. Its first paragraph proclaims a resounding thesis:

The concepts of obligation and duty—*moral* obligation and *moral* duty, that is to say—and of what is *morally* right and wrong, and of the *moral* sense of 'ought', ought to be jettisoned if this is psychologically possible; because they are survivals, or derivatives of survivals, from an earlier conception of ethics which no longer generally survives, and are only harmful without it. (*ERP* 26)

Aristotle has much to say about the virtues and vices, but he has no concept answering to our term 'moral'. It was Christianity, taking its moral notions from the Torah, that introduced a *law* conception of ethics. Conformity to the virtues and avoidance of the vices henceforth became a requirement of divine law.

Naturally it is not possible to have such a conception unless you believe in God as a lawgiver; like Jews, Stoics and Christians. But if such a conception is dominant for many centuries, and then is given up, it is a natural result that the concepts of 'obligation', of being bound or required as by a law, should remain though they had lost their root; and if the word 'ought' has become invested in certain contexts with the sense of 'obligation', it too will remain to be spoken with a special emphasis and a

Elizabeth Anscombe and Peter Geach, the most intellectually formidable philosophical couple of the twentieth century

special feeling in these contexts. It is as if the notion 'criminal' were to remain when criminal law and criminal courts had been abolished and forgotten. (*ERP* 30)

It is true, as philosophers have said since Hume, that one cannot infer an 'ought'—a moral 'ought'—from an 'is'; but that is because this 'ought' has become a word of mere mesmeric force, once the notion of a divine lawgiver has been dropped.

The most significant practical result of this, Anscombe maintained, is that philosophers have all become consequentialists, believing that the right action is the one with the best possible consequences. Every one of the best-known English academic ethicists 'has put out a philosophy according to which, e.g. it is not possible to hold that it cannot be right to kill the innocent as a means to any end whatsoever and that someone who thinks otherwise is in error'. This means that all their philosophies are incompatible with the Hebrew–Christian ethic, which held that there are certain things forbidden whatever consequences threaten. According to Anscombe, the differences between individual philosophers since Sidgwick are, in comparison with this incompatibility, unimportant and provincial.

The notions of duty, and of moral right and wrong, Anscombe proposed, should be discarded in favour of the notions of justice and injustice, which had a genuine content. Even of these notions it remained difficult to give a clear account, until we had a satisfactory philosophical psychology. For one cannot analyse the concepts of justice and virtue unless one has a satisfactory account of such terms as 'action', 'intention', 'pleasure', and 'wanting'. Anscombe herself made a monumental contribution to this area of philosophy in her book *Intention* (1957), which was taken as a model by many later investigators.

In the latter part of the twentieth century a variety of approaches to ethics was explored by English-speaking philosophers, and in Britain no single philosopher stood out as a prime exponent of ethical theory, as for a time Hare had done. In reaction to Hare's revival of Kantian morality a number of philosophers placed a renewed focus on themes of Aristotelian ethics. Thus Philippa Foot laid emphasis on the central role of virtue in morality, inspiring a school of 'virtue ethics', and Bernard Williams reminded philosophers of the great part played by luck in determining one's moral situation.

Foot's starting point is that the virtues are characteristics that any human being needs to have both for his own sake and for that of others. They differ from other qualities necessary for flourishing—such as health and strength, intelligence and skill—in that they are not mere capacities, but they engage the will. They concern matters that are difficult for humans, and where there are temptations to be resisted; but *pace* Kant moral worth is not to be measured by the difficulty of moral action. The really virtuous person is one who does good actions almost effortlessly: a really charitable person, for instance, is one who finds it easy, rather than hard, to make the sacrifices that charity calls for. Without the virtues the life of a human being is stunted, in the way that the life of an animal lacking a sense-faculty is stunted.

Williams began by recalling the way in which in the classical tradition happiness had been regarded as the product of self-sufficiency: what was not in the domain of the self was not in its control and so was subject to luck and the contingent enemies of tranquillity. In more recent thought, the ideal of making the whole of life immune to luck was abandoned, but for Kant there was one supreme value, moral value, that could be regarded as immune: the successful moral life was a career open not merely to the talents but to a talent that all rational beings necessarily possess in the same degree. Williams insisted that the aim of making morality immune to luck was bound to be disappointed. There is the constitutive luck of the temperament we inherit and the culture into which we are born: this sets the conditions within which our moral dispositions, motives, and intentions must operate. There is also—and Williams developed this theme in telling detail—the incident luck that is involved in bringing any project of moral importance to a successful conclusion.

As the century progressed philosophers began to focus their attention not so much on the higher-order questions such as the nature of moral language, or the relationships between principles, character, luck, and virtue, but on specific first-order issues such as the rightness or wrongness of particular actions: lying, abortion, torture, and euthanasia, for example. Foot and Williams played a significant part in this change of emphasis, which was also reflected in universities in the growth of such courses as medical ethics and business ethics.

Both Foot and Williams taught on both sides of the Atlantic. In the United States the most significant moral philosopher of the latter part of the twentieth century was John Rawls. Like Foot and Williams, Rawls was an enemy of utilitarianism, a system that he believed provided no safeguard against many forms of unfair discrimination. His project was to derive a theory of justice from the notion of fairness, which he did by introducing a novel version of social contract theory into ethics. Since the major implications of his theory concern political institutions rather than individual morality, his work will be considered later, in Chapter 11.

10

Aesthetics

The Beautiful and the Sublime

The person generally held to be the founder of aesthetics as an independent philosophical discipline is Alexander Gottlieb Baumgarten (1714–62). Certainly it was he who coined the word 'aesthetics', in a short treatise on poetry published in 1735. For Baumgarten, the purpose of art is to produce beauty, defined in terms of the ordered relationship between the parts of a whole. The point of beauty is to give pleasure and arouse desire. The finest beauty is to be found in nature, and therefore the highest aim of art is to imitate nature.

Other eighteenth-century philosophers sought to give a more precise analysis of beauty. Hume, in the section of his *Treatise of Human Nature* entitled 'Of Beauty and Deformity', offered the following definition:

beauty is such an order and constitution of parts, as either by the *primary constitution* of our nature, by *custom*, or by *caprice*, is fitted to give a pleasure and satisfaction to the soul. This is the distinguishing character of beauty, and forms all the difference betwixt it and deformity, whose natural tendency is to produce uneasiness. Pleasure and pain, therefore, are not only necessary attendants of beauty and deformity, but constitute their very essence. (ii. i. 8)

Later, Hume was dissatisfied with the idea that unexamined custom and uneducated caprice could determine beauty; he sought to make room, in aesthetic judgements, for correctness and incorrectness. In *The Standard of Taste* (1757) he argued that the criteria of judgement should be established by ascertaining which features of works of art were most highly pleasing to qualified and impartial connoisseurs.

Edmund Burke (1729–97) introduced into aesthetics, alongside the concept of beauty, that of sublimity. The sublime, as well as the beautiful, can be the aim of art: a feeling of beauty is a form of love without desire, and to feel something as sublime is to feel astonishment without fear. In *A Philosophical Inquiry into the Origin of our Ideas of the Sublime and the Beautiful* Burke sought to explain by what qualities objects inspire these feelings in us. He traced the feeling for the sublime to the fears and horrors implicit in the original instinct for self-preservation. The feeling for beauty, whose paradigm is a chaste appreciation of female perfection, derives, he maintained, from the need for social contact and ultimately from the instinct to propagate the race.

The treatise that dominated aesthetics in the nineteenth century was Kant's *Critique of Judgement* (1790). In his 'Analytic of the Beautiful' and 'Analytic of the Sublime' Kant sought to do for aesthetics what his earlier Critiques had done for epistemology and ethics. Human beings possess, in addition to theoretical understanding and practical reason, a third faculty, the capacity for judgement (*Urteilskraft*), the judgement of taste, which is the basis of aesthetic experience.

Agreeing with Burke, and disagreeing with Baumgarten, Kant sees disinterestedness as fundamental to the aesthetic response. 'Taste', he says, 'is the faculty of judging of an object or a method of representing it by an *entirely disinterested* satisfaction or dissatisfaction. The object of such satisfaction is called *beautiful*' (M 45).

Kant makes a distinction between two kinds of satisfaction: he calls sensual delight 'gratification' and reserves the notion of 'pleasingness' for the disinterested enjoyment of beauty. He writes, 'What gratifies a person is called pleasurable; what merely pleases him is called beautiful; what he values is called good.' Animals enjoy pleasure, but only humans appreciate beauty. Only the taste for beauty is completely disinterested, because the practical reason that determines goodness has reference to our own well-being. To point the difference, Kant remarks that while we can distinguish between what is good in itself and what is good only as a means, we do not make any parallel distinction between what is beautiful as a means and what is beautiful as an end (M 42).

A judgement of taste, Kant tells us, does not bring an experience under a concept, in the way that an ordinary judgement does; it relates the experience directly to the disinterested pleasure. Unlike an expression of

251

sensual pleasure, it claims universal validity. If I like the taste of Madeira, I don't go on to claim that everyone else should like it too; but if I think a poem, a building, or a symphony beautiful, I impute to others an obligation to agree with me. Judgements of taste are singular in form ('This rose is beautiful') but universal in import; they are, as Kant puts it, expressions of 'a universal voice'. Yet, because a judgement of taste does not bring its object under a concept, no reason can be given for it and no argument can constrain agreement to it.

Judgements of value are related to purpose. If I want to know whether an X is a good X, I need to know what Xs are for—that is how I tell what makes a good knife, or a good plumber, and so on. Judgements of perfection are similar: I cannot know what is a perfect X without knowing what is the function of an X. Judgements of beauty, however, cannot be quite like this, since they do not bring their objects under any concept X. However, Kant maintains that beautiful objects exhibit 'purposiveness without purpose'. By this he means perhaps that while beauty has no point, yet it invites us to linger over its contemplation.

This obscure thesis becomes clearer when Kant makes a distinction between types of beauty. There are two kinds of beauty: free beauty (*pulchritudo vaga*) and derivative beauty (*pulchritudo adhaerens*). The first pre-supposes no concept of what the object ought to be; the second does presuppose such a concept, and the perfection of the object in accordance therewith. The first is called the self-subsistent beauty of this or that thing; the second, as dependent upon a concept (conditioned beauty), is ascribed to objects with a particular purpose. A judgement of beauty without reference to any purpose that an object is to serve is a pure judgement of taste. A flower is Kant's regular paradigm of a free natural beauty. As for the other kind of beauty: 'Human beauty (i.e. of a man, a woman, or a child), the beauty of a horse, or a building (be it church, palace, arsenal or summer house), presupposes a concept of the purpose which determines what the thing is to be, and consequently a concept of its perfection; it is therefore derivative beauty' (M 66).

It is clear from this passage that Kant's aesthetic is much more at home with natural beauty than with the beauty of artefacts. But the problem he is mainly concerned with arises in both contexts. How can a judgement of beauty, a judgement that is not based on reason, claim universal validity? When I make such a judgement, I do not claim that everyone will agree with me, but I do claim that everyone ought to do so. This is only possible if we are all in possession of a common sensibility (*Gemeinsinn*)—a sensibility which, since it is normative, cannot derive from experience but must be transcendental.

Kant begins his 'Analytic of the Sublime' with a distinction between two kinds of sublimity, which he calls (not very happily) the mathematical and the dynamical. In each case the sublime object is vast, great, overwhelming; but in the mathematical case what is overwhelmed is our perception and in the dynamical case what is overwhelmed is our power. Whatever is mathematically sublime is too great to be taken in by any of our senses; it awakens in us the feeling of a faculty above sense which reaches out towards infinity. Whatever is dynamically sublime is something to which any resistance on our part would be vain, but which yet allows us to remain without fear in a state of security.

Bold, overhanging, and as it were threatening rocks; clouds piled up in the sky, moving with lightning flashes and thunder peals; volcanoes in all their violence of destruction; hurricanes with their track of devastation; the boundless ocean in a state of tumult; the lofty waterfall of a mighty river, and such like—these exhibit our faculty of resistance as insignificantly small in comparison with their might. But the sight of them is the more attractive, the more fearful it is, provided only that we are in security; and we willingly call these objects sublime, because they raise the energies of the soul above their accustomed height and discover in us a faculty of resistance of a quite different kind, which gives us courage to measure ourselves against the apparent almightiness of nature. (M 100–1)

Nature can be both beautiful and sublime, but art can only be beautiful. What, then, is the relation between beauty in nature and beauty in art? Kant's answer is subtle. On the one hand, nature is beautiful because it looks like art. On the other hand, if we are to admire a beautiful work of art, we must be conscious that it is artificial and not natural. Yet, Kant tells us, 'the purposiveness in its form must seem to be as free from all constraint of arbitrary rules as if it were a product of mere nature' (M 149). For the judgement of beautiful art taste is needed; for its production what is needed is genius.

The production of beauty is the purpose of art, but artificial beauty is not a beautiful thing, but a beautiful representation of a thing. Beautiful art can indeed present as beautiful things that in nature are ugly or repellent. There are three kinds of beautiful arts, each with their beautiful products. There are the arts of speech, namely rhetoric and poetry.

There are what Kant calls the formative arts, namely painting and the plastic arts of sculpture and architecture. There is a third class of art which creates a play of sensations: the most important of these is music. 'Of all the arts', says Kant, '*poetry* (which owes its origin almost entirely to genius and will least be guided by precept or example) maintains the first rank' (M 170).

It is interesting to compare Kant's ideas on aesthetics with those expressed a few years later by the English Romantic poets. In treating of works of art Kant as it were starts from the consumer and works back to the producer; he begins by analysing the nature of the critic's judgement and ends by deducing the qualities that are necessary for genius (namely, imagination, understanding, spirit, and taste). The Romantics, on the other hand, start with the producer: for them, art is above all the expression of the artist's own emotions. Wordsworth, in his *Preface to Lyrical Ballads*, tells us that what distinguishes the poet from other men is that he has a greater promptness of thought and feeling without immediate external excitement, and a greater power of expressing such thoughts and feelings:

Poetry is the spontaneous overflow of powerful feelings: it takes its origin from emotion recollected in tranquillity: the emotion is contemplated till, by a species of reaction, the tranquillity gradually disappears, and an emotion, kindred to that which was before the subject of contemplation, is gradually produced and does itself actually exist in the mind.

In giving expression to this emotion in verse, the poet's fundamental obligation is to give immediate pleasure to the reader.

Coleridge agreed with this. 'A poem', he wrote, 'is that species of composition, which is opposed to works of science, by proposing for its *immediate* object pleasure, not truth.' But in describing the nature of poetic genius Coleridge improved on both Kant and Wordsworth, by identifying a special necessary gift. Whereas Kant and earlier authors had regarded the imagination as a faculty common to all human beings—the capacity to recall and reshuffle the experiences of everyday life—Coleridge preferred to call this banal, if important, capacity 'the fancy'. The imagination, truly so called, was the special creative gift of the artist: in its primary form it was nothing less than 'the living Power and prime Agent of all human Perception, and as a representation in the finite mind of the eternal act of creation in the infinite I AM'. So Coleridge wrote in 1817 in the thirteenth chapter of his *Biographia Literaria*; and from that day to this critics and philosophers have debated the exact nature of this lofty faculty.

The Aesthetics of Schopenhauer

No philosopher has given aesthetics a more important role in his total system than Schopenhauer. The third book of *The World as Will and Idea* is largely devoted to the nature of art. Aesthetic pleasure, Schopenhauer tells us, following in Kant's footsteps, consists in the disinterested contemplation of nature or of artefacts. When we view a work of art—a nude sculpture, say—it may arouse desire in us: sexual desire perhaps, or desire to acquire the statue. If so, we are still under the influence of will, and we are not in a state of contemplation. It is only when we view something and admire its beauty without thought of our own desires and needs that we are treating it as a work of art and enjoying an aesthetic experience.

Disinterested contemplation, which liberates us from the tyranny of the will, may take one of two forms, which Schopenhauer illustrates by describing two different natural landscapes. If the scene I am contemplating absorbs my attention without effort, then it is my sense of beauty that is aroused. But if the scene is a threatening one, and I have to struggle to escape from fear and achieve a state of contemplation, then what I am encountering is something that is sublime rather than beautiful. Schopenhauer, like Kant, calls up various scenes to illustrate the sense of the sublime: foaming torrents pouring between overhanging rocks beneath a sky of thunderclouds; a storm at sea with the waves dashing against cliffs and sending spray into the air amid lightning flashes. In such cases, he says:

In the undismayed beholder, the two-fold nature of his consciousness reaches the highest degree of distinctness. He perceives himself, on the one hand, as an individual, as the frail phenomenon of will, which the slightest touch of these forces can utterly destroy, helpless against powerful nature, dependent, the victim of chance, a vanishing nothing in the presence of stupendous might; and, on the other hand, as the eternal, serene, knowing subject, who as the condition of every object is the sustainer of this whole world, the fearful strife of nature being only his own idea, and he himself free and apart from all desire and necessity in the contemplation of the Ideas. This is the full impression of the sublime. (*WWI* 205)

The impression produced in this way may be called 'the dynamical sublime'. But the same impression may be produced by calm meditation on the immensity of space and time while contemplating the starry sky at night. This impression of sublimity (which Schopenhauer, borrowing Kant's unhelpful term, calls 'the mathematical sublime') can be produced also by voluminous closed spaces such as the dome of St Peter's in Rome and by monuments of great age such as the pyramids. In each case the sense arises from the contrast between our own smallness and insignificance as individuals and a vastness that is the creation of ourselves as pure knowing subjects.

The sublime is, as it were, the upper bound of the beautiful. Its lower bound is what Schopenhauer calls 'the charming'. Whereas what is sublime makes an object of contemplation out of what is hostile to the will, the charming turns an object of contemplation into something that attracts the will. Schopenhauer gives as instances sculptures of 'naked figures, whose position, drapery, and general treatment are calculated to excite the passions of the beholder' and, less convincingly, Dutch still lifes of 'oysters, herrings, crabs, bread and butter, beer, wine, and so forth'. Such artefacts nullify the aesthetic purposes, and are altogether to be condemned (*WWI* 208).

There are two elements in every encounter with beauty: a will-less knowing subject, and an object which is the Idea known. In contemplation of natural beauty and of architecture, the pleasure is principally in the purity and painlessness of the knowing, because the Ideas encountered are low-grade manifestations of will. But when we contemplate human beings (through the medium of tragedy, for example) the pleasure is rather in the Ideas contemplated, which are varied, rich, and significant. On the basis of this distinction, Schopenhauer proceeds to grade the fine arts.

Lowest in the scale comes architecture, which brings out low-grade Ideas such as gravity, rigidity, and light:

The beauty of a building lies in the obvious adaptation of every part... to the stability of the whole, to which the position, size and form of every part have so necessary a relation that if it were possible to remove some part, the whole would inevitably collapse. For only by each part bearing as much as it conveniently can, and each being supported exactly where it ought to be and to exactly the necessary extent, does this play of opposition, this conflict between rigidity and gravity, that constitutes the life of the stone and the manifestation of its will, unfold itself in the most complete visibility. (*WWI* 215)

Of course, architecture serves a practical as well as an aesthetic purpose, but the greatness of an architect shows itself in the way he achieves pure aesthetic ends in spite of having to subordinate them to the needs of his client.

The representational arts, in Schopenhauer's view, are concerned with the universal rather than the particular. Paintings or sculptures of animals, he is convinced, are obviously concerned with the species, not the individual: 'the most typical lion, wolf, horse, sheep, or ox, is always the most beautiful also'. But with representations of human beings, the matter is more complicated. It is quite wrong to think that art achieves beauty by imitating nature. How could an artist recognize the perfect sample to imitate if he did not have an a priori pattern of beauty in his mind? And has nature ever produced a human being perfectly beautiful in every respect? What the artist understands is something that nature only stammers in half-uttered speech. The sculptor 'expresses in the hard marble that beauty of form which in a thousand attempts nature failed to produce, and presents it to her as if telling her "This is what you wanted to say"' (*WWI* 222).

The general idea of humanity has to be represented by the sculptor or painter in the character of an individual, and it can be presented in individuals of various kinds. In a genre picture, it does not matter 'whether ministers discuss the fate of countries and nations over a map, or boors wrangle in a beer-house over cards and dice'. Nor does it matter whether the characters represented in a work of art are historical rather than fictional: the link with a historical personage gives a painting its nominal significance, not its real significance.

For example, Moses found by the Egyptian princess is the nominal significance of a painting; it represents a moment of the greatest importance in history; the real significance, on the other hand, that which is really given to the onlooker, is a foundling child rescued from its floating cradle by a great lady, an incident which may have happened more than once. (*WWI* 231)

Because of this, the paintings of Renaissance painters that Schopenhauer most admired were not those that represented a particular event (such as the nativity or the Crucifixion) but rather simple groups of saints alongside the Saviour, engaged in no action. In the faces and eyes of such figures we see the expression of that suppression of will which is the summit of all art.

Schopenhauer's theory of art combines elements from Plato and elements from Aristotle. The purpose of art, he believed was to represent not a particular individual, nor an abstract concept, but a Platonic Idea. But whereas Plato condemned art works as being at two removes from the Ideas, copies of material things that themselves were only imitations of Ideas, Schopenhauer thinks that the artist comes closer to the ideal than the technician or the historian. This is particularly the case with poetry and drama, the highest of the arts. History is related to poetry as portrait painting is to historical painting: the one gives us truth in the individual, and the other truth in the universal. Like Aristotle, Schopenhauer concludes that far more inner truth is to be attributed to poetry than to history. And among historical narratives, he decides rather eccentrically, the greatest value is to be attributed to autobiographies.

Kierkegaard on Music

In Kierkegaard's works, the word 'aesthetic' and its cognates occur frequently. However, for him 'aesthetic' is an ethical rather than an aesthetic category. The aesthetic character is someone who devotes his life to the pursuit of immediate pleasure; and the pleasures he pursues may be natural (such as food, drink, and sex) no less than artistic (such as painting, music, and dance). Kierkegaard's main interest in discussing the aesthetic attitude to life (notably in *Either/Or*) is to stress its superficial and fundamentally unsatisfactory nature, and to press the claims of a profounder ethical, and eventually religious, commitment. But in the course of a detailed presentation of the aesthetic life he has occasion to discuss issues that are aesthetic in the narrower sense of being concerned with the nature of art. For instance, the first part of *Either/Or* contains a long section that is subtitled 'The Musical Erotic'.

The essay, which purports to be written by an ardent exponent of aesthetic hedonism, is largely a meditation on Mozart's opera *Don Giovanni*. Don Juan is the supreme personification of erotic desire, and Mozart's opera is its uniquely perfect expression. Music, we are told, is of all the arts the one most capable of expressing sheer sensuality. The rather unexpected reason we are given for this is that music is the most abstract of the arts. Like language, it addresses the ear; like the spoken word, it unfolds in time, not in space. But while language is the vehicle of spirit, music is the vehicle of sensuality.

Kierkegaard's essayist goes on to make a surprising claim. Though religious puritans are suspicious of music, as the voice of sensuality, and prefer to listen to the word of the spirit, the development of music and the discovery of sensuality are both in fact due to Christianity. Sensual love was, of course, an element in the life of the Greeks, whether humans or gods; but it took Christianity to separate out sensuality by contrasting it with spirituality.

If I imagine the sensual erotic as a principle, as a power, as a realm characterized by spirit, that is to say characterized by being excluded by spirit, if I imagine it concentrated in a single individual, then I have the concept of the spirit of the sensual erotic. This is an idea which the Greeks did not have, which Christianity first introduced to the world, if only in an indirect sense.

If this spirit of the sensual erotic in all its immediacy demands expression, the question is: what medium lends itself to that? What must be especially borne in mind here is that it demands expression and representation in its immediacy. In its mediate state and its reflection in something else it comes under language and becomes subject to ethical categories. In its immediacy it can only be expressed in music. (*E/O* 75)

Kierkegaard illustrates the various forms and stages of erotic pursuit by taking characters from different Mozart operas. The first awakening of sensuality takes a melancholy, diffuse form, with no specific object: this is the dreamy stage expressed by Cherubino in *The Marriage of Figaro*. The second stage is expressed in the merry, vigorous, sparkling chirping of Papageno in *The Magic Flute*: love seeking out a specific object. But these stages are no more than presentiments of Don Giovanni, who is the very incarnation of the sensual erotic. Ballads and legends represent him as an individual. 'When he is interpreted in music, on the other hand, I do not have a particular individual, I have the power of nature, the demonic, which as little tires of seducing, or is done with seducing, as the wind is tired of raging, the sea of surging, or a waterfall of cascading down from its height' (*E/O* 90).

Because Don Giovanni seduces not by stratagem, but by sheer energy of desire, he does not come within any ethical category; that is why his force can be expressed in music alone. The secret of the whole opera is that its hero is the force animating the other characters: he is the sun, the other

259

A paybill for the Prague premiere of Don Giovanni, which Kierkegaard argued was the most perfect possible opera.

characters mere planets, who are half in darkness, with only that side which is turned towards him illuminated. Only the Commendatore is independent; but he is outside the substance of the opera as its antecedent and consequent, and both before and after his death he is the voice of spirit.

Because music is uniquely suitable to express the immediacy of sensual desire, in Don Giovanni we have a perfect match of subject matter and creative form. Both matter and form are essential to a work of art, Kierkegaard says, even though philosophers overemphasize now one and now the other. It is because of this that *Don Giovanni*, even if it stood alone, was enough to make Mozart a classic composer and absolutely immortal.

Nietzsche on Tragedy

For the young Nietzsche it is not Mozart but Wagner whose operas are supreme. This is because of a shared debt to Schopenhauer. In 1854 Wagner wrote to Franz Liszt that Schopenhauer had come into his life like a gift from heaven. 'His chief idea, the final negation of the desire for life, is terribly gloomy, but it shows the only salvation possible.'[1] In his *The Birth of*

---

[1] A. Goldman, *Wagner on Music and Drama* (New York: Dutton, 1966).

Tragedy (1872) Nietzsche likewise bases his aesthetic theory on Schopenhauer's pessimistic view of life, taking as his text the Greek myth of King Midas' quest for the satyr Silenus.

When Silenus was finally in his power, the king asked him what was the best and most desirable thing for mankind. The daemon stood in silence, stiff and motionless, but when the king insisted he broke out into a shrill laugh and said 'Wretched, ephemeral race, children of misery and chance, why do you force me to say what it would be more expedient for you not to hear? The best of all things is quite beyond your reach: it is not to have been born, not to be at all, to be nothing. The next best thing is to die as soon as may be.' (*BT* 22)

Schopenhauer had held out art as the most accessible escape from the tyranny of life.

Nietzsche, too, sees the origin of art in humans' need to mask life's misery from themselves. The ancient Greeks, he tells us, in order to be able to live at all 'had to interpose the radiant dream-birth of the Olympian gods between themselves and the horrors of existence' (*BT* 22). There are two kinds of escape from reality: dreaming and intoxication. In Greek mythology, according to Nietzsche, these two forms of illusion are personified in two different gods: Apollo, the god of light, and Dionysus, the god of wine. 'The development and progress of Art originates from the duality of the Apolline and the Dionysiac, just as reproduction depends on the duality of the sexes'. (*BT* 14).

The prototype of the Apolline artist is Homer, the founder of epic poetry; he is the creator of the resplendent dream-world of the Olympic deities. Apollo is an ethical deity, imposing measure and order on his followers in the interests of beauty. But the Apolline magnificence is soon engulfed in a Dionysiac flood, the stream of life that breaks down barriers and constraints. The followers of Dionysus sing and dance in rapturous ecstasy, enjoying life to excess. Music is the supreme expression of the Dionysiac spirit, as epic is of the Apolline.

The glory of Greek culture is Athenian tragedy, and this is the offspring of both Apollo and Dionysus, combining music with poetry. The choruses in Greek tragedy represent the world of Dionysus, while the dialogue plays itself out in a lucid Apolline world of images. The Greek spirit found its supreme expression in the plays of Aeschylus (especially *Prometheus Vinctus*) and Sophocles (especially *Oedipus Rex*). But with the plays of the third famous tragedian, Euripides, tragedy dies by its own hand, poisoned by an injection of rationality. The blame for this must be laid at the door of Socrates, who inaugurated a new era that valued science above art.

Socrates, according to Nietzsche, was the antithesis of all that made Greece great. His instincts were entirely negative and critical, rather than positive and creative. In rejecting the Dionysiac element he destroyed the tragedians' synthesis. 'We need only consider the Socratic maxims "Virtue is knowledge, all sins arise from ignorance, the virtuous man is the happy man". In these three basic optimistic formulae lies the death of tragedy' (*BT* 69). Tragedy, in Euripides, took the death-leap into bourgeois theatre. The dying Socrates, freed by insight and reason from the fear of death, became the mystagogue of science.

Was it possible, in modern Germany, to remedy the disease inherited from Socrates, and to restore the union of Apollo and Dionysus? Nietzsche had no appreciation of the novel, which in the nineteenth century might be thought the genre most fertile of the beneficent illusion that in his view was the function of art. The novel, he thought, was essentially a Socratic art form, that subordinated poetry to philosophy. Oddly, he blamed its invention on Plato. 'The Platonic dialogue might be described as the lifeboat in which the shipwrecked older poetry and all its children escaped, crammed together in a narrow space and fearfully obeying a single pilot, Socrates . . . Plato gave posterity the model for a new art form—the novel' (*BT* 69). Nor had Nietzsche any high opinion of Italian opera, in spite of the combination of poetry and music it involved. He complained that it was ruined by the separation between recitative and aria, which privileged the verbal over the musical. Only in Germany was there hope of a rebirth of tragedy:

From the Dionysiac soil of the German spirit a power has risen that has nothing in common with the original conditions of Socratic culture: that culture can neither explain nor excuse it, but instead finds it terrifying and inexplicable, powerful and hostile—*German Music*, as we know it pre-eminently in its mighty sun-cycle from Bach to Beethoven, from Beethoven to Wagner. (*BT* 94)

The *Birth of Tragedy* peters out into a set of rapturous and incoherent programme notes to the third act of *Tristan und Isolde*. No one has condemned their weaknesses with more force than Nietzsche himself, who after he had emerged from the spell of Wagner prefaced later editions of the book with an 'Attempt at Self-Criticism'. There he recants his attempt to link the genius of Greece with a fictional 'German Spirit'. But he did not disown what he came to see as the fundamental theme of the book, namely, that art and not morality is the properly metaphysical activity of man, and that the existence of the world finds justification only as an aesthetic phenomenon.

Art and Morality

For Nietzsche, art is not only autonomous but is supreme over morality. At the opposite pole from Nietzsche stand two nineteenth-century aestheticians who saw art and morality as inextricably intertwined. One was John Ruskin (1819–1900), and the other Leo Tolstoy (1828–1910).

Ruskin regarded art as a very serious matter. In his massive work *Modern Painters* (1843) he wrote:

Art, properly so called, is no recreation; it cannot be learned at spare moments, nor pursued when we have nothing better to do. It is no handiwork for drawing-room tables, no relief of the ennui of boudoirs; it must be understood and undertaken seriously, or not at all. To advance it men's lives must be given, and to receive it their hearts.[2]

But the demands made by art could be justified only by the seriousness of its moral purpose: namely, to reveal fundamental features of the universe. Beauty is something objective, not a mere product of custom. The experience of beauty arises from a truthful perception of nature, and leads on to an apprehension of the divine. Only if an artist is himself a morally good person will he be able to deliver this revelation in an incorrupt form, and set before us the glory of God. But in a decaying society—as Ruskin believed nineteenth-century industrial society to be—both moral and artistic purity are almost impossible to achieve. Both the imaginative faculty that creates, and the 'theoretic' faculty that appreciates, are radically corrupt. Work is degraded by the modern division of labour, and the workman deprived of his due status as a craftsman seeking perfection.

Ruskin applied his moralizing theory of art to two arts in particular: painting and architecture. Painting, for him, is essentially a form of language: technical skill is no more than mastery of the language, and

---

[2] John Ruskin, *Selected Writings* (London: Dent, 1995).

263

the worth of a painting depends on the value of the thoughts that it expresses. Ruskin sought to bear out this contention by a close examination of the works of J. M. W. Turner. In *The Seven Lamps of Architecture* Ruskin set out the criteria by which he judged Gothic architecture superior to the architecture of the Renaissance and the baroque. The 'lamps' are predominantly moral categories: sacrifice, truth, power, obedience, and the like. For architecture, in his definition, is the art that disposes and adorns edifices so that the sight of them may contribute to man's mental health, power, and pleasure. And the essential element in mental health was a just appreciation of man's place in a divinely ordered universe.

For Tolstoy, art can be good only if it has a moral purpose. In *What is Art?* he described the price, in terms of money and hard labour, of the artistic ventures of his day, especially of opera. Such art, he maintained, could arise only upon the slavery of the masses of the people; and he asked whether the social costs involved could be morally justified. It was an art that appealed only to the sentiments of the upper classes, which extended no further than pride, sex, and ennui.

Tolstoy rejected the claims of earlier writers that the aim of art is beauty and that beauty is recognized by the enjoyment it gives. The real purpose of art was communication between human beings. While rejecting the Romantic idea that art must give pleasure, he agreed with Wordsworth that its essence was the sharing of emotion:

To take the simplest example: one man laughs, and another who hears becomes merry, or a man weeps, and another who hears feels sorrow. A man is excited or irritated, and another man seeing him is brought to a similar state of mind. . . . a man expresses his feelings of admiration, devotion, fear, respect or love, to certain objects, persons, or phenomena, and others are infected by the same feelings of admiration, devotion, fear, respect or love, to the same objects, persons, or phenomena. (*WA* 66)

Art in the broad sense of the world permeates our life, which is full of works of art of every kind, from lullabies, jokes, mimicry, the ornamentation of dresses, houses, and utensils, to church services and triumphal processions. But the feelings with which these works of art infect us may be good or bad. Art is only good if the emotions it injects are good; and those emotions can be good only if they are fundamentally religious and contribute to a sense of universal human brotherhood.

The emotions to be communicated by art must be emotions that can be shared by mankind in general, and not just by a pampered elite. Where this is not the case we have either bad art or pseudo art. Tolstoy is willing to accept that this judgement condemns many of the most admired works of music and literature—including his own novels. The greatest novel of the nineteenth century, he maintained, was *Uncle Tom's Cabin*, which spread the message of universal brotherhood across the boundaries of race and class.

Among the works of art Tolstoy condemned was Beethoven's Ninth Symphony. Does this transmit the highest religious feeling? No: no music can. Does it unite all men in one common feeling? No, Tolstoy replied: 'I am unable to imagine to myself a crowd of normal people who could understand anything of this long, confused, and artificial production, except short snatches which are lost in a sea of incomprehensibility.' It is true that the work's last movement is a poem of Schiller which expresses the very thought that it is feeling, in particular gladness, that unites people together. 'But though this poem is sung at the end of the symphony the music does not accord with the thought expressed in the verses; for the music is exclusive and does not unite all men, but unites only a few, dividing them off from the rest of mankind' (*WA* 249).

Art for Art's Sake

Tolstoy's moralistic view of art quickly became unfashionable in the twentieth century. The autonomy of art, if not its Nietzschean supremacy, was widely accepted: a work of art might be good art, and even great art, while being morally or politically deleterious. The artistic merit of a work was even held to redeem its ethical dubiety, and many countries repealed laws that forbade the production and publication of works of art that had a tendency to 'deprave and corrupt'.

One of the most influential of twentieth-century aestheticians was the Italian philosopher Benedetto Croce (1866–1952). In metaphysics, Croce was an idealist, and developed a Hegelian system along with Giovanni Gentile (1875–1944) until the two parted company in 1925 over the issue of Fascism. Gentile became a theoretician of Fascism, while Croce, who was a cabinet minister in both pre-Fascist and post-Fascist Italian governments, was the leading intellectual opponent of Mussolini in the 1930s.

For Croce, art occupies a position between history and science. Like history it deals with particular cases rather than general laws, but its particular cases are imagined, not real, and they illustrate, as science does, universal truths. Croce himself distinguished between four phases of his aesthetic theory, from the first volume of his *Filosofia dello Spirito* in 1902 to *La Poesia* of 1936. But several themes are common to every one of the phases of his thought.

The core of art, for Croce, is intuition. Intuition is not the same as feeling, whatever positivists might say: feelings need expression, and expression is a cognitive, not just an emotional, matter. Art in human beings, unlike emotion in animals, is something spiritual, not merely sensual. On the other hand, rationalist aestheticians are wrong to see art as something intellectual: it operates through images, not through concepts. Thus Croce distances himself from Romantics on the one hand and classicists on the other.

The artistic intuition is essentially lyrical. Croce explains what this means principally by contrasts. Art is not concerned with the True (as logic is) nor the Useful (as economics is) nor with the Good (as morality is). It has its own object, the Beautiful, that stands independently on equal terms with the other three. (For Croce, the notion of the Sublime was only a pseudo-concept.) An artistic expression is lyrical only if it is concerned exclusively with the beautiful. Thus a poem like Lucretius' *de Rerum Natura*, with its heavy scientific and moral messages, is not something lyrical, but merely a piece of literature. True poetry must have no utilitarian, moral, or philosophical agenda.

Views similar to Croce's were made familiar to the English-speaking world by R. G. Collingwood (1889–1943), who translated Croce's article on aesthetics for the 1928 edition of the *Encyclopaedia Britannica*. Collingwood, a classicist and archaeologist of distinction, became Wayneflete Professor of Metaphysics at Oxford in 1936. He is best known for his contributions to the philosophy of history, on which he was specially qualified to write, but his *Principles of Art* (1938) was a significant contribution to aesthetic theory.

Much of the book is taken up with explaining what art is not. Art is not mere amusement; even if much of what goes by the name of art is simply entertainment, true art is something different. Art is not a magical procedure like a war dance. By magic, Collingwood explains, he means a procedure for arousing emotion to some preconceived end, such as patriotic emotion or proletarian fervour. Most importantly, art must be distinguished from craft or technical skill. Art is not imitation or representation (*mimesis*), for that too is a craft. Of course, a great work of art will also be a work of craft, but what makes it a work of art is not what makes it a work of craft.

If art were a craft, we could distinguish in it between end and means. But if art has an end, it can only be the arousing of emotion; and this is not something that can be identified separately from the artistic activity, as a shoe can be identified separately from the act of cobbling. Art should not be seen as the activity of arousing emotion, but as the activity of expressing emotion. The true work of art is in fact the emotion in the artist himself. Successful artists conclude their success in their own imagination; the externalization of their images in a public work of art is merely a matter of craft.

The inner work, the true work of art, consists in raising something preconscious, an inarticulate feeling, into an explicit and articulate state. Following Croce, Collingwood accepted on this basis that imagination and expression were one and the same thing. It is through language that the preconscious is transformed into the articulate; and in this sense all artistic expression, in whatever medium, is essentially linguistic.

If art is the expression of emotion, Collingwood argues, then the distinction between artist and audience disappears.

If a poet expresses, for example, a certain kind of fear, the only hearers who can understand him are those who are capable of experiencing that kind of fear themselves. Hence, when someone reads and understands a poem, he is not merely understanding the poet's expression of his, the poet's, emotions, he is expressing emotions of his own in the poet's words, which have thus become his own words. As Coleridge put it, we know a man for a poet by the fact that he makes us poets. (*PA* 118)

Poet and reader share and express the same emotion: the difference is that the poet can solve for himself the problem of expressing it, whereas the reader needs the poet to show him how it is done. By creating for ourselves (aided or unaided) an imaginary experience or activity, we express our emotions; and this is what we call art.

Croce and Collingwood differed from Tolstoy because they regarded art as something distinct from and independent of morality. But all three writers shared a conception of art as expression of emotion. Most twentieth-century philosophers rejected the Tolstoyan view of the function of art as the communication of emotion. Wittgenstein, for instance, wrote:

There is *much* that could be learned from Tolstoy's false theorizing that the work of art conveys a 'feeling'. And indeed you might call it, if not the expression of a particular feeling, an expression of feeling, or a felt expression. And you might say too that people who understand it to that extent 'resonate' with it, respond to it. You might say: The work of art does not seek to convey *something else*, just itself. As, if I pay someone a visit, I don't wish only to produce such and such feelings in him, but first and foremost to pay him a visit—though of course I also want to be welcome.

The real absurdity starts when it is said that the artist wants others, in reading, to feel what he felt while writing. I can indeed think that I understand a poem, for example, that is, understand it in the way its author would want it to be understood. But what *he* may have felt while writing it isn't *any* concern of mine at all. (*CV* 67)

The independence of a work of art from its creator became a prominent theme, both in the English-speaking world and in continental Europe. American critics denounced as 'the intentional fallacy' any attempt to reach an understanding of a text on the basis of elements in its author's biography or psychology or motivation, rather than in properties to be discerned in the text in isolation. In France, philosophers went so far as to speak of 'the death of the author'. The text, they have argued, is the primary object; the notion of an author is rather an economic and legal construct. So far as interpretation goes, the reception of a text by generations of readers may be of greater significance than any item in the biography of the person who initially penned it.

The thesis of the death of the author has not been warmly welcomed in British philosophical circles. But the idea that in the interpretation of a work of art the author has no privileged status was anticipated by a nineteenth-century Englishman. The Victorian poet Arthur Hugh Clough wrote a controversial, some thought blasphemous, poem about the Resurrection, *Easter Day*. In a later poem he imagines himself questioned about its meaning: was it intended to be ironic or sarcastic? He responds:

Interpret it I cannot. I but wrote it.

11

Political Philosophy

Utilitarianism and Liberalism

In introducing his greatest happiness principle, Bentham was less concerned to provide a criterion for individual moral choices than to offer guidance to rulers and legislators on the management of communities. But it is precisely in this area, when we have to consider not just the total quantity of happiness in a community but also its distribution, that the greatest happiness principle, on its own, fails to provide a credible decision procedure.

Suppose that, by whatever means, we have succeeded in establishing a scale for the measurement of happiness: a scale from 0 to 10 on which 0 represents maximum misery, 10 represents maximum happiness, and 5 a state of indifference. Imagine that we are devising political and legal institutions for a society, and that we have a choice between implementing two models. The result of adopting model A will be that 60 per cent of the population will score 6, and 40 per cent will score 4. The result of adopting model B will be that 80 per cent of the population will score 10 and 20 per cent will score 0. Faced with such a choice, anyone with a care for either equality or humanity will surely wish to implement model A rather than model B. Yet if we operate Bentham's felicific calculus in the obvious manner, model A scores only 520 points, while model B achieves a total of 800.

The principle that we should seek the greatest happiness of the greatest number clearly leads to different results depending on whether we opt to maximize happiness or to maximize the number of happy people. The principle needs, at the very least, to be supplemented by some limits on the amount of inequality between the best off and the worst off, and limits on the degree of misery of the worst off, if it is not to permit outcomes that are gross violations of distributive justice.

Despite the problems with his grand principle, problems that he left for his successors to struggle with, Bentham did make very substantial contributions to political philosophy. He is seen at his best when he is, in the words of J. S. Mill, 'organising and regulating the merely *business* part of social arrangements'. On such topics he can write acutely and briskly, make shrewd distinctions, expose common fallacies, and pack a weight of argument into brief and lucid paragraphs. His treatment of state-imposed punishment is an excellent example of the way in which he puts these talents to use.

What, he asks, is the purpose of the penal system?

The immediate principal end of punishment is to control action. This action is either that of the offender, or of others: that of the offender it controls by its influence, either on his will, in which case it is said to operate in the way of *reformation*; or on his physical power, in which case it is said to operate by *disablement*; that of others it can influence no otherwise than by its influence over their wills; in which case it is said to operate in the way of *example*. (P 13. 1)

Punishment, being the infliction of pain, is as such an evil, so it should only be admitted in so far as it promises to exclude some greater evil. Bentham rejected the retributive theory of punishment, according to which justice demands that he who has done harm shall suffer harm. Unless the infliction of punishment has some deterrent or remedial effect either on the offender or on others, retribution is merely a rendering of evil for evil, and increases the amount of evil in the world without restoring any balance of justice.

It is true that the punishment of an offender, even if it has no deterrent or reformatory effect, may give a feeling of satisfaction to a victim, or to the law-abiding public. This, like any other pleasure, must be placed in the utilitarian scales. But no punishment, Bentham says, should be imposed merely for this vindictive purpose, because no pleasure ever produced by punishment can be equivalent to the pain.

Since the principal purpose of punishment was deterrence, punishment should not be inflicted in cases where it would have no deterrent effect, either on the offender or on others, nor should it be inflicted to any greater extent than is necessary to deter. Punishment, he says, must not be inflicted when it is inefficacious (cannot deter) or unprofitable (will cause more mischief than it prevents) or needless (where the mischief can be prevented by other means).

In the fourteenth chapter Bentham drew up a set of rules setting out the proportion between punishments and offences, based not on the retributive principle of 'an eye for an eye, a tooth for a tooth' but on the effect that the prospect of punishment will have on the reasoning of a potential offender. Bentham imagined a prospective criminal calculating the profit and loss that is likely to accrue from the offence, and regarded it as the function of the penal law to ensure that the loss will outweigh the profit. The law must therefore impose punishments that are sufficient to deter, but they should equally be no more than is necessary to deter. Punishment should, in Bentham's terms, be *frugal*.

While deterrence is the principal end of punishment, Bentham admits subsidiary purposes, such as the reformation or disablement of the offender. Reform, in the condition of most actual prisons, was and is unlikely to be achieved; but Bentham has some proposals for particular reformatory regimes. Imprisonment does have the effect of the temporary disablement of the offender, but obviously disablement is most efficaciously achieved by the death penalty. 'At the same time', Bentham observes, 'this punishment, it is evident, is in an eminent degree *unfrugal*; which forms one among the many objects there are against the use of it, in any but very extraordinary cases' (P 15. 19).

John Stuart Mill's political philosophy, like his moral philosophy, owed much to Bentham, but in this area too he felt obliged to temper the strict utilitarianism of his master. Bentham's system, with its denial of natural rights, would in principle justify, in certain circumstances, highly autocratic government and substantial intrusion on personal liberty. So too would the early forms of socialism with which Mill had flirted in his youth, which had given birth to the positivist system of Auguste Comte. In his mature years Mill attached supreme importance to setting limits to the constraints that social systems, however benevolent in principle, could place on individual independence. He described the Système de Politique Positive as a device 'by which the yoke of general opinion, wielded by an organised body of spiritual teachers and rulers, would be made supreme over every action, and as far as is in human possibility, every thought, of

Bentham's "auto-icon": his remains preserved in a waxwork in University College, London.

every member of the community'. He denounced Comte for proposing 'the completest system of spiritual and temporal despotism which ever yet emanated from a human brain'. In *On Liberty* he sought to set out a general libertarian principle that would protect the individual from illegitimate authoritarian intrusion whether motivated by utilitarianism, socialism, or positivism.

To safeguard liberty, Mill maintains, it is not sufficient to replace autocratic monarchy by responsible democracy, because within a democratic society the majority may exercise tyranny over the minority. Nor is it sufficient to place limits upon the authority of government, because society can exercise other and more subtle means of coercion.

There needs protection also against the tyranny of the prevailing opinion and feeling; against the tendency of society to impose, by other means than civil penalties, its own ideas and practices as rules of conduct on those who dissent from them; to fetter the development, and if possible, prevent the formation, of any individuality not in harmony with its ways. (*L* 130)

In order to place a just limit on coercion by physical force or public opinion we must affirm, as a fundamental principle, that the only part of the conduct of anyone for which he is accountable to society is that which concerns others. In the part which merely concerns himself, his independence should be absolute.

The most important application of this principle concerns liberty of thought, and the cognate liberties of speaking and writing. According to Mill, no authority, autocratic or democratic, has the right to suppress the expression of opinion. 'If all mankind minus one were of one opinion, and only one person were of the contrary opinion, mankind would be no more justified in silencing that one person than he, if he had the power, would be justified in silencing mankind' (*L* 130). This is because to suppress an opinion is to rob the whole human race. The opinion silenced may, for all we know, turn out to be true, because none of us is infallible. If it is not wholly true, it may well contain a portion of truth that would otherwise be neglected. Even an opinion that is wholly false has a value as offering a challenge to the contrary opinion and thus ensuring that the truth is not held as a mere prejudice or as a formal profession. Freedom of opinion, Mill concludes, and freedom of the expression of opinion, is essential for the mental well-being of mankind.

But freedom of opinion is not all that is needed. Men should be free to act upon their opinions, and to carry them out in their lives, without hindrance, either physical or moral, from their fellows. Of course the freedom should not extend to the right to harm others—even freedom of speech must be curtailed in circumstances where the expression of opinion amounts to an incitement to mischief. But ample scope should be given to varieties of character and to experiments in living, provided these concern only the individual's own affairs or the affairs of others 'with their free, voluntary, and undeceived consent and participation'. The individual's rule of conduct should be his or her own character, not the traditions or customs of other people. If this principle is denied, 'there is wanting one of the principal ingredients of human happiness, and quite the chief ingredient of individual and social progress' (*L* 185).

Without individuality, human beings become mere machines, conforming to a pattern imposed from without. But 'human nature is not a machine to be built after a model, and set to do exactly the work prescribed for it, but a tree, which requires to grow and develop itself on all sides' (*L* 188). If eccentricity is proscribed, damage is done not only to the individual constrained, but to society as a whole. We may all have something to learn from unconventional characters. 'There is always need of persons not only to discover new truths, and point out when what were once truths are true no longer, but also to commence new practices, and set the example of more enlightened conduct, and better taste and sense in human life' (*L* 193). Energetic and unorthodox characters are needed more than ever in an age when public opinion rules the world, and individuals are lost in the crowd. Genius must be allowed to unfold itself in practice as well as in thought.

What exactly does Mill have in mind when he commends 'experiments in living'? Sadly, he expounds his thesis by a series of eloquent metaphors rather than by offering examples of beneficial eccentricity. When he comes to offer practical applications of his principles, he confines himself to denouncing laws restricting humdrum activities of everyday people, not statutes constraining the development of genius. As examples of bad legislation, actual or hypothetical, he considers such things as prohibitions on the eating of pork and the drinking of spirituous liquors, or laws against travelling on the sabbath and restrictions on dancing and theatrical performances.

No doubt when Mill was encouraging nonconformity one example at the back of his mind was his own unconventional relationship with Harriet Taylor during the long years before their marriage. But, oddly, the one example he actually gives of an experiment in living is one of which he heartily disapproved: the Mormon sanction of polygamy. This experiment, he admitted, was in direct conflict with his libertarian principles, being 'a mere riveting of the chains of one half of the community, and emancipation of the other from reciprocity of obligation towards them' (*L* 224). However, since the world taught women that marriage was the one thing needful, he thought it understandable that many a woman should prefer being one of several wives to not being a wife at all. Mill was not commending polygamy; merely urging that Mormons should not be coerced into abandoning it. And it must be said that he had almost as much distaste for current English monogamy as for the institutions of Salt Lake City.

At the time of his own marriage in 1851 he wrote out a protest against the laws that conferred upon one party to the contract complete control over the person and property of the other. 'Having no means of legally divesting myself of these odious powers...I feel it my duty to put on record a formal protest against the existing law of marriage, in so far as conferring such powers, and a solemn promise never in any case or under any circumstances to use them' (*CCM* 396). He set out his objections to the English law of marriage at length in the pamphlet *On the Subjection of Women*. The legal subordination of one sex to the other was wrong in principle and a chief obstacle to human progress. A wife was simply a bond-servant to her husband; she was bound to give him lifelong obedience, and any property she acquired instantly passed to him. In some ways she was worse off than a slave. In a Christian country a slave had a right and duty to reject sexual advances from her master; but a husband can enforce upon his wife 'the lowest degradation of a human being, that of being made the instrument of an animal function contrary to her inclinations' (*L* 504).

The subjection of women to men had no other origin than the greater muscular strength of the male, and had been continued into a civilized age only through male self-interest. No one could say that experience had shown that the existing system of male superiority was preferable to any alternative; for no other alternative had ever been tried. Women had, by centuries of training from the earliest age, been brought to acquiesce in the system.

When we put together three things—first, the natural attraction between opposite sexes; secondly, the wife's entire dependence on the husband, every privilege or pleasure she has being either his gift, or depending entirely on his will; and lastly, that the principal object of human pursuit, consideration, and all objects of social ambition, can in general be sought or obtained by her only through him—it would be a miracle if the object of being attractive to men had not become the polar star of feminine education and formation of character. (*L* 487)

If women did wish to throw over their subjection, rebellion against their masters is harder than any rebellion against despots has ever been. Husbands have greater facilities than any monarch has ever had to prevent any

MILL'S LOGIC; OR, FRANCHISE FOR FEMALES.

"PRAY CLEAR THE WAY, THERE, FOR THESE—A—PERSONS."

A *Punch* cartoon of 1867 satirises Mill's crusade for equality between the sexes.

uprising against their power: their subjects live under their eyes and in their very hands. It is no wonder that the tyranny of males has outlasted all other forms of unjust authority.

Kierkegaard and Schopenhauer on Women

The significance of *On the Subjection of Women* in the climate of the time can be brought out by comparing it with the treatment of marriage and woman-hood in the works of two Continental philosophers, Kierkegaard and Schopenhauer. In Kierkegaard's *Either/Or* a ninety-page essay is devoted to affirming 'the aesthetic validity of marriage'—that is, to persuade the reader that entering into matrimony need not diminish, indeed may fortify, the raptures of first love. Romantic ballads and novels are quite wrong to portray love as a quest that surmounts obstacles and trials to achieve its goal in marriage: a wedding is the beginning, not the end, of truly romantic love. The essay takes the form of a letter to a romantic correspondent who has fundamental objections to the whole idea of a church marriage.

Kierkegaard imagines the objector saying:

The girl before whom I could fall down and worship, whose love I feel could snatch me out of all confusion and give me new birth, it is she I am to lead to the Lord's altar, she who is to stand there like a sinner, of whom and to whom it shall be said that it was Eve who seduced Adam. To her before whom my proud soul bows down, the only one to whom it has bowed down, to her it shall be said that I am to be her master and she subservient to her husband. The moment has come, the Church is already reaching out its arms for her and before giving her back to me it will first press a bridal kiss upon her lips, not that bridal kiss I gave the whole world for; it is already reaching out its arms to embrace her, but this embrace will cause all her beauty to fade, and then it will toss her over to me and say 'Be fruitful and multiply'. What kind of power is it that dares intrude between me and my bride, the bride I myself have chosen and who has chosen me? And this power would command her to be true to me; does she then need to be commanded? And is she to be true to me only because a third party commands it, one whom she therefore loves more than me? And it bids me be true to her; must I be bidden to that, I who belong to her with my whole soul? And this power decides our relation to each other; it says I am to ask and she is to obey; but suppose I do not want to ask, suppose I feel myself too inferior for that? (*E/O* 408)

Judge Vilhelm, whom Kierkegaard sets up as the defender of traditional marriage, urges his correspondent to accept that in marriage he cannot but be master, that his wife is no more a sinner than any other woman, and that accepting a third power means only thanking God for the love between bride and groom. At marriage the husband comes to understand that real love is daily possession throughout a lifetime, not the preternatural power of a brief infatuation; and his taking her as a gift from God, rather than as a conquest of his own, enables the wife 'to put the loved one at just enough distance for her to be able to draw breath' (*E/O* 411).

Vilhelm is emphatic that the only worthy motive for entering on marriage is love for the spouse. He lists, and rejects, other reasons why people marry or are urged to marry: that marriage is a school for character, that one has a duty to propagate the human race, that one needs a home. None of these motives are adequate, from either an aesthetic or an ethical point of view. 'Were a woman to marry', he tells us, 'so as to bear a saviour to the world, that marriage would be just as unaesthetic as immoral and irreligious' (*E/O* 417). Love is the one thing that will bring the sensual and the spiritual together into unity.

It is true that marriage, unlike romantic love, brings with it duties. But duty is not the enemy of love, but its friend. In marriage 'duty here is just one thing, truly to love, with the sincerity of the heart, and duty is as protean as love itself, declaring everything holy and good when it is of love, and denouncing everything, however pleasing and specious, when it is not of love' (*E/O* 470).

If *On the Subjection of Women* is a classic of feminism, and Judge Vilhelm's contribution to *Either/Or* was a classic defence of traditional marriage, Schopenhauer's *Essay on Women* of 1861 was a classic of male chauvinism. The natural purpose of women, the essay began, was to give birth, to care for children, and to be subject to a man, to whom she should be a patient and cheering companion. Women were better than men at nurturing children, because they were themselves childish: they lived in the present and were mentally myopic. Nature had provided women with sufficient beauty to allure a man into supporting them, but wisely took it away from them once they had produced a child or two, so that they should not be distracted from raising their families.

The fundamental defect of the female character, according to Schopenhauer, was lack of a sense of justice. As the weaker sex, they had to make their way by cunning. 'As nature has equipped the lion with claws and teeth, the elephant with tusks, the wild boar with fangs, the bull with horns and the cuttlefish with ink, so it has equipped woman with the power of dissimulation as her means of attack and defence' (*EA* 83). Women feel they are justified in deceiving individual men because their prime loyalty is not to the individual but to the species—to the propagation of the race that is their entire vocation.

Women are inferior to men not only in their powers of reasoning, but also in artistic talent and appreciation. It is not just that they chatter in the theatre at concerts (something that clearly annoyed Schopenhauer intensely); they altogether lack creative ability.

... the most eminent heads of the entire sex have proved incapable of a single truly great, genuine and original achievement in art, or indeed of creating anything at all of lasting value: this strikes one most forcibly in regard to painting, since they are just as capable of mastering the technique as we are, and indeed paint very busily, yet cannot point to a single great painting. (*EA* 86)

The worst type of woman is the *lady*, the woman who is set on a pedestal, treated with gallantry by men, and educated in arrogant haughtiness. A European lady is an unnatural creature, the object of derision in the East; and by her very existence she makes the great majority of her own sex deeply unhappy.

The law made a great mistake, Schopenhauer tells us, when it gave women equal rights with men without at the same time endowing them with masculine reasoning powers. By 'equal rights' Schopenhauer does not mean anything so outrageous as property rights or the suffrage; he simply means the institution of monogamy, which allows members of each sex to have one and only one marital partner. Polygamy, in fact, is a much more satisfactory arrangement: it makes sure that every woman is taken care of, whereas under monogamy many women are left untended as old maids or forced into hard labour or prostitution. 'There are 80,000 prostitutes in London alone: and what are they if not sacrifices on the altar of mono-gamy?' Polygamy is a benefit to the female sex, considered as a whole, and it regularizes the satisfaction of male desire. 'For who is really a monogamist? We all live in polygamy, at least for a time and usually for good.' Since every man needs many women, there could be nothing more just than that he should be free, indeed obliged, to support many women.

We may be grateful that it was Mill, and not Schopenhauer, whom future generations followed. Indeed, *On the Subjection of Women* has become antiquated as a result of its own success. The battle of which it was an early salvo has long been won, at least in the countries for whom Mill was writing. The marriage laws that Mill denounced have long been repealed, and in all matters of law women are now treated as in every respect the equals of men. And it has to be said that the cruel imprisonment that Victorian marriage law imposed on women is brought home with greater impact by the narrative and dialogue of novelists like Eliot and Trollope than by the ponderous earnestness of Mill's periods.

The issues discussed in Mill's *On Liberty*, by contrast, remain of the highest importance, though contemporary liberals often differ from Mill when they come to draw the line between warranted and unwarranted state interference with personal liberty. Most liberals accept parcels of legislation whose purpose is to promote an individual's own well-being rather than to protect others from harm: laws imposing compulsory insurance, or the wearing of protective headgear, for instance. If a modern liberal justifies this as designed to prevent the individual from becoming a charge on society, rather than as aiming at his own health and prosperity, it should be pointed out that the possibility of the poor and sick placing a burden on others assumes the existence of a network of social services provided at the taxpayer's expense—something for which Mill had a very limited enthusiasm.

On the other hand, Mill countenanced restrictions on liberty that most modern liberals would reject. He thought, for instance, that a government could legitimately limit the size of families, and he reconciled it with his libertarian principle on the following grounds: 'In a country either over-peopled, or threatened with being so, to produce children, beyond a very small number, with the effect of reducing the reward of labour by their competition, is a serious offence against all who live by the remuneration of their labour' (L 242). Many liberals share Mill's lifelong enthusiasm for population control by contraception (a cause for which he was willing to go, briefly, to prison). But when China introduced legislation to limit the size of families to a single child, most Western liberals reacted with horror.

Marx on Capital and Labour

At the same time and in the same city as Mill was writing classical works of liberal thought, Karl Marx was developing the theory of the communism that was to be for more than a century one of liberalism's greatest enemies. The basis of the theory was historical materialism: the thesis that in every epoch the prevailing mode of economic production and exchange determines the political and intellectual history of society. 'The mode of production of material life conditions the social, political, and intellectual life-process in general. It is not the consciousness of human beings that determines their being; on the contrary it is their social being that determines their consciousness' (CPE, p. x). There were two elements that determined the course of history: the forces and the relations of production. By the forces of production Marx meant the raw materials, the technology, and the labour that are necessary to make a finished product; as wheat, a mill, and a millworker are all needed to produce flour. The relations of production, on the other hand, are the economic arrangements governing these forces, such as the ownership of the mill and the hiring of the worker. Relations of production are not static; they alter as technology develops. In the age of the hand-mill, for instance, the worker is the serf of a feudal lord, tied to the land; in the age of the steam-mill he is the mobile employee of the capitalist. Relations of production are not matters of free choice; they are determined by the interplay of the productive forces. If, at any time, they become inappropriate to the productive forces, then a social revolution takes place.

Marx divided the past, present, and future history of the relations of production into six phases, three past, one present, and two to come. The past phases were primitive communism, slavery, and feudalism. The present, critical phase was that of capitalism. After capitalism's inevitable collapse, the future would bring first socialism and ultimately communism once more.

Following Engels, Marx believed that in the earliest stages of history human beings had been organized into primitive communist tribes, holding land in common, owning no private property, and ruled by a matriarchy. In the Iron Age, however, society became patriarchal, it became possible to accumulate private wealth, and slavery was introduced.

Slavery was the dominant economic feature of classical antiquity. Society was to be divided into classes: patrician and plebeian, freemen and slaves. Thus there began the story of class antagonism which was henceforth to be the fundamental feature of human history. The splendour of the classical culture of Greece and Rome was merely an ideological superstructure built upon the relations of production between the classes.

The ancient world gave way to the feudal system, with its relationships between lord and serf, and between guildsmen and journeymen. Once again, the philosophy and religion of the Middle Ages were an ideological superstructure sustained by the economic system of the age. From the serfs of the Middle Ages sprang the chartered burghers of the earliest towns: these were the first bourgeois, a middle class between the servile labourers and the aristocratic landowners. Since the time of the French Revolution the bourgeoisie had been gaining the upper hand over the aristocrats.

The modern bourgeois society that has sprouted from the ruins of feudal society has not done away with class antagonisms. It has but established new classes, new conditions of oppression, new forms of struggle in place of the old ones.

Our epoch, the epoch of the bourgeoisie, possesses, however, this distinctive feature: it has simplified the class antagonisms. Society as a whole is more and more splitting up into two great hostile camps, into two great classes directly facing each other; Bourgeoisie and Proletariat. (*CM* 3)

Marx believed that the capitalist society in which he lived had reached a state of crisis. The opposition between bourgeoisie and proletariat would become steadily stronger and lead to a revolutionary change which would usher in the final stages, first of socialism, in which all property would pass to the state, and finally to communism, after the state had withered away. The crisis which capitalism had reached, Marx maintained, was not a contingent fact of history; it was something entailed by the nature of capitalism itself. He based this conclusion on an analysis of the nature of economic value.

How is the value of a commodity determined? As a first step, we can say that a thing's value is the rate at which it can be exchanged for other commodities: a quarter of wheat may be worth so much iron, and so on. But the real value of something must be different from the countless different rates at which it can be exchanged with innumerable other commodities. We need a method of expressing the value of commodities that is common to, but distinct from, all the different particular exchanges between them.

As the *exchangeable values* of commodities are only *social functions* of those things, and have nothing at all to do with the *natural* qualities, we must first ask: What is the common *social substance* of all commodities? It is *labour*. To produce a commodity a certain amount of labour must be bestowed upon it, or worked up in it. And I say not only *labour*, but *social labour*. A man who produces an article for his own immediate use, to consume it himself, creates a *product*, but not a commodity. As a self-sustaining producer he has nothing to do with society. But to produce a *commodity* a man must not only produce an article satisfying some *social* want, but his labour itself must form part and parcel of the total sum of labour expended by society. It must be subordinate to the *division of labour within society*. (*VPP* 30)

To value a commodity, we should look on it as a piece of crystallized labour. How is labour itself measured? By the length of time the labour lasts. A silken handkerchief is worth more than a brick because it takes longer to make than a brick does. Marx states his theory thus: 'The value of one commodity is to the value of another commodity as the quantity of labour fixed in the one is to the quantity of labour fixed in the other' (*VPP* 31).

Two qualifications must be made to this simple equation. A lazy or unskilful worker will take longer to produce a commodity than an energetic and skilful one: does this mean that his product is worth more? Of course not: when we speak of the quantity of labour fixed in a commodity we mean the time that is *necessary* for a worker of average energy and skill to produce it. Moreover, we must add into the equation the labour previously worked up into the raw material of the commodity, and into the technology employed.

For example, the value of a certain amount of cotton yarn is the crystallisation of the quantity of labour added to the cotton during the spinning process, the quantity of labour previously realised in the cotton itself, the quantity of labour realised in the coal, oil, and other auxiliary matter used, the quantity of labour fixed in the steam engine, the spindles, the factory building and so forth. (*VPP* 32)

Naturally, only a proportion of the value of the spindle will be incorporated into the value of a particular quantity of yarn: the exact proportion will depend on the average working life of a spindle.

The value of a product at any given time will depend upon the productivity prevailing at that time. If an increase in population means that less fertile soils must be cultivated, the value of agricultural products will rise because greater labour is needed to produce them. On the other hand, when the introduction of the power-loom made it twice as easy to produce a given quantity of yarn, the value of yarn sank accordingly.

When value is expressed in monetary terms, it is called price. Since labour itself has a price, it too must have a value. But how is this to be defined? To answer this question we must note that what the labourer sells to his employer is not his actual labour, but his labouring power. If he is paid £10 for a sixty-hour week, he is selling for £10 his labouring power for sixty hours. But how are we to reckon the value of labouring power itself?

Like that of every other commodity, its value is determined by the quantity of labour necessary to produce it. The labouring power of a man exists only in his living individuality. A certain mass of necessaries must be consumed by a man to grow up and maintain his life. But the man, like the machine, will wear out, and must be replaced by another man. Beside the mass of necessaries required for *his own* maintenance, he wants another amount of necessaries to bring up a certain quota of children that are to replace him on the labour market and to perpetuate the race of labourers. (*VPP* 39)

It follows that the value of labouring power is determined by the cost of keeping the labourer alive and well and capable of reproduction.

To show how the capitalist exploits the labourer, Marx invites us to consider a case such as described above. Suppose that it takes twenty hours to produce the means of subsistence of the labourer for one week. He would, in that case, produce a value sufficient to maintain himself by working for twenty hours. But he has sold his working power for sixty hours. So over and above the twenty hours to replace his wages he is working a further forty hours. Marx calls these hours of *surplus labour*, and the product of those hours of labour will be *surplus value*. It is the surplus value that produces the capitalist's profit. The profit is the difference between the value of the product (six days' labour) and the value of the labourer's work (two days' labour). It is, Marx says, just as if he was working two days of the week for himself and working unpaid four days of the week for his employer.

As technology develops, and productivity increases accordingly, surplus value increases and the proportion of the labourer's work that is returned to him in wages becomes smaller and smaller. The surplus value in the output of a factory is shared between the landlord who takes rent, the banker who takes interest, and the entrepreneur who takes a commercial profit. All that goes to the labourer is the ever smaller sum that is necessary to keep him alive.

The very development of modern industry must progressively turn the scale in favour of the capitalist against the working man, and consequently the general tendency of capitalistic production is not to raise, but to sink the average standard of wages, or to push the value of labour more or less to its minimum limit. (*VPP* 61)

Given the inexorable tendencies of the capitalist system, it is futile to call for 'a fair day's wages for a fair day's work'. Only the total abolition of the cash nexus between employer and employee can achieve a fair return for labour.

The systematic exploitation endemic to the wages system is bound to reach a point at which the proletariat finds it intolerable and rises in revolt. Capitalism will be replaced by the dictatorship of the proletariat, which will abolish private property, and usher in a socialist state. Under socialism the means of production will be totally under central government control. The socialist state itself, however, will be only a temporary stage of the evolution of society. Eventually it will wither away to be replaced by a communist society in which individual and common interest will coincide. Just as Christian thinkers throughout the ages have given fuller accounts of hell than of heaven, so too Marx's descriptions of the evils of nineteenth-century capitalism are more vivid than his predictions of the final beatific state of communism. All we are told is that communist society will 'make it possible for me to do one thing today and another tomorrow, to hunt in the morning, fish in the afternoon, rear cattle in the evening, and write criticism just as I have a mind, without ever becoming hunter, fisherman, shepherd or critic' (*GI* 66).

Marx's analysis of surplus value is thought-provoking and contains profound philosophical insights. But considered as a predictive scientific theory, which was how Marx wished it to be taken, it has a fatal flaw. We are offered no convincing reason why the capitalist, no matter how great his profits, should pay the labourer no more than a subsistence wage. But that claim was an essential element in the thesis that revolution was an inevitable consequence of technological development within a capitalist system. If Marx's hypothesis had been correct, revolution would have occurred soonest in those states in which technology, and therefore exploitation, was progressing fastest. In fact the first communist revolution occurred in backward Russia, and in the developed countries of western Europe employers soon began, and have since continued, to pay wages well above subsistence level. But to be fair, the improvement in the condition of the working classes would not have taken place without the heightened awareness of the wretched state of factory labourers to which the work of Marx and Engels made a significant contribution.

Among the many philosophers who wrote in the wake of Marx and Engels the most influential was V. I. Lenin, the leader of the Russian Revolution of 1917. Lenin's influence was exercised not so much through his philosophical writings, though he was the author of two works on materialism and its epistemology, as through his leadership of the Communist Party. Against other Russian communists who believed in waiting for the inevitable dissolution of capitalism, he insisted that the birth-pangs of the new order should be hastened by violent revolution. He insisted that the party should be led by an authoritarian elite, whose ideas would shape, rather than be shaped by, economic change. Soviet democracy was to be marked not so much by the rule of the majority as by the use of force, on behalf of the majority, against the minority.

A photo post-
card showing
Karl Marx
shortly before
his death.

K. Marx

Closed and Open Societies

Lenin was disappointed when other nations failed to follow Russia's example and rise up against their capitalist rulers, but he explained the failure of Marx's predictions of their economic collapse by their imperialist exploitation of colonies as an outlet for excess capital and a source of cheap labour and raw materials. Imperialism, he famously said, was the monopoly stage of capitalism. Lenin's successor, Josef Stalin, was content to see his task as the preservation of socialism in one country, and the power of the communist elite was sustained and preserved by the patriotic fervour of the nation's struggle against Nazi Germany from 1941–5.

Neither Hitler's Germany nor Mussolini's Italy produced any lasting work of political philosophy. It is a mistake, however, to class the two ideologies together under the heading 'Fascism'. True, both Hitler and Mussolini were nationalist dictators who believed in a totalitarian state, but the leading idea of Nazism was racism, while the corporatism that was a central doctrine of Italian Fascism had nothing to do with race. Corporatism was intended to be a vocational organization of society in which individuals were grouped for purposes of representation according to their social functions. The corporate state would regulate relations between capitalists, workers, the professions, and the Church in such a way as to avoid the conflicts between classes that led to revolution. This was a different kind of political creed from the idea that one race was superior to all others and should dominate or eliminate them. Of course, Hitler and Mussolini were wartime allies; but so were Stalin and Churchill.

The Second World War did, however, produce one classic of political philosophy: *The Open Society and its Enemies*, by the Austrian exile Karl Popper. If a political organization is to flourish, Popper maintained in this book, its institutions must leave maximum room for self-correction. Just as science progresses by the constant correction of inadequate hypotheses, so society will only progress if policies are treated as experiments that can be evaluated and discontinued. Two things, therefore, are important: that the ruled should have ample freedom to discuss and criticize policies proposed by their rulers; and that it should be possible without violence or bloodshed to change the rulers, if they failed to promote their citizens' welfare. These are the central features of an open society, and they are more important elements of democracy than the mere election of a government by a majority. An open society is at the opposite extreme from the centrally controlled polities of wartime Germany, Italy, and Russia.

Popper did not rule out, however, all forms of government intervention. Unbounded tolerance could lead to intolerance, and unrestrained capitalism could lead to unacceptable levels of poverty. Incitement to intolerance should therefore be considered as criminal, and the state must protect the economically weak from the economically strong.

This, of course, means that the principle of non-intervention, of an unrestrained economic system, has to be given up; if we wish freedom to be safeguarded, then we must demand that the policy of unlimited economic freedom be replaced by the planned economic intervention of the state. We must demand that unrestrained *capitalism* give way to an *economic interventionism*. (*OSE* ii. 125)

Unlimited economic freedom was in any case a contradiction in terms: unlimited freedom of the labour market could not be combined with unlimited freedom of workers to unite.

In the two volumes of his book Popper attacked two philosophers whom he saw as enemies of the open society: Plato and Marx. His detailed critique of some Platonic political institutions was perhaps no more than a useful corrective to the fatuous admiration for the *Republic* that had been fashionable in British universities since the time of Benjamin Jowett. The critique of Marx, however, was something much more effective and influential. Popper's principal target was Marx's belief that he had discovered scientific laws that determined the future of the human race, tendencies that worked with iron necessity towards inevitable results. Popper showed how the course of history since *Capital* had in fact falsified many of Marx's specific would-be scientific predictions.

Marx's determinism was only one example of a more general error that Popper pilloried in a later book, *The Poverty of Historicism* (1957): 'I mean by "historicism" an approach to the social sciences which assumes that *historical prediction* is their principal aim, and which assumes that this aim is attainable by discovering the "rhythms" or the "patterns", the "laws" or the "trends" that underlie the evolution of history.' Besides Marxism, early Christian belief in an imminent Second Coming, and Enlightenment belief in the inevitability of human progress, offer examples of historicism. All forms of historicism, Popper showed, can be refuted by a single argument. What form the future will take will depend, *inter alia*, on what form scientific progress will take. If, therefore, we are to predict the future of society we must predict the future of science. But it is logically impossible to predict the nature of a scientific discovery; to do so would entail actually making the discovery. Hence, historicism is impossible, and the only meaning we can find in history, past or future, is that given it by free, contingent, unpredictable human choices.

The most sustained attempt to set out a systematic theoretical structure for the type of liberal democracy aspired to by most Western states was made by John Rawls (1921–2002) in his book *A Theory of Justice* (1971). Utilitarianism, Rawls argued, was insufficient as a foundation for a liberal state because it placed welfare over justice, ignoring what he called 'the priority of the right over the good'. 'Each person possesses an inviolability founded on justice that even the welfare of society as a whole cannot override. Therefore, in a just society the rights secured by justice are not subject to political bargaining or the calculus of social interests' (*TJ* 66). Instead of utilitarianism, Rawls proposed as a basis for determining the inalienable freedoms a novel kind of social contract, a thought-contract like a thought-experiment.

Imagine that there are as yet no social institutions, but we are all initially equal. In this 'original position' we are ignorant of the facts that will determine our position in the society to be designed. We do not know our race, sex, religion, class, talents, and abilities; we do not even know how we will conceive the good life. Under this 'veil of ignorance' we are to draw up a constitution on the basis of a rational desire to further our own aims and interests, whatever they may turn out to be. Because of our ignorance of the factors that are going to distinguish us from others, we are driven, in this imaginary position, to an equal concern for the fate of everyone.

The participants in this constitution-building, Rawls maintains, would choose to abide by two principles of justice. The first principle is that each person should have the right to the most extensive basic liberty compatible with a like liberty for all. The second principle is that social and economic inequalities are to be attached to office and positions that are open to all in fair competition, and that these inequalities are justified only if they can be arranged so that they are to the benefit of the worst off. If the two principles come into conflict, the principle of equal liberty trumps the principle of equal opportunity.

Rawls sees it as obvious that no one in the original position would agree to a system that incorporated slavery, for fear that when the veil of ignorance was lifted he would find himself a slave. But he also uses his two principles to operate upon a number of more contentious issues, such as intergenerational justice and civil disobedience. In a pluralistic society, he maintains, there is little chance of achieving total unanimity in ethics; the most we can hope for is a set of shared values. But by discussion of, reflection on, and adjustment to our moral judgements Rawls hopes that we may achieve what he calls 'an overlapping consensus' on ethical issues.

The goal that Rawls holds out is a state of 'reflective equilibrium'. The initial intuitions of different citizens will clash with each other, and indeed a single individual's intuitions may be inconsistent among themselves. However, if we reflect upon these intuitions and endeavour to articulate them into defensible principles we may advance towards coherence and consensus. As we do our best to deal with intuitions that are recalcitrant to the rules we have formulated, we may hope to achieve an ever more harmonious set of moral principles for ourselves and our society.

12

God

Faith vs. Alienation

Hegel regarded his system as a sophisticated and definitive presentation of philosophical truths that had been given fluctuating and mythical expression in the world's religions. In the first half of the nineteenth century the two most important reactions to the Hegelian treatment of religion came from opposite points of the philosophical compass. While Ludwig Feuerbach (1804–72) regarded Hegel as excessively sympathetic to religion, Søren Kierkegaard (1813–55) thought him impudently disrespectful of it.

In criticizing Hegel, Feuerbach made use of the Hegelian concept of alienation, the condition in which people treat as alien something that is in fact part of themselves. The fundamental idea of his *Essence of Christianity* (1841) is that God is a projection of the human mind. Humans are the highest form of beings, but they project their own life and consciousness into an unreal heaven. Men take their own essence, imagine it freed from its limitations, project it into an imagined transcendent sphere, and then venerate it as a distinct and independent being. 'God as God, that is, as a being not finite, not human, not materially conditioned, not phenomenal, is only an object of thought' (*EC* 35).

Whatever Hegel may say about Spirit, for Feuerbach the real essence of man is that he is a material being and part of nature. 'Man', he said famously, 'is what he eats.' But man differs from other animals; and the great difference that marks him out is his possession of religion. Awareness of his dependence on nature makes man initially deify natural objects like trees and fountains. The monotheistic idea of a personal God arises when humans become conscious of themselves as possessing reason, will, and love. In religion, man contemplates his own latent nature, but as something apart from himself.

Religion is the disuniting of man from himself; he sets God before him as the antithesis of himself. God is not what man is—man is not what God is. God is the infinite, man the finite being; God is perfect, man imperfect; God eternal, man temporal; God almighty, man weak; God holy, man sinful. God and man are extremes: God is the absolutely positive, the sum of all realities; man the absolutely negative, comprehending all negations. (*EC* 33)

Feuerbach agrees with Hegel that religion represents an essential, but imperfect, stage of human self-consciousness. But Hegel's own philosophy, according to Feuerbach, is yet another form of alienation: it is the last refuge of theology. By treating nature as posited by the Idea it offers us only a disguised version of the Christian doctrine of creation. We must set Hegel on his feet, and place philosophy on the solid ground of materialism.

Like Hegel's doctrine of alienation, Feuerbach's criticism of religion and idealism had a great influence on Marx and Engels. But Marx regarded not religion but capitalism as the greatest form of alienation—it was money, not God, that was the capitalist's object of worship. Religion, said Marx, is the opium of the people. By this he did not mean that religion was a pipe-dream (though he believed that it was) but that belief in a happier afterlife was a necessary stupefacient to make labour under capitalism bearable. 'Religious suffering is at one and the same time the expression of real suffering and a protest against real suffering. Religion is the sigh of the oppressed creature, the heart of a heartless world and the soul of soulless conditions. It is the opium of the people' (*EW* 257).

While Hegel and Schopenhauer regarded traditional religious beliefs as popular allegorical or mythical presentations of philosophical truths that were accessible only to an enlightened elite, and while Feuerbach and Marx regarded them as the illusory projections of alienated consciousness, Kierkegaard always placed faith at the summit of human progress, and regarded the religious sphere as superior to the regions of science and politics. Ethics, too, he taught, must be strictly subordinated to worship.

For centuries, ever since Plato's *Euthyphro*, philosophers had debated the relationship between religion and morality. Does the moral value of an action depend simply on whether it is prescribed or prohibited by God? Or is it only because some actions are already of their own nature good or bad that God commands or forbids them? Thomas Aquinas had held that all the Ten Commandments belonged to a natural law from which not even God could offer dispensation. Duns Scotus, on the other hand, maintained that God could dispense from the law against murder and had done so when he ordered Abraham to sacrifice Isaac.[1]

In *Fear and Trembling* Kierkegaard adopted a new approach to this thorny topic. He too took the Genesis story of Abraham and Isaac as the test case for his discussion.

God did tempt Abraham and said unto him, Abraham: and he said, Behold here I am.

And he said, Take now thy son, thine only son Isaac, whom thou lovest, and get thee into the land of Moriah; and offer him there for a burnt offering upon one of the mountains which I will tell thee of.

And Abraham rose up early in the morning, and saddled his ass, and took two of his young men with him, and Isaac his son, and clave the wood for the burnt offering, and rose up, and went unto the place of which God had told him.

Then on the third day Abraham lifted up his eyes and saw the place afar off.

And Abraham said unto his young men, Abide ye here with the ass; and I and the lad will go yonder and worship, and come again to you.

And Abraham took the wood of the burnt offering, and laid it upon Isaac his son; and he took the fire in his hand, and a knife; and they went both of them together.

And Isaac spoke unto Abraham his father, and said My father: and he said Here am I, my son.

And he said, Behold the fire and the wood: but where is the lamb for a burnt offering?

And Abraham said, My son, God will provide himself a lamb for a burnt offering: so they went both of them together.

And they came to the place which God had told him of; and Abraham built an altar there, and laid the wood in order, and bound Isaac his son, and laid him on the altar upon the wood.

And Abraham stretched forth his hand, and took the knife to slay his son. (Gen. 22: 1–10)

[1] See vol. I, pp. 291–2; vol. II, pp. 273–4.

Gustav Doré's 1866 representation of the sacrifice of Abraham.

There is undoubtedly something heroic in Abraham's willingness to sacrifice Isaac—the son for whom he had waited eighty years, and in whom all
his hope of posterity rested. But in ethical terms, is not his conduct
monstrous? He is willing to commit murder, to violate a father's duty to
love his son, and in the course of it to deceive those closest to him.

Biblical and classical literature, Kierkegaard reminds us, offers other
examples of parents sacrificing their children: Agamemnon offering up
Iphigenia to avert the gods' curse on the Greek expedition to Troy, Jephtha
giving up his daughter in fulfilment of a rash vow, Brutus condemning to
death his treasonable sons. These were all sacrifices made for the greater
good of a community: they were, in ethical terms, a surrender of the
individual for the sake of the universal. Abraham's sacrifice was nothing of
the kind: it was a transaction between himself and God. Had he been a
tragic hero like the others, he would, on reaching Mount Moriah, have
plunged the knife into himself rather than into Isaac. Instead, Kierkegaard
tells us, he stepped outside the realm of ethics altogether, and acted for the
sake of an altogether higher goal.

Such an action Kierkegaard calls 'the teleological suspension of the
ethical'. Abraham's act transgressed the ethical order in view of his higher
end, or *telos*, outside it. Whereas an ethical hero, such as Socrates, lays down
his life for the sake of a universal moral law, Abraham's heroism lay in his
obedience to an individual divine command. Moreover, his action was not
just one of renunciation, like the rich young man in the gospel abandoning
his wealth: a man does not have a duty to his money as he does to his son,
and it was precisely in violating this duty that Abraham showed his
obedience to God.

Was his act then sinful? If we think of every duty as being a duty to God,
then undoubtedly it was. But such an identification of God with duty
actually empties of content the notion of duty to God himself.

The whole existence of the human race is rounded off completely like a sphere,
and the ethical is at once its limit and its content. God becomes an invisible
vanishing point, a powerless thought, His power being only in the ethical which is
the content of existence. If in any way it might occur to any man to want to love
God in any other sense, he is romantic, he loves a phantom which if it had merely
the power of being able to speak, would say to him 'I do not require your love. Stay
where you belong'. (*FT* 78)

If there is to be a God who is more than a personification of duty, then there must be a sphere higher than the ethical. If Abraham is a hero, as the Bible portrays him, it can only be from the standpoint of faith. 'For faith is this paradox, that the particular is higher than the universal.'

Even if we accept that the demands of the unique relationship between God and an individual may override commitments arising from general laws, a crucial question remains. If an individual feels called to violate an ethical law, how is he to tell whether this is a genuine divine command or a mere temptation? Kierkegaard insists that no one else can tell him; that is why Abraham kept his plan secret from Sarah, Isaac, and his friends. The knight of faith (as Kierkegaard calls Abraham) has the terrible responsibility of solitude. But how can he even know or prove to himself what is a genuine divine command? Kierkegaard merely emphasizes that the leap of faith is taken in blindness. His failure to offer a criterion for distinguishing genuine from delusive vocation is something that cries out to us in an age when more and more people feel they have a personal divine command to sacrifice their own lives in order to kill as many innocent victims as possible.

Kierkegaard's silence at this point is not inadvertent. In his *Philosophical Fragments* and his *Concluding Unscientific Postscript* he offers a number of arguments to the effect that faith is not the outcome of any objective reasoning. The form of religious faith that he has in mind is the Christian belief that Jesus saved the human race by his death on the cross. This belief contains definite historical elements, and Kierkegaard asks, 'Is it possible to base an eternal happiness upon historical knowledge?', and he gives three arguments for a negative answer.

First, it is impossible, by objective research, to obtain certainty about any historical event; there is always some possibility of doubt, however small, and we never achieve more than an approximation. But faith leaves no room for doubt; it is a resolution to reject the possibility of error. No mere judgement of probability is sufficient for this faith which is to be the basis of eternal happiness. Hence, faith cannot be based on objective history.

Second, historical research is never definitively concluded: it is always being refined and revised, difficulties are always arising and being overcome. 'Each generation inherits from its predecessors the illusion that the method is quite impeccable, but the learned scholars have not yet achieved success.' If we are to take a historical document as the basis of our religious commitment, that commitment must be perpetually postponed.

Third, faith must be a passionate devotion of oneself, but objective inquiry involves an attitude of detachment. Because belief demands passion, Kierkegaard argues that the improbability of what is believed not only is no obstacle to faith, but is an essential element of faith. The believer must embrace risk, for without risk there is no faith. 'Faith is precisely the contradiction between the infinite passion of the individual's inwardness and the objective uncertainty.' The greater the risk of falsehood, the greater the passion involved in believing. We must throw away all rational supports of faith 'so as to permit the absurd to stand out in all its clarity, in order that the individual may believe if he wills it' (P 190).

If the improbability of a belief is the measure of the passion with which it is believed, then faith, which Kierkegaard calls 'infinite personal passion', must have as its object something that is infinitely improbable. Such was the faith of Abraham, who right up to the moment of drawing the knife on Isaac continued to believe in the divine promise of posterity. And his faith was rewarded, when God's angel held back his hand and Isaac, liberated from the pyre, went on to become the father of many nations.

Few believing Christians have been willing to accept that Christianity is infinitely improbable, and non-believers are offered by Kierkegaard no motive, not to say reason, for accepting belief. Paradoxically, his irrationalism has been most influential not among his fellow believers, but among twentieth-century atheists. Existentialist thinkers such as Karl Jaspers in Germany and Jean-Paul Sartre in France found attractive his claim that to have an authentic existence one must abandon the multitude and seize control of one's own destiny by a blind leap beyond reason.

The Theism of John Stuart Mill

In England, religious thought took a very different turn in the writings of John Stuart Mill, published some fifteen years after the *Concluding Unscientific Postscript*. Jeremy Bentham and James Mill had ensured that religious instruction should form no part of John Stuart's education. Accordingly, in his autobiography, Mill says he is 'one of the very few examples in this country of one who has, not thrown off religious belief, but never had it'. Possibly because of this, he did not feel the animus against religion that many other utilitarians have felt. In his posthumously published *Three*

Essays on Religion he took a remarkably dispassionate look at the arguments for and against the existence of God, and at the positive and negative effects of religious belief.

While dismissing the ontological and causal arguments for God's existence, Mill took seriously the argument from design, the only one based upon experience. 'In the present state of our knowledge', he wrote, 'the adaptations in Nature afford a large balance of probability in favour of creation by intelligence.' He did not, however, regard the evidence as rendering even probable the existence of an omnipotent and benevolent creator. An omnipotent being would have no need of the adaptation of means to ends that provides the support of the design argument; and an omnipotent being that permitted the amount of evil we find in the world could not be benevolent. Still less can the God of traditional Christianity be so regarded. Recalling his father, Mill wrote in his autobiography:

Think (he used to say) of a being who would make a Hell—who would create the human race with the infallible foreknowledge, and therefore with the intention, that the great majority of them were to be consigned to horrible and everlasting torment. The time, I believe, is drawing near when this dreadful conception of an object of worship will be no longer identified with Christianity; and when all persons, with any sense of moral good and evil, will look upon it with the same indignation with which my father regarded it. (*A* 26)

We cannot call any being good, Mill maintained, unless he possesses the attributes that constitute goodness in our fellow creatures—'and if such a being can sentence me to hell for not so calling him, to hell I will go'.

But even if the notion of hell is discarded as mythical, the amount of evil we know to exist in this world is sufficient, Mill believes, to rule out the notion of omnipotent goodness. Mill was indeed an optimist in his judgement of the world we live in: 'all the grand sources', Mill wrote, 'of human suffering are in a great degree, many of them almost entirely, conquerable by human care and effort' (*U* 266). Nonetheless, the great majority of mankind live in misery, and if this is due largely to human incompetence and lack of goodwill, that itself counts against the idea that we are all under the rule of all-powerful goodness.

Mill's essay *Theism* concludes as follows:

These, then, are the net results of natural theology on the question of the divine attributes. A being of great but limited power, how or by what limited we cannot even conjecture; of great and perhaps unlimited intelligence, but perhaps also more narrowly limited power than this, who desires, and pays some regard to, the happiness of his creatures, but who seems to have other motives of action which he cares more for, and who can hardly be supposed to have created the universe for that purpose alone. Such is the deity whom natural religion points to, and any idea of God more captivating than this comes only from human wishes, or from the teaching of either real or imaginary revelation. (3E 94)

If that is the case, what can be said about the desirability or otherwise of religious belief? It cannot be disputed, Mill says, that religion has value to individuals as a source of personal satisfaction and elevated feelings. Some religions hold out the prospect of immortality as an incentive to virtuous behaviour. But this expectation rests on tenuous grounds; and as humanity makes progress it may come to seem a much less flattering prospect.

It is not only possible but probable that in a higher, and above all, a happier condition of human life, not annihilation but immortality may be the burdensome idea; and that human nature, though pleased with the present, and by no means impatient to quit it, would find comfort and not sadness in the thought that it is not chained through eternity to a conscious existence which it cannot be assured that it will always wish to preserve. (3E 122)

Creation and Evolution

By the time Mill's Essays were published in 1887, religious believers felt under threat more from evolutionary biology than from empiricist philosophy. On the Origin of Species and The Descent of Man were greeted with horror in some Christian circles. At the meeting of the British Association in 1860, the evolutionist T. H. Huxley, so he reported, had been asked by the Bishop of Oxford whether he claimed descent from an ape on his father's or his mother's side. Huxley—according to his own account—replied that he would rather have an ape for a grandfather than a man who misused his gifts to obstruct science by rhetoric.

The quarrel between Darwinian evolutionists and Christian fundamentalists continues today. Darwin's theory obviously clashes with a literal acceptance of the Bible account of the creation of the world in seven days. Moreover, the length of time that would be necessary for evolution to take place would be immensely longer than the 6,000 years that Christian

John Stuart Mill with his stepdaughter Helen who published posthumously his writings on religion.

fundamentalists believe to be the age of the universe. But a non-literal interpretation of Genesis was adopted long ago by theologians as orthodox as St Augustine, and many Christians today are content to accept that the earth may have existed for billions of years. It is more difficult to reconcile an acceptance of Darwinism with belief in original sin. If the struggle for existence had been going on for aeons before humans evolved, it is impossible to accept that it was man's first disobedience and the fruit of the forbidden tree that brought death into the world.

On the other hand, it is wrong to suggest, as is often done, that Darwin disproved the existence of God. For all Darwin showed, the whole machinery of natural selection may have been part of a creator's design for the universe. After all, belief that we humans are God's creatures has never been regarded as incompatible with our being the children of our parents; it is no more incompatible with us being, on both sides, descended from the ancestors of the apes.

At most, Darwin disposed of one argument for the existence of God: namely, the argument that the adaptation of organisms to their environment exhibits the handiwork of a benevolent creator. But even that is to overstate the case. The only argument refuted by Darwin would be one that said: wherever there is adaptation to environment we must see the immediate activity of an intelligent being. But the old argument from design did not claim this; and indeed it was an essential step in the argument that lower animals and natural agents did not have minds. The argument was only that the ultimate explanation of such adaptation must be found in intelligence; and if the argument was ever sound, then the success of Darwinism merely inserts an extra step between the phenomena to be explained and their ultimate explanation.

Darwinism leaves much to be explained. The origin of individual species from earlier species may be explained by the mechanisms of evolutionary pressure and selection. But these mechanisms cannot be used to explain the origin of species as such. For one of the starting points of explanation by natural selection is the existence of true breeding populations, namely species.

Many Darwinians claim that the origin and structure of the world and the emergence of human life and human institutions are already fully explained by science, so that no room is left for postulating the existence of activity of any non-natural agent. Darwin himself was more cautious. Though he believed that it was not necessary, in order to account for the perfection of complex organs and instincts, to appeal to 'means superior to, though analogous with, human reason', he explicitly left room, in several places of the second edition of *On the Origin of Species*, for the activity of a creator. In defending his theory from geological objections he pleads that the imperfections of the geological record 'do not overthrow the theory of descent from a few created forms with subsequent modification' (*OS* 376). 'I should infer from analogy', he tells us, 'that probably all the organic beings which have ever lived on this earth have descended from some one primordial form, into which life was first breathed by the Creator' (*OS* 391).

Indeed, Darwin claims it as a merit of his system that it is in accord with what we know of the divine mode of action:

To my mind it accords better with what we know of the laws impressed on matter by the Creator, that the production and extinction of the past and present inhabitants of the world should have been due to secondary causes, like those determining the birth and death of the individual. When I view all beings not as special creations, but as the lineal descendants of some few beings which lived long before the first bed of the Silurian system was deposited, they seem to me to become ennobled. (*OS* 395)

It was special creation, not creation, that Darwin objected to.

When neo-Darwinians claim that Darwin's insights enable us to explain the entire cosmos, philosophical difficulties arise at three main points: the origin of language, the origin of life, and the origin of the universe.

In the case of the human species there is a particular difficulty in explaining by natural selection the origin of language, given that language is a system of conventions. Explanation by natural selection of the origin of a feature in a population presupposes the occurrence of that feature in particular individuals of the population. Natural selection might favour a certain length of leg, and the long-legged individuals in the population might outbreed the others. But for this kind of explanation of features to be possible, it must be possible to conceive the occurrence of the feature in single individuals. There is no problem in describing a single individual as having legs *n* metres long. But there is a problem with the idea that there might be just a single human language-user.

It is not easy to explain how the human race may have begun to use language by claiming that the language-using individuals among the population were advantaged and so outbred the non-language-using

Darwin's theory of evolution portrayed in Punch's Almanac for 1882, twenty two years after the publication of *The Origin of Species*.

individuals. This is not simply because of the difficulty of seeing how spontaneous mutation could produce a language-using individual; it is the difficulty of seeing how anyone could be described as a language-using individual at all before there was a community of language-users. Human language is a rule-governed, communal activity, totally different from the signalling systems to be found in non-humans. If we reflect on the social and conventional nature of language, we must find something odd in the idea that language may have evolved because of the advantages possessed

303

by language-users over non-language-users. It seems almost as absurd as the idea that banks may have evolved because those born with an innate cheque-writing ability were better off than those born without it.

Language cannot be the result of trial and error learning because such learning presupposes stable goals that successive attempts realize or fail to realize (as a rat may find or fail to find a food pellet in maze). But there is no goal to which language is a means: one cannot have the goal of acquiring a language, because one needs a language to have that wish in.

If it is difficult to see how language could originate by natural selection, it is equally difficult to see how life could originate that way. However successful natural selection may be in explaining the origin of particular species of life, it clearly cannot explain how there came to be such things as species at all. Darwin never claimed that it did; he did not offer an explanation of the origin of life.

Neo-Darwinians, by contrast, often attempt to tell us how life began, speculating, say, about electrical changes in some primeval organic soup. These explanations are of a radically different kind from those that Darwin put forward to account for evolution. Neo-Darwinians try to explain life as produced by the chance interaction of non-living materials and forces subject to purely physical laws. These accounts, whatever their merits, are not explanations by natural selection.

Natural selection and intelligent design are not incompatible with each other, in the way that natural selection is incompatible with the Genesis story. But though 'intelligent design' may be used in political circles as a euphemism for biblical fundamentalism, in the sheer idea of an extra-cosmic intelligence there is nothing that commits one to a belief in the Judaeo-Christian, or any other, religious revelation. To be sure, discussion of the possibility of such an intelligence does not belong in the science classroom; if it did, the intelligence would not be an extra-cosmic one, but a part of nature. But that is no reason why philosophers should not give it serious consideration.

The most fundamental reason in favour of postulating an extra-cosmic agency of any kind is surely the need to explain the origin of the universe itself. It is wrong to say that God provides the answer to the question, 'Why is there something rather than nothing?' The question itself is ill-conceived: the proposition 'There is nothing' cannot be given a coherent sense, and therefore there is no need to ask why it is false. It is not the existence of the universe that calls for explanation, but its coming into existence. At a time when philosophers and scientists were happy to accept that the universe had existed forever, there was no question of looking for a cause of its origin, only of looking for an explanation of its nature. But when it is proposed that the universe began at a point of time measurably distant in the past, then it seems perverse simply to shrug one's shoulders and decline to seek any explanation. In the case of an ordinary existent, we would be uneasy with a blithe announcement that there was simply no reason for its coming into existence. Unless we accept a Kantian view of the limitations of reason, it seems irrational to abandon this attitude when the existing thing in question is all-pervasive, like the universe.

Newman's Philosophy of Religion

If one accepts that the origin of the universe needs some explanation outside itself, that is not of itself sufficient to amount to a belief in God as defined in the great monotheistic traditions. Nor, even according to some believers, is it necessary. So devout a philosopher as John Henry Newman could write, 'It is indeed a great question whether Atheism is not as philosophically consistent with the phenomena of the physical world, taken by themselves, as the doctrine of a creative and governing power' (US 186).

For Newman, the justification of religious faith came from quite different sources, as he explained in *The Grammar of Assent*. 'Faith', for Newman, has a quite precise sense. Faith in God is more than just belief that there is a God: Aristotle believed in a prime mover unmoved but his belief was not faith. Faith in God was not necessarily total commitment to God: Marlowe's Faustus, on the verge of damnation, still believes in redemption. Faith contrasted with reason and love; the special feature of a belief that makes it faith is that it is a belief in something as revealed by God, belief in a proposition on the word of God. Such was Newman's conception of faith. It is a Catholic conception, different from the Lutheran one that we encountered in Kierkegaard.

Faith, understood as belief rather than commitment, is an operation of the intellect, not of the will or emotions. But is it a reasonable operation of the intellect, or is it rash and irrational? Newman accepts that the testimony on which faith is based is in itself weak. It can only convince someone who has an antecedent sympathy with the content of the testimony.

> Faith ... does not demand evidence so strong as is necessary for ... belief on the ground of Reason; and why? for this reason, because it is mainly swayed by antecedent considerations ... previous notices, prepossessions, and (in a good sense of the word) prejudices. The mind that believes is acted upon by its own hopes, fears, and existing opinions. (*US* 179–80)

Newman is well aware that his stress on the need for preparation of the heart may well make faith appear to be no more than wishful thinking. He emphasizes, however, that the mismatch between evidence and commitment, and the importance of previous attitudes, is to be observed not only in religious faith, but in other cases of belief.

> We hear a report in the streets, or read it in the public journals. We know nothing of the evidence; we do not know the witnesses, or anything about them: yet sometimes we believe implicitly, sometimes not: sometimes we believe without asking for evidence, sometimes we disbelieve till we receive it. Did a rumour circulate of a destructive earthquake in Syria or the South of Europe, we should readily credit it; both because it might easily be true, and because it was nothing to us though it were. Did the report relate to countries nearer home, we should try to trace and authenticate it. We do not call for evidence till antecedent probabilities fail. (*US* 180)

Two objections may be made to Newman's claim that faith is reasonable even though acceptance of it depends not so much on evidence as on antecedent probabilities. The first is that antecedent probabilities may be equally available for what is true and for what merely pretends to be true. They supply no intelligible rule to decide between a genuine and a counterfeit revelation:

> If a claim of miracles is to be acknowledged because it happens to be advanced, why not for the miracles of India as well as for those of Palestine? If the abstract possibility of a Revelation be the measure of genuineness in a given case, why not in the case of Mahomet as well as of the Apostles? (*US* 226)

Newman, who is never more eloquent than when developing criticisms of his own position, nowhere provides a satisfactory answer to this objection.

Secondly, it may be objected that there is a difference between religious faith and the reasonable, though insufficiently grounded, beliefs to which we give assent in our daily lives. In Newman's own words, Christianity is to be 'embraced and maintained as true, on the grounds of its being divine, not as true on intrinsic grounds, nor as probably true, or partially true, but as absolutely certain knowledge, certain in a sense in which nothing else can be certain'. In the ordinary cases, we are always ready to consider evidence that tells against our beliefs; but the religious believer adopts a certitude that refuses to entertain any doubt about the articles of faith.

Newman responds that even in secular matters, it can be rational to reject objections as idle phantoms, however much they may be insisted upon by a pertinacious opponent, or present themselves through an obsessive imagination.

I certainly should be very intolerant of such a notion as that I shall one day be Emperor of the French; I should think it too absurd even to be ridiculous, and that I must be mad before I could entertain it. And did a man try to persuade me that treachery, cruelty, or ingratitude was as praiseworthy as honesty and temperance, and that a man who lived the life of a knave and died the death of a brute had nothing to fear from future retribution, I should think there was no call on me to listen to his arguments, except with the hope of converting him, though he called me a bigot and a coward for refusing to enter into his speculations.

On the other hand, a believer can certainly investigate the arguments for and against his religious position. To do so need not involve any weakening of faith. But may not a man's investigation lead to his giving up his assent to his creed? Indeed it may, but:

my vague consciousness of the possibility of a reversal of my belief in the course of my researches, as little interferes with the honesty and firmness of that belief while those researches proceed, as the recognition of the possibility of my train's oversetting is an evidence of an intention on my part of undergoing so great a calamity. (GA 127)

There is no need to follow in detail the arguments by which Newman does his best to show that the acceptance of the Catholic religion is the action of a reasonable person. He maintains that the enduring history of Judaism and Christianity through the vicissitudes of human affairs is a phenomenon that carries on its face the probability of a divine origin. But it does so, Newman admits, only to someone who already believes that there is a God who will judge the world.

But what reason is there in the first place to believe in God and a future judgement? In response, Newman makes his celebrated appeal to the testimony of conscience:

If, on doing wrong, we feel the same tearful, broken hearted sorrow which overwhelms us on hurting a mother; if, on doing right, we enjoy the same sunny serenity of mind, the same soothing satisfactory delight which follows on our receiving praise from a father, we certainly have within us the image of some person, to whom our love and veneration look, in whose smile we find our happiness, for whom we yearn, towards whom we direct our pleadings, in whose anger we are troubled and waste away. These feelings in us are such as require for their exciting cause an intelligent being. (*GA* 76)

It is difficult for members of a post-Freudian generation to read this passage without acute discomfort. It is not the mere existence of conscience—of moral judgements of right and wrong—that Newman regards as intimations of the existence of God. Such judgements can be explained—as they are by many Christian philosophers as well as by utilitarians—as conclusions arrived at by natural reason and common sense. It is the emotional colouring of conscience that Newman claims to be echoes of the admonitions of a Supreme Judge. The feelings that he eloquently describes may indeed be appropriate only if there is a Father in heaven. But no feelings can guarantee their own appropriateness in the absence of reason.

Earlier, we noticed parallels between the accounts of belief given by Newman and Frege. Frege himself had no great interest in philosophy of religion. There is, however, one passage in the *Foundations of Arithmetic* that is of great importance to anyone interested in the possibility of proving the existence of God. Frege sets out an analogy between existence and number. 'Affirmation of existence', he says (*FA* 65), 'is in fact nothing but denial of the number nought.' What he means is that an affirmation of existence (for example, 'Angels exist' or 'There are [such things as] angels') is an assertion that a concept (for example, *angel*) has something falling under it. And to say that a concept has something falling under it is to say that the number belonging to that concept is not zero.

It is because existence is a property of concepts and not of objects, Frege says, that the ontological argument for the existence of God breaks down. That is to say, that-there-is-a-God cannot be a component of the concept

God, nor can it be a component of that concept that-there-is-only-one-God. If in fact there is one and only one God, that is a property, not of God, but of the concept *God*.

Frege's argument was taken by many later philosophers—including Bertrand Russell—as giving the death-blow to the ontological argument. But the matter is not so simple. Frege has not shown that it is never possible to make an inference, as the ontological argument does, from the components of a concept to its properties. Frege himself infers from the components of the concept *equilateral right-angled triangle* that it has the property of possessing the number zero. Perhaps, one may argue, there may also be cases where one can infer from the component characteristics of a concept to existence or to uniqueness. Moreover, if, as some later logicians have done, one is prepared to allow into one's ontology not only actual but also possible objects, then existence is indeed a property of objects: it is precisely what makes some of them actual and not possible.

The Death of God and the Survival of Religion

Two years before Frege published his criticism of the ontological argument, Nietzsche had announced in *The Gay Science* that God was dead, that belief in the Christian God had become incredible. He did so, however, in the tones not of a philosopher, but of an evangelist; he was not offering arguments against a thesis, but proclaiming the greatest of good news. 'At last the horizon lies free before us, even granted that it is not bright; at least, the sea, *our* sea lies open before us.' The Christian God, with his commands and prohibitions, had been hitherto the greatest obstacle to the fullness of human life. Now that he is dead we are free to express our will to live.

Nietzsche had no patience with those thinkers—particularly in England—who tried to preserve Christian morality while denying the Christian faith. He was particularly scornful of that 'moralizing little woman' George Eliot, clinging on to respectability after being emancipated from theology.

Christianity, Nietzsche says, is a system, a coherent and *complete* view of things. If you break off one of its principal concepts, the belief in God, then you shatter the whole thing; you have nothing essential left in your fingers. Christianity presupposes that man does not—*cannot*—know what is good for him, and what is evil: he believes in God, and God alone knows these things. Christian morality is an imperative; its origin is transcendental; it is beyond any criticism, any right to criticize; it is true only if God is truth—it stands and falls with the belief in God (*TI* 45).

The idea of a moral law without a lawgiver is vacuous. English people who believe that they can detect good and evil by intuition merely reveal how much they are still under the hidden influence of the Christianity they have thrown off. While a healthy morality would fulfil 'the decrees of life', conventional morality is anti-natural and fights our vital instincts. 'In saying "God looks at the heart" it says no to the lowest and highest of life's desires, and proclaims God as the enemy of life ... The saint, in whom God is well pleased, is the ideal castrato ... Life ends where "the kingdom of God" begins' (*TI* 23).

One person who took seriously Nietzsche's criticism of saintliness was William James. For Nietzsche, he observed, the saint represents little but sneakingness and slavishness. He is the sophisticated invalid, the degenerate par excellence, the man of insufficient vitality; his prevalence would put the human type in danger. Poor Nietzsche's antipathy, James said, was sickly enough, but the clash he describes between two ideals is real and important. 'The whole feud', James wrote, 'revolves essentially upon two pivots: Shall the seen world or the unseen world be our chief sphere of adaptation? and must our means of adaptation in this seen world be aggressiveness or non resistance?' (*VRE* 361). James devoted five of his 1902 Gifford lectures to a defence of the value of saintliness. But the defence was qualified. 'Abstractly the saint is the highest type', he concluded, 'but in the present environment it may fail, so we make ourselves saints at our peril' (*VRE* 10).

The Varieties of Religious Experience is not a work of philosophy, of whose powers in this area James was sceptical, nor of anthropology, since it is based not on fieldwork but on written sources. It is more like a Kama Sutra guide to the experiences of those who have sought release and satisfaction in religion. (Not that James welcomed any assimilation of religion to sex. 'Few conceptions are less instructive', he wrote, 'than this re-interpretation of religion as perverted sexuality'; *VRE* 33.)

Besides saintliness, James surveyed religious phenomena such as the sense of sin, the experience of conversion, and mystical states. The treatment of saintliness and conversion left unanswered the question, 'Is the

Philosophers have long discussed proofs and disproofs of God's existence; but the rise and fall of religions has been due less to argument than to custom and coercion. This is a 1974 receipt for payment of a fine levied in the U.S.S.R "for belief in God".

sense of divine presence a sense of anything objectively true?' Mysticism, James concluded, was too private and too various to make any claim to universal authority. In the last lectures of his series he asked whether philosophy could stamp any warrant of veracity upon the religious man's sense of the divine.

James had little hope of any help from traditional proofs of God's existence, whether the argument to a first cause, or the argument from design, or the argument from morality to a lawgiver. 'The arguments for God's existence', he wrote, 'have stood for hundreds of years with the waves of unbelieving criticism breaking against them, never totally discrediting them in the ears of the faithful, but on the whole slowly and surely washing the mortar from between their joints' (*VRE* 420).

James listed the attributes of God that theologians had striven over the centuries to establish: his self-derived existence (aseity), his necessity, his uniqueness, his spirituality, his metaphysical simplicity, his immensity and omnipresence, his omniscience and omnipotence. James has a brief, nononsense, pragmatist's way with these conceptions of natural theology. To develop a thought's meaning, he stated, with a salute to Peirce, we need only determine what conduct it is fitted to produce, and that conduct is for us its sole significance. If we apply this principle to God's metaphysical attributes, we have to confess them destitute of all intelligible significance.

Take God's aseity for example; or his necessariness; his immateriality; his 'simplicity' or superiority to the kind of inner variety and succession which we find in finite beings, his indivisibility, and lack of the inner distinctions of being and activity, substance and accident, potentiality and actuality, and the rest; his repudiation of inclusion in a genus; his actualized infinity; his 'personality', apart from the moral qualities which it may comport; his relations to evil being permissive and not positive; his self-sufficiency, self-love, and absolute felicity in himself:—candidly speaking, how do such qualities as these make any definite connection with our life? And if they severally call for no distinctive adaptations of our conduct, what vital difference can it possibly make to a man's religion whether they be true or false? (*VRE* 428)

So much for God's metaphysical attributes. But what of his moral attributes, such as holiness, justice, and mercy? Surely these are, from the point of view of pragmatism, on a different footing: they positively determine fear and hope and expectations, and are foundations for the saintly life. Well, perhaps these predicates are meaningful; but dogmatic theology has never produced any convincing arguments that they do in fact belong to God. And modern idealism, James believed, has said goodbye to dogmatic theology for ever.

It is not reason, he maintained in conclusion, that is the source of religion, but feeling. Philosophical and theological formulas are secondary. All that philosophy can do is to assist in the articulation of religious experience, compare different expressions of it, eliminate local and accidental elements from these expressions, mediate between different believers, and help to bring about consensus of opinion. The theologians' enumeration of divine epithets is not worthless, but its value is aesthetic rather than scientific. 'Epithets lend an atmosphere and overtones to our devotion. They are like a hymn of praise and service of glory, and may sound the more sublime for being incomprehensible' (*VRE* 437–9).

In a world governed by science and its laws, is there any room for prayer? James distinguishes between petitionary prayer, and prayer in a wider sense. Among petitionary prayers, he makes a further distinction between prayers for better weather, and prayers for the recovery of sick people. The first are futile, but not necessarily the second. 'If any medical fact can be considered to stand firm, it is that in certain environments prayer may contribute to recovery and should be encouraged as a therapeutic measure' (*VRE* 443).

Taken in a wider sense, prayer means 'every kind of inward communion or conversation with the power recognized as divine'. This, James maintains, is untouched by scientific criticism. Indeed, the whole upshot of his investigation of religious experience is that 'religion, wherever it is an active thing, involves a belief in ideal presences and a belief that in our prayerful communion with them, work is done, and something real comes to pass'. But is this belief *true*, or is it a mere anachronistic survival from a pre-scientific age? Any science of religion is as likely to be hostile as to be favourable to the claim that the essence of religion is true.

But science, James thinks, need not necessarily have the last word. Religion is concerned with the individual and his personal destiny, science with the impersonal and general. 'The God whom science recognizes must be a God of universal laws exclusively, a God who does a wholesale, not a retail business' (*VRE* 472). But which is more real, the universal or the particular? According to James, 'so long as we deal with the cosmic and the general, we deal only with the symbols of reality, but *as soon as we deal with private and personal phenomena as such, we deal with realities in the completest sense of the term*' (*VRE* 476). It is absurd for science to claim that the egotistic elements of experience should be suppressed. 'Religion, occupying herself with personal destinies and keeping thus in contact with the only absolute realities which we know, must necessarily play an eternal part in human history' (*VRE* 480).

James is willing, in conclusion, to call the supreme reality in the universe 'God'. But his positive account of God is extremely nebulous; it is similar to Matthew Arnold's definitions of God as 'the stream of tendency by which all things seek to fulfil the law of their being' or 'an eternal power, not ourselves, that makes for righteousness'. James's woolliness of expression, however, is only to be expected, since he regarded religion as essentially a matter of feeling, and feelings as essentially inarticulate. But it disappointed many of his friends, who regarded him, on other topics, as a model of candour and precision. 'His wishes made him turn down the lights', said his old friend Oliver Wendell Holmes, Jr., 'so as to give miracle a chance.'[2]

---

[2] Letter of 1 Sept. 1910, quoted in Louis Menand, *The Metaphysical Club* (London: Flamingo, 2001), 436.

Freud on Religious Illusion

Freud, on the other hand, wanted to turn up the lights on the dark corners of the soul in order to rid the world of enchantment. Religion, he maintained, was an illusion; and he used 'illusion' in a precise sense as a belief determined by human wishes. Illusions, for Freud, are not necessarily false beliefs, as delusions are, but they are beliefs undetermined by evidence; if they are true it is by a happy accident. 'For instance, a middle-class girl may have the illusion that a prince will come and marry her. This is possible; and a few such cases have occurred.' Freud's definition means that he can maintain that religion is an illusion while, in theory at least, leaving open the question of the truth-value of religious beliefs. It is unlikely, he thinks, that the Messiah will come and found a golden age; but religious doctrines can no more be disproved than they can be proved.

Religious ideas, Freud says in *The Future of an Illusion*, are not the result of experience or ratiocination.

They are illusions, fulfilments of the oldest, strongest and most urgent wishes of mankind. The secret of their strength lies in the strength of those wishes.... The terrifying impression of helplessness in childhood aroused the need for protection—for protection through love—which was provided by the father; and the recognition that this helplessness lasts throughout life made it necessary to cling to the existence of a father, but this time a more powerful one. Thus the benevolent rule of a divine Providence allays our fear of the dangers of life; the establishment of a moral world-order ensures the fulfilment of the demands of justice, which have so often remained unfulfilled in human civilization; and the prolongation of earthly existence in a future life provides the local and temporal framework in which these wish-fulfilments shall take place. (*FI* 47–8)

Though Freud disowns any pretension to refute religious claims, he clearly thinks it would be better for all concerned if religion withered away. Religion has rendered great service by helping to tame human instincts. But in the thousands of years it has held sway it has achieved very little. There is no evidence that men were in general happier when religious doctrines were universally accepted, and they were certainly no morally better than they are nowadays. The growth of the scientific spirit has decisively weakened the hold of religion. 'Criticism has whittled away the evidential value of religious documents, natural science has shown up the errors in them, and comparative research has been struck by the fatal resemblance between the religious ideas which we revere and the mental products of primitive people and times.' (*FI* 63).

Thus far Freud's criticism of religion, as he himself insists, owes nothing to psychoanalysis. But, ever since *Totem and Taboo* in 1913, he had propounded a psychoanalytic narrative of the origin of religious morality. In the earliest ages, he reported, humans lived in hordes, each horde being ruled by a primal father who enslaved the other men and possessed all the women. One day the men banded together and slew the primal father and established taboos against murder and incest. The primal crime left an inheritance of guilt, so that humans deified the murdered father in their imaginations and determined to respect his will henceforward. Religion, on this view, is the universal obsessional neurosis of humanity.

Like the obsessional neurosis of children it arose out of the Oedipus complex, out of the relation to the father. If this view is right, it is to be supposed that a turning-away from religion will occur with the fatal inevitability of a process of growth, and that we find ourselves at this very juncture in the middle of that phase of development. (*FI* 71)

Freud tells us that the time has come to replace the effects of repression by the results of the rational operation of the intellect. But what he is doing is not at all replacing religion with science, but substituting for the myth of Adam's fall another myth of no greater credibility as a historical narrative. His later writings diminished, rather than increased, any plausibility that *Totem and Taboo* may have possessed. In *Moses and Monotheism* he maintained that the prehistoric primal murder had been twice repeated in historic times—once when the Jewish people murdered Moses (did they, now?) and once when they murdered Jesus. Thus 'there is a real piece of historical truth in Christ's resurrection, for he was the resurrected Moses and behind him the returned primal father of the primitive horde, transfigured and, as the son, put in the place of the father' (*SE* xxiii. 89–90).

Philosophical Theology after Wittgenstein

God is hardly mentioned in Wittgenstein's *Tractatus Logico-Philosophicus*: no doubt he is among the things whereof one should keep silent. But throughout his life, Wittgenstein, though he early gave up his Catholic faith, took religion very seriously. 'To believe in God', he wrote in a notebook during the First World War, 'means to see that life has a meaning.' But believing in God was not a matter of assenting to a doctrine. The Gospels do not provide a historical basis for faith.

Christianity is not based on a historical truth: rather, it offers us a (historical) narrative and says: now believe. But not: believe this narrative with the belief appropriate to a historical narrative; rather, believe through thick and thin, which you can do only as a result of a life. Here you have a narrative; don't take the same attitude as you take to other historical narratives. Make quite a different place in your life for it. (*CV* 32)

Wittgenstein was most opposed to the idea that Christianity was reasonable, and that its reasonableness was established by a branch of philosophy called natural theology. Philosophy, he thought, could not give any meaning to life; the best it could provide would be a form of wisdom. But compared with the burning passion of faith, wisdom is only cold grey ash.

But though only faith, and not philosophy, can give meaning to life, that does not mean that philosophy has no rights within the terrain of faith. Faith may involve talking nonsense, and philosophy may point out that it is nonsense. Having in the *Tractatus* urged us to avoid nonsense by silence, Wittgenstein after his return to philosophy said, 'Don't be afraid of talking nonsense' (*CV* 56). But he went on to add: 'You must keep an eye on your nonsense.'

The logical positivists shared the view that religious language was nonsense; but they felt for it none of the paradoxical respect accorded it by Wittgenstein. A. J. Ayer, in *Language, Truth and Logic*, offered a brisk proof that religious language was meaningless and that 'God' was not a genuine name. A religious man, he tells us, would say that God was a transcendent being who could not be defined in terms of any empirical manifestations. But in that case, 'God' was a metaphysical term:

To say that 'God exists' is to make a metaphysical utterance which cannot be either true or false. And by the same criterion, no sentence which purports to describe the nature of a transcendent god can possess any literal significance.

It is important not to confuse this view of religious assertions with the view that is adopted by atheists, or agnostics. For it is characteristic of an agnostic to hold that the existence of a god is a possibility in which there is no good reason either to believe or disbelieve; and it is characteristic of an atheist to hold that it is at least probable that no god exists. And our view that all utterances about the nature of

God are nonsensical, so far from being identical with, or even lending any support to, either of these familiar contentions, is actually incompatible with them. For if the assertion that there is a god is nonsensical, then the atheist's assertion that there is no god is equally nonsensical, since it is only a significant proposition that can be significantly contradicted. (*LTL* 115)

For some years, believing philosophers were alarmed by verificationist arguments against religious doctrines, and strove to defend their meaningfulness without making much effort to demonstrate their truth. Towards the end of the twentieth century, however, some natural theologians recovered confidence and were much less defensive in their attitudes. Typical of this phase is Alvin Plantinga, first of Calvin College, Grand Rapids, and later of Notre Dame University.

For instance, Plantinga has offered a sophisticated restatement of the ontological argument. In a simplified version his revision goes like this. Let us begin by defining the property of maximal excellence, a property that includes omniscience, omnipotence, and moral perfection. Obviously God, if he exists, has maximal excellence in the actual world. But maximal excellence is not sufficient for Godhead: we need to consider worlds other than this one.

Those who worship God do not think of him as a being that happens to be of surpassing excellence in *this* world but who in some other worlds is powerless or uninformed or of dubious moral character. We might make a distinction here between *greatness* and *excellence*; we might say that the *excellence* of a being in a given world W depends only upon its ... properties in W, while its greatness in W depends not merely upon its excellence in W, but also upon its excellence in other worlds. The limiting degree of greatness, therefore, would be enjoyed in a given world W only by a being who had maximal excellence in W and in every other possible world as well.[3]

Maximal greatness therefore is maximal excellence in every possible world, and it is maximal greatness, not just maximal excellence, that is equivalent to divinity or Godhead. Anything that possesses maximal greatness must exist in every possible world, because in a world in which it does not exist it does not possess any properties. If it is possible for maximal greatness to be instantiated, then it is instantiated in every world. If so, then it is instantiated in our world, the actual world; that is to say, Godhead is instantiated and God exists.

[3] Alvin Plantinga, *The Nature of Necessity* (Oxford: Clarendon Press, 1974), 214.

Plantinga's argument obviously depends on the coherence of the apparatus of possible worlds, and on a solution having been found to the problem of transworld identity. He believes that he has found such a solution, and he presents it at considerable length in his book. But it should also be remarked that in the case of a possible God, rather than of a possible human, the problem does not seem so pressing; it seems foolish to put to Plantinga the question, 'Which God are you proving the existence of?' It remains the case, however, as Plantinga himself points out, that the whole argument depends on the truth of the premiss that it is possible for maximal greatness to be exemplified—that is to say, in his terms, that it is exemplified in some possible world.

Bertrand Russell, in his *History of Western Philosophy*, maintained that there were instances where philosophy had reached definitive answers to central questions. He gave as one example the ontological argument. 'This as we have seen was invented by Anselm, rejected by Thomas Aquinas, accepted by Descartes, refuted by Kant, and reinstated by Hegel. I think it may be said quite decisively that as a result of analysis of the concept "existence" modern logic has proved this argument invalid' (p. 752). Plantinga's reinstatement of the argument, using logical techniques more modern than any available to Russell, serves as a salutary warning of the danger that awaits any historian of logic who declares a philosophical issue definitively closed.

CHRONOLOGY

CHRONOLOGY

ABBREVIATIONS
AND CONVENTIONS

Works cited are quoted by page number unless otherwise specified.

Anscombe

ERP   *Ethics, Religion and Politics* (Oxford: Blackwell, 1981)

Ayer

LTL   *Language, Truth and Logic*, 2nd edn. (London: Gollancz, 1949)

Bentham

B   *The Works of Jeremy Bentham*, ed. John Bowring, 10 vols. (New York: Russell & Russell, 1962)

P   *Introduction to the Principles of Morals and Legislation*, ed. J. H. Burns and H. L. A. Hart (London: Athlone, 1982); cited by chapter, section, and/or subsection

Brentano

PES   *Psychology from an Empirical Standpoint*, ed. Oskar Kraus, 2 vols. (Hamburg: Meiner, 1955)

Collingwood

PA   *Principles of Art* (Oxford: Clarendon Press, 1938)

Darwin

OS   *On the Origin of Species*, Oxford World's Classics (Oxford: Oxford University Press, 1996)

Davidson

EA   *Essays on Actions and Events* (Oxford: Oxford University Press, 1980)

ITI   *Inquiries into Truth and Interpretation* (Oxford: Oxford University Press, 1984)

ABBREVIATIONS AND CONVENTIONS

Derrida

Diff.   *Writing and Difference*, trans. Alan Bass (London: Routledge & Kegan Paul, 1978)

G   *Of Grammatology*, trans. G. C. Spivak (Baltimore, Md.: Johns Hopkins University Press, 1976)

P   *Positions*, trans. A. Bass (Chicago: Chicago University Press, 1981)

SP   *Speech and Phenomena* (Evanston, Ill.: Northwestern University Press, 1973)

Engels

See under Marx.

Feuerbach

EC   *The Essence of Christianity*, trans. G. Eliot (New York: Harper, 1957)

W   *Sämtliche Werke*, 12 vols. (Stuttgart: Bolin, 1959–60)

Frege

BLA   *The Basic Laws of Arithmetic: Exposition of the System*, trans. Montgomery Furth (Berkeley: University of California Press, 1964)

CN   *Conceptual Notation and Related Articles*, trans. T. W. Bynum (Oxford: Oxford University Press, 1972)

CP   *Collected Papers on Mathematics, Logic and Philosophy*, ed. B. McGuinness (Oxford: Blackwell, 1984)

FA   *The Foundations of Arithmetic*, trans. J. L. Austin (Oxford: Oxford University Press, 1950, 1980)

PW   *Posthumous Writings* (Oxford: Blackwell, 1979)

Freud

EI   *The Ego and the Id* (London: Hogarth Press, 1962)

FI   *The Future of an Illusion* (Garden City, NY: Doubleday, 1964)

NIL   *New Introductory Lectures on Psychoanalysis* (London: Hogarth Press, 1949)

SE   *The Standard Edition of the Complete Psychological Works of Sigmund Freud*, 24 vols. (London: Hogarth Press, 1981)

Husserl

CCH   Barry Smith and David Woodruff Smith (eds.), *The Cambridge Companion to Husserl* (Cambridge: Cambridge University Press, 1995)

ABBREVIATIONS AND CONVENTIONS

CM   *Cartesian Meditations* (Dordrecht: Kluwer, 1988)

Ideas   *Ideas Pertaining to a Pure Phenomenology*, 3 vols. (Dordrecht: Kluwer, 1980, 1982, 1989)

LI   *Logical Investigations*, ed. J. N. Findlay, 2 vols. (London: Routledge, 2001)

James

T   *The Meaning of Truth* (New York: Prometheus Books, 1997)

VRE   *Varieties of Religious Experience* (London: Fontana, 1960)

Kant

M   *Critique of Judgement*, ed. J. C. Meredith (Oxford: Oxford University Press, 1978)

Kierkegaard

E/O   *Either/Or*, trans. A. Hannay (Harmondsworth: Penguin, 1992)

FT   *Fear and Trembling*, trans. A. Hannay (Harmondsworth: Penguin, 1985)

P   *Papers and Journals: A Selection*, trans. A. Hannay (Harmondsworth: Penguin, 1996)

SD   *Sickness unto Death*, trans. A. Hannay (Harmondsworth: Penguin, 1989)

Marx

C   *Capital*, ed. D. McLellan, Oxford World's Classics (Oxford: Oxford University Press, 1995)

CM   Karl Marx and Friedrich Engels, *The Communist Manifesto*, ed. D. McLellan, Oxford World's Classics (Oxford: Oxford University Press, 1992)

CPE   *Critique of Political Economy* (Moscow: Progress, 1971)

EW   *Early Writings* (Harmondsworth: Penguin, 1975)

GI   *The German Ideology*, ed. C. J. Allen (London: Lawrence & Wishart, 1920, 2004)

TF   *Theses on Feuerbach* (New York: Prometheus Books, 1998)

VPP   *Values, Price and Profit*, ed. E. M. Aveling (New York: International Publishers, 1935)

Mill

3E	*Three Essays* (London: Longman, 1887)
A	*Autobiography*, ed. J. Stillinger (Oxford: Oxford University Press, 1969)
CCM	*The Cambridge Companion to Mill*, ed. J. Skorupski (Cambridge: Cambridge University Press, 1998)
CW	*The Collected Works of John Stuart Mill*, ed. John M. Robson, 33 vols. (Toronto: University of Toronto Press, 1963–91)
L	*On Liberty and Other Essays*, Oxford World's Classics (Oxford: Oxford University Press, 1991)
SL	*A System of Logic*; many editions; cited by book and section number
U	*Utilitarianism*, ed. M. Warnock (London: Collins, 1962)

Newman

GA	*The Grammar of Assent*, ed. I. Ker (Oxford: Oxford University Press, 1985)
US	*University Sermons* (London: Rivington, 1844)

Nietzsche

BGE	*Beyond Good and Evil*, trans. M. Faber, Oxford World's Classics (Oxford: Oxford University Press, 1998)
BT	*The Birth of Tragedy*, trans. S. Whiteside (Harmondsworth: Penguin, 1993, 2003)
GM	*The Genealogy of Morals*, trans. D. Smith, Oxford World's Classics (Oxford: Oxford University Press, 1996)
TI	*Twilight of the Idols*, trans. D. Langan, Oxford World's Classics (Oxford: Oxford University Press, 1998)
WP	*The Will to Power* (New York: Vintage, 1968)
Z	*Thus Spoke Zarathustra* (Harmondsworth: Penguin, 1961)

Peirce

CP	*Collected Papers of Charles Sanders Peirce*, 8 vols. (Cambridge, Mass.: Harvard University Press, 1931–58)
EWP	*The Essential Writings of Charles Peirce*, ed. E. C. Moore (New York: Prometheus Books, 1998)
P	*Pragmatism* (New York: Prometheus Books, 1997)

ABBREVIATIONS AND CONVENTIONS

Popper

OSE   *The Open Society and its Enemies*, 2 vols. (London, 1945)

Quine

FLPV *From a Logical Point of View* (Cambridge, Mass.: Harvard University Press, 1953)

WO   *Word and Object* (Cambridge, Mass.: MIT Press, 1960)

Rawls

TJ   *A Theory of Justice* (Cambridge, Mass.: Harvard University Press, 1971)

Russell

A   *The Autobiography of Bertrand Russell, 1872–1916* (London: Allen & Unwin, 1967)

AM   *The Analysis of Mind* (London: Allen & Unwin, 1921)

IMP   *Introduction to Mathematical Philosophy* (London: Allen & Unwin, 1917)

PM   *The Principles of Mathematics* (Cambridge: Cambridge University Press, 1903; 2nd edn., 1927)

PP   *The Problems of Philosophy* (London: Oxford University Press, 1912)

Ryle

CM   *The Concept of Mind* (London: Hutchinson, 1949)

CP   *Collected Papers*, 2 vols. (London: Hutchinson, 1949)

Sartre

BN   *Being and Nothingness*, trans. Hazel Barnes (London: Routledge, 1969)

EH   *Existentialism and Humanism* (London: Methuen, 1947)

Schopenhauer

EA   *Essays and Aphorisms*, trans. R. J. Hollingdale (London: Penguin, 2004)

WWI *The World as Will and Representation*, trans. E. F. Payne, 2 vols. (New York: Dover, 1969); all quotations are from volume I.

Sidgwick

ME   *Methods of Ethics* (London: Macmillan, 1901)

ABBREVIATIONS AND CONVENTIONS

Strawson

I   *Individuals* (London: Methuen, 1959)

Tolstoy

WA *What is Art?* (Oxford: Oxford University Press, 1966)

Wittgenstein

BB *The Blue and Brown Books* (Oxford: Blackwell, 1958)

CV *Culture and Value* (Oxford: Blackwell, 1980)

NB *Notebooks 1914–1916* (Oxford: Blackwell, 1961)

OC *On Certainty* (Oxford: Blackwell, 1969)

PG *Philosophical Grammar*, trans. A. Kenny (Oxford: Blackwell, 1974)

PI   *Philosophical Investigations*, trans. G. E. M. Anscombe (Oxford: Blackwell, 1953, 1997); part I cited by paragraph, part II by page

TLP *Tractatus Logico-Philosophicus* (London: Routledge, 1921, 1961); cited by paragraph

Z   *Zettel* (Oxford: Blackwell, 1967)

BIBLIOGRAPHY

General

The *Routledge History of Philosophy* contains five volumes that overlap with the period of this volume. They are volume VI, *The Age of German Idealism*, ed. Robert Solomon and Kathleen Higgins; VII, *The Nineteenth Century*, ed. C. L. Ten; VIII, *Continental Philosophy in the 20th Century*, ed. Richard Kearney; IX, *Philosophy of Science, Logic and Mathematics in the 20th Century*, ed. S. G. Shanker; and X, *Philosophy of Meaning, Knowledge and Value in the 20th Century*. The *Routledge Encyclopaedia of Philosophy* also contains many articles about the people and topics treated here.

Titles marked 'AP' appeared in the Routledge series Arguments of the Philosophers, and titles marked 'PM' appeared in the Oxford series Past Masters.

COPLESTON, F. C., *A History of Philosophy*, vols. vii–ix (London: Burnes Oates, 1963–75)
KENNY, A., *A Brief History of Western Philosophy* (Oxford: Blackwell, 1998)
—— (ed.), *The Oxford Illustrated History of Western Philosophy* (Oxford: Oxford University Press, 1994)
KNEALE, W. and M., *The Development of Logic* (Oxford: Oxford University Press, 1962)
MACINTYRE, ALASDAIR, *A Short History of Ethics* (London: Macmillan, 1966)
—— *After Virtue: A Study in Moral Theory* (London: Duckworth, 1981)

Bentham

The Collected Works of Jeremy Bentham, ed. J. H. Burns, J. R. Dinwiddy, and F. Rosen (London: Athlone, 1968–)
Introduction to the Principles of Morals and Legislation, ed. J. H. Burns and H. L. A. Hart (London: Oxford University Press, 1982)

DINWIDDY, J. R., *Bentham* (Oxford: Oxford University Press, 1989)
HARRISON, ROSS, *Bentham* (London: 1983) (AP)
HART, H. L. A., *Essays on Jurisprudence and Political Theory* (Oxford: 1982)

Mill and Sidgwick

The Collected Works of John Stuart Mill, ed. John M. Robson, 33 vols. (Toronto: University of Toronto Press, 1963–91)
Mill, *On Liberty*, Oxford World's Classics (Oxford: Oxford University Press, 1991)
Mill, *Principles of Political Economy*, Oxford World's Classics (Oxford: Oxford University Press, 1994)

BIBLIOGRAPHY

The Cambridge Companion to Mill, ed. J. Skorupski (Cambridge: Cambridge University Press, 1998)

Sidgwick, *Methods of Ethics* (1874); the most convenient edition is (London: Macmillan, 1901)

ALEXANDER, EDWARD, *Matthew Arnold and John Stuart Mill* (London: Routledge & Kegan Paul, 1965)

BERLIN, ISAIAH, *Four Essays on Liberty* (London: Oxford University Press, 1969)

CRISP, ROGER, *A Guidebook to J. S. Mill's Utilitarianism* (London: Routledge, 1997)

MACKIE, J. L., *The Cement of the Universe* (Oxford: Oxford University Press, 1973)

RYAN, ALAN, *The Philosophy of John Stuart Mill*, 2nd edn. (New York: Macmillan, 1988)

SCHULTZ, BART, *Henry Sidgwick, Eye of the Universe* (Cambridge: Cambridge University Press, 2004)

SKORUPSKI, JOHN, *John Stuart Mill* (London: Routledge, 1989) (AP)

Schopenhauer

Schopenhauer's works are available in several German editions, of which the most recent is *Werke in fünf Banden. Nach den Ausgaben letzter Hand*, ed. Ludger Lütkehaus, 5 vols. (Zurich: Haffmans Verlag, 1988).

The most convenient recent English edition of his main work is *The World as Will and Representation*, trans. E. F. Payne, 2 vols. (New York: Dover, 1969).

English translations of other works include:

Essays and Aphorisms, trans. R. J. Hollingdale (London: Penguin, 2004)

Essay on the Freedom of the Will, trans. K. Kolenda (Indianapolis: Bobbs-Merrill, 1960)

On the Fourfold Root of the Principle of Sufficient Reason, trans. E. F. Payne (La Salle, Ill.: Open Court, 1974)

The Cambridge Companion to Schopenhauer, ed. Christopher Janaway (Cambridge: Cambridge University Press, 1999)

GARDINER, PATRICK, *Schopenhauer* (Bristol: Thoemmes Press, 1997)

HAMLYN, D. W., *Schopenhauer* (London: Routledge & Kegan Paul, 1980) (AP)

MAGEE, BRYAN, *The Philosophy of Schopenhauer* (Oxford: Clarendon Press, 1997)

TANNER, MICHAEL, *Schopenhauer: Metaphysics and Art* (London: Phoenix, 1998)

Kierkegaard

There is a twenty-volume edition of Kierkegaard's works in Danish, which has gone through three editions. A complete English edition, translated by Howard V. Hong and others, is being published in twenty-six volumes by Princeton University Press. In England, Penguin have published translations of several of his works by Alastair Hannay (*Fear and Trembling* (1985); *The Sickness unto Death* (1989); *Either/Or* (1992); *Papers and Journals: A Selection* (1996))

BIBLIOGRAPHY

The Cambridge Companion to Kierkegaard, ed. Alastair Hannay and Gordon D. Marino (Cambridge: Cambridge University Press, 1998)

GARDINER, PATRICK, *Kierkegaard* (Oxford: Oxford University Press, 1998) (PM)
HANNAY, ALASTAIR, *Kierkegaard* (London: Routledge, 1991) (AP)
POJMAN, LOUIS, *The Logic of Subjectivity: Kierkegaard's Philosophy of Religion* (Tuscaloosa: University of Alabama Press, 1984)
RUDD, A., *Kierkegaard and the Limits of the Ethical* (Oxford: Oxford University Press, 1993)

Marx

The first complete edition of the works of Marx and Engels in German was published by the East German authorities in 1968 (*Marx-Engels Werke*). An English translation of this edition was commenced by the London publishers Lawrence & Wishart. English translations of the major works have appeared in the Marx Library (New York: Random House; Harmondsworth: Penguin) between 1974 and 1984. A convenient abridgement of *Capital*, edited by David McLellan, appeared in Oxford World's Classics in 1995.

The Cambridge Companion to Marx, ed. Terrell Carver (Cambridge: Cambridge University Press, 1991)

BERLIN, ISAIAH, *Karl Marx*, 4th edn. (Oxford: Oxford University Press, 1978)
KOLAKOWSKI, LESZEK, *Main Currents in Marxism*, trans. P. S. Falla, 3 vols. (Oxford: Oxford University Press, 1978)
MCLELLAN, DAVID, *Karl Marx: His Life and Thought* (New York: Harper & Row, 1973)
SINGER, PETER, *Marx* (Oxford: Oxford University Press, 1980) (PM)
WHEEN, FRANCIS, *Karl Marx* (London: Fourth Estate, 1999)

Darwin

On the Origin of Species is available in many editions, notably Oxford World's Classics and Penguin Classics. Recent philosophical discussions of his work appear in the following:

RUSE, M., *Taking Darwin Seriously: A Naturalistic Approach to Philosophy* (Oxford: Oxford University Press, 1986)
SOBER, ELLIOTT, *Philosophy of Biology* (Oxford: Oxford University Press, 1993)

Newman

Newman's major philosophical work is *An Essay in Aid of a Grammar of Assent* (ed. I. Ker (Oxford: Oxford University Press, 1985)). There is a good Past Masters biography by Owen Chadwick (Oxford: Oxford University Press, 1983).

GRAVE, S. A., *Conscience in Newman's Thought* (Oxford: Oxford University Press, 1989)

BIBLIOGRAPHY

Nietzsche

The critical edition of his collected works is *Kritische Gesamtausgabe Werke*, edited by G. Colli and M. Montinari, 30 vols. in 8 parts (Berlin: de Gruyter, 1967–). A more convenient German edition is *Werke in Drei Bänden*, edited by Karl Schlechta (Munich: Carl Hansers, 1965). The following works have been translated into English by Walter Kaufmann and published in New York by Random House: *Beyond Good and Evil* (1966), *The Birth of Tragedy* (1967), *On the Genealogy of Morals* (1967), *The Gay Science* (1974). Several of Nietzsche works, including *Thus Spake Zarathustra*, are available in Oxford World's Classics and Penguin Classics.

DANTO, ARTHUR, *Nietzsche as Philosopher: An Original Study* (New York: Columbia University Press, 1965)

HOLLINGDALE, R. J., *Nietzsche* (London: Routledge & Kegan Paul, 1973)

SCHACHT, R., *Nietzsche* (London: Routledge & Kegan Paul, 1983)

Peirce

The *Collected Papers of Charles Sanders Peirce* were published in eight volumes by Harvard University Press between 1931 and 1958. A new, chronological edition has been under way since 1982, published by Indiana University Press. Meanwhile, there are accessible collections of his main papers in the two-volume *The Essential Peirce*, edited by N. Houser and C. Kloesel (Bloomington: Indiana University Press, 1992–4) and in the one-volume *The Essential Writings*, edited by E. C. Moore (New York: Prometheus Books, 1998)

BRENT, J., *Charles Sanders Peirce: A Life* (Bloomington: Indiana University Press, 1993)

HOOKWAY, CHRISTOPHER, *Peirce* (London: Routledge, 1985) (AP)

Frege

The most widely available works of Frege in English are the following:

Conceptual Notation and Related Articles, trans. T. W. Bynum (Oxford: Oxford University Press, 1972)

The Foundations of Arithmetic, trans. J. L. Austin (Oxford: Oxford University Press, 1950, 1980)

Collected Papers on Mathematics, Logic and Philosophy, ed. B. McGuinness (Oxford: Blackwell, 1984)

The Basic Laws of Arithmetic: Exposition of the System, trans. Montgomery Furth (Berkeley: University of California Press, 1964)

DUMMETT, MICHAEL, *Frege: Philosophy of Language* (London: Duckworth, 1973)

—— *The Interpretation of Frege's Philosophy* (London: Duckworth, 1981)

—— *Frege: Philosophy of Mathematics* (London: Duckworth, 1991)

KENNY, A., *Frege* (London: Penguin, 1995; Oxford: Blackwell, 2000)

James

The Principles of Psychology of 1890 has been reissued many times: a convenient reprint is the Dover paperback (2 vols. in 1; New York, 1950). *Varieties of Religious Experience* is also available in many editions, including one by Collier Macmillan of London in 1961.

AYER, A. J., *The Origins of Pragmatism* (London: Macmillan, 1968)
BIRD, G., *William James* (London: Routledge & Kegan Paul, 1987) (AP)

British Idealists and Critics

AYER, A. J., *Language, Truth and Logic*, 2nd edn. (London: Gollancz, 1949)
BRADLEY, F. H., *Appearance and Reality* (Oxford: Oxford University Press, 1893)
—— *Ethical Studies*, 2nd edn. (Oxford: Oxford University Press, 1927)
GREEN, T. H., *Prolegomena to Ethics* (Oxford: Oxford University Press, 1883)
MCTAGGART, *The Nature of Existence* (Cambridge: Cambridge University Press, 1910, 1927)
MOORE, G. E., *Principia Ethica* (Cambridge: Cambridge University Press, 1903)

BALDWIN, THOMAS, *G. E. Moore* (London: Routledge, 1990)
GEACH, PETER, *Truth, Love, and Immortality: An Introduction to McTaggart's Philosophy* (London: Methuen, 1979)
WOLLHEIM, RICHARD, *F. H. Bradley* (Harmondsworth: Penguin, 1959)

Russell

Among the more important of Russell's copious publications are *The Principles of Mathematics* (Cambridge: Cambridge University Press, 1903; 2nd edn., 1927); 'On Denoting', *Mind*, 14 (1905) (often reprinted); *The Problems of Philosophy* (Oxford: Oxford University Press, 1912); *Our Knowledge of the External World* (London: Allen & Unwin, 1914); *Introduction to Mathematical Philosophy* (London: Methuen, 1917); *The Analysis of Mind* (London: Allen & Unwin, 1921); *Human Knowledge: Its Scope and Limits* (London: Allen & Unwin, 1948)

AYER, A. J., *Bertrand Russell* (Chicago: University of Chicago Press, 1988)
PEARS, D. F., *Bertrand Russell and the British Tradition in Philosophy* (London: Fontana, 1967)
SAINSBURY, MARK, *Russell* (London: Routledge, 1979) (AP)

Wittgenstein

Wittgenstein's entire *Nachlass* is available in transcription and facsimile in electronic form, in a text established by the University of Bergen and published by Oxford University Press (Oxford, 1998). *Tractatus Logico-Philosophicus* was published by Routledge & Kegan Paul in London in 1921; a new translation by D. F. Pears and Brian McGuinness was published in 1961. Other writings of Wittgenstein were all published posthumously by Blackwell at Oxford, including *Notebooks 1914–1916* (1961); *Philosophical Investigations* (1953, 1997); *Philosophical Remarks* (1966); *Philosophical Grammar* (1974); *Culture and Value* (1980); *Remarks on the Philosophy of Psychology* (1980); *Last Writings on the Philosophy of Psychology* (1982, 1992); *On Certainty* (1969). A comprehensive and scholarly commentary on the *Philosophical Investigations* was produced by G. P. Baker and P. M. S. Hacker between 1980 and 1996. In 1994 I published with Blackwell an anthology of texts under the title *The Wittgenstein Reader*. A second edition appeared in 2006.

ANSCOMBE, G. E. M., *An Introduction to Wittgenstein's 'Tractatus'* (London: Hutchinson, 1959)

KENNY, A., *Wittgenstein* (Harmondsworth: Penguin, 1973; Oxford: Blackwell, 2006)

KRIPKE, SAUL, *Wittgenstein on Rules and Private Language* (Oxford: Blackwell, 1982)

PEARS, DAVID, *The False Prison* (Oxford: Oxford University Press, 1997, 1998)

RUNDLE, BEDE, *Wittgenstein and Contemporary Philosophy of Language* (Oxford: Blackwell, 1990)

Analytic Philosophy

An excellent overview is given by P. M. S. Hacker in *Wittgenstein's Place in Twentieth Century Analytic Philosophy* (Oxford: Blackwell, 1996). Important works by individual analytic philosophers are listed below.

ANSCOMBE, G. E. M., *Intention* (Oxford: Blackwell, 1957)

AUSTIN, J. L., *How to Do Things with Words* (Oxford: Oxford University Press, 1961)

DAVIDSON, DONALD, *Essays on Actions and Events* (Oxford: Oxford University Press, 1980)

—— *Inquiries into Truth and Interpretation* (Oxford: Oxford University Press, 1984)

FØLLESDAL, DAGFINN, *Referential Opacity and Modal Logic* (London: Routledge, 2004)

GEACH, PETER, *Mental Acts* (London: Routledge & Kegan Paul, 1958)

QUINE, W. V. O., *From a Logical Point of View* (Cambridge, Mass.: Harvard University Press, 1953)

—— *Word and Object* (Cambridge, Mass.: MIT Press, 1960)

RAWLS, JOHN, *A Theory of Justice* (Cambridge, Mass.: Harvard University Press, 1971)

RYLE, GILBERT, *The Concept of Mind* (London: Hutchinson, 1949)

—— *Collected Papers* (London: Hutchinson, 1949)

STRAWSON, P. F., *Individuals* (London: Methuen, 1959)

Freud

Freud's works are collected in German in *Gesammelte Werke*, edited by A. Freud and others (Frankfurt am Main: S. Fischer Verlag, 1960–87). In English there is *The Standard Edition of the Complete Psychological Works of Sigmund Freud*, 24 vols. (London: Hogarth Press, 1981). All the most significant works are easily accessible in *The Penguin Freud Library*, edited by A. Richards and A. Dickson.

The Cambridge Companion to Freud, ed. J. Neu (Cambridge: Cambridge University Press, 1991)

GAY, P., *Freud: A Life for our Time* (New York: Norton, 1988)

LEAR, JONATHAN, *Freud* (London: Routledge, 2005)

RIEFF, P., *Freud: The Mind of the Moralist* (Chicago: Chicago University Press, 1979)

WOLLHEIM, R., *Sigmund Freud* (Cambridge: Cambridge University Press, 1971)

—— and HOPKINS, J. (eds.), *Philosophical Essays on Freud* (Cambridge: Cambridge University Press, 1982)

Husserl

The critical edition of Husserl's works was inaugurated in 1950 with the publication of *Cartesianische Meditationen*. Since then twenty-eight volumes have appeared, edited first by Leo van Breda, and later by Samuel Ijsseling. It is now published by Kluwer (Dordrecht). The most useful English translations are *Logical Investigations*, trans. J. N. Findlay, 2nd edn. (London: Routledge, 2001); *Ideas Pertaining to a Pure Phenomenology and to a Phenomenological Philosophy*, First Book, trans. F. Kersten (The Hague: Nijhoff, 1982); Second Book, trans. R. Rojcewicz and A. Schuwer (Dordrecht: Kluwer, 1989); Third Book, trans. T. E. Klein and W. E. Phol (Dordrecht: Kluwer, 1980); *Husserl, Shorter Works*, ed. and trans. P. McCormick and F. Elliston (Notre Dame, Ind.: University of Notre Dame Press, 1981).

The Cambridge Companion to Husserl, ed. Barry Smith and David Woodruff Smith (Cambridge: Cambridge University Press, 1995).

BELL, DAVID, *Husserl* (London: Routledge, 1989) (AP)

DREYFUS, H. L. (ed.), *Husserl, Intentionality and Cognitive Science* (Cambridge, Mass.: MIT Press, 1982)

MOHANTY, J. N., and McKENNA, W. R. (eds.), *Husserl's Phenomenology: A Textbook* (Lanham, Md.: Centre for Advanced Research in Phenomenology, 1989)

SIMONS, PETER, *Philosophy and Logic in Central Europe from Bolzano to Tarski* (Dordrecht: Kluwer, 1992)

Heidegger

A *Gesamtausgabe* of Heidegger's works is planned in approximately 100 volumes. Some seventy have now been published by Klostermann (Frankfurt am Main). English translations of the major works include: *Being and Time*, trans J. Stambaugh (Albany, NY: SUNY Press, 1996); *Basic Writings*, ed. D. F. Krell (New York: Harper & Row, 1977); *What is Philosophy?*, trans. W. Kluback and J. T. Wilde (New Haven, Conn.: College & University Press, 1958)

The Cambridge Companion to Heidegger, ed. C. Guignon (Cambridge: Cambridge University Press, 1993)

DREYFUS, H. L., *Being-in-the-World: A Commentary on Heidegger's 'Being and Time' Division I* (Cambridge, Mass.: MIT Press, 1991)

MULHALL, STEPHEN, *On Being in the World: Wittgenstein and Heidegger on Seeing Aspects* (London: Routledge, 1990)

PÖGGLER, OTTO, *Martin Heidegger's Path of Thinking*, trans. D. Magurshak and S. Barber (Atlantic Highlands, NJ: Humanities Press, 1987)

STEINER, GEORGE, *Martin Heidegger* (Chicago: University of Chicago Press, 1987)

Sartre

La Nausée (Paris, 1938), trans. Robert Baldick as *Nausea* (Harmondsworth: Penguin, 1965)

L'Être et le néant (Paris, 1943), trans. Hazel Barnes as *Being and Nothingness* (London: Routledge, 1969)

L'Existentialisme est un humanisme (Paris, 1946), trans. Philip Mairet as *Existentialism and Humanism* (London: Methuen, 1948)

CAWS, P., *Sartre* (London: Routledge, 1979) (AP)

COOPER, DAVID, *Existentialism, a Reconstruction* (Oxford: Blackwell, 1990)

WARNOCK, MARY, *The Philosophy of Sartre* (London: Hutchinson, 1965)

Derrida

De la grammatologie (Paris, 1967), trans. G. C. Spivak as *Of Grammatology* (Baltimore: Johns Hopkins University Press, 1976)

L'Écriture et la différence (Paris, 1967), trans. Alan Bass as *Writing and Difference* (London: Routledge & Kegan Paul, 1978)

Positions, trans. Alan Bass (Chicago: University of Chicago Press, 1981)

NORRIS, CHRISTOPHER, *Derrida* (London: Routledge, 1987) (AP)

ROYLE, NICHOLAS, *Jacques Derrida* (London: Routledge, 2003)

ILLUSTRATIONS

ILLUSTRATIONS

ILLUSTRATIONS

Endpapers Boris Anrep 'Lucidity' (left) and Boris Anrep 'Curiosity' (right)
© The Anrep Family Estate and The National Gallery, London

In a few instances we have been unable to trace the copyright holder prior to publication. If notified, the publishers will be pleased to amend the acknowledgements in any future edition.

INDEX